Jim & Marg.

Remain blessed in
the Lord.

— Fr. Anthony

The **Life GPS** system & Tonic

KEEPING HUMAN RELATIONSHIPS TOGETHER:

Self Guide to Healthy Living
[Studies in Spiritual Psychology vis-a-vis Human Values]

Anthony O. Nwachukwu

iUniverse, Inc.
Bloomington

Keeping Human Relationships Together:
Self Guide to Healthy Living
[Studies in Spiritual Psychology vis-a-vis Human Values]

iUniverse books may be ordered through booksellers or by contacting:

iUniverse
1663 Liberty Drive
Bloomington, IN 47403
www.iuniverse.com
1-800-Authors (1-800-288-4677)

*Because of the dynamic nature of the Internet, any Web addresses or links contained in this
book may have changed since publication and may no longer be valid. The views expressed
in this work are solely, exclusively and originally those of the author.*

ISBN: 978-1-4502-0521-4 (sc)
ISBN: 978-1-4502-0522-1 (e)

Printed in the United States of America

Dedication

To

Teenage Boys and Girls

(To duly & diligently decide, choose, act well &
enjoy their future)

THE OPEN LETTER ON "LIFE GPS @ CONGRESS.ORG"

TO: President Barack Obama (D-US), 1ˢᵗ term
April 28, 2010 (letter slightly edited)

The general topic of this message is
Children/Families:

<u>Subject:</u>
The Life GPS system for Change
-"Keeping Human Relationships
Together: Self Guide to Healthy Living
[Studies in Spiritual Psychology vis-a-
vis Human Values]"

Dear Mr. President,

I am a Catholic Priest, from the Igbo Tribe of Nigeria, Ahiara Diocese Mbaise, serving as a Missionary to the Catholic Church in the US, especially in New York and the First African to serve as Faculty and Prof. of Counseling Psychology & West African Studies at Graduate Theological Foundation, Indiana, (Affiliate of Oxford University, England & Centro Pro Unione, Rome, Italy), and a Specialist in Spiritual Psychology.

In your mail to me dated Wed. 11/05/08, through infobarackobama. com, and I quote: *"I'm about to head to Grant Park..., but I want to thank you first....You made history every single day during this campaign – I want to thank you who gave your time, talent, and passion to this campaign...you believe it's time for change".*

Yes, I believe society needs change for the best. After I finished reading your mail, I felt the need myself to add speed to the publication of a survey that has taken me over 20 years to develop, aimed at the change and values you promised in your campaign. If I made any substantial contribution during your campaign, it was basically to advise you and other Politicians to keep your hearts to your faith in God. Any governance that lacks God's Presence or Sound Moral Life must surely fail. Thus, this open letter invites you to read my survey and encourage others to do the same because there is no Presidency or Governance that is above God and His Creation - Nature. Therefore, rule with God and Respect for His People and Environment or Eco-Spirituality. You do not need anyone to praise or love you if you are doing the right thing or God's work. For: "Nobody keeps honest relationship with the one he or she deceives". No wonder, divorce rates are higher among those who have divorced before and are more likely to divorce again than those who have not. Be cautious Mr. President. Friendship is not equal to Leadership but Love and the devil/enemy works more on our weakness. Love is the only weapon that weakens the devil because it never fails or disappoints. It is the language the Dump and Deaf, Life and Death can hear. Be a Politician, but play no politics with God's people please. God is Love, a Presence, not a "discovery". To love is to act, show, demonstrate a commitment, a science of sharing and sacrificing self. Every leadership position demands it.

We are all aware that society is facing the most economic and natural disaster in history, coupled with incessant cases of indiscipline, immorality in an unqualified magnitude, teenage fighting, and bullying, sexing, social and domestic violence, torture and serial killing of innocent souls. You rightly noted on 9/9/09, during your address to Congress on Health Care Reform that *"the problems of society are not only economic but also "Moral Issues"*. Again, remember what you noted at the University of Notre Dame on 05/17/09 and I quote: "*We must find a way to live together as one human family, in the spirit of the Gospel until we touch each other's hearts….aiming at the law that binds all people irrespective of religious affiliations" etc.* Which way Mr. President? There are so many ways already to chaos because of lack of moral order? You know it. Society is sick. Then, the question is: "What do we do?" As a matter of great concern, I am deeply compelled to request you, the First American Black and God-made President, to assist me through this survey fight for the values of right decisions, choices, and behaviors, particularly among our teens, in manners most appropriate to you. My worries as such include the following:

1. "Why have our teenage boys and girls continued to get involved in domestic and social violence, bullying and fighting at schools? We must bring them back from their long journey (Prodigal case) of sin and protect them against worlds of fantasies and illusions.

2. Why do most teenage girls constantly give themselves in for sex as against common sense and the speeches you have given them?

3. Why has sex, though priceless gift, which has no Religion, Church, or U-Turn, lost respect among rational [human] beings?

4. Why "I love you" is not "I am in love?" Does puppy love last? Is it not mere act of man (brutal) to demand a favor for sex, especially in married life? The devil has really joined humanity in procession.

5. Why are some parents afraid to take charge of their children?

6. Why have most ministers of the Gospel tagged God for sale, a cheap commodity for the market place? Why has frustration levels remained in the increase? Times of "kneeling theology" are over. Society needs doers of the Word of God.

7. Why have some Priests or Ministers of the Gospel Message continued to get involved in sex scandals, abusing minors or in cases of pedophilia, entrusted to their care?

8. Why priests/ministers need self-assessment test at this year of the priests or 21st Century Christianity?

9. Why do [only] ordinary human beings become Saints and not angels?

10. Why are Atheists and Bastards equally loving children of God?

11. Why religion is not a choice of chance or an option for heavenly rewards?"

12. Why should God not be subjected to philosophical debates but experienced as He is?

13. Why do spirits of the dead operate in the physical world? I have concrete evidence for this assertion.

14. Why God should not be taken by surprise or mystified?

15. Why is prayer an insult to God when a supplicant has no remorse for sin? Why has Moral Instruction or Spiritual Psychology not part of Educational Objective and System?

16. Why is God a friend of silence and not noise - in noise we hear ourselves, in silence we hear God?

17. Why love, at times, sleeps in the same bed with hatred?

18. Why kids don't follow adult conversations but interpret them?

19. Why does nature not forgive us?

20. Is there any magic or miracle in a relationship one is not ready to maintain or keep? Or can a man expect his wife to be honest when he is greedy and selfish?

Consequently, our survey: "Keeping Human Relationships Together: Self Guide to Healthy Living [Studies in Spiritual Psychology vis-a-vis Human Values]" first published 2010 by iUniverse, has addressed all these concerns and more, raised here. This epoch-making venture is mainly dedicated to our teenage boys and girls.

Please do read this book and determine whether or not it should be made public in the families, school systems, and individual relationships. In this manner, [as the finest group on the planet, living within the same parenthesis of eternity] we can assist in curbing the dearth of indiscipline in individual lives, relationships, governments, families and school systems.

Permit me to send you the summary also. As for the 10% royalty with iUniverse, as I have done in the past, it will be donated to alleviate sufferings among individuals in society.

Available at Amazon.com, barns & nobles.com and iUniverse.com]

Summary of Survey/Book

This 'Life GPS system & Tonic' is a survey, scientifically designed and validated to study the creative integration of spiritual psychology and insightful probing in the workings of the human mind, behavior, values and complexities for holistic realization of the individual person at the moment. The book is unique, revolutionary and radical in scope and content in the sense that it does not only promote the need to keep society, college students, our children out of trouble, but it goes to the root of the illusions and projections that impact negatively on its attainment.

Relationship is basically life & anything that threatens a person's relationship affects him or her life in a very drastic way. Society appears terribly inundated with various emotional frustrations, loss of jobs, anxieties, depressions, panic attacks, broken relationships, homes, marriages, abandoned children, conflicting ideologies, juvenile delinquencies, indiscipline, teen fighting, bullying, domestic and social violence, natural disasters, etc. Most parents are afraid to teach, correct or care for their children. Educational systems suffer from moral aridity and in many government quarters, nobody takes responsibilities for atrocities committed on daily basis. Worse still, some ministers of the Gospel message or religious leaders have tagged God for sale, for their own selfishness. In many Churches, neuroses and mental cases, that deserve medical attention, are being praised as holiness and spiritual virtues.

Today, our teens seem to joke with the most sacred gift of sex, which naturally hears and speaks only one language - "let's go". In the midst of all these hypocritical atmospheres and religious masquerading, politicking, inordinate rush for fame and wealth, both society and individual relationships suffer. Faith only works in action and I assure you: "God, heaven, hell is real". Salvation is within our actions.

Hiding in the hood of a monk makes no sense. Cafeteria type of religion has to stop. Ministers cannot be like the African watermelon, that is whitish inside and greenish outside. Praying for a better tomorrow when today is neglected is madness or an insult to God. Of course, prayer does not change God but you. Claiming to be busy, praying when your attention is urgently sought in your relationship is demonic and pharisaical. Nobody is beyond God's favor or love, be him or her an atheist or a prostitute. Every child is precious, whether by wedlock, a prostitute or a mad person.

Therefore, spiritual psychology examines issues from long-term benefits and perspectives that guide the moment. It offers society and individuals some action alert vitamins, impulse controls, high consciousness, internal energies, inner strengths, emotional muscles, spiritual connections or self-affirmation and strong sense of who they are. Each person has to understand a bit of him or herself, trust in his or her nature and capacity to adapt, build and resuscitate lost hopes and live.

Every relationship needs some sacred space, moral, intellectual virtue or emotional intelligence in order to visualize in the future the consequences of one's present decisions, choices and actions or the self-perceived ability to reflect on the right course of action. There is no CP, no capital P or partner in any human relationship, no pretence or neutrality, either you have one or you don't. We are our own relationships. When "I love you" equals "I want you", relationship collapses. Education of the mind is essential - transmission and inculcation of values of right behaviors. Puppy love does not last. No partner is a spare part supplier of needs, a piece of furniture one can replace at will, an 'agency theory' where a third party can be delegated, an object under one's shoe that can be thrown away once one removes one's feet from it or a COMD business, an hourly or monthly affair. So long as feelings have no banks, they must be expressed, either peacefully or confrontationally. To relate is to treat as valid, to recognize, to appreciate and to fix one's shoes to avoid hurting others and be at home with self and society.

We teach and tell others how to relate with us. Relational attires or dresses only cover the body and not the heart. Openness, sincerity of heart, sound moral lives are the engines, the individual internal system memories, energy and power manifestations of healthy relationships. Possibly, something is keeping you uncomfortable or destroying your relationship, and at times, that something is you, your unhealthy life styles. To break a bad habit, first, acknowledge there is a problem and create the will to change. Any issue that created problem in your relationships in the past, must not be allowed to play a role in the future because the devil [who does not go on vacation] does not know what we have in mind till we invite him in what we say and do. All the same, the devil we know is better than the "angel" we do not know because the world does not come down to us. We assert ourselves first and move to it. To change others, we must adjust our tone of response and change ourselves first. Always create an environment or atmosphere in which your partner is likely to agree with you because each individual story differs and people behave true to types. There is no miracle in any relationship one is careless about or cannot maintain or keep.

The book is more of a Life GPS system and tonic, an academic manual for teachers, individual life companion, a daily Vitamin for partners, a compendium of moral instructions for college students and parents, a handbook of self-supervision, authentic religious advocate, a challenge to 21st Century priests and ministers, a good news for those who have no religion, atheists, a big guide to teenage boys and girls, therapeutic for the depressed and individuals suffering from emotional frustrations. To be peaceful is to be just, truthful, and avoid hurting others. Relationships grow on what we say 'yes' to and not what we say 'no' to - flexibility is essential in any level of human relationship.

Let us, all work hard, be happy with ourselves, and always remember to stop and smell the flowers and experience the joy of living together as God's own family on earth.

Thank you so much Mr. President for your time and patience.

- The Author
[Prof. Anthony O. Nwachukwu]

Promotional Blurb for Father's Book

"The Reverend Father Anthony Odinakachi Nwachukwu, Ph.D., Psy.D., has ventured into unchartered territory in this provocative and stimulating study of the creative integration of spiritual psychology and the West African mind. His insightful probing into the inner workings of the human mind and spiritual development as epitomized in human relationships is a major contribution to the related fields of West African studies, spiritual psychology, and religious consciousness".

John H. Morgan, President
Ph.D. (Hartford), D.Sc. (London), Psy.D. (FH/Oxford)
Senior Fellow of Foundation House, Oxford.

Advisory Board Member
Centre for Religion in Public Life
Oxford University

Karl Mannheim Professor of the History and Philosophy of the Social Sciences
Graduate Theological Foundation

Sir Julian Huxley Distinguished Research Professor
Cloverdale College

Dodge House
415 Lincoln Way East
Mishawaka, IN 46544.

The Foundation
1-800-423-5983 (U.S. & Canada)
574-255-3642 (International)
574.255.7520 (fax)
www.gtfeducation.org

The College
1-800-470-1822 (U. S. & Canada)
www.cloverdalecollege.org

*

"If discipline [i.e. - doing the right thing when no one is watching] and sound moral living are the measurements for solid education, self-fulfillments, religious practices and healthy relationships, then, the book has said it all. It has, not only, provided the various management strategies that resuscitate broken relationships, but also, created conscious inner strengths that keep the healthy ones alive, both in the private and public sectors. I recommend that everybody joins Nwachukwu in this timely opportunity and the 21st century campaign for sound radical changes in the individual lives and society".

Anthony J. Grieco,
MD, MACP, Professor of Medicine, NYU School of Medicine

*

"The African erudite author once more avails every reader of his psychological insight into the secrets of maintaining a healthy relationship. While promoting a positive and optimistic attitude, he gets to the root of the illusions, presumptions and projections that impact negatively on its attainment. The author's reflections in a way seem to have translated the Tillichian idea of the paradoxical co-existence of the good and the bad into its psychological, ethical and practical relevance. I highly recommend this book to everyone who is out to make his life a success story".
Dr.-theol. Sylvester I. Ihuoma,
Delegate for Africans, University of Muenster, Germany.

*

"Wow! This book is more of the GPS system that guides each individual life". It is actually a book for every rational person".

Joan Bareth,
(NM, NYU)

*

"Many authors have written on a variety of related subjects on human relationships. But this book practically touches on every aspect of human life, political, socio-religious, spiritual etc and this makes it unique for everybody to read".

Mr. Andrew Clerico
(Fixed Income Portfolio Manager, NY)

*

"Sex has no religion – I agree. Your book is as exciting as the Action Alert Tonic – AAT you have provided for the young generation and society. Congratulations!"

Dr. Innocent E. Gubor
(Upstate University, SYR, NY)

*

"This is fascinating. The book is a guarantee for healthy living. Read it".

Dr. Theresa Adaeze Okere,
Chief Consultant, Head of Department, Anesthesia, FMC, Owerri, Imo State, Nigeria

*

"To the question being asked by so many today regarding the incessant social and domestic violence of our young generation – 'what do we do?' – Anthony Nwachukwu has, in a very skillful, appealing and professional manner provided an answer in his book. He outlines how the failure to acknowledge and appreciate the value of one's own life inevitably leads to the devaluing of the lives of others, and provides a wonderful working tool to fight the resulting epidemic of immorality and crime among today's youth. This superb book, with its formula for radical change in individual lives and society, is essential reading for general readers, religious leaders, youth and youth workers, and mental health professionals – in short, for all who care about this enormously important issue".

Dr. Charles D. Mayer
Episcopal Priest and Pastoral Psychotherapist, New York, NY

*

"Fantastic! This is the stuff society, individuals; the school systems, especially our children need at this time. The book is an unchallengeable and unique contribution towards the educational, spiritual, emotional and sound moral growth of our families, children in particular, and society, at large. I wish and hope this book is going to be made available to Nigeria, every nation, ethnic group, person, irrespective of race, color, age or gender. Many Congratulations!"

Ugoeze (Dr.) Josephine Nwachukwu Udaku,
KSM, JP, MFR, President, National Council of Catholic Women Organization of Nigeria (NCCWO).

*

"Everyone needs to be happy and maintain peaceful relationship. But most often, it does not work out that way. The main reasons being that, many people sacrifice these basic needs for wants and other factors that unconsciously militate against their honest efforts. The author, an African scholar, intimately versed in his culture and field of specialization, has, in this book, provoked a 21st Century campaign that is energizing, self-convincing, educative, informative, challenging and avails people of all cultures, linguistic and tribal groups, color, gender, status, etc. the techniques they need to achieve peace and happiness in their various levels of relationships. In his own words: 'We, either, have healthy relationship or we don't - 'there is no neutrality or a capital P in relationship".

Aman A. Acholonu
Writer & Commentator on historical and Current Affairs in Igboland of Nigeria, based in USA

*

"Wow! Dr. Nwachukwu has said it all: 'Each person is his or her own relationship.' I have always tried and maintained equilibrium in my marital and professional relationships. But, after reading this book "Keeping human relationships together", I was so amazed to discover how ignorance and little things could drastically affect and destroy one's cherished relationship. This is what it really means to hit the nail at the head. I can't understand how any person, college student, parent and single, youth – a young boy and girl, perpetrators of violence in society today, an addict, a victim of depression, broken home, sex abuser, a politician, religious, atheist, whoever, after reading this masterpiece, will not be moved to self-supervise, reflect and realize the need to appreciate the beauty of life, hard work, and "TJP" in his or her relationship. The saying goes just as this book "a good market sells itself". The book is precisely written, for a change of attitudes, new visions, appreciation of one another. Don't wait to be told about it. Grab your own copy today and digest it for life".

Prof. Christian Chibundu Anyanwu
Department of Social Sciences
Medgar Evers College of the City University of New York.

*

"This book is a 'must-read' for anyone who loves him or herself. The title may be repulsive to those who have risked their lives in one form of relationship or the other. On the contrary, the book is a search light, the LIFE GPS for resuscitating lost hopes and providing a lasting context to begin and enjoy life afresh".

Engr. (Dr.) Reginald Aguh,
Cranfield University, England, FH/Oxford, Facilities Engineering Manager, SPDC, Nigeria, Lead Facilities Engineer, TX.

*

"It was Abraham Lincoln who once said: 'Remember in the depth and even agony of despondency that you will feel well again'. I believe, the book has offered individuals the spiritual and material guidelines to overcome fears, anxiety, depressions and build in their capacity to live".

Prof. Anthony Nnamdi Okere,
Acting Vice Chancellor, Imo State University, Nigeria.

*

"This is a wonderful first book I have ever read on such an enriching subject – Spiritual Psychology".

Robison Stephen,
BA, MPS, MSN, RRT, Respiratory Care, NYUMC

*

"At last, society is offered a life tonic, that, not only energizes, but also, reassures vitality in the Government, families, individual lives and the classrooms".

Philip Rodriguez
Patient Advocate, NYUMC

*

"We can no longer fold our hands and watch our children perish in social and domestic violence. The book has skillfully suggested the strategies to fight lack of discipline in society, especially among teenage boys and girls. It wants to bring them back from the negative effects of global village syndrome so that they can enjoy the peace life offers them on daily basis".

Msgr. Walter Neibrzydowski,
Retired Pastor/Teacher, You Tube Channel @ www.youtube.com/frwalter1 & Manhattan Cable Show, Channel 57, Time Warner, Channel 84 RCN, Tuesday @ 10:30 AM

Contents

Foreword

That humanity seems to have attained great feat and apogee in science and technology is indubitable. Unfortunately, the same cannot be said of human relationships. To separate the physical from the spiritual creates a metaphysical quagmire because man is a composite of body and soul at least in the Aristotelian –Thomistic intellectual tradition. The two must go together. Ironically, many have emphasized one over the other. This is the crux of the matter.

Today, our society is inundated with countless instances of broken homes, marriages, friendships, abandoned children, companies, ministries and all forms of atrocities. Geometrically, a lot of people suffer from depressions and anxieties because they have lost the sense of identity and belongingness. Some don't even trust their nature any more. Most people are literally sad today of nothing. Energies are wasted in futility, no planning, no agenda; and suspicion seems to abound in many quarters. An individual tends to easily get angry especially when the good behavior he or she expects from others is not exhibited. Hence, it is plausible to assert that there is no perfect relationship anywhere. Moreover, some ministers of Gods' words have tagged Him for sale, a cheap commodity for the market place. No wonder, in some religious circles, neuroses have been rewarded and "praised as holiness". Wow! Where then lie the human dignity and rationality?

Consequently, Nwachukwu has ex-rayed the human characteristics, dynamics, traits and dispositions and has come up with amazing management strategies and therapies that can easily assist people value themselves as 'important human documents'. The book: "Keeping human Relationships together: Self Guide to healthy Living" is timely and urgent, particularly at the 21st century. It has magical transforming effects on human behaviors. The book is a must-read because relationship is basically the true test for living, the embodiment of what it means to exist. One does not really live but merely exists outside healthy relationships. No one lives in a vacuum. Even when one does not want to relate with anybody, one still needs to know and understand that ones joy and sadness, success and achievements are within ones making. We are our relationships.

On a special note, college and research students will tremendously benefit from this book. It offers them the scientific design and methodology. For married couples, the book is a daily vitamin, a challenge to 21st Christian ministers, a welcoming news to those who have no religion, the downtrodden, the dejected, a big guide to the younger generation, reinforcement to those who may not be academically gifted but versed in creative intelligence. It is revival for those who seem to have lost their lives in one form of depression, anxiety or the other.

The book is dedicated to all men and women of good conscience, young and old, who make efforts to maintain healthy relationships among the groups they find themselves. Therefore, I strongly recommend that this educational manual, individual life companion be made available in every school library, home and office. The author's linguistic fluidity is evident and this renders the book readable and easily comprehensible.

Prof. Christian Chibundu Anyanwu
Department of Social Sciences
Medgar Evers College of the City University of New York.

GRATITUDES

I am singularly indebted to all the experts, professionals and individuals whose works; materials, Websites, TV Shows, ideas and resources I cited here for the development of this historic masterpiece for human healthy relationships. My filial gratefulness also goes to all those whose scientific findings and contributions, substantially constituted the main Instrument for data collections of the survey.

I am ever grateful to God and Mary, the Mother of Jesus, my parents, Ezeji and Mrs. Francis Nwachukwu for inculcating in me the virtue of humility and values of right decision, choice and behavior.

On a very special note, I am most thankful to the Catholic Church, her Ministers – Bishops, especially, my Beloved Bishop V. A. Chikwe, Monsignors, Priests, Religious and Lay, my family, teachers, friends, Staff of GTF and Pastoral Care Professionals whose lights of love and team work have constantly and continually shown me the path to humility, truth, justice and peace – God, my spiritual source energy.

More importantly, I am very appreciative of all those who read drafts and offered Praises/Blurbs, critical and analytical insights to this publication. In this light, I singularly and unflinchingly thank Dr. John H. Morgan, President of Graduate Theological Foundation, Indiana and Cloverdale College; USA, an affiliate of Oxford University and Centro Pro Unione, Rome for supervising and spurring me to the publication of this book on Spiritual Psychology –SP, which is not for or against any faith or religious system, but sound moral life.

May God guide and bless you as you read this book - Keeping your heart in your faith, believing that things that matter most in life are little and often neglected.

Prologue

* * * * *

Welcome to the panorama of human relationships, the rewarding-inward journey of life.

"Everything has been figured out except how to live"
– Jean Paul Sartre

Life is one. To live and enjoy one's life is basic and a matter of great concern. In this book, we made assiduous efforts to assist each person realize and utilize this value by studying human characteristics and dynamics typical of rational beings. The human 'body' is the center of openness. People need to understand a bit of themselves first, trust in their nature and inner strengths before they can amicably relate with others. Through Internet resources, libraries and fieldworks, we examined the influences individual characteristics exert on their relationships. In order to achieve our desired objectives and justify the need for spiritual psychology (SP) in this capacity, like in any other scientific and systematic investigation, we approached the issue of human relationships from the psychological and ethical perspectives.

First of all, we designed the area and population of our study. After that, we proceeded with sample and sampling technique, instrument for data collection, assembling, developing, validating, presenting, analyzing, measuring and interpreting our instrument for the survey. Eventually, the results we obtained from the analysis, generally guided us to develop this book. They equally assisted us map and ascertain the best skills, tools, techniques and management strategies people could individually employ to bring positive changes and avoid conflicts in their lives and relationships.

Obviously, relationship is as old as humanity. Experts and professionals have written volumes on this area of study and are still making their contributions. Yet, by the time anyone has patiently gone through the pages of this book, he or she shall come to the conclusion that it is not so much the fighting dog that counts as the fight in the dog. The need for self-mastery is the prime target that runs throughout this book. For instance, when things happen unexpectedly, we have to adjust to the circumstances and move ahead to fix them if we can.

Therefore, our approach in this survey appears somewhat entirely different, practical, inspirational, discursive, inviting, challenging, revolutionary, unique, bold and original. It is symmetrically designed in a manner in which the reoccurring ideas and words in the book are carefully chosen and organized to gradually and consistently elicit some impressive responses and changes in the reader. Substantially, we adopted the Heraclitian and Tillichian ideas of the paradoxical co-existence of the good and bad. Opposites necessarily exist. Life is an ongoing process governed by elements of change. A notorious criminal today may become a saint tomorrow. Uniformity is not unity but can lead to it. When relationship appears enjoyable, one or unified, there is still an element of diversity because unity or oneness is not identity. No condition has a time frame. Every view in this book has its context.

Each person is unique and must be respected accordingly. Probably, in Heraclitus' common sense-truth of change, "cold things warm up, the hot cools off, wet becomes dry, and dry becomes wet" (IEP). Experiences differ, and to condemn a person or partner because of a single mistake is wrong. No wonder, he insists that no one can step into the same river twice because every other thing on the planet may change except change itself (Wikipedia, the free Encyclopedia). You are your own change, value and self, irrespective of what others think of you. For instance, expecting what you hate in another person, especially in a marital relationship, which constituted 60% of the over all analysis of our survey on relationships, is the energy that keeps you healthy. According to Heraclitus: "If you do not expect the unexpected, you will not find it" (IR, July 2, 2009) and to exist authentically, cheerfully with longevity is always to expect the unexpected. Surprises are important values of life. Always watch out and be prepared to contend with them. Love, at times, resides with hatred.

Spiritual psychology (SP) is also interpretative and does not leave any stone unturned. Everybody must put on his or her thinking cap and face the challenges of the moment. Since spiritual psychology is a practical application of moral and psychological values to concrete human situations, it is objectively critical of religious practices and behaviors that are not in conformity with ethical principles in general. Faith only works in actions, and being responsible for one's actions is maturity. SP is a clarion call for each person to create a conscious "time-line-exercise" according to Mayer in Morgan (2009:119) or inner strength for assessing his or her weaknesses and growths in life because the seed of healthy relationship gradually grows from self. We ought to know when we are on the right track, derailing or beyond the edge. This is what it means to respect values and to be in touch with oneself and others – to know one's lane and keep to it. SP is an urgent call to live on the spiritual and higher level of consciousness - living your best life that is acceptable to Created order, God & 'Man'.

Furthermore, the book is not limited to any particular level or type of human relationship. Generally, it provides the modules for workability, scholarship, understanding, flexibility and adaptability in every human relationship. More importantly, this is not a textbook on Spiritual Psychology or Religion as such, but an honest attempt to apply psychological and ethical values on human dynamics, characteristics, belief systems, behaviors and relationships. Examples and indentations are readily provided in many cases to drive home the message. In this book, indentations and some highlights in-between the pages are deemed necessary for the sake of emphasis and easy accessibility. However, they are employed according to the author's choice and discretion and do not follow any specific procedure. Such words as "partner, party, individual, people, are interchangeably applied here and the reader is at liberty to appropriate the one that best describes his or her own situation. The use of the third person singular and possessive pronouns like "he or she, his or her, him or herself" was adopted for the sake of emphasis too. However, the prologue features the following *highlights* that punctuate the entire work:

I. Delusional cases vis-à-vis spiritual growth

Healthy relationship creates and revitalizes life. The emphasis here is not that people have not been relating to one another or do not know the importance of relationships. Rather, the main thrust of the book centers on its ability to diligently examine, guide and sustain the various conditions and possibilities that unexpectedly create conflicts in human relationships. For instance, a mental and lunatic problem or behavior can easily be praised as an act of holiness. This state of life generates problems in relationships. In Kinzer's own words, it is possible that "what is actually an emotional problem can disguise itself as a spiritual virtue" (1980:26) because "there is a spiritually hopeful part of us and a dangerously hostile part" (Bly, R.1992: 159). In his writing, entitled "Why Shakespeare is for all Time", Dalrymple Theodore noted: "Shakespeare reminds us of the line between good and evil running down the center of all human beings" (IR). Spiritual psychology guides individuals to constantly understand and monitor this line in order to avoid strife in their relationships. In support of Kinzer, Bly & Dalrymple, Sharon wrote:

> *Much of your negative life experience is likely related to ineffective behavior that fails to solve life's challenging problems and leads to undesired effects such as psychosomatic illness, depression, anxiety, and various other difficulties (2004:247).*

For instance, how can a person aspire to improve the economic situations of society or help others when his or her own house is on fire? Some religiously poise to engage in charitable works, fight for egalitarian society, world peace and good economy et cetera when they are reluctant and lazy to work. Commendably, doing good acts is generally a practical demonstration of charity and love. But, when a lazy person engages in acts of charity without the physical resources to back them up, he or she is in denial and afraid to accept his or her deplorable condition or may be soliciting for assistance to him or herself. This is the problem that faces society in various angles. For instance, how can any government succeed in taking guns out of the streets when teenage boys and girls have not been adequately cultured in sound moral life and education? It is like employing a thief who is not ready to quit stealing to guard a bank. It is sheer psychotic, mental, and a waste of time and energy for one to do things just to please others when it is greatly inconvenient to him or her. That is why, it is also wrong for a person to engage in assisting others when he or she is expected to be at his or her workplace. A Latin adage explains this better "caritas non obligat in magna comodo, that is, "charity does not oblige in great inconvenience" Misplacements of values in relationships are dangerous. Spiritual psychology, in this sense, classifies such charitable acts as mismanaged priorities that do not bring joy and peace to self and society or encourage interpersonal relationships. Every reasonable person is obliged to make appropriate contributions to the progress of his or her environment, family, society, firm, organization, religious affiliation, group and relationship. That is what healthy relationships are all about. Nonetheless, our actions should always and transparently be organized as fragrant aroma that joyously uplifts our spirits and internal energies and those of others. It is wrong to travel by the right train but on a wrong track.

II. Unresolved issues color personal feelings

A "hungry man is an angry man" is a popular aphorism among the Igbo of Nigeria. Love is not deceitful. Thus, the book offers some therapeutic guidelines, impulse controls and healings to individuals, groups, establishments, and families who engage in a variety of relationships. Undoubtedly, "traumatic events impact not only on our psychological functioning, but also on our body chemistry" (Flannery, 1995:43). In order to balance individual body chemistry, spiritual psychology poises to bring about higher consciousness to society and individuals towards assisting them change their thoughts, attitudes and address some of their unresolved issues in relationships. By 'unresolved issues' here we include all psychological stressors triggered by memories of past and present events such as divorce, forced marriage, broken relationships, bereavement, loss of jobs or friendships, post traumatic effects, alcoholism, disappointments, postpartum depressions, sexual abuses, emotional and physical, et cetera. These factors create stress in human relationships. In a general sense, Jamison observed:

> *We all carry burdens with us that others don't suspect. And those burdens color how we feel and how we think... and affect whether or not we are able to risk and grow [in our relationships-mine] (1989:36).*

Unfortunately, these burdens consciously or unconsciously affect individuals and their relationships. This is a big challenge for spiritual psychology and calls for self-orientations. There are a couple of things we can do to deal with burdens. First of all, we must acknowledge them along with our weaknesses and mistakes, seek reconciliation with ourselves and neighbors, and the world by trying to do things right. In James's own view, we must "be quick to listen but slow to speak and slow to rouse your temper" (James 1: 19). Moreover, a burden shared with others is a burden solved. Collective efforts in relationship are self-rewarding. But, staying in the way of others' dreams is self-damaging.

III. Everyone else is unique: "You are your own survival self"

Our being humans or who we are, is not an accident or a risk. We must take control of our feelings, emotions and channel them to meaningful ends. To this effect, the book aims to revive and resuscitate those unconscious strengths, emotional muscles, and energies in individuals that may assist them to steadily navigate through every day management challenges and crisis moments. Tapping into one's internal or inner strengths helps to keep one timelessly healthy. In the words of Jamison: "You do have power. Yes you do. It comes from the very center of yourself—your kernel—the part of you that is unique" (1989:43). Everybody needs this survival personality inside him or her despite the inevitable storms that gradually unfold in relationships. Each person is unique and behaves differently. Never give up in making your future, choosing the best path of life that does not constitute obstacles to others, and follow your heart.

Puppy love does not last

In one of Tyra's Shows, I felt emotionally wounded when some girls admitted that they gave themselves in for sex as ways of building their self-esteems. Unknown to girls in general, self-esteem issues are the ways they appreciate and perceive themselves. They do not dependent on any person or thing, man, woman or affluence. If you say: "I am" others will recognize you. Doing things always, I repeat, to please people is not meritoriously an act of sacrifice but a sign of fear, cowardice and immaturity. It is sickness when a person can no longer derive joy from his or her looks or being. I still wonder if our young men and women ever take a moment and reflect on what the primary goal of this life is all about. For instance, it is very simple for a young man to tell a girl, "I really love you", without being in love with her. Falling in love is easy but staying in it can't be possible without a crisis or sacrifices. A puppy love does not last, especially when it is made under the influence of drug and alcohol. Therefore, spiritual psychology urges young girls and boys to attune and reactivate their faith in themselves. Self-identity is important in relationships. Moreover, it is impossible for any human being to be happy, progressive and self-reliant without spiritual connections to him or herself, society and the world around him or her. Spiritual connection is self-affirmation in one's importance, beliefs and behaviors that are not dependent on matter. It is precisely why the Christian Bible says: "Cut off from me, you can do nothing" (Jn.15: 5). This "me", refers to a spiritual value, source of joy, love, peace and progress. We all need to have the feeling of joy, love, peace and being progressive in our lives, irrespective of our relationships with others. This self-image is not sought outside oneself. But, we can share it with other people who fully appreciate us, as we really deserve.

The world does not come down to us; we assert ourselves first and work up to it. The praises some men lavish on women, at times, are emotional traps, set for selfish motives. The powers to confront unhealthy emotions come from within and not from outside. We must always come to terms with our negative self-images and shape our future with positive self-affirmation that overcomes fears and anxieties. For instance, you are your own personality and I am mine. These differences are basic, normal, and inevitable and can create problems in relationships if they are not properly studied and guided. According to Shlemon, representing the Christian faith, noted:

> *No single prayer, spiritual exercise or meditative technique*
> *can possibly touch all the unhealed areas within us. The*

> *process of healing the inner person is a journey, which we travel throughout our Christian lives as we gradually become infused with the light of God's love (1982:13).*

The process calls for understanding, tolerance, caution, flexibility, acceptance, love, unity and open-mindedness. As McDonald and McDonald would have it: "In this process...the strengthened self begins to take a more active role, functioning as an internal guidance system...to transcend the limits of life and the discomfort of change. Life is then built upon foundations that last, and these flow from within" (1997:12). Certainly, once the human spirit is uplifted in good work, it touches the realm of the sacred and spirituality, and begins to enjoy a lasting renewed feeling of energy. Paradoxically, spiritual psychology prepares each person for the rainy days, especially when life is on the right path. Real success must have a fulfillment. There is no fulfillment for any success or achievement that is made from illicit means or bad will. To prepare the future of tomorrow, our children, there is every need to incorporate sound moral education in the school curricula. One's actions, whether positive or negative, determine one's personality, future and survival rate. But, to achieve survival and progress in relationships, the individual personality has to be positively in alignment with them. Honesty is both therapeutic and medicinal. In achieving a survival strategy, Knaus, citing from the Editors of Bottom Line Publishers, noted:

> *To break a problem habit, you need to create a 'will to change'...a command effort that allows experimenting with change, accepting its difficulty and moving ahead again even after inevitable backsliding... Deflect your attention from the habit to something else (1998:51).*

Each person is his or her own personality and survival. The "will to change" entails some radical decision, determination, courage and humility on the principal agent. This clarion call compels us to examine the principles of cognitive-behavioral therapy. According to Capuzzi & Gross: "The manner in which people think and feel affect their lives" (2003:214; in Odikanoro, V. 2008:4 -20) and relationships. For instance, "Physicians have long known that a patient who expects to get pain relief from a pill often does, even though it is a placebo containing no medication" (Norman, 2007:191). This self-consciousness guides individuals or partners to expect the unexpected in their relationships even when things plausibly sound friendly and welcoming. It equally calls for the purification of individual hearts in order to avoid passing judgments on someone or a partner one has not studied or has not really come in contact with. Worse still, it is wrong for people or parties to base the judgments of their actions on hearsays and rumors that have not been verified. All is well that ends well.

The Johari window model of Joseph Luft and Harry Ingham, created in the US in 1955 is of classic importance here. The Johari window is a cognitive psychological tool or skill that can help individuals especially in corporate settings, students and peer groups to understand one another better for smoother relationships. Partners in marriage can equally learn from this model. The window is in a form of house with 4 rooms and each of these rooms contains vital pieces of information that assist participants or inmates to self-supervise themselves. By "rooms" here, we refer to individual qualities or values. For instance, 2 rooms have information that is accessible to others while 2 hold information that is unknown to others. The first room represents part of our life patterns that others know about us and we know them too. The second room specifies those qualities (blind spot quadrants) only known by others but unknown to us, for which they blame or praise us. By implication, many a time, this is the room that creates conflicts in relationships because unrealistic minds or individuals do not want to hear about their ugly sides or stories. The third room points to our unconscious or subconscious selves, which mysteriously remain unknown both to others and us. The fourth room represents our private lives we know about but keep only to ourselves (IR). In other words, Johari widow typology has great relevance in interpersonal relationships and calls for caution in judging others because we live by what we say, do and our values.

As a guide, spiritual psychology insists that it is wrong for a person to imagine his or her partner to be bad till he or she has exhausted his or her positive sides, windows or kind dispositions. It is impossible to fully understand what piece of being a human is. Possibly, something might

9

be keeping you uncomfortable or destroying your relationship, and at times, unknowingly, that something is you, yourself, nature, unhealthy imaginations, choices and habits. For instance, it is practically hard to satisfy a dependent, family member, friend, neighbor, partner or person whose material expectations and appetites are higher than your own. Getting worried over the attitude of an ungrateful person or partner is of no use. Create joy for yourself. It is only you that is you on the planet.

The world is never limited by our worries. Cautiously and always create an atmosphere and peaceful environment where healthy relationships can thrive. The best way to achieve this goal is by reinforcing, encouraging and appreciating the efforts of others, no matter how little. Mindfully, despite some of the unwelcoming circumstances of life and human imperfections, partners should always channel their strengths, goals, dreams, potentials and deliberations on choices that are in agreement with their set goals and resources. On no account should people allow the 'smoke of Satan' [unnecessary anger] or suspicion infiltrate into their relationships because individual goals and preferences will always differ. This is why each person should have a strong sense of him or herself; morally do the best he or she can and validate him or herself irrespective of the standards others have set for themselves. Some people judge others based on their limited knowledge of the true fact. Partners deserve the best in every relationship, especially when they understand their "ultimate edges" the vital step-by-step precautions of Anthony Robison, they must take to their desired goals (IR, 2009).

IV. Making real the presence of God and each other in relationship

Life is basically relationship. Again, relationship, like life, is of divine origin, ontologically linked to the family, society, others and especially to its source as noted here: "Let us make man in our own image, in the likeness of ourselves" (Gen. 1:26). God has always maintained a covenant relationship with humanity. This is a covenant of *"taba"* [friendship], and *"hesed"* [love or solidarity], in which man responds, *"yada"* [to serve God] faithfully in accordance with the terms of the covenant. Love, in this context, is not about feelings but expressions

10

of gratitude and praises for the joys that come from loving and being loved. Thus, God initiated a covenantal relationship and communion with humankind to show us his love. Covenant, as employed in this book, is a solemn promise that demands actions on both sides. It is a commitment in which one declares one's life and relationship for God and allows God take control of one's life and relationship. In this way, the human families form a union of people that represents the presence of God in their relationships and world. In this context, while spiritual psychology does not support or oppose the same sex marriage, it emphasizes that sexual orientation is not a matter of choice but a divine and biological reality. The choices we make of things, often, do not change their reality. That a person wants something does not mean he or she can have it.

God is life GPS – Listen carefully
"Your destination is at your hands!"

Parties in any level of relationship also need a personal covenant. God is like the GPS system. He continues to assist us navigate our life journey towards the road to integrity, accountability, probity, peace, sound moral life, hard work, learning, hope, joy and love. One can still choose otherwise. At times, we misinterpret the GPS, make mistakes, yet, it does not blame or abandon us, instead, if we listen carefully and pay attention, it automatically reconnects us on the right path to accomplish our set objectives. Whatever God, our Life GPS begins or starts, with our cooperation, he will definitely finish. According to William: "God continually acts in the universe to draw all of us into community with the Trinity and with one another" (Vol. 11, No. 3. 1990:9). According to the Book of Second Chronicles:

> *If my people who bear my name humble themselves, and pray and seek my presence and turn from their wicked ways, I myself will hear from heaven and forgive their sins and restore their land (7:14).*

For believers, here lies the whole emphasis on human relationships. Accepting and loving one another, as fulfillments of Gods' love and covenant with us is a platitude. Our land or society is already chaotic.

Anything that seems to have consistently created problem for us in the past should not be allowed to play any role in our future. In each of the covenant relationships, God has always invited individuals for a friendly dialogue, which reached its perfection in the person of Christ, the Sacramental expression of God's love. Matrimonial relationship in the Catholic Church is also a Sacrament. Uninterested love is equally sacramental.

In the words of Hellwig: "Sacrament is an embodiment. Human persons cannot meet or experience God except as embodied" (1981:136) in the person of Jesus Christ. So long as human beings are created in God's image, [relationships] according to religious traditions, therefore they become the embodiment of the divine presence, the branches of the Vine [John 15.5] in each other and the world around them. This was precisely why Fulton Sheen in Marlin, G referred to the "Sacraments" as "the drama of God" (1989:278). For the Catholics, these are Liturgical Dramas, Actions through which graces and stability are inwardly implanted into our souls and relationships. The moment individuals shun God and discipline in their relationships they suffer "spiritual aridity" and the nightmares are always dreadful, mental, poisonous and suicidal. For instance, how can one believe in God when one does not have a place for him in one's heart, home and relationship? Believing "in one God" and remaining divided in our relationships is like praying the "Our Father" for forgiveness when we are not ready to forgive others. R - G or M = BSA. That is: Relationship minus God or Morality is equal to Brute Animals or Bachelor of Spiritual Death. Moreover, the devil does not know our plans or thoughts until we invite him in what we say and do. Therefore, when we utter foul and morally offensive words, the devil cashes in immediately and assists us put them into actions. Evil intentions sleep in the same bed with the devil. The devil we know is better than the 'angel' we do not know. When we consult with God for anything, be it sickness, loss of friendships, emotional stress, disappointments, we must leave it there with him.

V. Avoid being held in a tight corner: Relate freely

Definitely, it is not proper to feel insecure in any relationship. If occasion of insecurity arises, calmly relax your mind and deal with it. First, examine your previous attitudes or roles in the matter, the impacts they have on others and be ready for adjustments if possible. To sincerely enter into healthy relationship with others, whether it is covenantal, contractual, consensual, natural or accidental, one must be ready to listen to the opinions of others and be there for them in all circumstances possible. It is necessary that people joyously maximize every moment and opportunity in their relationships to exercise freedom. In this sense, Sanford remarks:

> *We need relationships in which we can just be ourselves, where others will relate to us just as human beings, the professional aspect is not part of the relationship…. When people relate to us in terms of our profession rather than who we are as people, we speak of the relationship as a 'transference' (1982:41-42).*

Relationship is one of the key focal points of metaphysics, especially with regard to its dynamics, the fulfillment of what it means to be and the realization of life. It aims at experiencing the warmth of humanness and unity in one another, the presence of God in us, and allowing others to experience him in us. Relationships are the continuing presence of God's goodness, values, care and love in our lives, in each other and the world, even for unbelievers. Unless individuals are freely able to realize, utilize and make real the presence of God or Goodness in one another, in their homes, work places, government quarters, et cetera, life will always be meaningless. This natural disposition for self-supervision, I refer to as emotional intelligence or "wisdom". Emotional intelligence or Wisdom in this context is the ability for an individual in any relationship to visualize in the future the consequences of his or her present decisions and actions. In reference to wisdom in marital relationship, Clerico A. in an interview, noted: "Relationship is all about two persons sacrificing parts of themselves to contribute in loving appreciation to their new life together-giving away of independent existence and simultaneously taking up the responsibility to fully share in all that life has to offer, either joyously or painfully" (Nov. 26, 2009). Relationship remains a shared identity of joy and sorrow, loss and gain. Freely, it embraces both the positive and negative qualities of each person or partner. In support of the above views, Johann observes:

> *When love is interested, when the attraction is based on a*
> *motive of profit or need, it has no difficulty in finding words*
> *to justify it. When "I love you" equals "I want you," the*
> *expected satisfaction of the want is reason enough for the love*
> *(1966:19).*

Basing human relationship on narrow-mindedness or self-centeredness is hazardous. Anything that threatens relationship equally affects the individual lives in a very drastic and dramatic way. In Hybels's words: "A stockpile of God's blessings has been poured into our lives. When we live in the awareness of all God has given us, it spills over to others" (1996:19). This is what relationship is all about, freely living in the presence of God's innumerable gifts, blessings and turning them into a community of peace without force or being ordered around.

VI. Peace, the soul of relationships: Without it, we merely exist and do not live

Eventually, to exist is one thing and to live, another. We merely exist in the absence of Truth, Justice and Peace - TJP. But we live when there is unruffled state of mind encompassed in deep sense of identity and belongingness. In the words of Fulton Sheen:

> *Peace means a right conscience, not a dictatorship over the*
> *proletariat... not the overthrow of society; it means loving our*
> *enemies, not despising them; it means something in the inside*
> *of a man's soul, not something outside like a sickle and a*
> *hammer (1989:221-222).*

We need each other to create and live in peaceful relationships. That is why the fullness of life in relationship is primarily realized when we experience the serenity and peace of God within ourselves. Paths to peace do not count so much on the details of actions or wrong behaviors that initially led to the altercation. In peace, the mind only recollects positive memories that energize progress. There is peace when we choose well, work hard, shape our destinies, priorities and plan within our reach. We must allow others to be and live their lives. That was the point Hawkins David meant when he wrote: "It is a relief to let the mind become silent and just 'be' with the surroundings. Peace results, and appreciation and calm prevail…. The well-disciplined mind should only speak when requested to perform a task" (2006:234). In this way, we embody peace and joy in our relationships and the world around us. There is no peace in any relationship, without truth and justice. Most often, these singular heartfelt gestures of open-mindedness and sincerity are highly rewarded and reciprocated in a variety of ways, particularly when partners understand themselves and their limitations. But, at some other times, they are not. That is the unpredictability of life and no person has control over it. As long as we put our best selves in every moment of our relationships, our lives effervescently remain rewarding to us, others and society. Relationship is like a religious cell group system. As Cho P, once put it: "Each cell group becomes a nucleus of revival in its neighborhood, because the cell group is where real life is to be found in that neighborhood" (1978:58). In other words, healthy relationship can be compared to what Cho Paul noted here about cell groups in the following words:

> *When a home cell meeting [relationship] is full of life, and when people [partners] are happy and sharing their faith and witnessing to what the Lord has done in their lives; other people are drawn to them. Unbelievers [others] become curious. They want to know why this little [poor] group of Christians is so joyful when all around them there are so many troubles (1978:58-59).*

VII. No 'CP'- capital 'P' [Partner] in healthy relationship – No neutrality

Consequently, the book reminds us that each person is his or her own relationship. Whichever way one makes one's bed does one lie on it. Every tree falls along the sideway it bends. The good and evil we attach to our actions and our relationships are just names that signify our appetites and choices. We may not fully understand ourselves except in those actions that define our values and personalities. Basically, we reflect who we are and how we relate to others by our actions. Eventually, it is our personal values, our lives, positively or negatively, that we bring or relate to other people because; *nemo dat quod non-*

habet, that is, "no one gives what he or she has not". In this light, the book has illumined the 'vertical' and 'horizontal' aspects of man *qua tale,* his or her potentials, dispositions and aspirations. In view of these studies, we have come up with guidelines of shared identities and ocean of findings from which individuals can draw their behavioral maps and patterns to avoid toxic relationships. To maintain a healthy relationship, always watch your mouth, as regards what to say, when and how you say it. Human relationships are essentially guided by the same principles but uniquely experienced from different levels. For, what's good for the goose is good for the gander. Generally, there is no "CP", that is, capital "P", person or "partner" in relationships especially within the marital circles or friendships. Every person is indispensable for relationship to work. All forms of controlling and domineering mentality typical of egocentric individuals or animals easily crash relationships. To avoid having relationships go up in flames, each person should see his or her partner as a soul mate and not as spare parts supplier of needs. Relationships are not presumptuous. There is no neutrality in any healthy relationship. Either, one has a relationship or not. However, constructive initiatives are readily welcomed in all levels of relationships.

The concept of "marital relationship" in Africa partly appears challenged here. Unlike in the western world where there is equality of gender, it is a taboo in Africa. The situation is underscored in this biblical context: "…. as Christ is head of the Church…so is a husband the head of his wife; and as the Church submits to Christ, so should wives to their husbands, in everything" (Eph. 5: 21-22). The bible explicitly made no distinctions of the kind of husbands meant here. Even though Jesus is fighting infidelity of the age, the teaching is normal in the African understanding of marital relationship, the worthiness of some husbands notwithstanding. The African women generally and gladly cash in this circumstance and take pride for being provided for and protected by men or their husbands. As such, they do all within their powers to reciprocate the gesture. Initially, the situation raised no dust on both sides. Traditionally, for instance, when the economy was booming, women were not meant to suffer or engage in strenuous manual labors. Due solely to the fact that Africans place much premium on life, the primary function of women is to stay home, do some farming, clean the house, wash clothes, prepare the food, look after the house and take care of the children. The men virtually provide the needs of the family. Comparatively, most women from the western world would definitely prefer the African option, staying at home without having to spend sleepless and strenuous days and nights working. However, abuses came into the system because of selfishness and greed of some men. Moreover, the mortality rate of the men complicated the system and rendered the less working class widows redundantly hopeless. Eventuality is the mother of invention. Such women have to survive.

Generally, acting the man as husband in a marital relationship or the woman instead of a wife is always dangerous. For, all husbands and wives are men and women respectively, but not all men and women are husbands and wives. Good husbands and wives are gifts. Some friendships are gifts too. As it were, things are changing; today some African women, especially the learned work, financially take care of their homes, train their kids, favorably compete with men, and fight for their "empowerment and emancipation". Undoubtedly, many women are unconsciously and unjustly dominated by the tyranny of some illiterate and selfish men. As a consequence, spiritual psychology, through educational approach and research, aims to protect, restore the equality, right and peace of the human person irrespective of gender or race. All the same, equality of status and gender has not been anything to be grasped in Africa. Conventionally, the African men perceive their right over women, generational.

VIII. Imperfect human beings are everywhere

Eventually, spiritual psychology hereby studies the gloomy darkness of hatred and the apparent conflicts and misconducts in relationships and investigates why they seem to have divided the individual and society today. Moreover, each person is unique and behaves true to type despite religious affiliations and belief systems. This 'uniqueness', which is inherent in each person calls for caution because human relationship is as imperfect as humanity itself. Imperfections are everywhere. We also need to remember those we stand on their toes, or have offended, assassinated their characters and denied their fundamental rights.

There is no absolute order in any relationship. This is not to say that some relationships cannot stand as models or be trusted within certain circumstances. Paradoxically, no matter how diligent, caring, reliable we may be in our relationships, following our hearts and obeying our consciences; some people will always criticize and hold different opinions about us. This is one of the natural and relational growing edges. We must expect this possibility in any relationship, even from our colleagues and best friends. Our enemies, most often, avoid us and do not easily succeed in harming us but friends do. Inevitably, we have to take the Heraclitian and Tillichian ideas of the paradoxical co-existence of the good and the evil very seriously. Society at large, especially individuals and partners in particular, should be aware of this paradox in their relationships. Naturally, amidst love, joy, progress and peace, hatred, sadness, failure and quarrel co-exit. Prudence is essential here. Therefore, partners should carefully and jointly stick to the roads to love and peace that ultimately guide all healthy relationships. Healthy relationship does not take a break. It has to be consistent.

IX. Memories of negative past events frustrate the present

Occasionally, as noted already, we encounter ingratitude in the midst of our generosity and hatred or envy among our best friends. To build healthy relationship, we have to be ready to deal and cope with such behaviors. When faced with such situations, we recall the letter of St. Paul to the Romans (12:14-21), which is consoling and encouraging. Inasmuch as there is no art to measure the depth of the human mind, we must try to do our best and leave the rest for eternity. Being misjudged in our actions or relationships is normal. We do not owe apologies to anybody for our being misunderstood for conventionally doing what we ought to do (Wisdom 2:12). Besides, we must not allow the memories of our negative past events frustrate our present life. Instead, it is better we think of our positive life styles, a life full of authentic relationships and memories and move forward. Positive memories are vital ingredients of life and they motivate fruitful accomplishments. Keep on doing good and let nature take its course.

Humility and openness are the keys to progress and healing. Happy is the person who is contented with the least he or she has. The quest for worldly glories is not a priority in relationships. Rather, the weight of one's personality, one's riches and level of one's learning are often evaluated by the nature of relationships one keeps. We cannot solve our problems by running away from them and talk of doing good when there are evils to be avoided or build healthy relationships when old wounds have not been healed. We can always learn to start a healthy relationship afresh by first of all acknowledging where we went wrong because we may be the principal agents or causes of the bad behaviors we seem to hate and encounter in others. That is why the best way to break bad habits is to admit that there is a problem. In many cases, we are our own worries and headaches.

X. The world is large enough: Waste no time or Do not look for good reasons to win a case

In one of the writings of Fulton Sheen, he recommended that each person should perceive and live every day as his or her last. This idea propelled us into the study of the various images of relationship that lead to healthy living. Openness is indispensable in every relationship and our bodies are the center. The expressions and impressions we show to others determine whether they are invited in our lives or not. Gabriel Marcel, a French Philosopher in Dr. Uwasomba's work, used the symbol of door in his phenomenological studies to demonstrate this view. For instance, an open door lets us into a room, a hall, a theatre etc. But a closed one shuts us out and the one that is kept ajar, creates the sense of insecurity as whether we are free to enter or not (2009). Playing the 'hide and seek' games in relationship is dangerously self-damaging. Diplomacy is not always helpful in relationships but courtesy is. For instance, one of the doctors we interviewed here in New York told us that he had often admitted being at fault and apologized to his wife in trivial issues just to avoid raising any voice in their relationships. At the same time, the readiness to accept apologies in relationships is grace while rigidity of heart damages both the relationship and the soul of the unforgiving partner. According to James: "Everyone who knows the right thing to do and does not do it commits a sin" (Jam. 4:17). It is better we try to do the good or the right thing and fail than succeed in doing nothing. Staging or setting traps for others as a way to test their love is diabolical. Once a mistake has already been made, it automatically becomes a thing of the past and little or nothing can be done to change it. Possibly, the only way out is to focus on the future with optimism and courage. Mistakes are best corrected from where they are discovered and "what is not there cannot be counted" (Eccl. 1:15). To live in peace is more glorious than to look for good reasons to win or justify cases. In my interview with Prof. Iwuchukwu Boniface of Imo State University, Nigeria, in November 14, 2009, he said:

> *Do not waste time organizing how to retaliate or fight your enemy. Instead, use that time to organize how to move ahead in more important things in life. In other words, while your enemy is static waiting for a big fight and victory, you would have gone so far, addressing other important issues to enjoy a better day. It will practically be late for your enemy to realize that he has wasted all his useful moments, waiting only to fight himself and herself.*

Procrastination is not always helpful in a relationship that counts on immediate actions and results. Calmly and politely tell your partner/s how you feel at each moment, state and level of your relationship. While we need distractions at times in relationships, disturbances kill. Therefore, whenever we let our partners know our feelings, we must at the same time expect the unexpected by remaining positive and acting as if our wishes had been granted. The evil one or the devil uses, acts and speaks through our best friends to upset us. The world itself is wide enough to accommodate everybody. Every deed, whether it is good or bad has its own effects and rewards, if not now, later.

XI. Human life continues on its explorative journey

One day at a time leads to eternity. Therefore, we should gladly maximize all the possible and beautiful avenues that help us come to terms with society and ourselves. Appreciating one another, and realizing that we are all within the parenthesis of eternity (empty we came to the world and empty shall we return) irrespective of our religious, socio-political and personal differences, is a must in every relationship. No wonder a 5th century BC philosopher, Anaximander once remarked in William: "All things must in equity again decline into that whence they have their origin" (1926:35). Come what may, life continues on its explorative journey, ultimately returning to its origins. Our lives should, therefore, touch others in positive perspectives. According to Jamison: "We all live in groups, all kinds of groups: families, schools, offices, factories, clubs, social circles. And within all these groups we each occupy a position and have influence in relation to the other members of the group" (1989:5). This is why Jesus calls humanity to form an inner moral unity with one another, which is his own unity with the father (Jn.17: 21-22). God himself is a mystery. He created humanity, for those who believe, in his own image. In a sense, human beings are mysterious and daily unfold themselves that way in their relationships. This is why every relationship is experienced differently and shaped by it's own story and belief. For instance, as a Catholic priest and celibate, I relate to people that way whether they agree with my life choice or not, irrespective of the common values, love, respect and reasons that bind us together.

XII. Need man be man if he claims no responsibility for his actions?

From a different angle, it is necessary to note that in this book, we interchangeably used the words "religious", "moral" and "ethical" unless where we considered some distinctions necessary. The same applies to the words "Heaven, Eternity, EIDN – Eternal Identification Number, Good work and Values". However, as a matter of great concern, as already noted, we approached human relationship from psychological and ethical perspectives because it involved rational beings and actions. The approach and its implication as they concern every person appear to offer some solutions to the increasing conflict; disunity and misunderstanding that exist in many relationships today. Therefore, our in-depth study of the different psychological, ethical, moral principles, human reasoning and judgments [conscience] as regards human behaviors go a long way to enhance the scholarship of this book. As observed in Tavris and Aronson's book:

> *The reality was…that I was alone not because of my politics but because I did not know how to live in a decent way with another human being (2007:183-184).*

We are all aware that society and most people have been infected with irresponsible attitudes as the result of bad associations, religious, racial and economic differences. Human existence and life merely become animalistic and meaningless if no person claims responsibility for his or her actions. In this vein, the book identified the enormity and nature of such disorientations and the possible measures that can be applied to eradicate them. Being responsible for our secret or public speeches, actions and deeds whether they are offensive or commendable graciously makes us human beings in all levels of relationships.

XIII. Life teaches: To be religious is not being spiritual

Life has no duplicate and abhors debates. One can be so religious without mindful of what it means to relate and care for others. It is only when one incorporates good work and behavior with theology that one aspires to spirituality. Spirituality is stewardship – the best application of one's talents and resources for the good of oneself and others. We shall revisit this point later. However, it is one thing to approach the issue of relationship from a psychological perspective and another to underline the kind of psychology that is didactic and appropriate for achieving the desired goals. There are as many psychologies as there are human enterprises and behaviors. In a book like this, we employ a psychology that studies and examines the individual behaviors and relationships in view of their socio-religious belief systems. By "religious belief systems" here, we do not refer to any particular religion because healthy relationships can exist without religious affiliations. Moreover, even if one does not believe in religion or have any, one still believes in something that is sustainable and foundational in one's relationship and being. By implication, whatever keeps one in alignment and balanced with healthy relationship, whether it is clear or not, may serve as one's belief system or religion. In a practical sense, we are our own religion and belief systems. When individuals freely stick to and believe in whatever appeals to them, life irrevocably, sooner or later, teaches and proves to them the reality and implications of their costly choices.

In the words of Erik: "Whoever says he has religion must derive a faith from it which is transmitted to infants in the form of basic trust; whoever claims that he does not need a religion must derive such basic faith elsewhere" (1980:67). Whether everyone or the whole world believes in religion or not, historically and intrinsically, it does not change what it is or its mission. The few people, who totally embrace religion as the foundation of their lives, care less about all these theological debates and jargons. As Fr. Pellegrino J. would have it: "Truth has nothing to do with numbers" (IR, 8/23/09). The sacrifices of Elijah and the 450 prophets of Baal quickly come to mind here (1Kings 18: 20-27). For instance, that abortion is legalized in many parts of the globe today does not make it morally acceptable by everybody. There are so many people in society, married couples, families who naturally do not practice abortion whether legalized or not. Such legalizations do not set the standards for sound moral actions. For instance, one of the professionals, Ms. Rose Nwachukwu, Head Mistress, Central School Umunama, we interviewed in Nigeria made the following remarks about abortion:

> *It seems abortion rate is higher among the unmarried or singles than the married. Besides, to abort a child is not about the baby, but me, because it makes me irrational and think I have no self-continence and the right to exist or live myself. Now, if I cannot assist this little baby enjoy the same life like myself, how do I validate my own existence and expect others to assist me in anything? Animals do not have brains like me, yet they do not abort their off springs like humans, rather, they nurse them jealously. This is an unfortunate situation, solving a natural problem through the most unloving and dirty way. God, please forgive us, 4/3/98.*

We cannot wish or pray for a better tomorrow when we do not take advantage of our today. I would have wished these issues were left at the hands of the individuals and the Church and not with the government. Has anybody raised questions as regards how the deadly issue of HIV has resisted medical science? However, whether there is a general consensus as regards the introduction of religion or moral instructions to public school systems, colleges, universities or not, religion continues to guide and sustain the faith of so many students and their families today. Majority does not always guide human relationships. This is where every human institution, academic, ministry needs spiritual psychologist. Today, majority of our young generation do not show any interest in religion or religious practices and services. Visit the Churches and Crusades; most of them are mainly filled with elderly people. These are the same youths who wish to grow and enjoy longevity. In Africa, old age or gray hair is a blessing and not a curse. Religion has always had huge influence in people's relationships.

Conclusively, it is sheer selfishness, self-deception and hypocritical for a youth to consciously and freely live his or her youthful life exhibiting less interest in religious matters only to come back to frequent religious services at his or her old age. We do not doubt that these youths can repent whenever their spirit or conscience is reactivated in grace. There is always time for self-supervision. Imperatively, spiritual psychology proactively advocates the introduction of "Moral Instructions" in all schools, colleges and universities. It should be one of the elective classes or courses offered in Colleges and Universities.

Educate the child and change society – Oprah

Only posterity will tell of society that lacks the foundation of moral education. For instance, Imo State Government of Nigeria has recently announced the handing over of High and Secondary schools back to the Church because, both the education and moral lives of the young generation have terribly been messed up. The good news is that the Government took over these schools over forty years ago from the Church and has now realized the need for discipline and sound moral education in the lives of our teenage boys and girls. Some parts of the western world, must one day, come back to the Church for spiritual edification in both schools and society by introducing Moral Instructions or spiritual psychology in the schools. Even though some people have sharply criticized the proverb "spare the rod and spoil the child", naturally there is need to guide each child irrespective of his or her wonderful dispositions. Ineluctably, discipline has to be enforced, directly or indirectly because nobody tells a person with hearing impairment that there is commotion in the Market Square, Playground or Park. Imo State has seen it now, thanks to the present Government. The rod has been spared from the child in many cultures and families; today society is generally suffering the effects in one head

24

injury, social, religious violence or the other. Moreover, a relationship based purely on physical application of interests, appetite and reasons that are devoid of moral values will definitely suffocate. Due mainly to this sad trend, Dr. Nwachukwu Udaku citing Garbner, lamented:

> *No wonder George Garbner a renowned TV researcher wisely remarks: The more time one spends 'Living' in the world of television the more likely one is to report perceptions of social reality (that) can be traced to television's presentations of life and society (2009:71).*

If a child were, ab initio, taught the need to respect and preserve the dignity of human life, he or she could not have turned into a terrorist. Terrorism also exists in many forms. A Latin adage says: "Initiarum pervum sunt" meaning that 'things are small when they begin'. If it is normal and lawful for a child to call the police and fight his or her parents simply because he or she is ordered to behave well and keep good company, what else will such a child not do to have his or her ways in society? The mentality of opening fire and shooting innocent souls and abduction for no just cause did not start one day. Our homes, associations, schools and environments could easily and locally be a nursing ground and the beginning of terrorist's mission. On this note, Heraclitus remarked:

> *Good character is not formed in a week, or month. It is created little by little, day by day. Protracted and patient effort is needed to develop good character (IR).*

Prevention is always better than cure. Teach the child to respect others and it will surely respect itself. In Oprah's own words: "Educate a child and save and change the whole village" (12/01/09). An action becomes religious when it addresses practical issues that spiritually uplift the needy of society.

The glories of technology should not rule out or discourage respect for one another. It is counterproductive to advance in science and technology when most of those who are the prime beneficiaries of the scientific age cannot differentiate between moral actions that destroy and those that promote human lives. We are living witnesses of what I describe and refer to as "DOCMI" that is, 'Deliberate Opportunity Cost for Moral Irreversibility'. "You cannot have your cake and eat it" has been adopted in this book as a warning signal. Society cannot expect to enjoy a brighter future, full of love, safety and peace, an organized system of education free from immorality, clean politics and interpersonal relationships when "Moral Instructions" have directly and lawfully been abrogated from many institutions and colleges. How can natural moral laws become appendages to human made or civil laws? While spiritual psychology strongly promotes civil laws because of the bad eggs in society, they should inevitably co-exist pari passu with natural moral laws that guide individual consciences and actions. Credibility is always the rule in relationships and good name is better than gold.

The Christian Bible expressed it better: "…make every part of your body into a weapon fighting on the side of God; …since you are living by grace and not by law" (Rom. 6:13-14). It is self-rewarding to adhere more to the reasons for the law than its letters. The ills we experience today because of lack of discipline are the opportunity cost for the irreversible peace society would have enjoyed. The President of the United States of America, Barack Obama, in his presidential address to Congress on Health Care Reform, observed that all the problems the world is facing today are not physical but "moral issues" (Sept. 9, 2009). These are moral issues because many people have refused to behave true to their nature as rational beings. In many health matters today, sickness has been insured instead of health itself because of greed. Even in Africa, it costs more to bury the dead than maintain the living. Human beings cannot enjoy any peace of mind without sound moral life. Morality shapes our aspirations, both present and future as rational beings. Joking with this fundamental value is to play with fire.

Ultimately, it is difficult if not practically impossible to define a person through his or her claims on religious affiliations without sound moral life. A person can strongly believe in God without historically being identified with any religion that emphasizes membership. Similarly, one can sound so religious or pietistic and totally lacks moral virtues, values and spirituality. This is not to diminish or negate the irreplaceable role of religion in society. It is ultimately impossible to be spiritual without being practically oriented, as a sign of one's belief system, either in oneself, source, destiny, others or religion. In a simple analysis, a person's behavior essentially gives clues to his or her nature, level of religious practices and spirituality. Spirituality is the embodiment and synthesis of religion in action. In the words of Msgr. Walter Niebrzydowski in his Versus-Verses-Series, "Religion devoid of spirituality degenerates into a club. Spirituality married to religion generates a community" (10/30/09). Practically, to be religious is not being spiritual and vice versa.

Contextually, spiritual psychology is concerned more with those religious practices whose denials are intrinsically contradictory. It is within this understanding that we conceive man as a religious animal - *homo religiousus (religious man)*. Spirituality, as we shall see later incorporates the minutest details of our values, beliefs and actions. Any religious belief that does not lead to practice lacks spirituality. Our emphasis here also presupposes the question: "can any form of life be lived or religion practiced without psychology?" In issues like this, sentiments have no place. While religion generally precedes "beliefs" in God, religion in turn, is nourished and animated by beliefs that are concretized in actions. That means we worship what we believe in and practice or carry out that belief the way we are. For instance, none of our states in life, stature, riches or poverty, education or illiteracy is an obstacle in practicing our belief systems or worshipping God. Eventually, it is spiritual psychology that holistically guides the individual to realize the importance and need to achieve his or her objectives in life by being conscious of what he or she does and how he or she goes about them for meaningful results.

XIV. Relationship is "W-a-w"-whole and whole and not half and half

In order to make human relationship healthy, it has to be cherished in its entirety. Very little thing can provoke suspicion. Usually, we relate and interact the way we are. For instance, our gender, sex or age [genetic, environmental or hormonal], stature or 'character' play important roles in our relationships. Nothing counts more in healthy relationships than self-consciousness. Nonetheless, religion as an organized system plays vital roles too. It can change our life styles and guide our relationships but hardly our nature. Hence, faithfulness or fidelity in general is a characteristic test for healthy relationships and religious practices. The human nature is such that one falls at a time and rises also. To be constantly aware of this weakness, even in our relationships, is grace. Therefore, religion should not be an obstacle to human relationships. Individuals can relate and live together without being denominational or having formal religion. Yet, whether religion is revealed or born by association, relationship is basically the measurement, test and foundation. Any religion that lacks sound morality is already dead.

We are deeply concerned here with whatever guides parties to establish healthy relationships in their lives and society. While we do not doubt the importance of religion in this regard, spiritual psychology is designed to analyze the spiritual and inner attitudes, dispositions and abilities of individuals to adapt to the world around them. This amazing ability to adapt to our world goes a long way to enhance our relationships. For instance, how does a devoted religious believer who is infected with life-threatening disease perceive God in the face of such excruciating pains and death? How does a caring husband or wife feel when his or her beloved partner surprisingly cheats on him or her? Or, how do the children of separated parents react as they watch their parents quarrel and angrily yell at each other? These are sad moments, but they create potential occasions for greater spiritual maturity and call for supportive presence and prudence since relationships primarily run on the electricity and network of emotions and feelings. This is the time to say: "Wait a minute". Take a deep breath, examine your actions, ask self-reflected questions and quit bad habits.

Sex is not Love and vice versa

This is why life is larger than logic. Not even religion can automatically heal the hurt created by infidelity especially in marital relationships. Infidelity in sexual issues is of two categories. When it is planned and aimed at hurting the other person, it becomes critical and more precarious. In a situation like that, it points to unresolved issues that have never been given any attention in relationship. This is bad. It can also be circumstantial, a mistake which just happened with no intention to hurt one's partner. Yet, these are challenging moments in our lives when personal convictions and beliefs take the upper hand. A reasonable partner will always employ wisdom and moral virtue by weighing the consequences of his or her decisions and actions to avoid being erratic, sporadic and rash in his or her judgments. Emotional intelligence, the self-perceived ability to reflect on the right course of action, is needed here. Cheating, especially when it is premeditated, is grievously and totally the summary of "a let down". It points to the question: "what can you do?" Nothing hurts more in relationships than that. However, this is the time to recollect that relationship is simply "W-a-w", that is, whole and whole. In this instance, because spiritual psychology examines issues from a long term benefits and perspectives that guide the moment, would want partners to consider the following alternatives: For instance, "does it worth the game for me to part with this my cherished and long life partner because he or she cheated on me? What circumstances could have precipitated and been responsible for this act? What is the primary motive for this emotional injury and infliction? What about our kids and future? Could my partner be sick and needed medical attention? Oh my God! Is this mess intentional or accidental? It is too much for me to bear. Would I have preferred him or her dead in the process?" Unbearably, the situation is hurtful for any sensible partner. Our view of love may change with events, but love itself does not change. The case of Joseph whose wife seemed to have cheated is a big guide here. For instance, the Bible says:

> *...before they came to live together she was found to be with child.... Her husband Joseph; being a man of honor and wanting to spare her publicity, decided to divorce her informally (Mat. 1:18-19).*

Few questions come to mind here: "What is the primary reason for Joseph to hide a crime that is punishable by death? Why did he put the safety of his wife first before his hurt? If you were in Joseph's position, how would you have handled the issue?" Did the fact that Mary was with a child through the Holy Spirit make any sense to Joseph when such 'atrocious act' has never been recorded anywhere before? Who is the Holy Spirit for Joseph and by what authority has he to intrude in his relationship? This is where spiritual maturity comes in again. In many life moments like these, when all hopes seem to have vanished, this is when spiritual psychology concretely surfaces in the light of Heraclitian and Tillichian paradoxical co-existence of the good and bad with positive thoughts that assist one deal with one's hurtful feelings. Religion historically plays the same role in the face of insurmountable problems for those who are practically sincere with it. Mistakes and hurts can easily be forgotten when the spirit is at work or in control of the body.

Retrogressively, spiritual psychology reminds the wounded partner to consider the many faithful years they lived together, the favorable things they received and shared, how they stood by each other amidst all odds, especially when all friends and relations deserted them, how they risked their lives to save each other, even at sickness et cetera. Ask yourself these questions: "Must I crucify him or her for this particular sin? Or, has he or she been in this habit? Where lies the concept of love and forgiveness? Did he or she mean to cheat actually? When my love does not go beyond physical appearances and human frailties, can I still claim one?" Eventually, it becomes important to note that fidelity is a universal value that is not limited to carnal relationships. It is an offence against one's nature, conscience and being to do so. As such, "love" and "sex" are two different values. While sex can be an expression of romantic (eros) or philia love, most often, it is not equivalent to love. Humans share erotic love with other living beings and creatures. "Philia love", according to Kant in Nwachukwu "is pathological because it is based on affection and attraction" (1993:10). What happens to love when physical attractions fade? It is also described, as 'unitive' love in married state. Sex is naturally a physical reality and common to all living creatures. On the contrary, love, especially "agape", the Christian aspect, "virginal" and "appreciative" is a value shared by both rational beings and the supernatural. It goes beyond physical bounds and makes sex more meaningful.

Therefore, for a partner to base his or her judgment of fidelity on sex alone clearly indicates that love has never existed in his or her relationship. Moreover, when a person reveals the secret of his or her partner to a third party who may not be in good terms with his or her partner, it is worse than having sex with him or her. Partners should always notify each other ahead of time when their relationship appears exothermic. In the foregoing discussion, love entails forgiveness. Love survives and leads sex and not, the other way round. It is only within this understanding that married relationships can survive affairs. According to Herbert George in Yancey's book: "He who cannot forgive another breaks the bridge over which he must pass himself" (1997:82). Experiences have shown that in anger, one can easily bite the finger that feeds one, but when severe hunger strikes, one may silently die of shame. It is better to keep and maintain the partner one has espoused his or her weaknesses than taking the risk of engaging in a new one whose behaviors are uncertain. Condemning a partner because of a single mistake or hoping to replace him or her, as piece of furniture because of what appears newest, best and promising is always regrettable. There is an adage among the Igbo of Nigeria that says: "It is only when one has married a second wife or husband that one can compare which one is better in assisting one live or die". At times, to enter into divorce one needs to think first because, as a third party in relationship, it can ruin one's life forever.

It takes more to be a parent than make a baby – Be careful relating with kids

In the case of the children of separated parents, for instance, the emotional and heavy weight of their parents' rancor and acrimony lie on them. No wonder Whitehead Barbara remarked: "In the divorce literature, however, children inhabit a shifting and uncertain social world" (1997:126). In this instance, spiritual psychology tries to assist these children of uncertain social world to understand themselves and positively appreciate the world. Therefore to relate well with kids, give them enough space to get themselves together, always be aware that a lot of things go within them. Involve them in any conversation, event or activity that concerns them, allowing them play some role models and carefully and spontaneously pick, build on their interests, and follow their lead. (Cf. pds.kids.org). For instance, kids that have lost a parent, either through untimely death or divorce, normally seek immediate attentions, easily get angry and feel disappointed with the world. They are not to blame because there is no other way to express their feelings.

The best response to this situation by a sensible parent is not to get angry about the kid's unusual behaviors but invite them to talk about the loss or divorce. Every moment with kids at this tender age could have long impacts on their future and character formation. Even in the Catholic Church, the impression priests create to children at their first participation at the Sacrament of Reconciliation (Confession/ Counseling) may encourage or discourage them for life with the Church. Every child is God's own, whether by a prostitute or whoever.

Reinforcing children for the little efforts they make motivates them to try many other possibilities. Kids came into the world with great joy. They constantly show this by looking at the faces of adults to share the same unconditional love with them and learn the principles of earthly and happy life. Unfortunately, most of them quickly fall victim to the sins of parents and society. For the preverbal [infants], use eye contact, reading, touching, singing, clapping hands and massaging. In eye contact with them, always try to follow their gaze, trying funny different things and do not keep them on one activity for so long because they easily get bored. Always allowing them to have enough rest. It is always phenomenal and monumental to allow them perceive your positive sides, smell and feel your warmth and love. Besides, children grow with both the positive and negative impressions they made early in their lives while adults tend to forget most of their memories as they grow older.

Adults, especially parents must generally avoid any scandalous activity before their children. As observed in this book, kids may lack the power of words, but they interpret and take note of all facial expressions, moods, tone of words, feelings, and all these have great impacts on their relationships later in life. Babies in their mother's womb equally feel the warmth or hatred of their parents before they are born. Never frown your face when interacting with kids except when they do something wrong. Generally, kids have no malice, prejudice or hatred for any one because they have not imbibed that from the adults. It is only when society furnishes them with her ills that they begin to express ill feelings. For instance, people have the right to make their decisions, but often, they lack the ability to control the consequences. Failure to take note of these little behavioral patterns creates problems in relationships. Moreover, on no condition should a person make mention or caricature of his or her partner's stature or height, weight or ugly looks in public. But they can always suggest to each other the best ways to keep fit and healthy. Naturally, it does not take as much to make a baby as to be a mother or father. Any 'beautiful looking person' that lacks good manners is as ugly and dangerous as a hardworking person that lacks respect, honesty and accountability. Naturally, stature is nobody's business, big or slim.

XV. Research students form unique relationship with their work

In line with scientific writing and presentation, this book provides a good study guide and working tool for college students and researchers in the development of their works. As we shall see later, relationship is like a research work in which the conclusion systematically agrees with the introduction. Any research work that is not concluded is like a relationship that is never fulfilled or asking a person who has lost both arms to clap for Jesus or God. As Hayes John would have it:

> *A common method of problem solving is a means-end analysis... When the starting and ending positions are agreed by clients, [researchers/partners-mine] moving from the current to the desired situation is easier to accomplish (1994:180-182).*

In this manner, students who are engaged in scientific research will tremendously benefit from this book. They will not only benefit from the points of view of acquiring scientific skills in the fields of research and academia but also adequately arm themselves with the principles that guide their relationships. For relationships to be healthy, just like in any scientific investigation, they have to follow certain parameters that keep them out of trouble and temptations. Elaborating more on such "perimeters" for scientific writing, Morgan John added: "The danger for the creative mind is to imagine too much, too broadly" (2007:4).

Inevitably, based on what Morgan has noted, human relationship is akin to research work and comparable to it. As a form of science, each person should systematically study the behavior and feeling of the other,

33

analyze the results of his or her findings in order to identify what needs to be encouraged or dropped to achieve healthy relationship. That is to say, scientific work or research is not about continuous writing, volumes or living together but design and organization. Scientific work is not about the researcher as such, but the findings based on systematical and methodological approach. Likewise, every human relationship is a process designed to lead individuals to appreciate one another. Just as every research work has to be objective, human relationship, though, operating on a subjective level, needs organization, openness and objectivity. Our relationship can only be possible when our lives, like any research work, are properly and objectively organized. Cosmetic decorations are not the soul of relationships, but the skillful attitudes that make them meaningful and worthwhile.

XVI. Relationship is science: It has to be systematic, consistent and focused

For a research work to be meaningful and scientific, it must be focused, with an introduction and valid conclusion. In the same way, our relationship must be focused. A research student should have a clear vision of his or her perimeters: the background, (the thesis statement or the hypothesis), purpose of study, scope of his or her investigation, significance, a reference group (literature), a methodology, a design for data collection, analysis, presentation, interpretation, measurement, et cetera. Such ideas or visions have to be inviting and challenging to the reader/audience. The researcher has to be married to his or her ideas, objectively represent and become part of the position he or she has adopted in his or her work. In this way, a researcher strives to become a professional in his or her own specialty because no researcher can exhaust any field of study. Principally, this is why we cannot expect an ideal relationship anywhere. Each person is bound to know his or her partner. It is a movement from inside out. The eyes of relationship might be too tiny to see everything. The little efforts individuals make on daily basis in a given relationship constitute the hands that rock its foundation and scientifically make it a living experience.

Therefore, at this point, there is need to categorically study an important aspect of human relationship. This is the phase that challenges every step we take to ensure healthy relationship. Science, like relationship, "is a process", series and "sequence of operations", actions, "which gives a desired result" (Dict. Def.) or taken to accomplish a desired goal. It is a process of self-evaluation and a clarion call to reexamine some of the conflicting ways we perceive ourselves in relation to others. Generally, in every research work, we call "the statement of problem", chapter one, which the book attempts to address here. Therefore, the statement of the problem of human relationship, hypothesis or thesis statement constitutes chapter one of this book or survey.

Chapter one

* * * *

The statement of problem

In a nutshell, this chapter exposes the factors that could affect the beautiful faces of human relationships. It poses a fundamental concern or hypothesis: "It is possible for human beings to amicably relate with one another" hence, the choice of our topic "Keeping human relationships together: Self Guide to healthy living". This is essentially the statement of what it means to have a lively relationship. Raising these concerns over healthy human relationships today presupposes that something has gone or is going wrong somewhere in society, school systems, among individuals in their relationships. In order to fix it, this chapter examines those factors that are responsible and why they are so important as parts of the investigation tools. Due to the nature of the investigation, the statement of problem will be reflected in almost every section of the book and the background is going to take more pages than other parameters. Getting started, we ex-rayed the factors within the following parameters, numbered A to D:

A. Background of the study

In the words of Morgan J., "attrition does not just happen; it happens because something went wrong" (2003:62) either with the individual or society or both of them. Similarly, in support of Morgan, Sheffield Anne made the following remarks: "Since nobody sets out to deliberately sabotage his or her own spirit and courage, it follows that if you are demoralized, someone else has initiated the process" (2003: 144).

Our young boys and girls should not allow any association, group or friendship to mislead them. Some complexities in human nature, to a great extent, create problems in individual relationships as underlined in the above observations. Therefore, spiritual psychology, not only creates the awareness that assists individuals guide against attritions and demoralizing events, but also provides them with the tools they need to accomplish their life goals. Such tools include; optimism, self-confidence, trust, flexibility, consistency, focus, and integration of sound ethical principles in their lives. For instance, a concerned village titled man and judge, Ezeji [Nze] Emmanuel Nwachukwu on his annual address to the people of Umuchie Community in Ezinihitte Mbaise L.G.A. of the Igbo of Nigeria noted: "If every person were to be straightforward, open, truthful and honest, the world would have been better, morally shaped and ordered than it is today" (1/1/09). Nwachukwu, in unequivocal terms, has raised a danger signal that some people are not measuring up to expectation, either in their actions or relationships.

Besides, nobody likes to be labeled an unscrupulous person, yet bad behaviors geometrically abound in society. The tortoise would want to have a tail, but its shell is an impediment. Most of us have different kinds of shells, either of anger, hypocrisy, religious masquerade, hatred, jealousy et cetera that constitute obstacles in our relationship. In order to fight this shell of selfishness and hypocrisy, spiritual psychology, advocates for a soft shell that encourages peace, love and tolerance in society. This is the only way healthy human relationship can be achieved in our society. On this premise, we sampled and examined "three groups" of people in society who constitute major factors and background of our study, particularly as they differently affect relationships. We have them in every culture. There are more groups with different peculiarities and personality types.

❖ The first groups of people are the "neo- Epicureans". They propound the philosophical system of hedonism that pleasure is the highest or supreme good and conceive the world as an end itself. Thus, they do whatever it takes to fully enjoy the physical world regardless of tomorrow.

37

❖ The second groups are the "neo-Scholastics" [e.g. Thomas Aquinas] who appreciate the world as a gift from God and an opportunity to enjoy a greater life hereafter.

❖ The third group belongs to the camp of Plato who perceives the present world as shadows of the real One; therefore, they strive to live their entire earthly lives in pursuit of the real.

In the above scenario, the moral decisions, formation and judgment of conscience, behaviors and nature of relationships of these three groups of people towards others are eventually determined by their belief systems and life styles. We said it already, the very life we lead influences and determines the nature of our relationship. That is why the various faces of human relationship presented in the book are meant to be guiding beacons to understanding oneself and others.

World-oriented & Epicurean Life	Inclusive & Other-Oriented Life.	Heaven-oriented & Self-centered spirituality
↓	↓	↓
A	B	C

(The above figure is an illustration of Spirituality or Life Goal Typology of three groups of people who fervently seek meaningful relationships in their lives).

These behavioral patterns are generally found in every relationship and the world today. The question still remains: "Why do people who share the same human heritage, class and gender, bound by the same laws of nature not only behave differently from one another, but also from the universally ethical principles that are conventionally accepted?" Ihuoma E., an Igbo of Nigeria and Ezinihitte indigenous writer, referring to the situation among his own people appeared to have summarized our statement of problem or the instability of human relationship in these words: "Why is it that the Igbo Christian today is prepared to give God his due at Mass and service on Sunday, and at the same time he gives Amadioha his due when he goes home" (1990:13). Double-dealing attitude is sin.

The emphasis on the above quotation is on the word "today". Ihuoma has indirectly made a sharp distinction between the Traditional and Christian religion and how the two have presently dichotomized the basic values of the Igbo people. The word "Amadioha" is an oracle, and a Traditional religious substitute for the one true Almighty God of Igbo people and Christians in general. A closer examination of what Ihuoma had pointed out here guides us to appreciate the syncretistic life styles that create devastating effects in many relationships. Such problems seem to have rocked the fabric of the religious belief systems of most people in society, especially the people of Ezinihitte in Igbo of Nigeria, Imo State. The point is that, both the negative and positive values of religion and morality of the people have been mixed up to the extent that it is hard to identify true Christians among the Traditionalists.

Who is fooling whom in relationship – A trustworthy partner or deceiver?

Painfully to note, if a person can double deal with matters related to truth or God by making faith and justice a game of chance, we can generally imagine what happens in human relationships. With reference to the Igbo of Nigeria, the question remains: "Who is to blame", the missionaries who initially poured the waters of Baptism on the people without proper catechesis or the people themselves who hesitantly accepted the new ways without raising many questions? Misrepresentation always leads to confusion and creates problems in relationships. That was the situation when the person of Jesus Christ was introduced to the Igbo people of Nigeria. For instance, when a person cannot represent his or her partner well in public, no matter how the two claim to love each other in the house, there is problem in that relationship. The good names we give others at their back is better than the gifts of gold and silver we offer them in their presence. A dishonest partner unconsciously fools him or herself.

Misrepresentation compels individuals, couples, partners in business, friends et cetera to be objective in their judgments and have clear visions of what they need in their relationships. Sincerity is expedient in every relationship. For a man to promise his fiancée heaven and earth just to woo her to amateur relationship is not accidental. Dinsmore Charles seems to be addressing this issue when he writes about the "sins of impulse and sins of settled habits.... sins of the flesh are less culpable than sins of the spirit" (IR). It is evil for a person to willfully enter a relationship he or she has no intention to keep or maintain. This boils down to what Dinsmore refers to as "sins of settled habits or of the spirit". The Catholic Church refers to these as "sins against the Holy Spirit" which "will not be forgiven either in this world or in the next" (Mt. 12:32). (Cf. CCC, 1994:456, #1864). The Catechism is explicit on the 6 sins against the Holy Spirit, namely: Despair – C.C.C # 2091, Presumption of God's mercy – C.C.C. # 2092, Impugning the known truth, Envy the spiritual good of another, Obstinacy and Finally, Impenitence. Since some sins are forgiven in the next world, from what the Bible has noted, does that not encourage us to pray for our dead brothers and sisters?

It is catastrophic, scandalous, fatal and unforgivable, to say the least, for an individual to consciously and knowingly plan to put another person into trouble or deceive him or her in the pretence of love and friendship or relationship. Solid relationship entails an orientation, a skill grounded in openness and readiness to learn and adapt. For instance, when an individual has a problem and tells the truth, the matter lively becomes part of his or her motivating and encouraging past experience. But, when the person tells lies, the same lie constantly becomes part of his or her demoralizing future engagements. This is where spiritual psychology, essentially employing human conscience, plays an irreplaceable role in human relationships. Each person represents an entity. One is either a human being or an animal at a time and behaves accordingly. Dependable relationship must nurse reliability, consistency and trust.

Necessarily, the book thoroughly examines if every person has conscience or whether it is relative and secondary to human beings. This concern assisted us in ascertaining and appreciating the cultural diversities we encounter in human behaviors today. As a matter of fact, we approached the statement of problem principally from three perspectives. These problems are encountered in every aspect of human relationship and call for serious attention and consideration in this order:

1. The problems, which generally and internally arise from the nature of man or woman him or herself, basis of his and her actions, judgments and formation of conscience;
2. From the enormity and magnitude of the present day conflicts, physically resulting from immoral practices and lack of discipline in society. We largely drew our examples from the USA and the Igbo land of Nigeria with particular reference to Ezinihitte people.
3. From the problems and disorders that affect human relationships due to wrong approaches or inadequate methodology of missionary activity: The Nigerian case. Surprisingly, this section seems to have constituted 40% of the statement of the problem in this section.

1. The problems generating from the nature of man:

We have already observed in this book that man is a bundle of possibilities. He is capable of many things, good and evil. His freedom to choose is limitless. No matter the role an individual plays in a given relationship, the formation and application of his or her conscience are responses to moral order or presuppositions of some knowledge of morality. Shatesbury, in this light presents "conscience as the consciousness of wrongdoing, not of rightdoing" (Shatesbury, in Inquiry 11, 2,1).

On the same par, the Internet Free Encyclopedia observes that:

> *Doing good to your neighbor (partner-mine) does not arouse the conscience to speak, but wickedness inflicted upon the innocent is sure to make the conscience scream (IR, 2007).*

The message is that if human relationships have been cordial and harmonious, nobody would have bothered to talk or write about them. Wickedness inflicted at any level of human relationship is a revolution to nature itself, devastating the fabric of human existence. It is inconceivable to speak of human relationships without certain knowledge of moral standards. This, again, boils down to our earlier assertion that every human society as we understand it cannot exist without some norms or laws, written or unwritten, that guide the affairs of her citizens. In this sense, conscience and morality, which involve doing the right thing at the right time, *age quod ages*, dating as far back as the Greek civilization, are very important. Unfortunately, many people do not listen to, comply with or utilize the formidable roles of morality in their behaviors and relationships. The net result of this fundamental let down is responsible for a large portion of the animalistic inclinations and conflicts that besiege society today. No sensible individual can just open fire and begin to shoot and kill innocent people. For a reasonable driver to ensure his or her safety and those of his or her passengers, he or she should have at the back of his or her mind that all other drivers on the way are either drunk or sleeping at the steering and anticipate that very little mistake can cause an accident. This disposition should guide and feature in our relationship to avoid unlikely surprises. This is precisely why a psychological approach to this fundamental dimension of man, conscience and its value in human relationship is of classic importance in our survey.

Has humanity any common identity of values?

Practically, the urgency and statement of problems facing this book are clear. Despite the magnitude of religious practices and emphasis being laid on religion today, according to Raab, why are there no changes in peoples' lives and relationships? The question that stares us in the face is: "What impact then has religion made in society and the lives of individuals?" Why have the records of crimes and violence continued to be in the increase today despite the emphasis on religion? To what extent have religion and belief systems in the Supernatural influenced human choices between evil and good? Besides natural resources like air and water, even though water is sold in the market today, has humanity any common identity in the right direction? Where lies the feasibility of a race that no longer owes gratitude to a source, be it a force, spirit or God. We are all aware, according to Chinua Achebe that things have fallen apart and the center cannot hold any longer because of misplaced priorities and lack of moral order.

Today, a majority of the politicians who are charged with the governance of their people have excessively become greedy, avaricious, egoistic, inordinate and insatiable in search of wealth regardless of what happens to the constituencies. Some of them simply use convincing arguments and promises to propagate and achieve their egoistic intentions and objectives. They seem to do all these to maintain worldly relationships that count on material possessions. What do we say of people who market religion as commodities? Why cannot the awesomeness of the Supernatural or God who could punish evil and reward good deeds influence the ways the human person relates and behaves? Or, have the Omniscience and Omnipotence of God been incapacitated or rendered useless when the tomorrow of society is uncertain? Have we scientifically drawn conclusion that human beings are now and completely dependent on themselves? In situations like this, the need for spiritual psychology springs up and urges people to remain on the path of truth and justice. It is better to die with glorious and healthy memories than die in misery and regret.

To reasonably achieve the holistic objectives of spiritual psychology, the importance of psychology in general cannot be overemphasized. We live and reflect our psychologies as individuals in our actions, as we relate and interact with others. Based on the diversities and differences of these individual actions, there is need for a psychology that directly and easily addresses the burning issues in human relationships. Our field of study elaborately incorporates a psychology that functionally guides the individual person to self-supervise him or herself in his or her relationships. We refer to this branch of study as "Spiritual Psychology". Spiritual Psychology properly understood in this book is on the area of psychological practice. It is applied in all human situations to assist individuals become changed agents in themselves, their environment, community, organization, profession and interactions with others irrespective of religion, race, sex, culture and language. With spiritual psychology, relationships are not exclusive of positive past memories, which create favorable aspirations towards future goals, hopes and expectations for better life. There is enormous need to urgently approach the issue of human relationships from a global context, especially today that there are transferences of cultural values in both market industries, communications and at all levels of human interactions.

The survey we made in this section of the chapter is indicative of how peoples' good intentions in relationships, at times, can unconsciously turn into destructive and misleading weapons. The borderline points to the need to respect other people's values. When an act is bad in itself, its best intention cannot be justified. Stealing to feed the hungry is wrong. Respect of value means remaining and keeping to one's own lane and also being aware of each other's lane. Any act of benevolence or kindness diligently extended to another person should be executed or carried out according to the needs and convenience of the recipient. For instance, it is not proper for an individual to invite his or her partner for recreational reasons and discussions when he or she is already late for an appointment or for a delicious meal when the partner is so weak and needs some rest. To insist on doing good to your partner when he or she is indisposed is a sign of unresolved issue in one's personality development and insecurity.

Human relationships can be risky and delicate if not objectively guided and straightened by truth and justice. This is why spiritual psychology frowns at many religious practices of the age. As Knitter would have it:

> *I would suggest that one of the major reasons why there is so much disunity and lack of peace in today's world is because the religions of the world have not done their job (1992:283).*

Therefore, the book raises a lot of challenging questions for different levels of relationships that remain unanswered here. The in-depth study of the individual dynamics assists each person to create some self-awareness and vigorously examine and fight the itching factors that may constitute diversities and awful experiences in his or her relationships. Envisaging a situation where what appears like gold is not, pragmatically disposes individuals and leads them to common understanding, unity and positive results among the human family. Spiritual psychology does not perceive moral behaviors as an "a priori synthesis" or a probability, what will happen in future, but as what have already and concretely manifested themselves in human actions. This is because every rational being has the natural tendency or inclination (*conatus essendi*) for good or evil. Ethically speaking, spiritual psychology studies and organizes these natural tendencies and inclinations as vital tools and values for the enhancement of the individual person and society. As an essential aspect of achieving societal goals, Maxfield Carol (2007), in her address to Spiritual Care Givers entitled "Listening is the best thing you can do" remarked that 'by knowing what to expect in any situation one is better prepared to establish' healthy relationship with others. Consequently, we need to imagine the weight our behaviors and actions have on others and ourselves.

Unfortunately, our failure to take cognizance of how others feel and react to our behaviors creates major problems in interpersonal relationships. A denial of the reality of morality or conscience in human lives is anthropologically an entailment of the non-reality of human existence itself. For instance, when we say that conscience or morality primarily belongs to man, we do not mean that it has a secondary relation to other animals. Rather, we mean that it is typically man or woman because the two are inseparable. As it were, the application of the promptings of conscience in human relationship is functionally part and parcel of the anatomic and physiological components of man and woman. Especially, at this fashionable age, many people seem to play 'hide and seek' games and put veils over their obligations and responsibilities in relationship. According to St. Paul: "For law abiders there was no law" (Rom. 6:10). In Pauline context, for law abiders, there is little or no need for scientific study of the phenomenon of human relationship. Instead, it could have conventionally been taken for granted that people would always obey their consciences, behave rightly and build healthy relationships. Contrarily, it is commonly evident to our senses regarding what is happening in society and individual relationships today, that many people behave entirely different from others in moral matters. This is problematically a threat and danger signal to interpersonal co-existence. While there can be certain forms of rules in relationships, rules should not destroy love, which is the foundation of every relationship. Actually, no good can be accomplished in relationships where love is hidden behind any rule or law. In this sense, law is not the basis of relationships, but openness and love.

The syllogistic judgments of individuals in their relationships always differ due to the non-uniformity of moral applications to behaviors. For instance, when an object at a distance is viewed from different

Anthony O. Nwachukwu

locations, it might give varying reflections and images. As earlier on observed, when groups of people experience an event at the same time, often times, they interpret the event differently, let alone when the event is experienced at different times. These differences in moral judgments, whether they are intended or accidental urgently underline the relevance of the inclusiveness of spiritual psychology in human industry. Anscombe, representing a widely held position noted: "We must always remember that an object is not what, what is aimed at, is the description under which it is … called that object" (958:65). For instance, a well-sculptured human object could mistakenly be taken or addressed as a human being when in actual fact it is a beautiful piece of art. In other words, if a well-dressed gentle man turns out to be an idiot, his attire may not define or say anything about his character and personality but his actions will. Naturally, it is always possible that a bad person can become a better partner in his or her relationship by taking bold steps to correct his or her mistakes.

Unnecessary Suspicions may lead faithful partners to infidelity

Suspicion is human but not necessary in healthy relationships. In effect, human relationship is determined; not by the looks and appearances of the individuals involved, but by the ways they sincerely coat, present, demonstrate and act it out to themselves and to the outside world. For instance, how will a young man feel when, unannounced, arrives his house and sees his wife opening the door for another man who just jumps out of the house and vanishes? Such moments call for spiritual psychology and maturity to give a partner's action some benefits of doubt, or "a despite of". Perhaps, the best and general way, though unnatural, to handle such a situation is NOT to allow instincts cast doubts on the trust one has for one's cherished relationship with one's partner. Rather, as in the case at hand, the man should remain cheerful and quickly say to his wife: "Honey, anything the matter, I hope it is okay? Come on in, I have great stories for you". Any mature boss in an office, husband or wife, should intuitively act in a reassuring manner as if nothing is amiss. Relationship can just be fun at times. Besides, to cheat one's partner is to cheat oneself and entire family.

46

A sensible person should not keep her husband or his wife in suspense as why a man jumped out of the house, but tell him or her right away what happened. For instance, the woman in our story should immediately explain the situation as the case at hand: "Honey, I am sure you saw the man running out of the house. Can you imagine, the company you called few days ago for our light sent an electrician to fix it today? I tried to get to you but could not. Unfortunately, no sooner did the man start the job than his wife called and informed him that their son had a terrible motor accident. He left his tools here and ran away. You nearly met him". The incident described here leaves no room for suspicion and calls for trust and fidelity in relationship. Even if the situation is different or falsely narrated, the person should always and promptly let his or her partner know why a visitor jumped out of their house. Silence in this situation is an affirmation that something has gone wrong and may lead to severe conflicts when revisited.

Hitherto, most people do not have access to the internal squabbles; conflicts, trials and sacrifices their partners and workers go through to maintain healthy relationship. In the example just cited, very little thing could have triggered off an unquenchable mistrust and before the matter gets resolved, would have damaged a lot of things. Moreover, another friend of the family who saw the man jump out of the house could have equally called the husband in question and alerted him of such august visitor, adding injuries to the real story. In this light, many honest people have been fired from their jobs and marriages torn to shreds because of misrepresentations. Nothing hurts more in human relationships than a person or partner being falsely accused on a matter he or she is completely innocent. But no partner is innocent of any suspicious behavior or an accusation that has not been clarified and proved. Therefore, maturity in relationship includes the ability to avoid creating such occasions for unnecessary suspicions and bickering. Individuals should freely and reasonably try and maximize their energy, time and resources to what encourage healthy living. In this light, Carl Anderson observes:

> *If the history of the human race has taught us nothing else, it should at least have taught us that freedom in this instinctual sense is utterly illusory. It is freedom of the tyrant, who is caged*

47

> *by the fear and hatred of his own subjects, of the libertine,*
> *who is the slave of his desires; of the nihilist, who cries with*
> *Nietzsche, "Nothing is true; all is permitted (2008:26).*

Partners should not allow instincts, the id, (the selfish part of man) dominate their relationships. Maturity is also equal to patience and tolerance, especially in handling each other's shortcomings and mistakes.

It is not in doubt that the issue of moral obligation is required in every relationship. As Paulin would have it, "the concomitant awareness of the obligation attaching to the concepts of good and evil is an essential part of the awareness of their basic meaning" (Paulin, 1992:135). One can theologically assert that the evildoer, many a time, understands the magnitude of his or her actions. The written troubles and intentions of the brain are not easily and completely razed out. Good behavior is never an accident. Rather, it is a personal, conscious sacrifice and efforts one makes on behalf of oneself and others. In our context, according to Whitson: "sin", though very attractive in nature, "is the refusal to believe...a refusal to accept truths revealed" (1995:60). Unfortunately, this refusal to accept and recognize the genuine efforts some partners make on daily basis creates serious problems in their relationships. Relationship has its own language. Failure to apply the right steps and judgments to complement the little efforts each partner makes in his or her relationship adversely boomerangs. Most of the emotional and interior sufferings people encounter today point to the natural consequences of their own actions. Heart-felt concerns for the welfare of others are the keys to global healthy relationship. Therefore, emotional intelligence is necessary in relationships. We must always try to open the door of our hearts to allow others come in and share with us the riches of sound moral living.

Confrontations serve as recipes in many relationships

In this light, spiritual psychology recommends that partners morally avoid keeping certain matters secret, especially where there is trust. It does not matter if one is misunderstood for being honest and open. Again, this depends on individuals. Some people are naturally suspicious. To tell them of the visit of a friend who simply knocked on the door, greeted and left, will always metamorphose into great suspicion. In this way, faithful partners have been forced into sexual infidelity because of unnecessary accusations and suspicions. Suspicion is a sign of insecurity. People need to avoid it. Honesty is self-rewarding and every good act begets itself. At times, circumstances might deny some people of the truth they are entitled to, in a particular issue. The manner, in which we handle issues in our relationships, helps us to relax with our environment or run crazy. This attitude justifies the position of some psychoanalysts like Romero and Kemp who maintain that the suppression of human unpleasant memories to the subconscious leads to some mental disorder. For instance, if your partner is a drunkard and you hate it, you must not wait to politely express your feelings to him or her. Being silent over unwelcoming attitudes of one's partner gradually stagnates relationships. At times, friendly confrontation is necessary. As Tavris and Elliot expressed it:

> *In good marriages, a confrontation, difference of opinion, clashing habits, and even angry quarrels can bring couple closer, by helping each partner learn something new and by forcing them to examine their assumptions about their abilities or limitations. It isn't easy to do this (2007:183).*

As Romero and Kemp put it "destroying or chasing away something unpleasant gives us almost the same result as running away ourselves" (2007:169). An idle person cannot expect luxury. The only antidote in avoiding human troubles, whether they are mental or otherwise, is our preparedness to call a spade a spade, accept our responsibilities and face the consequences of our actions. We can only reach this level of emotional intelligence or self-actualization in our human relationship when we are disciplined and honest ourselves. We teach people how to treat us. In spiritual psychology, the word "discipline" means our willingness to do the right thing at all times, especially when nobody is watching. This is a call for consistency and moral orderliness. Doing that, which you consider morally the best, even when you act ignorantly, will always bring you joy and life. It is within the darkest secret of our sincere lives that miracles and mysteries happen.

When God says: "Yes" or "No", nobody can alter it
– Jonah/Tyra's Case

The Christian or Traditional God of the Igbo is the God of Impossibility. He creates a way where there is none. The case of Jonah comes to mind. Whether it sounds funny or not, it is true. To accomplish God's work, at times, it may take unusual procedures. In human judgment, Jonah felt, like the rest of us or our children that it was better to escape from the teachers, school assignments, parents, moral instructions, God and hide in Lagos, Germany or Tarshish for our own personal goals, avoid doing our home work, hiding from parents and teachers than to go and assist others and the people of Nineveh to repentantly enjoy healthy relationship with themselves, society and God. His sleeping in the belly of the fish for 3 days and 3 nights is indicative that when God says 'yes or no', nobody can alter it (Jonah 2:1).

Besides, the stories two young women narrated at Tyra's Show on Tuesday, October 13, 2009, that they became aware of their 9 months pregnancies only at those very unexpected moments of giving birth, are really convincing that there is a Mighty Force in control of this planet. Shockingly, one of them admitted that she started birth control at the age of 14 and both agreed they were never expecting to have any babies. Luckily, two of them have been elevated by eternal circumstances from friendship to a more stable state of marital relationship. Science is free to hold its own opinion in this instance but God controls all human knowledge. Our enemies or strangers can also save us in moments of great need. The story of the Good Samaritan is handy, (Lk. 10:29-36). Despite the tremendous advantages of science and technology today, there are still so many unanswered questions and mysteries enveloping the world. Relationship simply demands steadfastness and focus. Referring to the application of human conscience for human stability, Genicot recommends: "When conscience feels certain, whether it be correct or mistaken, one is always obliged to follow it, when it enjoins or forbids... recommends or permits ... one is entitled to it" (1931: 290). But, in many cases, these basic facts are neglected and consciously or unconsciously lead to mishaps and ugly surprises in many human relationships. Incredibly, the most confusing aspect of human relationship, particularly on the political level is that some of those in leadership positions who claim to be champions of truth and justice are victims of the mess or immoral behaviors they are elected to clean up. This is a major problem that plagues society.

Nevertheless, the obligation to self-supervise does not permit an illusion in any judgment we make of our actions or encourage complacency or self-righteousness in the name of being a good person. It is necessary to note that the human conscience, whether it is activated or not, is the interior witness and a fearless judge of the individual motives and actions. Basically, it is a source of comfort or remorse especially when one behaves contrary to established moral values and standards. For instance, a partner who finds it difficult to face his or her responsibility in the house will never have peace of mind, no matter his or her excuses and reasons. Here lies the irrevocable value of conscience in human relationship. Going back to our spirituality typology as a way of guiding relationships, we have these analyses to make of the three groups A, B and C that represent the attitudes of most of us:

A. People in this group seem to maintain a type of conscience and relationship that primarily dances to selfish inclinations or listens to urges as their highest good. We have this group of people in every walk of life, irrespective of religious affiliations or systems. Unfortunately, it is very hard to build healthy relationship among people in this group.

B. Those in this group stand between the extremes of life. They believe and adhere to inclusive conscience and relationship that give the convenience of others the benefit of doubts or a priority. The behaviors and relationships of those in this group, therefore, point to a holistic and relational spirituality.

C. Those in this group seem to draw their spiritual maps or judgments for actions and relationships from the analysis and conviction that God is their only final judge. For instance, this is a situation in which an individual in his or her frantic efforts to attend an early prayer meeting on Sunday morning abandons his or her sick partner in the house. A holier-than-thou attitude has always led to dangerous ends in relationships.

Morgan in Shaw J., seemed to be addressing those in this group when he wrote:

> *We are all called to a level of responsibility, accountability and duty, which precludes …excuses and dependence on an outside source for making the world and our lives better. We are the ones, only us, you and me, says Sartre". It is with us in community and as individual selves that the world's hopes and dreams are deposited and can, if we work hard, without excuses, become reality, (J., 2006:25).*

Whichever way we may examine or analyze the above passage; there is room for further clarifications. That is to say, while it does not concern us to know everything, it is worth noting that our own particular lives, responsibilities and destinies have been committed to our care. According to Beecher in New York Times, noted: "It is true that a man must tolerate infelicities in his party, but when its spirit goes counter to his whole conscience, then it is his duty to maintain the sovereignty of his individuality" (2/25/1886). Problems emanate whenever the sovereignty of an individual is threatened or violated in any relationship. Human relationship calls for caution, examination and consideration at any level of its growth. The choices we make in our relationship equally count here. To whom, for instance, do we ascribe our faults when we cannot make careful distinctions between what is desirable or repulsive in our individual choices and relationships? But where do we classify those who do not care about the unpleasant situations of their relationships? When people who are criminal-minded; dubious, deceitful, unfaithful in relationships begin to sugarcoat their behaviors, there is always going to be a problem. Or when a criminal who is released from jail refuses to listen to anybody or seek help from a counselor, he or she is surely going back there for more years. Rudeness in relationship is evil. This is where society has to be very cautious with such people in their groups and companies. Being rude to sensitive issues that affect global relationships, like lack of attentive listening ear, coming late to common meetings or dinner and laughing or feeling unconcerned when others are upset et cetera are signs of primitiveness and uncertainty. A wise person may look foolish in his or her actions.

History is repeating: In Noah's days, at the peak of merriment, the flood unexpectedly swept all away – Let us avoid the hand writing on the wall (Daniel. 5:5)

Put differently, why is it hard for some partners to emulate the good behaviors of others, practice sound moral principles of peace, unity, love and imbibe the authentic teachings of religion, unadulterated? One does not need to have religion to act religiously. Something is either wrong with humanity or hidden somewhere which is hard to unfold. Could it be as John's Gospel expressed it: "Men have shown they prefer darkness to the light because their deeds are evil" (John 3:19)? What is the meaning of life then if one prefers darkness to light, destruction to peace, sadness to happiness, curse to blessing? Preferably, any person who chooses to navigate this earthly journey alone, without seeking supernatural or human assistance is likely going to paint an ugly history for self and posterity. Or have we come to the conclusion that humanity evolved? While I do not intend to discuss the issue of evolution here, "The things of the world and the things of faith derive from the same God", who is the author of all things (Vatican 11, GS 36:1)? Amazingly, humanity has a beginning from a source that is self-existent and each person has been called to participate in this endless life of love and peace in his or her relationship. The Church is not against faith and science or any systematic research in any branch of knowledge as long as it is carried out in a truly scientific manner and does not override moral laws. Belief systems and science should not be obstacles to healthy relationship. The admonition of his holiness, Pope Benedict XVI, during his Papal visit to America is supportive of the above views: "There is no conflict between science, ethics and religion. It is a matter of choice between the sciences that dehumanize the human person and the sciences that uplift the human situation" (4/17/08). Of what significance is science then if it dehumanizes those for whom it meaningfully exists? Or, can man become a slave to his own creativity and innovations? In the light of the Papal admonition and belief systems, a Scientist, Engr. Dr. Aguh Reginald noted:

> *Science is part and parcel of the human history... It is of classic importance to note that the choices we make determine, to a great extent, the foundation upon which our*

> *lives [relationships-mine] are built. Choices prioritize our decisions and actions (H/Oxford, 2008)*

Certainly, how can life be meaningful and enjoyable without a source that is permanently convincing, reassuring, reasonable and necessary? Science has widened and bettered the scope of human knowledge and condition. We should appreciate it. Yet, as already noted, there are so many other things, events and realities in our world that are beyond all scientific investigations and remedies. The forces of nature, for instance, such as earthquakes, tornados, tsunamis et cetera, challenge us in many circumstances. In humility, humanity is inevitably and unquestionably compelled to accept a divine intervention in our relationships and totally surrender to that unbeatable source of our being. Mother earth challenges every aspect of human knowledge, intelligence and technology.

History has continued to repeat itself because humanity seems to be deaf to the signs of the times. Let us remember the story of Noah as the Christian Bible expressed it: "As it was in Noah's days, so will it be when the son of Man comes. For in those days before the Flood, people were eating, drinking, taking wives, taking husband, right up to the day Noah went into the ark, and they suspected nothing till the Flood came and swept all away" (Mt. 24:37-39). For instance, why has the issue of global climate change or warming become topical among world leaders toady? Scientists have predicted that global forces of nature are driving our earth's climate to an uncomfortable direction. Time has come for united efforts and global solidarity in identifying the beauty of creation and its source. Appreciations and reinforcements are the energies that build solid relationships.

In our limitations, it is pointless pretending to usurp or arrogate to ourselves powers we have no control of. There are reasons for most of the recent natural disasters, baffling deaths and economic recession being experienced in our times. There are so many unborn and stillbirth babies. Life needs a celebration as gratuitous gift. The moment a person bites the very finger that feeds him or her, there is no point surmising whether he or she is going to die of hunger or not. Most people smile at evil and frown when challenged with discipline. Time has also come when each person should take cognizance of his or her fellow travelers in the inevitable homeward pilgrimage. We have absolute freedom to choose between alternatives. Interestingly, the dilemma of freedom lies on the fact that, it has plunged and drowned many people into deep oceans of wrong choices. As such, individual freedom needs to be kept on hold for effective and collective realization of the meaning of life and healthy relationships. There are so many other problems that emanate from human nature, which the book has to address too.

If God is dead for you, why waste time talk about him or bring in science?

The greatest mistake of the century is for humanity to believe and accept "the death of God" theology. If God is dead, why talk about him in the first place? Naturally, people spend time on what they value and cherish. Why is it that many theologians have devoted their precious time arguing, debating and comparing a non-existent being with the living? Belief systems tremendously affect the stories partners share in their relationships. The inroad of science and technology in our times should be appreciated at all levels of our relationships. All the same, every person is entitled to his or her own belief. For instance, according to Dietrich Bonhoeffer: "Our coming to age forces us to a true recognition of our situation vis-à-vis God. God is teaching us that we must live as man who can get along very well without him. The God who is with us, is the God who forsakes us…before God and with him, we live without God. God allows himself to be edged out of the world and on the cross" (1954:163).

For many believers, Traditions, Cultures, Jewish and Christians, such observations are contradictorily obnoxious, pharisaical and misleading. For Bonhoeffer, man has become a microcosm onto him-self and does not seek assistance in his relationships beyond the physical world in which he probably owns, lives and dies. Amazingly, in his own words, if he believes that "God is teaching us that we must live as man" whether we "can get along very well without him" or not, he has automatically admitted and acknowledged that God initiates, teaches, commands and orders the course of human journey. The way we get about it is our choice. Moreover, "living as man" entails the realization of what it means to be that man, harmoniously relating, interacting, and building relationships that are compatible with healthy living. There are a lot of flaws and contradictions in "the death of God" theology. On the same trend, the American Methodist Student Magazine, *Motive* once ran the obituary of God in these words: "God, creator of the universe, principal deity of the world's Jews, ultimate reality of Christians and most eminent of all divinities, died yesterday during a major surgery undertaken to correct a massive diminishing influence" (1965:9; Fannon P., 1968:24).

Surely, "nobody has seen God" (1Jn.4: 12). He is timeless and ageless – Eterminabilis. How could God go for surgery, except the god of the Student Magazine that did so. Such comments as "God, creator of the universe.... died yesterday during a major surgery undertaken to correct a massive diminishing influence", reveal the extent humanity has abandoned her source. For instance, today there is every need to embrace peace, unity and love of neighbor as guiding beacons in relationships, yet many prefer the darkness of wars and terrorism. Why have "Moral Instruction" and Spiritual Psychology, which are essentially and practically designed to mould and form the future generation been discouraged in the school systems? Humanity has already started reaping the fruit of "the death of God" ideologies. Some kids no longer respect, even their own parents, let alone their teachers and seniors. For them, life selfishly means "me" and no one else. These animalistic tendencies, not only influence their relationships, but also indicate the manner they suffocate and kill their source. This ugly situation led Dr. Nwachukwu Udaku to say:

> *It is good to encourage civilization but not to use civilization to backup evil things that manifest these days. Possibly you are among the parents who are concerned about the way our children are getting almost out of control behaviorally these days or do you belong to those who say it is a civilized world? The world is a global village so whatever is done in the United States is encouraged in our remote towns and villages. If you belong to this group, you are among those who fold their arms and watch values being misplaced. Or do you belong to those who are timelessly working to nip this current menace in the bud? (2009:59)*

According to the "death of God" theologians, man is now living in an era where God has become the helpless amputee of history. Subjectively, in Harvey Cox's own view: "Life is a set of problems and not an unfathomable mystery…man perceives himself as the source of whatever significance the human enterprise holds" (1965:72). This position is generally not true. A tree does not make a forest. No one has it all. We live and interact as families and need each other to progress and advance. Unfortunately, the sacred seems to have been absorbed into the process and activity of a material world in which man becomes a need fulfiller and problem solver. Secularization is the product of human and selfish invention. In support of these radical ideas of godlessness, Friedrich Nietzsche made the following remarks: "God is dead! God stays dead! And it is we who have killed him" (1910:125). The death of God for him is a redemptive event because man has been liberated from an alien transcendence and can now give unconditional affirmation to the immanent reality of his own life. Killing God here does not necessarily refer to homicide but to the un-limitedness of human freedom. In the light of Nietzsche's thought, man must learn to live without God as a human problem solver. This is very dangerous because most of human proposals and aspirations do not come through or hold water.

It is undoubted that God gave man freedom and dominions over the earth, to be fruitful, multiply, fill the earth, subdue and conquer it (Gen.1: 28). For one to exercise this freedom and maturity in accepting responsibility for one's actions, one is fundamentally bound to acknowledge the source of one's being, through thanksgiving and appreciation. Man and his existence are simply gifts of God. Ingrates exist, we know. But, who has failed in his or her relationship because he or she is an honest person, truthful, just, trustworthy, open and hardworking? Even if a person seems to have temporarily failed because of human frailties, nemesis will always catch up with evildoers. "The death of God" theologians have challenged us to keep on doing the good work God has initiated in us through love.

Today, science and technology and the ugly monster of "secularization" (Keller in Rahner. 1975:1554-1561) seem, for some people, to have invaded and substituted God and his unique roles in their relationships.

The experience of the Transcendence is rapidly shifting to mundane and a "this – worldly faith" and thereby setting fire to many relationships. Do we call this religious "nominalism"-the belief or doctrine that general or abstract words do not stand for objectively existing entities and that universals are no more than names assigned to them? (IR). Along these scientific sentiments, V. M. Andrew recorded the following:

> *Lord, it is pretty difficult to believe in you now, when it is out of fashion. Science has usurped your place...Now-a-days... men have set foot on the moon and soon they will be in Mars. Test-tube babies will greet us soon. Artificial rains are on the way. Memory pills and such wonder drugs are in the market all speak of the wonders of science, and who is there who cares for you. Do you think Lord; these things will not have any influence on me? I am confused, Lord: I wonder if I still believe in you (1973:9-10).*

Accepting V. M. Andrew's position is self-contradictory and condemning. On no circumstances should science usurp God's place because no one became a scientist at birth. The act of conception and giving birth is fundamentally beyond all scientific and technological advancements. Scientific knowledge is a process that demands the cooperation of others and development of the human mind for comprehension and practice. Therefore, turning around to attack the source of scientific knowledge is the highest display of affected ignorance. The modern consciousness of person's greatness, achievements, power over him or herself and the universe alarmingly needs to be guided by spiritual psychology. These materialistic tendencies of "who cares or anything goes" are indications of moral emptiness of the age and have destroyed many relationships already.

There is so much inhumanity to man, hatred, tale bearing, assassination of characters, hypocrisy of all forms et cetera even in God's vineyards. Has the Gospel message been determined by material tendencies and scientific age? How can material-oriented ministry guarantee a healthy relationship? Today, both the natural and positive laws are flouted with a wave of the hand. Nobody seems to be listening to the voice of reason. Society is gradually plunged into spiritual aridity and the joyous music of life turned into catastrophes. Insensitivity is an enemy to healthy relationship. The few saving voices are not heard. The sound contributions of a majority of people remain marginalized. How can healthy relationship be built on shaky and slippery foundations? The world seems to have fallen into the worst economic disaster in history because of selfishness and greed. Spiritual psychology, therefore, calls each person to take a break, look back, and consider what it would mean to live alone in the world or in isolation without any relationship. To err is human but persistence in error is diabolical. Mistakes are natural but refusal to make efforts to avoid them is demonic. It is normal to see our best friends or partners unexpectedly persecute us even when we are full of appreciations for them. But instead of duplicating mistakes, we should simply utilize such moments to foster solid relationships. We should always turn ingratitude and politicking into opportunities for greater anthropological advancements and awareness for closer understanding of the human nature. These ideals can only be reached in truth, justice, trust and love.

"Thank you" costs nothing but can buy everything

Fortunately, when a bad partner runs out of gas, he or she seeks peace. Spiritual psychology calls for consistency in every act that promotes sound relationships. In this light, to build relationships solely on physical appearances, chemical dependence and instincts always ends up in emotional disasters. When things seem to be going normal in relationships, it is an inevitable period to back them up with reasonable reinforcements for continued motivation. The sense of appreciations is necessary in human relationships. For instance, in relationships, the expression "thank you very much" costs nothing but can buy everything. This is where prayer becomes vital for believers in oneself and in God. In the words of Yancey: "Through the medium of prayer we go to our enemy, stand by his side, and plead for him to God" (1997:89). As if Emmanuel Ede was referring to spiritual psychology when he spoke of African Metaphysics, it "is designed to uphold man's beholdenness to God rather than proclaiming man as the rational absolute" (2006:12). A costly mistake the modern age can make is to think that we are builders of a world nobody knew when it began. If Christ were not God, his death could have been equal to one death, but he died for the entire human race. Practical life situations should guide us come to terms with our world and ourselves in every relationship we find ourselves. Unfortunately, the situation appears different today, thereby creating a major problem for society.

However, some people make honest efforts to build healthy relationships in order to enjoy a better world. To fully maximize the beauty of this world to our own advantages, it has to be clear to our senses that we are part and parcel of an established system in which every person plays an important role. We know it. Earthly enjoyment is ephemeral, limited, transient, and momentary in nature. As it were, life could be meaningless, frustrating and baseless if there were no better place that guarantees eternity of peace and joy. Therefore, there is need to strike a balance between the various groups of people in society. Respecting peoples' values and working together for common objectives will help us build a better society and harmonious relationship. To bail the cat is the problem. Let us appreciate each other in manners that are meaningful and loving.

Pretense normally fills the eyes of relationships with tears

For instance, it is no longer news that so many happy married couples, families, friends and peers have suddenly separated. Some have even attempted to kill one another. The big question that stares everybody on the face is, when and how did such ill-wind start blowing in the first place? Who is responsible? There can be no end to such enquiries. Philosophical anthropology teaches that man is a bundle of possibilities as indicated earlier on. He is the architect of his relationship. In the words of William Shakespeare in Macbeth, "A fool thinks himself to be wise, but a wise man knows himself to be a fool.... There is no art to find the mind's construction in the face". (Act 1 Scene 4. 11-12). Foolishness is of two types here. A person, who refuses to listen to others, remains a fool in every relationship irrespective of how educated or rich he or she claims to appear. But a wise person always tries to own his or her responsibilities and learn from his or her mistakes. No wonder the Bible noted that "God's foolishness is wiser than human wisdom, and God's weakness is stronger than human strength" (1Cor. 1:25). It is evident to our senses that someone may have evil in his or her heart when his or her mood disguisedly looks friendly. The Psalmist indicated this when referring to a traitor. Thus: "His speech is softer than butter but war is in his heart" (Ps. 55:20-21). The Psalmist elaborately held:

> *If an enemy has done this I could bear his taunts. If a rival had risen against me, I could hide from him. But it is you, my own companion my intimate friend, how close was the friendship between us? We walked together in harmony, in the house of God. Ps.55: 12-14.*

Relationship is not pretentious. It is real life. What could "walking in harmony in the house of God," mean in the above quotation for us today? Dr. Iwuala Ishmael reacting to the above Psalm observed: "This is a pathetic or sorrowful lamentation, expression of anxiety for a friend who feels seriously betrayed, wounded and disappointed by an intimate friend" (FH/Oxford, 2009). Relationship here calls for a re-definition as regards what friendship is all about for the individual. It is sad acting the good guy in relationships when the opposite is the case. Better be a man and quit evil than pretending to be friendly only to destroy innocent souls in the name of relationship. These are problems emanating from human nature and most of our young boys and girls easily fall victim to them.

The case of Julius Caesar and his intimate friend, Brutus quickly comes to mind also. This is the simple truth about some human relationships. There is need to expect the unexpected in every relationship and be ready to stomach insults and hurts to allow the world move on. Of course, the world keeps on moving irrespective of how we fashion our lives and relate to each other. The fact that Brutus, mercilessly tortured, held and raised the dagger to the face of his bosom friend Caesar, eliminating and stabbing him to death was the ultimate level of betrayal. Who could imagine how Julius Caesar felt when he was shouting to his friend Brutus: *"Et tu Brute*, and you Brutus?"* (Act 111, Scene 1). Now, how do we feel when we are in trouble like Caesar, to see our friend, who should have been a source of relief and peace of mind to us, coming, turning around and holding a sword against us and the basic moral principles of life, relationship, health and harmony? Here lies the dilemma and the most ugly face of human relationship, thereby filling the eyes of relationship with an uncontrollable tear. Some relationships are problematically more of a lamentation than blessings; hence, the urgent need to finish reading this book.

Consequently, spiritual psychology adopts a unique measurement for what constitutes morally good or bad act in the individual. The suitability of human relationship generally lies on the application of moral values and principles to concrete human situations. As it were, spiritual psychology, not only, raises the question of "why" we apparently have diversities in society but also embarks on finding out the best options for sustaining and healing the wound of divisions in every relationship. Due principally to the relative tendencies associated with most moral behaviors, the course adopts a universally accepted moral standard and measurement as a guide to our relationships. This is important because a behavior that is culturally considered immoral in one community or among individuals may be accepted and celebrated as a model by others.

Human relationship is non denominational

In a situation where there are clashes of interests, preferences and choice points, it is difficult for individuals to navigate through the tempest of their relational differences. Therefore, the ethical and moral principles regarding the sacredness, dignity and spirituality of human life coupled with authentic religious values as evidenced in concrete human situations are the measurements and standards of this book. The book is as non denominational as human relationship both on the individual, group and cultural levels. It is holistic and all embracing. Call this measurement "a code of human Spirituality" or a necessary call to order, which, in McGrath's own words: "Is a quest for a fulfilled life and authentic life, that involves taking the beliefs and values of Christianity and weaving them into the fabric of our lives, so that they animate, provide the 'breath' and 'spirit' and 'fire' for our lives" (1999:9). This is a measurement that corresponds with the Christian ethics and values. Linzey in Shaw & Morgan, in appropriation of these values in the Christian context observed:

> *The life and teaching of Jesus specifically in his "ethic of inclusive moral generosity" extended to the poor, the vulnerable, the*

outcast, and those normally beyond the boundaries of social concern, (2006:23).

Only those who are conscious of their weaknesses and limitations can adequately appreciate human relationship in its true meaning. As we earlier on noted in the book, relationship includes the various areas in which individuals find themselves. There is relationship in everything under the earth, in oneself, science, finance, marriage, religion, government, and industries among individuals and groups et cetera. We live and operate in relationships, the nature and level of individual relationships notwithstanding. The borderline is the ability to identify with the ethic of inclusiveness, instead of exclusiveness, moral generosity that respects all boundaries. These are target points of spiritual psychology, which some individuals seem to violate today by their ugly behaviors.

2. The magnitude of problems resulting from immoral practices in society:

The second issue the book handles in the background of the statement of problem is the enormity and levels of conflicts experienced in society today due to immoral behaviors. These immoral behaviors also originate from the ferocious and individual characteristics as we discussed above. However, this section centers more on the evidences of such moral, religious, social violations in society. The young generation is hereby called upon to guide themselves by joining and emulating good lives, associations and peer groups. To be physically young is temporal, but one can emotionally remain a kid for life. It is permanently regrettable and maniacal to be childish at one's adulthood. The cultivation of positive life styles and values at youthful age is an ocean of riches that never dries away. The youths who nurture good behaviors whenever the opportunity strikes, later, live to proudly tell their stories with great joy and enthusiasm. Being the future of tomorrow, it is a must that the young ones try their best to remain disciplined for successful and progressive future. Based on these vital issues, the National President of the Catholic Women Organization of Nigeria, Dr. Nwachukwu Udaku has this to say to the youths:

Children and teenagers now observe with their very eyes what happens in the world of adults. They are exposed to the

> *adult world of adultery, addiction, incest or any vice you can name. After all the exposures, gradually, they begin putting to practice what – they have seen adults do. The Igbos do say that Nwata etoghi eto wara ogodo, ikuku kuwe, o buru nwata burukwa ogodo ya – a child that starts doing what he is not yet mature to do, he or she plays a dangerous game because the winds of life realities will surely not spare such a child (2009:66).*

It will be late for most of these teenagers to realize the damage they have unconsciously inflicted upon themselves due to foolhardiness. Immoral associations and behaviors have never paid anybody in his or her life.

Apparently, we drew some examples from different cultures particularly, USA and the Igbo of Nigeria to justify our position here. We are living witnesses that there are various cases of immoral behaviors abounding in many relationships and society today. These immoral behaviors range from hypocrisy, infidelity, advanced fee fraud, (OBT), tricks, lies, tale bearing, lack of respect, embezzlements and mismanagement of public funds, cheating, IM in the Nigerian context (cover up mentality due to familiarity), lying, greed, sex abuses, high ring prostitutions, drug addiction, truancy, fighting, rancor and acrimony, examination malpractices, betrayal, impersonations, cultism, alcoholism, highway robbery, kidnapping, terrorisms, homicide, suicide and hired assassins, et cetera. These are concrete problems that tend to destroy interpersonal relationships. Immorality, especially hypocrisy paralyzes and completely chokes human relationships. Ehusani summarizing the situation at college levels noted:

> *Our schools and colleges have lost their sacred character as formation centers, and have rather become breeding grounds for thieves, thugs, touts, secret cultists, gangsters, rapists and prostitutes. We hear these days of school children beating up their teachers, sacking their principals, and burning their libraries (2002:14).*

Worse still, some of the government agencies that are meant to protect the peace and safety of the people seem to have become institutions of crimes and indiscipline. In the Nigerian context for instance, the government seems to be the most corrupt, dishonest, selfish and perpetrator of crimes in different quarters and levels of Nigerian society. The situation is far from the Socratic formula or dialectic approach where a person is blameless in following an erroneous conscience. That is to say in the Nigerian case, in Aquinas view, "where there is ignorance (invincible) that a man is in no way to blame for the ignorance itself, he is wholly free from blame", (949: Art 2). Partners need to know this too. On the contrarily, most of the perpetrators of these evils and immoral behaviors in relationships and society are quite aware of what they are doing. For instance, the magnitude of corruption in Nigeria today has calamitously metamorphosed into the consciousness of the young generation that, according to Ogunu "cases of impersonation abound in Nigerian Institutions" (2002:10).

This is where the problem has become hydra-headed, especially in matters of trust in relationship. Referring to examination malpractices among the students of Nigerian higher Institutions of learning in the same writing, Ogunu observed: "Our students devise as daily routine new tricks to beat supervisors and examiners". According to the same source: "Some female students use the "sanitary pad" method, whereby they hide their prepared notes in sanitary pads, and wear them to the examination hall. When the Invigilator's attention is focused on other candidates, such female students disentangle the notes and try to copy" (2002:10). Based on such awful habits and practices, one wonders whether these students have any form of conscience in the first place. Secondly, it is obvious that such students will find it impossible to build any reliable relationships anywhere in their lives. A person who enjoys cheating others hardly gives it up.

We have so many things to wonder about regarding the future of our young ones. Or has the collective psyche of our young people been brutally battered and wounded to the extent that it has become part of their lives? Parents, teachers and society must come out. According to Wade Carole in Dr. Nwachukwu Udaku:

> *The following account by Carole Wade an American Psychologist may add to convince you: In a Connecticut town,*

> *a group of teenage boys looking for excitement telephoned an order for Chinese food so that they could rob the deliveryman. When he refused to hand over the food, one of the teenagers shot him to death. Later the boys calmly ate the food (2009:68-69)*

It is also true that some schoolteachers, principals, lecturers and some parents, particularly in most educational systems in society at the higher or secondary schools levels are involved in these examination malpractices, especially in Nigeria. Ehusani had this to say as regards the situation in some Nigerian States: "Teachers and principals organize cheating at external examinations, and parents usually contribute to "settle supervisors and invigilators" (2002: 14). Is this attitude not the climax and foundation of building the most atrocious human relationship? When evil intentions are the bases of any relationship, be it in families, couples, ministries, government quarters, among individuals, groups of people, friends, the net results are always the stagnation of peace and progress of society at large. As one adage puts it: "When the elephants fight, the grasses suffer". Bad will is carcinogenic to relationship and many are victims to it.

Again, Ilo, reacting to the same shocking and immoral behaviors in society today, made the following remarks: "We are daily being fed with tangled tales of rapes, adultery, child sex abuse (pedophilia), sexual harassment among others" (1997:7). This ill has grown and gone global. Why do some use rape as a weapon for choice? It is no longer news that some of the secondary or high school and University students indulge in one immoral relationship or the other for selfish ends. Regarding sexual immoralities in our schools, Ilo lamented, thus:

> *Many right-thinking Christians are worried that the immoral lives of our students would destroy future families, lead to marital infidelity spread sexually transmitted diseases... destroy the goals of University education (1997:8).*

By implication, according to Ilo, there are as "many right-thinking Christians" as there are unreliable Ones. How can society infected with corruption build lasting and trustworthy relationships? Worse still, the infidelity Ilo spoke about here is number one killer disease in all levels of human relationship, especially in marital states. Spiritual psychology is thereby constrained to investigate into the apparent causes and reasons why human beings, the finest creature on the planet, created in God's image, choose to cheat and deceive in their relationships. One may wonder if the reasons are traceable to economic, religious, greed, hate or lack of faith in ones life or partner? No! Lack of sound moral instruction in the training and education of children is the principal cause.

Unbelievable! Death toll on the increase: Case of teenagers – Need for spiritual psychology/sound moral education in the school systems

Moreover, referring to the school children in a State in Nigeria for instance, Abubakar observed: "A junior secondary school student at the Maimalri Government Day Secondary School, Maiduguri claimed to have killed about 48 people for ritual purposes in Maiduguri alone, and three people outside the state capital" (2001:15). If we mean to cite juvenile delinquencies and criminal cases of society and our children in this book, we shall need to write another one. The awful event that took place in the USA, at Virginia Tech. in April 16, 2007 regarding the shooting by young student Mr. Seung-Hui Cho that left 33 people dead, is still fresh in our minds. What of the atrocious deed of manslaughter of the 11-year-old Pennsylvania boy, Jordan Brown who killed his father's pregnant fiancée Kenzie Houk with a shotgun (NY Post, 2/22/09)? What of the barbaric act of Jiverly Wong 41, who killed 13 innocent souls in Binghamton, Syracuse in New York, before he took his own life (NY Post, 4/5/09)? Can any one imagine the horror of the terrorist's attack of September 11, 2001? Again, the murder of the young girl, Annie Le whose body was found on Sunday, September 13, 2009, the day of her wedding by Raymond Clark 3rd, a Yale Mouse Keeper, is unimaginably heart breaking (NY Times, 9/1809). As already observed, such sad stories are told worldwide on daily basis, particularly in Europe, America and Africa. It is hard to imagine how bad characters have devastated various relationships and society at large. I feel, to squarely deal with these crime rates, violence and evils in society 'Moral Instructions' within the area of spiritual psychology should compulsorily be introduced in all levels of the school curricula.

An urgent call to parents to take charge of their children - Panel

On the same issues of social and domestic violence, Dominic Carter, Inside City Hall, Host/Senior Political Reporter/NY1, News Warner Cable TV, on October 8, 2009 nearly shed tears because of how a 16-year-old Derrion Albert of Chicago was beaten to death like a rat on Thursday, September 25, 2009. At that TV news, Dominic Carter angrily posed a fundamental and practical question: "Now, what do we do, the matter is getting out of hand?" Unanimously, the panelists, Eric Adams, Keith Wright and Jackie Rowe-Adams (who has also lost 2 children to gun violence and co-founder of Harlemmothersave. com) bitterly blamed parents for their failures to guide their children. They insisted that parents should not be afraid to take charge of their children and that it was time various communities came out and took control of the situation. There must be some parameters for monitoring and guiding the young ones. For instance, certain movies, video games and pornographic programs available in various facilities, to mention but a few, should be restricted from kids to avoid 'scandals of the weak'. That was the point Dr. Nwachukwu Udaku meant when she remarked:

> *Mean-world syndrome is the tendency to view the world as a battlefield, where survivals-of-the-fittest is the norm; a place where aggression and violence are the only ways to solve problems. As such, prolonged consumption of violence and other base behaviors in movies and TV programmes increase particularly in children and teenagers the acceptance of such inappropriate ways of living and achieving one's goals (2009:73).*

Dominic Carter, even, cited a dimensional case where he never stayed late at night outside their home because of "the rod" and how his father would treat him. When kids grow, they mimic their parents and values. For instance, how can a child speak of God or religion, when he or she never heard his or her parent mention that? The warning signals the Panelists raised for parents are: "Whenever your child no longer fears and respects you in whatever he or she says and does, let it be noted that your child as turned into something else and you could fall victim to his or her crimes one day". This is essentially why we dedicated the book to the benefits of young people. Let us heed Michael Gerson, in what he calls "cultural revival" that when things are tough, people connect with their cherished values" (IR). There is no other time to come together than now.

Moreover, research and experience have shown that a child with poor family upbringing constitutes a nuisance in society and at school environment. For instance, a reckless parent who drives drunk, walks half naked, eats in inappropriate manners, and talks carelessly without minding the implication of his or her words and actions can hardly raise a responsible child. Nwachukwu Udaku, citing Linus Okwu in his Home Media in Nigeria, noted:

> *One mother expresses herself this way: I can't even resist the TV. I come in, the first thing I do is to switch on the TV, stager to the seat until deep into the night while maid makes food for the children before they sleep. Imagine, no single time for the family; the husband and children. Possibly both the husband and the children may not be different also. Such homes as this have almost nothing to share together as a family. In short, there is no home here (2009: 72-73).*

Teaching a child to behave well at school, social or religious gatherings when his or her parents are irresponsible at home is like putting on a beautiful reading glass on a person completely born blind from birth. On this point, Rev. Dr. Desmond Nwanne Chilagorom observed: "Parents should not only expect their children to obey them, to accede to what is for their own good…. They should create a family atmosphere that can help children to learn from experience what is good and in accordance with conscience to be obedient to one's superior…personal example of parents to their children gives more insight on what is expected of their children than verbal instructions" (2006:133). When one does not care for oneself or about how one looks like, one cannot be expected to care for others. Put differently, the Christian Bible said:

> *Can people pick grapes from thorns, or figs from thistles? In the same way, a sound tree produces good fruit but a rotten tree bad fruit. A sound tree cannot bear bad fruit, nor a rotten tree bear good fruit. .... I repeat, you will be able to tell them by their fruits (Mt. 7:16-20).*

Rationalizations in matters of mores will always lead to bitter ends. Society can be peaceful and enjoyable if each person decides to take the right steps to healthy self-reflection and supervision. Blaming the government and the politicians for their failures to provide enough infrastructures when our wants have already gotten in the ways of our needs is like having one's cake and expecting to eat it also. Spiritual psychology hereby calls every Dick and Harry to join in this vital campaign for order and peace in our school systems, individual families, lives and society. As long as bad character is not formed in a day, both parents and children can decide to take a break and ask valid questions on how they can gradually come out of such bad habits. When society looses the sense of shame and no longer cares about how individuals should behave in public, indiscipline will surely become the order of the day.

However, on the third level of the background of the statement of problems, as a case study, we systematically reviewed the disorientations, ugly influences, which the incarnation of the Gospel message created in the long-lived relationships of the Igbo of Nigeria. The study gave us access to clearly understand how half-baked approaches to sensitive matters like belief systems; personal values and feelings could easily soil human relationships. As the situation unfolded, we focused more on the socio-religious and cultural innovations and differences that seemed to have darkened the future, hope, peace, progress, and moral principles of a people who had maintained a common identity of oneness. The problem is so devastating that we examined the impact Christianity in particular has on the cultural values of the people. Nigeria, a purely cultural-religious people, is examined here as a case study.

3. Problems that affect human relationships due to wrong approaches or inadequate methodology of missionary activity: The Nigerian case:

The primary reason for treating this issue in details is to demonstrate the importance of jointly approaching and viewing a common problem in relationship. The tone of an advice determines its consideration. The missionaries who introduced Christian religion to Nigeria did not actually mean to destroy the people. They came as superiors to introduce the main reliable religion to a people who needed the light of God. But, unknown to them, the Igbo of Nigeria had practiced a living religion that sustained them for ages. In this light, the missionaries unconsciously created notable disorders in the cultural identity of the Igbo people. Generally, to enter into other people's world of feelings, it is always necessary for the individual to devote some time to study them and what constitutes their identity as such. A little elucidation of the backgrounds of the moral and religious practices of the Igbo of Nigeria, particularly the people of Ezinihitte is urgent at this point. Call it an introduction of a people who, for ages, serve as models for healthy human relationships. Our survey on this regard is based on the historical evidences and inroads of the missionaries to the peaceful people of the Igbo land of Nigeria and the damages done thereupon. The missionaries in their zeal to bring Christianity to the people "intentionally" or unintentionally planted the 'seed of syncretism' that has dangerously affected the religious consciousness and relationships of the people till date. "The failure to deal with problems of human growth" according to Au, Wilkie, "weakens apostolic effectiveness" (1989:219). In this sense, it appeared as if Emile Louis Victor de Lavelaye in Mead Frank, S., referred to the situation at hand when he remarked:

> *If Christianity were taught and understood comfortable to the spirit of its Founder, the existing social organism could not exist a day (1965:55).*

As it were, Christianity was never taught or understood by the people because of the manner in which it was presented to them. Therefore, we are constrained in this book to weigh the consequences and impacts of such missionary activities in that part of the globe, Igbo of Nigeria, especially in the area of their cherished values. As an African and a certified counselor, writing about keeping relationships together, I particularly feel concerned with the manner in which my people's culturally established relationships got jeopardized by Christianity, call it western civilization or evangelization. Chinua Achebe expressed it better. Thus:

> *Does the white man understand our custom about our land? How can he when he does not even speak our tongue? But he says that our customs are bad; and our own brothers who have taken up his religion also say that our customs are bad. How do you think we can fight when our own brothers have turned against us? The white man is very clever. He came quietly and peaceably with his religion. We were amused at his foolishness and allowed him to stay. Now he has won our brothers, and our clan can no longer act like one. He has put a knife on the things that hold us together and we have fallen apart (1994:176).*

Denominationally, the situation escalated to a point where religious bigotry seemed to have tremendously influenced and affected the relationship of the people, especially the Igbo of Nigeria. Ironically, there is no gainsaying that, factors such as individual cultures, upbringing, environments, and associations influence relationships. But the swift influence the people encountered on account of improper implantation of the Gospel message seemed to have adversely affected their belief systems. No culture is meaningless, particularly to the people for whom it exists. Generally, for a culture to be meaningful, it has to be dynamic, lively and flexible and not static. Paradoxically, flexibility is equally an indispensable value in relationship. It was as a result of these classic reasons, that we drew part of our population and some samples for the survey mainly from the Middle Class of the Igbo of Nigeria. The most interesting aspect and resultant effects of the improper introduction of Christianity to the Igbo of Nigeria hinges on the fact that a minister of the Word of God in Igbo land of Nigeria can at the same time get involved in fetish practices. The above abnormal scenarios are traceable to the failure of the missionaries to catechize the people first before they introduced the Gospel message to them. Nowhere in the dream world does relationship thrive in confusion. Thus, in this book, we largely treated such practices, intended or not, as disorders and the hurricane that seemed to scatter the unity, peace and relationship of the people in question.

The book, eventually, considered the inherent diversities in human relationships as ways of responding to a common good or goal. Extensively, these diversities guided us to the study of an aspect of human relationship, namely Conscience. Call it an aberration or an oversight; this book carefully examined the culture of the Igbo of Nigeria as a case study to understand the possible causes of frictions and conflicts within human relationships in general. Knowledge builds on knowledge. Our study of the culture of the Igbo of Nigeria throws some lights on how best the individuals can, first and foremost, realize their own values and then respect other peoples' boundaries. By sharing positive values from other cultures, individuals are disposed to put on their thinking caps as regards the best ways they can relate to the global community. Inconsistency does not encourage any healthy relationship, religious practice and progress. The study therefore raises questions, as whether every person is a human being. Or has humanity been likened to the Biblical rich man whose soul was demanded on the very night he felt most comfortable in his life (Lk.12: 16-21)? God called him "fool" because he failed to realize the main source of his being and good harvest. This could also serve as a warning to those who brag with their wealth and do not care to share with others, especially the needy.

Within this understanding, we presented and studied the effects of the Christian religion on the people, with particular reference to the sharp division it has brought to them at large. Today, the Igbo Christians of Nigeria are disorientated and dichotomized in their beliefs as regards what constitutes Traditional or Christian values. In this way, Christianity introduced two basic belief systems among the people, whereby a Christian who confesses strong faith in Christ, equally keeps and adheres to his or her traditional values. Lamentably, we do not need to go to any particular culture to understand the magnitude of disservices; disorders, disorientations and conflicting positions create in human relationships. It is better one keeps to what energizes one because the devil does appear and disguise himself in different attires, at times, as an angel just to obstruct human recognitions.

Nonetheless, after we examined some of the religious and traditional practices of the Igbo of Nigeria for instance, we discovered the various damaging effects the Christian religion seemed to have had on their relationships. Such situations are akin to many cultures of the world too. Interestingly, the Igbo people of Nigeria tenaciously believe in one God and in such moral principles and values as truth, justice, peace, hospitality, unity, love, honesty, humility, respect for the elderly, human life and dignity et cetera. But, with the advent of Christianity, which came in form of civilization, surprisingly some people started opposing the Traditional and moral values. Faith in one God of the ancestors began to face sharp criticisms. These are really misnomers, disorders and problems facing the book.

The confusion in question emanated from civilization that was muddled and presented within the context of evangelization without adequate catechesis by the evangelizers. The missionaries did not do any fieldwork or study the culture of the people and its implications before they launched their evangelical mission. Ilogu Edmund well expressed this view in this way:

> *With the arrival of the Missionaries and traders from 1857 onwards, the neat pattern became disturbed. Plurality of religious and value concepts appeared for the first time to start the rapid change that has been going on in Igbo land ever since then, although more rapid at the periods than others (1974:63).*

Moreover, those Nigerians who assisted the missionaries in interpreting and translating the Christian messages were not educated enough for such evangelical and academic functions. The interpreters, as it were, equally share blames for the disorders and effects of the unexamined inter- and multi-cultural encounters. The importance of studying the characteristic, behavioral patterns, ways of life of other people cannot be overemphasized in any relationship. There should be no rush in any level of human relationship. For instance, while we encourage unity, peace and healthy relationships among individuals, relating and contracting businesses with a notorious criminal who is unbending is unpleasant.

In a way, the book raises serious concerns as whether the Igbo of Nigeria would have been better off today without Christianity than painfully sacrificing their religious and cultural values at the altar of the Christian message. As Levi-Strauss, C. puts it: "Each of us is a kind of crossroad where things happen" (1979:4). Now, things have happened. Therefore, each of us must be ready to expect the unexpected in the other. These concerns tantamount to the classic importance of studying other peoples' cultures, particularly that of the Igbo of Nigeria vis-à-vis the western cultures.

The major question that dominated greater part of this section is: "Was the evangelization of the Africans or the Igbo of Nigeria the same as their civilization?" Unfortunately, as noted already, evangelization came to the people in the context of civilization and they welcomed it from materialistic perspectives. This created an unsolvable problem in the sense that most of the people would always approach the Christian religion from its instrumental dimensions. They emphasize the material benefit it offers them while intrinsically relying on the Traditional values and religion that guarantee their safety on earth and eternity in the world to come. In a more practical fashion, Onwubiko O. seems to be referring to this problem when he noted: "In traditional African societies, there were no atheists. This is because religion, in the indigenous African culture, is not an independent institution. It is an integral and inseparable part of the entire culture.... This is because social morality is dependent on religion" (1991:23). Pricelessly, if the Igbo of Nigeria have lacked anything in their lives, it is not in the area of religion. In support of Onwubiko, Elizabeth Isichei recorded about a German Missionary in Aboh in 1841 concerning the same Igbo people, in these words:

> *The Igbos are in their way a religious people - the word 'Tshukwu' (Chukwu-God) is continually heard. Tshukwu is supposed to do everything... Their notions of some attributes of the Supreme Being are, in many respects, correct, and their*

> *manner of experiencing striking. God made everything: He made both black and white is continually on their lips. Some of their parables are descriptive of the perfections of God (1977:24).*

Correspondingly, the target of spiritual psychology substantially reflects the view Isichei has underlined above, particularly on the equality of human values and feelings. In this light, the book extensively tries to dig out the main source of disorder in society and how to reduce conflicts in human relationships. For instance, today, the Igbo of Nigeria are unconsciously reaping the fruits of two religious worlds that emanated from the missionary activities in their land. The book is blunt on this point. Relationships are sacrificially all about sensitivity to the values and feelings of others because everyone needs some space. Rigidity is a virus that gradually eats up human relationship. We justified our position in this section of the book by briefly juxtaposing the culture of the Igbo people of Nigeria with that of the westerners. We are, at this point compelled to ask: "Who are the Igbo of Nigeria?"

The Igbo of Nigeria at a glance and their cosmology

Nigeria is located in West Africa and shares land borders with the Republic of Benin in the West, Chad and Cameroon in the East, and Niger in the North. The territory of the Igbo land shares boundaries with Igala in the North, Isoko in the East, Ijawu/Itsekiri in the West and Urobhro in the South. The Igbo people of East-Southern Nigeria are generally homogenous – one language, one color, one belief system with slight dialectical differences, hence a bit heterogeneous. The picture thus presented here represents a model for trustworthy relationship. It is important to note that the word "Igbo" or "Ibo" can stand for a noun, an adjective, singular or plural. The homogeneous nature of the people of Igbo land of Nigeria necessitated the limited range of our focus to Ezinihitte people in particular. They share the same socio-religious, moral and ethical principles. The homogeneity of their moral conduct makes this section interesting because the truth of their religious practices is purely dependent on moral standards.

The entire cosmology, spirituality, epistemology and anthropology of the Igbo people are geared towards finding the best ways to meaningfully enjoy healthy relationships here on earth as to continue them in eternity with their ancestors. Their communal, collectivistic, interdependent structure marks them out from the rest of the western culture or world that tends to emphasize individualistic and independent lifestyles. These lifestyle differences have their own problems in human relationships. As Kinzer would have it: "Thus, the general shift in society from committed personal groupings [such as kinship and neighborhood groups] to more impersonal institutional settings has probably increased our modern problems with self-worth" (1980:25). The impersonal institutional settings have compounded the problems facing the Igbo of Nigeria today. These are groups of people who always and remarkably put smiles on their faces amidst difficulties and pains. To be fair and truthful in relationship is culturally divine for the people. Infringements and violations to their natural identity as descendants of a common ancestral heritage are serious taboos. Commenting on the ontological dimension and solidarity of the Igbo of Nigeria, Basden made the following observations:

> *The ontological community denotes first and foremost ontological quality of human relations. It is ontological in so far as all members of the community are believed to descend from a common ancestor. Every man is linked to his parents on the natural level. His parents in turn are bound to their grand-parents, etc. This link which binds all members of the same family by propagation is broadened to include all members of the community or clan who are believed to be descendants of the same ancestor. Everyone considers himself as member of a definite community and as part of the whole, (1966:122).*

Basden has said it all. The Igbo share one cultural identity. Anything that happens to a member of the family or community equally affects the rest of the people. In the words of Ilogu, we read: "Communality is the essence of the gods. They are the common possessions and guardians of all. No one sins to the gods alone. Punishment for one man is visited on all. The blessings of the gods are also shared by all" (1975:34-43). It is not a sweeping generalization to say that the morality and religion of the Igbo of Nigeria are the same and one thing. Their entire cosmology and belief systems, as I noted in one of my books, are deeply rooted "within the ambience of ancestral, community life or in solidarity with the Umunna or community" (2002:341). For the people, morality is synonymous with life. It is a pattern of life bequeathed to them by their ancestors. In this perspective, the level of relationship that exists between Igbo people is indescribably superb. There is order in everything under the sun, between gender, age and class. A violation of the moral order of the land affects not only the humans but also vegetation and livestock. Virtue is highly rewarded as the normal ways of living and sound moral qualities are inevitably considered as parts of their common heritage.

Therefore, any religion whether it is Christian or Traditional that violates the ethical standards of the Igbo people is perceived as a threat to the ancestors who are the role models of religion and morality as cited in my PhD dissertation, (HF/Oxford, 2007). It was on this basis that Odiegwu D. noted:

> *African Traditional religion practiced by some Africans before the advent of Christianity in the continent has immense symbols, values that could enrich us as Christians today (1997:36).*

Eventually, there is need to examine some of these Traditional or cultural values that seem to have conflicted with the Christian principles among the people of today due to wrong approaches. The analysis also guides us to ascertain the magnitude of problems most people encounter in their individual relationships. Till this day, the problems of "who are really fooling whom" remain unsolved among the people? The Igbo Christians are divided among themselves. While some are Traditional religionists in the Christian attire, others are Christian fundamentalists in the Traditional fashion. In a nutshell, the problem sprang from the challenges of cross-cultural transference and encounter of the crossroads of two cultures, the western versus the African. There was, ab initio, no clear distinction between the two religions and cultures. Due to this lack of clarity, the book generally studied them within the context of the influence of western civilization on the Igbo in general.

On a more serious note, we considered a few of the basic religious values and practices of the Igbo of Nigeria that were violated by the missionary activities and influences of western civilization. These are problems that have attracted not only the attention of westerners themselves but also constituted the problems in question among the Igbo of Nigeria today. Every relationship is a world of its own. The effects of entering into another person's world without proper orientation and information, as noted earlier, are living witnesses of how people can easily destroy the healthy relationships of others. In reference to the Nigerian case, Ilo Chu Stan observed: "There were obviously many things that the missionaries did, which in the light of today's thinking would be considered inappropriate. Whatever way of life or custom the missionaries did not understand, they often condemned in Africans as fetish and pagan" (2006:73). It is wrong to condemn the 'attitude' of a person, whose culture is still unknown to you. To relate with others or incarnate the Word of God to a people like the Igbo of Nigeria, without a thorough study of their culture is always a big risk. Generally, such oversights create similar problems in every stratum of human relationships as the ones handled here. In this light, Norman, D. observed:

> *The conventional answer of scientists has been that the human brain, from which all thought and action emanate, produces culture…Culture is not just produced by the brain; it is also by definition a series of activities that shape the mind. We become cultured through training in various activities, such as customs, arts, ways of interacting with people…learning of ideas, beliefs, shared philosophies, and religion (2007:287).*

As a guide to healthy human relationship, therefore, it is necessary to study the possible unintentional effects of a person's 'good will' and properly channel them to the right directions. That is precisely what this survey is all about as regards the incarnation of the Gospel message to the Igbo of Nigeria. Consequently, the missionary's failures to integrate the Christian values to the fundamental values and culture of the people are studied and presented in this section, numbering 1 to 13, as Violations or disorders. They are mainly the focus of the background of the study among the three major factors in the statement of problem.

The aspects of the cultural values of the Igbo of Nigeria studied here include:

1. The Council of Elders/Association of first sons *(Ndi Opara)*

This is a council constituted by elders of proven character in the community. Good character is a sine qua non in every healthy relationship. One becomes a member of the council of elders not by election, appointment or religious affiliation but by age and good moral standard. Unlike today, money seems to constitute the criteria for leadership in certain quarters. This council meets every eight-market day to look into common problems that might affect interpersonal relationships or destabilize the morality of the land. Likewise, every relationship needs some moments set apart for planning. To this effect, Dr. Udaku remarked:

> *Movies and TV at meal or other family relation moments deprive the members of the joy and opportunity of interacting and relating fully, interestingly and actively with one another. Parents in this kind of family neither truly understand their children in order to give them the proper information they require, nor can the children develop sound and vital love and understanding to become friends with one another (2009:72)*

In the case of the Council of elders, Meek noted: "The elders were a body of mediators and referees than of prosecutors and judges, and the community was Republican in the true sense of the term, that is, a corporation in which government was the concern of all" (1943:130). Whenever relationship becomes selfish and not directed to the conveniences of both parties, it collapses. According to an indigenous writer from Ezinihitte, Onwubiko: "The elders have their practical effect in the maintenance of custom and tradition" (1999:23).

Actually, "the associations of the first sons" which means *ndi opara* play almost the same role as the council of elders. The expression *ndi opara* is always in the plural form. All the well-behaved elderly male children besides the first sons, *ndi opara,* are automatically members of the council. That is why each family has an "elder" who might be that way by age, sound moral life or divine. For instance, every first male among his siblings belongs to the group of *ndi opara*. A father who is the second or third son of his own parents might not enjoy the privileges and rights of *ndi opara*, which is available to his own first son. However, the father of that first son may enjoy the privilege of belonging to the council of elders by age or moral standard and holds the *Ofo na Ogu*, meaning "truth and justice" the symbol of authority of his family till death. At the death of a father, the first son eventually takes up the responsibility of looking after his father's compound and holds the *Ofo na Ogu*. The *Ofo na Ogu* is ancestral power of governance over the family or community and there has never been any confusion as who holds it for any period of time. Such a situation helps to ensure peaceful relationships among the community or compound concerned. It equally works well in many families when responsibilities and duties are clearly shared.

Unfortunately, confusion emerged into the soil of the Igbo land of Nigeria with the advent of Christianity and civilization. Just like in human relationship, education regarding the culture and values of any people is important. For instance, the missionaries did not spend time to observe the policies, politics, social and religious systems of the people, rather they rashly branded everything fetish and heathen. As a consequence, the revered institution of the above elders became battered. A titled and retired teacher, Nze Ogbonna from Ezinihitte of Igbo land of Nigeria representing large opinion of his people, in my interview with him, described the situation in these words: "The community is now against itself. Today, the educated and the so-called Christians are trying to nip all our customs and traditions in the bud" (4/20/01). Again, some people, especially the youths and Christian fanatics flout the role of these elders. As it stands in Ezinihitte of Igbo land, a wealthier son irrespective of his position in the family can now fight for the natural birthright that belongs only to the first son, thereby committing abominations. This is not simply a problem but an offence, a crime against the ancestors and the land. Worse still, some elderly people, for economic reasons seem to hide or close their eyes against the truth and secretly support the wealthy sons. What a negative impact on the people's belief systems and relationship? This is a typical scenario of a cultural kingdom rising against itself.

A clearer elaboration of the meaning of *Ofo na Ogu* may throw more light to the extent of violation in question. There is no gainsaying that in human relationship; a person alone can keep the glue of love and peace that holds two people together. One person at a time has to be the sacrificial lamb for peace to reign in relationships because good manners and self-sacrifices are the highest rules of grace. Every relationship shares its own equality and operates on its level.

2. The Symbol of Authority and Justice *[Ofo na Ogu]*

The significance of *Ofo na Ogu* in the socio-political and religious life of the people is a matter that remains for posterity. Authority here does not literally refer to political leadership and power to rule and control but understood in the context of proven integrity, probity, accountability and truthfulness. Not only does *Ofo na Ogu* stand for "justice" and "truthfulness", in the religious and day-to-day life of the people, they equally serve as the yardstick for settling, deciding conflicts of any sort and measuring the interpersonal relationship of the community. These values are feared as gods. Practically speaking, any act that is devoid of *Ofo na Ogu* is generally believed to have evil effects. Hence, our people say, *Omeni jidekwa Ofo na ogu*, that is, "whatever anybody has to do, let him have justice and truth in it". In a sense, this is what Benson referred to as "remembered wellness" as discussed in this book. It is impossible to have a healthy relationship without *[Ofo na Ogu]* justice and truthfulness. This is not only justice in the ordinary sense of the word. Rather, it is "justice" in a strict sense, by which eternity, our God or ancestors control human affairs. It is a symbol of equity. The entire concept of justice and fairness in deciding disputes and adjudication of disagreements through *Ofo na Ogu* could be represented by a carved object held by the elder called "Ikenga". As a staff of office, according to Amam A. Acholonu, in my interview with him, it is properly named 'ikenga' meaning "the power with which I operate" (10/19/09).

Ofo na Ogu are religious values that help both the Traditionalists and Christians in Ezinihitte understand the need for upright and sincere lives, just as the Christian Bible generally does in the lives of Christians. All the same, many Christians may disregard the Bible when carrying out their evil intentions, but not when the value of *"Ofo na Ogu"* is invoked. By implication, all human relationships should be guided by these principles of justice and truthfulness. We do not need to belong to any religious affiliation to live upright lives. To have peace in one's relationship is of classic importance and self-rewarding.

Specifically, the Traditional *Ofo* includes these three: The ancestral One (*Ofo Ndichie*); that of a medicine man or chief priest of a shrine (*Ofo Nwadibia or Ezemmuo)* and the One belonging to titled men (*Nze na ozo)*. To hold an *Ofo*, which is in a form of carved object, is to hold *Ogu*. Any object or symbol could be used for it today. *Ofo* is the symbol of Authority and (*na*) *Ogu* means Justice or Truthfulness. The two are interchangeable. The *Ofo*, in one of my books, is "the authority of the ancestors that is being handed down from one generation to the other" (2002:129). Unlike the Traditional *Ofo,* we have the *ofo* with small letter *"o"* representing the staff of office denoting the authority of the custodian. This can be handled by anybody, man or woman in that particular office as seen in the government quarters. According to Emean, while the *"Ofo Nwadibia, Nzenaozo, Ezemmuo"* can be thrown away at the death of the custodian, *Ofo Ndichie* passes from one *Opara* to another for posterity, (1998:22).

However, today the object, *Ofo* may not be physically used by most people, yet the concept is applied in every level of the people's relationships, even in the settlement of land cases or misconducts in the community. No wonder Uchendu V. C. remarked: "Community spirit is very strong among the Igbos. Almost from the first born, the individual is aware of his dependence on his kin group and his community" (1965:34). This communal spirit and life define the Igbo people of Nigeria as such. Every human relationship requires one form of *Ofo* - Authority or the other, *Ogu* - truthfulness or sincerity as a value that survives earthly existence. Justice and truthfulness in the African context have to be clearly noted, and these are the values that should sustain society, particularly our young generation. Unlike in the Christian sense or understanding, they are highly dreaded and respected as spiritual values whose violations attract instant punishment on the offender or community as a whole. Until recently, the Igbo of Nigeria did not need any civil court, law enforcement agencies and police Departments to settle their conflicts and cases, no matter the magnitude. The issue of healthy or unhealthy relationship was out of the question. Couples, individuals, leaders, farmers, teachers, et cetera had no serious grounds for misunderstanding each other. On a practical perspective, every human culture, government or relationship needs to incorporate these values of justice and truthfulness in its entirety.

Unfortunately, today contradictions have emerged within the Christian Gospel of peace, love, unity and forgiveness. Things have drastically changed that most people are entrapped in syncretism. Hardly do we distinguish Christians from Traditionalists in matters of greed, robbery, cheating, adultery, high sense of materialism, inordinate desires and selfish ambitions towards affluence and riches. The Traditional and Christian values are so mixed up that many people are confused regarding their religious and ancestral identity. The issue of *Ofo na Ogu* has been messed up. A lot of people have kicked against it, especially some of the Christians who prefer the use of the Holy Bible to the *Ofo*. Most of the youths flout Traditional values that prevent them from promiscuity and immoral practices, like carelessly mingling with the opposite sexes. Some no longer care about who is an elder. Such immoral acts as incest, theft, fighting, slander, and disrespect of gray hairs now abound in un-quantifiable levels. Even some of the elders themselves who are meant to be the custodians of justice and order in the community have equally derailed.

The attitudes of the council of elders and members of the first sons raise a lot of dust today, especially when and where one of their members dies. They make life unbearable for the affected family by compulsory and unnecessary items the family has to pay regardless of their economic background. The items may include money, goats, rams, kola nuts, and hot drinks, certain quantity of particular foodstuff or dish. Such behaviors have forced some to ask if these elders have consciences at all or are really honest and truthful to the ancestors they claim to be representing. What a violation then? Unfortunately, the people believe and point it out that this ugly situation causes rampant and untimely death among them these days. No death is worse than bad life.

In a sense, the basic principles for healthy relationships of the people have been abused. This is where our three groups of individuals as outlined in this book manifest their real qualities. In Ezinihitte of Igbo of Nigeria in particular and society at large, while many people do not care about what the Traditionalists or Christians are doing, some try to bring balance and congruity in the system, others emphasize only the spiritual dimension either in the Traditional or the Christian perspectives and values. These three groups of minds function in many relationships. One person may not care whether relationship crashes or not, while another lavishes time giving reasons based on religious preference instead of keeping it moving; the other patiently fights to heal all the wounds of hurts, anger and division. For the people in question, the object of their relationships generally and beliefs in the life-hereafter consists in their deep belief in God, whom they call *Chukwu*, "the spirits (*Mmuo*), and ancestors "*Ndichie*" (Arinze, 1970:8). The people of the Igbo of Nigeria strongly maintain that relationship is of divine origin and each of their belief systems is an indispensable value for keeping it alive. Thus, human relationship requires a belief in something, either in God, a remembered wellness in terms of such values as *ofo na ogu* or justice and truthfulness, oneself or in the other. In a sense, this has everything to do with religion, which describes our connection to God as the one thing that exists.

3. Belief in God *[Chukwu]*,

The Igbo people of Nigeria principally practice monotheism. Even before Christianity came to this part of the globe, Igbo people of Nigeria worshipped the Supreme Being, *Chukwu* as Isichie Elizabeth earlier observed of the German missionary (1841) in Igbo land. The name "*Chukwu* in Parrinder, stands for God Almighty" (1969:26-36), which is etymologically derived from two Igbo words: '*Chi*' and '*Ukwu*'. *Chi* with the capital letter "C" stands for God – Who, not only gives life to the individual but also assures his marked relationship and identity to the community. When *Chi* goes with the small letter "c" it points to the destiny of men and women (Basden, 1966:147). The word *Ukwu* means "great", God Almighty, hence we speak of *Chukwu,* the Supreme God of creation and salvation. These are solid relationships of spiritual values, which both the Christians and the Traditionalists agree to. In the Old Testament of the Christian Bible, for instance, Moses tells the Israelites that: "Your God is the God of gods, the Lord of lords" (Dt.10: 17). The above statement seems to apply and speak of smaller gods that minister under the umbrella of the Great God of Christianity and the Igbo of Nigeria. In both Traditions, there is only one Supreme God.

In human relationship, there is no capital P or partner as we saw earlier on. Relationship is not based on age differentiations, as regards who is senior, junior, richer, poorer or more educated, but on who is ready to understand, care more, make more sacrifices, endure more to maintain the relationship.

As it were, when *Chukwu* or God is considered strictly as the Creator, the people call him *Chineke*, the God who creates, *Onye-Okike* – He, who alone creates (Ikenga-Metuh, 1981:24), but as the controller of the Universe, he is called *Osebuluwa,* the sustainer of the world, for without him, the world would not exist. Within the context of prayer he is addressed as *Obasi-din'elu* (the sky God). For the Christians, *Chukwu* is the only name of God they know today which implies life in itself. It is hard to imagine what a Christian, an individual or a Traditionalist can claim in religion today that is more important than building healthy relationship with oneself and others as implicated in their God-related names.

Igbo versus Christian names and implication for life - Theophoric

The peoples' Theophoric or God-related names mean much to them and explain how deeply; religiously and faithfully they are committed to their identity with the Supernatural. The Igbo of Nigeria believe and act their names in their lives. Such names do influence their relationships also. For instance, despite the apparent disagreements that exist between the Christians and the Traditionalists, almost everybody has "theophoric", a God-related and oriented name. These are names that illustrate the reality and the benevolence of God in practical terms. Such names include: *Nwa-chukwu* (the child of God), *Odinaka-Chi* (one's destiny/being is at God's hands), *Chukwu–di* (God is) *Chi-Nonso,* (God is present, especially when one is in need), *Chi-nwendu* (Only God owns life), *Chi-bu-ndu* (God is life), *Chi-amaka*

(God is good), *Olu-chi* (God's handiwork), *Chi-bu-ike* or *Ike-chi* (God is power or God's power), *Chi-nedu* (God leads), *Ekechi* (Destiny or the life derived from God) et cetera. As Ilogu would have it, "*Ekechi* refers to God-given lot to man" (1975:41). For more details, consult Nwachukwu, 2002:134.

As hitherto said, violations arose when the missionaries came. First of all, they disregarded these Theophoric names and started baptizing the people with foreign names that meant nothing to them. Unfortunately for the missionaries, these names had, not only established the basis of the peoples' lives for decades but also given meanings to their existence. They equally introduced the concept of "God" without any reference to "*Chukwu*", which the people already knew as their God. The missionaries thus missed many opportunities they would have capitalized upon to carry out their message. For instance, the people were forced to believe in the names of saints that had no significance in their lives, business with them or link with their destinies and ancestors. By such missionary activities, confusions were created in the peoples' belief systems.

4. Belief in other Arch-Deities

Majority of the people are basically influenced by polytheistic tendencies. The idea arises from the reverence the people have for the Big God. The Mighty God of the Igbo of Nigeria has Delegates or Lieutenants who take control of other human needs. This belief or practice is so prevalent in the peoples' religious consciousness that today most Christians show equal reverence to other gods or the ancestors as they would, to the Big God.

In other words, there are a host of other gods working in collaboration with *Chukwu,* the Supreme God in maintaining order in the relationship of the people. These gods include *Ala* [the Earth godess, spirit or mother], *Ogu* [the god of justice], *Ofo* [the god of righteousness], *Ahianj-oku-ukwu* [the god of Agriculture], *Amadioha* [the god of Thunder, Lighting, and vengeance against evil doers], *Ajala* [the first Son of *Ala*], *Umumiri* [the god of the river], *Igwe* [the sky god], *Emeregini* [the first son of *Ogu*] et cetera (Nwachukwu, J. U. 2/4/89).

Among the pantheon of divinities that reign in Ezinihitte are also *Ogwugwu, Ekiri, Agwu,* [the god of might, courage and valor]. With this litany of gods, it becomes evident that the Igbo people of Nigeria, particularly Ezinihitte, have strong belief, not only, in the Supreme and Almighty God but also in His agents. As a matter of fact, if the word "Pagan", according to Oxford Advanced Learner's Dictionary of Current English, means any person who does not believe in any of the chief religions of the world, it then means there were no pagans in Ezinihitte, or Igbo of Nigeria, even in pre-colonial years.

Again, with the involvement of the people of Ezinihitte (Igbo) of Nigeria with the colonial masters and other regions in Nigeria who traded on slaves, they came in contact with gods other than theirs. According to Edward Nwachukwu in my interview with him:

> *Among those gods, are Amadioha-Ozuzu in Etche, Ojukwu in the Rivers State, Igwe-kala in Umunoha of Mbaitolu, Onyi Ora in Nri near Oba, Agbala at Awka all in Anambra State, Imo–miri Ochi and the long Juju of Aro-chukwu known as chukwu Abiayamah in Abia State. Some call it Chukwu Abiama. This very Juju, Voodoo or Agbara of Aro-Chukwu was regarded as the most dreadful and powerful in the then Eastern Region, (4/8/ 2000).*

Besides these gods, each village or town in Ezinihitte has a god dedicated to her own market day. The most powerful of all these gods in Ezinihitte is *Ala-Ogbaga* at Chokonze in Ezinihitte Mbaise of Igbo land of Nigeria. Infiltration of these gods in Ezinihitte compounded the conflicts the people have today regarding the proper religious values they need in their relationships as community of believers in the great God, *Chukwu.*

It is interesting to note that despite the fact that Ezinihitte people of Igbo land, East of the Niger has produced the largest number of Rev. Fathers, Sisters and Brothers, including Bishops, Vicar Generals, Monsignors et cetera, most Christians still revere and consult *Ala-Ogbaga* for various needs and reasons. Ala-Ogbaga kills instantly if one is found guilty. So nobody can afford to lie before this particular deity. This is the highest level of disorder in the peoples' belief systems. Where then lies the success of Christianity in this part of the globe? As it stands, these new belief systems and syncretistic practices are the major sources of socio-religious conflicts among the people today. In a situation where one pays allegiance to many forces, the formation of conscience and its application to moral principles become unnecessarily entangled. At this point, one can imagine the nature of relationships society or an individual is expected to build when it seems there is no agreed system of doing things.

5. Belief in Spirits

Parrinder rightly stated: "The belief in spirits is one of the basic qualities of West African religion" (1969:26-36). Among the lgbo in general and Ezinihitte in particular, spirits are called *Ndi-Mmuo* – the invisible beings that are not seen or perceived. They are primarily in the invisible world called *Ala-Mmuo* - land of the spirits. This is in sharp contrast to the 'home of the living'- *Ala-Madu*. In his own observation, using the criterion of habitation, Ejizu presents the universe into two hemispheres: "The world of man and the world of spirit–beings" (2000:49). The most significant feature of this perception and ordering of reality in terms of space is that according to Uchendu, there is constant interaction between the world of man and the world of the dead; the visible and invisible forces (1965:11-12). This interaction in my own assessment is very much perceivable. In lkenga-Metuh's view, there are two kinds of spirits, the non-human spirits and the human spirits (1981:60-82). The non-human spirits include "*Chukwu* (God), *Ndi-Mmuo* (the spirits created by God) the spirit forces (ibid 1981:60-82). The belief systems of the three groups of people in our spirituality typology are well reflected here.

Other non-human classes of spirits include the spirits of *Ndi-ichie,* (Ancestors), the invisible powers and principalities that are supernatural in nature but manifest in human situations. So many people in Ezinihitte believe that witches, sorcerers, diviners, water spirits, *Ndi-otu* (secret societies), medicine men, et cetera, do possess supernatural powers. Beliefs in these spirits are essentially enshrined in the psychology of the people and they deeply influence their relationships.

With the amplification of the Good News of the Kingdom in Igbo land, the significance of the spirits took a different appellation; the Holy Spirits and the Guarding Angels emerged, relegating the peoples' concepts of spirits to the background. The people had never doubted the nature, effects and powerful roles of the spirits in their entire lives. But when the Christian message surfaced, no mention of the individual and the Holy Spirits was made in reference to the peoples' own spirits that protected them. Again, the peoples' beliefs in the spirits got entangled with the introduction of the new ones by the missionaries to the extent that many of the people today have lost the sense of such formidable values in their lives. However, as regards believing in the spirits, the people still and strongly believe in the spirits of their ancestors and beloved dead ones.

Moreover, many of the Christians publicly oppose the Traditional understanding of spirits, like spirits of the ancestors, the dead, telepathy [as always experienced and evidenced when a partner sneezes], spirits of productivity et cetera. Pretentiously, those Christians secretly have recourse to the same beliefs in spirits especially at times of sickness and great needs. This is a major problem, a violation and equally a threat to lively relationships among the people.

6. Belief in Self-God *[Chi]*

In Ezinihitte of Igbo land of Nigeria, every individual is believed to possess a spirit, a transcendental 'self-god' or guardian angel known as *Chi* who guides and leads him or her through the upheavals of life. The Catholic Church teaches the same faith. Idowu calls this the "inner man", the "essential person" and this is usually conceived as something, which man obtains from deity himself and ultimately, the account of how man uses his talent must be rendered before deity (Idowu, 1976:60). We can now understand the need for spiritual connections in one's life. According to Azorji: "Because God created human beings, each has its own *Chi* [divineness]" (1976:172). For lkenga-Metuh, *Chi* is characterized as the immanent presence of God in man or man's guardian angel in life (1981:68-69). All these spirits remind us of the "remembered wellness" of Benson and that quality in every person that endures in the face of hardship, difficulties, sickness and losses in relationships. This is one's survival personality.

According to Iwe: "Transcendence and immanence – transcendentally *Chi* is the divinely endowed spirit of God which functions as a guardian spirit, Personal to each human being" (2000:21). Simply put, "*Chi* is man's spiritual self, the guardian spirit of each individual person through life (Ejizu, 2000:57). "*Chi*" simply means 'spirit'. This value is not limited to any culture and can also be likened to human conscience as studied and presented in this book. The individual spiritual-self plays vital roles in influencing his or her behaviors and relationships. To lack this spirit makes a human being more of a brute animal. For instance, we can now imagine why, in a group of ten students, while nine of them simultaneously react the same way to a particular event or stimulus, only one reacts differently. At times, the matter may not be strictly psychological or neurotic, but something beyond somebody's psychosomatic adjustments. Spiritual psychology matters in situations like this, because an emptiness of the spirit is the fullness of matter.

The understanding among Ezinihitte people regarding *Chi* underlines their belief in the superiority of the Supreme *Chi,* God, over the whole universe. In support of this view, Arinze remarks: "No Ibo man will put God on a level with any *alusi* [evil spirit] be that spirit ever so powerful" (1970:10). Though, *alusi* or evil spirit in Arinze's view is generally synonymous with spirits, but in Ezinihitte, they refer only to non-existent gods or man-made gods.

In effect, we are compelled to make some distinctions between good spirit [*Chi-Oma*] and bad spirits [*Chi-Ojoo*]. Among the people of Ezinihitte a person's morality and behavior are equally based and interpreted in the context of bad or good spirits. Most of the people of Ezinihitte believe that one's *Chi* or spirit could be benevolent, [*chi-oma*] or malevolent (*Chi Ojoo*). There is in Ezinihitte, as in other parts of Igbo land, the belief that nothing good or bad can come anybody's way without the consent of his or her *Chi*. This explains why the nomenclature of Ezinihitte is replete with other personal Theophoric names like *Chi-ma* [God knows, that is, his or her self-god, knows], *Chi-kwe* [if his god permits), *Chi-jioke* [one's fortunes are at the hands of one's God], *Chiawuotu* (people's gods differ), *Chi-naaka* [only God decides], *Chi-nasa* [only God answers] et cetera.

One's *Chi* is held responsible and seen as being instrumental to one's fortune or misfortune. That is the reason behind the self-exclamation "Oh my God!" especially when something abruptly happens to a person. It has everything to do with one's destiny or personal spirit. Society constantly lives in the mystery of mysterious creation without knowing it. It dawns on her only when the unexpected takes place. In Ezinihitte, it is common to hear people say or suggest '*Uwa gi na Chi gi bu otu*'. That is, 'your life and your destiny [god] are one and the same thing'. The people equally have an adage which says that" *Ofu nne na-amu ma ofu chi adigi eke*' Literally speaking, this means that 'children are born of one mother but they are not created by one *Chi* or god'. The implication is that, even, among the children of one mother, each of them has his or her distinctive *Chi* or spirit and characteristics (traits) different from others. These distinctive spirits that characterize each individual equally have much influence in his or her relationships. This spirit value should assist individuals from any culture to appreciate the spirit manifestations of their partners and lead to global awareness of personal differences and destinies in human relationships.

The distinctions are essential as they guide our relationships in understanding why people behave differently in society at large and the Igbo land of Nigeria in particular. Among the Igbo of Nigeria, a person with a 'malevolent spirit' or "*Onye chi-ojoo*" is always despised and isolated. The person is easily spotted in the midst of others through the history of his or her numerous misfortunes, hardships, failures, mistakes, forgetfulness, illness and the inability to fit in well in any group. The issue of benevolent and malevolent spirits in the western world is scientifically bracketed as psychotic cases or characteristics. For instance, among Igbo people, if a person with such spirits happens to be among groups of people who encountered motor accidents like in the case of Jonah or fell victims to bandits while on a journey or expedition, he or she is singled out and blamed for such misfortunes or mishap. Interestingly, victims of malevolent spirits often acknowledge and admit their situations as such. Generally, these tendencies in which an honest person is blamed for occurrences that are beyond his or her control, urgently call for attention in spiritual psychology and individual relationships. Within the framework of the morality of the people, the one looked at, as having malevolent spirit or "*Onye chi-Ojoo*" may not have the grounds to prove otherwise thereby getting gripped by the sense of guilt. This tendency of prejudgment or misjudgment has to be avoided in relationships.

Painfully observed, "how can people with malevolent spirits be expected to make valid judgment of conscience and respond to the morality of the land as to establish solid relationships?" For instance, why must a person with malevolent spirit or *"Onye Chi-Ojoo"* who is ambitious to make progress in life, at times, be subjected to offer sacrifices to propitiate the malignant god responsible for his or her ordeal? Again, before he or she makes the sacrifices as such, a diviner of an oracle, *Dibia Anya Nzu* [a native doctor with *Odo* or clay on his eyes) has to be consulted to know who is responsible, the victim or his or her grand or great grand parents. It is the same victim that carries the burdens of the sacrifice and items to be involved. In Ezinihitte, people believe that one's *Chi* is the same as one's 'destiny' or *"Akaraka"*. These are the main reasons why most families in Ezinihitte are ritually graded in certain perspectives. For instance, in one of my commentaries concerning marriage, I noted certain questions that can help us understand the socio-religious differences among the people of Ezinihitte.

These equally belong to the images of healthy relationships as regards the initial Traditional nuptial enquiries before any marriage is contracted. Sadly, these enquiries are mainly conducted on the part of the female partners to determine their fitness, suitability and socio-religious morality. Once a man is wealthy and handsome, little or no enquiries are made. These are problems that face spiritual psychology. People have got to trust in themselves irrespective of the stigma society places on them. While I do support nuptial enquiries in general, why must the emphasis be centered on women alone and excludes the men? Thus, before any Ezinihitte man in Igbo land of Nigeria offers his hands in marital relationships, the following enquiries must be made and completed regarding the family history of the would-be wife:

> *Are they "Osu or Outcasts? Are they "Njoku" or thieves? Do they die at child deliveries? Are they mental? Are they "Ume" or die young? Do they have "aka oku" or industrious? Are they associated with "Mmuo Miri or water spirit etc? These are*

> *the questions that determine the continuity of a Traditional marriage, (1994:9).*

In a nutshell, I have just enumerated in my former book the various areas in which individuals with malevolent spirit or *chi-ojoo* or *akara-chi ha* [their destinies] can be categorized. The diversity in destinies or *Chi* tends to create conflicts in behaviors, traumas, disorders, and lack of harmony and trust, which also affects human relationships. These diversities or qualities equally determine one's status in Ezinihitte because the people strongly believe that *"akaraka di iche iche"* [the mark on each person's palm is different from the one on another person's palm]. To this, Mozia says, *"Akalaka* refers to the individual destiny which each person's guardian spirit helps him or her to attain" (1987:189). In Ezinihitte of Igbo land, there is always a capital P in relationship. An Ezinihitte 'person' concretely lives out his or her belief in every relationship as the senior or junior.

Eventually, the incarnation of the Gospel message among the Igbo people of Nigeria presents another problem. The central message of the missionaries, we believe, is a call to holiness, sound morality, love, peace and unity in relationships. Unfortunately, they failed in their approach to such sensitive spiritual values. The nuptial enquiries the people carry out, as a strong means of ensuring healthy relationships as I remarked in that my earlier book was turned down. They simply introduced and presented the Christian marriage as a Sacramental union, between Christian adherents - man and woman regardless of emphasis on procreation. They did not explore the Traditional values of marriage as a participation in the creative nature of their God - procreation, meaning and role of the individual personal *"chi"* or self-God and the basic marriage enquiries et cetera, as the springboard of their evangelization. The reality of God or gods for the people has never been foreign to them. The evangelizers would have recorded more success if they had tapped into what the people already had or knew and moved from there - the known to the unknown. That would have assisted the people understand and appreciate the unique realization of one's personal God in the Christian marriage. The belief in self-God is practically a powerful, operational and functional value that would have helped the people perceive themselves as reflections of

Gods' presence in their marriages. Alas! The evangelizers ignored that important aspect of their missionary target.

Furthermore, the sharp and dangerous demarcations the people have between their destinies in the context of benevolent and malevolent spirits directly oppose and contradict the Christian message and healthy relationships. Yet, the missionaries completely left it untouched. That was a mismanagement of the Gospel message. In this light, one wonders whether the Christian message brought positive changes in the lives of the people or a confirmation of received theologies that failed to address peoples' spiritual problems at the moment. All the same, most of the Igbo Christians who do not publicly believe in Self-God or accept its existence personally and proudly take and give these self-God-related names to their children up till today. Then, the question remains: Who is fooling whom? This is also a problem the book has set out to address.

7. Belief in ancestors *[Ndichie]*

We deem it necessary to re-emphasize the importance of the ancestors here due to its peculiarity in the lives of the people. The concept of *Ndichie* [ancestors] is another significant feature in the "old'" religion of Ezinihitte people that does not die. We call it "old" because the ancestors define the religion of the people as such. The Ancestors are the role models and torchbearers of the Igbo of Nigeria, particularly Ezinihitte people. This belief generally grew out of the belief and understanding that a good person in Igbo land never dies. This is, of course, in line with the Christian teaching (Jn.11: 25-26). Death is only a passage to the other world. It is not the end of the story for Christ's followers. Azorji calls this "Ila-ulo – a going home" (1976:177). The ancestors are those who have safely reached their home with their Creator like the Saints in the Catholic Church. In this way, one's earthly existence and style of life determine whether one joins them or not. Emphatically, it is the belief of an average Ezinihitte man or woman that the ancestors profoundly do influence the lot or fate of the living relations. Ezinihitte people of the Igbo of Nigeria believe that the ancestors guide and protect them, their offsprings on earth and intervene on their behalf with the gods in the spirit world.

In support of the above fact, Ejizu in Azorji says that the ancestors represent another section of the same community [Platonic-oriented-mine] in the spirit world and the concern of the living is equally their own concern (1976:177). The ancestors are properly called *Ndichie*, [The ancients] or the first people, *Ndi-Mbu*, [the first generation] of founding fathers. The people, including me emulate and consult them in prayers.

There is need to note also that not all dead fathers are ancestors. In the Christian context, for instance, only "the souls of the just" and not the souls of the dead "are in the hands of God' (Wis. 3: 1-1). In Azorji's view: "Ancestors are those who died at a good old age and received grand funeral celebrations (rite of passage), those who were rightly buried by their community, *Umunna*" (1976:177). Ezinihitte people believe that when a person dies, his spirit simply hovers or wanders between the physical world and the spiritual world till it is received or welcomed into the company of the ancestors. This is why Osuji sees the rite of passage as a conditio sine qua non for entry (1977:166-173). In this stance, Basden expressed his amazements as regards why:

> *The Ibo will endure everything demanded of him in this life, will put up with hardships, the misbehavior of his children, indeed everything, in order to ensure that his burial will be properly performed. His whole future welfare depends upon this; hence it takes at all times almost prominent place in a man's calculation (1975:117).*

To put up with temptations, trials and difficulties in relationships in view of greater rewards, joys, peace, even here on earth, particularly in eternity is the highest level and practical demonstration of faith and life commitment. The sentiments Baseden has raised here are very striking for a materialistic world like ours. In other words, this rite of passage, typical of many religions of the world has many implications for healthy relationships. For instance, many people especially the Ezinihitte of Igbo land aspire and advocate for good moral behaviors in order to be saved or join their ancestors. We equally need these qualities to maintain healthy relationships here on earth because a person who had no peace on earth cannot be expected to enjoy it elsewhere.

Am I really a reincarnation of my grand father? – Yes!

The ancestors are believed to reincarnate into the families as new children. In Igbo land generally, every person is a representation of one dead member of the family that lived a good life. For instance, I am personally known and addressed by my family [very devout and fervent Catholic] as my own grand father. Even though, I do not, in physical qualifications believe in reincarnation, I strongly agree with the people that the memories of a person who led good life on earth live forever. Their physical bodies may not be there, but their spirits and good works influence the present. Hence, my mother fondly called me *"Nna Di M"* meaning 'the father of my husband'. As for many Ezinihitte people, there is no doubt where one goes after death due mainly to the type of relationship and life one has been maintaining on earth. For instance, of what significance is a human person who lacks order, peace, discipline and sound moral life? In effect, for two parties who have varying belief systems to relate peacefully, one or two of them have to shift positions in order to accommodate the good and bad effects of the change (Le Chatellier's principles). One partner has to be the uninitiated, the nucleus of peace terms in that relationship. This is where and when spiritual maturity and God-filled spiritual orientation play a vital role in our relationships.

Nonetheless, Ezinihitte people believe that ancestors protect life and property and ensure the continuity of *Umunna* (community) solidarity here on earth. The people equally give to their children such reincarnated names as *Nnenna* (the mother of one's father], *Nnanna* (the father of one's father), *Nna-nneya* (his mother's father), *Ogonnaya* (one's father's in-law) et cetera. These names portray their unshakeable beliefs in reincarnation. Their external ritual worship is also an additional confirmation of how much they value their relationships and eternity with God or ancestors.

The issue of *"Nladu"* that is, getting to the abode of the ancestors or salvation is paramount in the socio-religious lives of the people of Ezinihitte as a community. Every individual in Ezinihitte as such, needs the assistance of the community to attain salvation with the ancestors or God by respecting each other. This assistance can only be possible through mutual cooperation and observance of the religious and "moral laws" of the land [*Omenala*], which were handed down by God to the community through the ancestors. It is with such an understanding that Osuji makes the following observations:

> *The concept of salvation for the Igbo includes union with one's "Umunna" Community, living upright life, dying in a very good age, and having children through whom the lineage, the torch of life for one's group is not extinguished, being accorded full burial rites after death... salvation for the Igbo is dynamic, elastic as life itself. This is well manifested in one's relationship first with Chineke, then the ancestors and love within the "Umunna" Community (1977:68).*

The understanding of "*Nladu*" or salvation among the Ezinihitte people affirms that the purpose of relationships and life for them is both communitarian and eschatological. Their entire lives, culture, religion, whatever defines them as a people are geared towards "*Nladu*" or salvation. This is primarily why the Traditionalists claim to know God more than their Christian counterparts.

The problems that sprang with the Christian message as regards the ancestors anchored on the fact that the missionaries were myopic in utilizing the wonderful spiritual values of the people for their work of evangelization. For instance, the concept of ancestors is well known to Christianity, yet the peoples' belief in them was not given any attention. In the Old Testament for instance, Abraham, Isaac and Jacob are ancestors to the Christian and Jewish religions. Why was Jesus not presented as a Proto (Brother) Ancestor? That could have easily assisted the people digest the Christian message with firm convictions. Even the concept of the peoples' *Umunna* –community (ecclesia) and solidarity' would have been a strong strategy to drive home the idea of unity and connectedness in human relationships. But the missionaries failed in this aspect too. The idea of salvation (*Nladu)* that prominently featured in the religion of the people was not explored either. For them, there is no salvation elsewhere outside the Christian message, which is misleading. Principally, salvation begins from self.

Shockingly, the peoples' widespread belief in reincarnation, which was directly incompatible with the Christian message, was not addressed. Many writers on Igbo Traditional religion and psychology have pointed out some inconsistencies and contradictions in the belief in reincarnation or *Ilo-Uwa*. The Igbo people's beliefs in reincarnation, though wrongly and traditionally construed, would have helped them appreciate the more, the reality of Christ's resurrection episode. Yet, such a sensitive issue meant nothing to the missionaries. It is going to take Christianity many decades to convince the people otherwise and wipe off that belief from their minds. As it stands, the people have been brought to a cross road of faith dilemma. Many Christian fanatics neither believe in the ancestors and their influences on human affairs nor keep to the authentic teachings of the Christian religion. These attitudes have generated a lot of conflicts and discords among the people. It becomes misleading when most of these Christians who disagree with Traditional beliefs in reincarnation still retain and answer the names of the reincarnated members of their families. Even up till date, most of the middle names the Igbo Christians of Nigeria give to their children are these reincarnation-related ones. They equally invoke or employ these native names in prayers. The people significantly value their Igbo or native names that identify them as such, more than the Christian and foreign ones as noted earlier. These issues compound the possibility of building healthy relationships, especially in the areas of valid judgments of conscience and conformity to the moral standards. Coming into relationships with preconceived ideas and expectations is not helpful. Society needs to learn and grow together as life unfolds itself.

8. Ritual Worship

Ritual worship, simply understood in Igbo of Nigeria especially in Ezinihitte, refers to the way the people establish a relationship with the invisible world. To be precise, ritual worship or cultic action is the faith of the people celebrated and expressed in symbols or the way they realistically are before their ancestors or God. These are focal points of spiritual psychology. Any group activity performed in the name of God falls within ritual worship (Mulago, 1981:171-179). To offer sacrifices to *Chukwu* is an entry into his presence, a way to establish relationship with him. They do this in variety of ways just as a person may invite his or her partner with a simple smile:

i. Through Sacrifices

In Ezinihitte, the people offer sacrifices to *Chukwu* or their God as a way of self-fulfillment and salvation through his agents, intermediaries or mediators who are human beings invested with the power to communicate with the spirits or the Great God, *Chi Ukwu*. Initially when Christianity came to Ezinihitte, adherents to the new religion regarded and revered the early missionaries as equal to their Traditional mediators and agents of the spirits or God. Unfortunately things changed on daily basis and it became evident that Christians created the chaos and disorders in the community. For instance, even up to today, it is safer to trust or keep community money with non-Church goers than most Christians. This is how religious conflicts crept up. As Gordon in Pastoral Psychology, expressed it:

> *It is a well-established fact in social science that on the average, churchgoers (especially ministers of the Churches-mine) in our country harbor more racial, ethnic, and religious prejudices than non-churchgoers (1967:20).*

In this light, Gordon supported my stand on one of my books when I observed: "There is nothing the Church does today that is alien to the devil" (1999:24). These are problems that face this survey. The head of every clan in Ezinihitte offers compulsory sacrifices on *Orie-ukwu* market day, the Traditional Sabbath day of the people. It falls once in a week of eight days. Each family repeats the sacrifice in grandier styles during the all-important ceremonies of *iro-ofo* - celebrating and revitalizing the spirit of truthfulness, *Ime ogu* - justice and *Iri ji* - New Yam festivals. Ezinihitte is particularly known for *Igo Oji* (Kola nuts) and *Iri Ji* (Yams). Though, the celebration of *iro-ofo* and *Ime ogu* in many parts of Igbo land seems to have died, the moral implications and principles are still adhered to. The implication of the celebration of *Igo Oji* – presenting kola nuts to welcome visitors and *Iri Ji* – feeding oneself, others and strangers is at the heart of human relationships.

Ancestors are always remembered during the presentation of kola nuts in gatherings of friends, in-laws, kinsmen and visitors. The elderly person who "prays over the kola nuts" *Igo Oji* invites the ancestors to share the kola nuts with the living. At every meal the elderly person equally repeats the invitation. I wonder how many people say the grace before meals these days.

Hitherto, *Igo Oji,* presentation of kola nuts in Ezinihitte has taken a wider dimension whereby different towns, communities, Government Officials are invited to participate in their cultural heritage and global relationships that unite the living and the dead. A Bishop may say the opening prayer. Yet, this is a celebration that originated from the Traditional belief and religion and not from Christianity. A special feast day in honor of the ancestors, the *Iro-ofo,* the revitalization of the spirit of truthfulness launches and heralds the planting season. It also serves to thank God for the previous harvest. In pre-colonial and even colonial period, there used to be mass return of family members who were expected to partake of the sumptuous feasting and reconciliation of 'aggrieved' dead members of the community and family before embarking on the impending farming activities. As part of the ritual, even up till today, many families do not attempt to eat the new yam till the official ceremony is performed or *Orie-ukwu* market day. Experiences should guide and teach us on daily basis. For instance, if partners use milk on a regular basis, it is wrong for the partner who discovers that the milk is almost done to use it without, first of all, trying to buy more.

The people in a way practiced 'polytheism', due to the reasons noted already. They show reverence to other small gods believed to be agents and instruments of peace of the Supreme God, *Chukwu.* Ukpong, referring to the religious worships and sacrifices in general, stated:

> *Cultic actions are not categorized in vertical terms of the higher and lower but in qualitative terms of the more potent and less potent....sacrifice is conceived as a cultic action that is most potent in establishing communication with the spiritual beings. It is not therefore reserved to God alone but can be offered to all and any spirit-being when contact with such beings is required (1983:200).*

From what Ukpong just noted, we can deduce the magnitude of disorientations that emerged from the missionary activities in Igbo land of Nigeria. Rightly noted, it is obvious that the religious life of the people of Ezininhitte is immensely characterized by their ritual worships. Traditionally, due to the lived values and experiences of the people and the seeming hypocritical attitudes of most Christians today, the Christian religion will always remain foreign and shallow in Igbo land. This sounds funny and misleading. But it is true. For instance, when a person imposes his or her values and beliefs on his or her partner, building healthy relationship is always impossible. Why did the missionaries not capitalize on the peoples' numerous ritual worships to introduce the celebration of the Eucharist, prayer sessions, a word of prayer, fellowship and communion worships typical of many Christian sects today? Again, due saliently to the polytheistic tendencies of their religion, the people strongly assert that the ancestors bequeathed to them complete priestly craft, that is, those who can foresee future events, well ordered ritual worships, sacred chants and oracle incantations, rules and standards of morality, social behaviors directly derived from the gods. But, branding every Traditional practice and worship as fetish, heathen and so forth by the missionaries created dichotomy and divisions in the peoples' relationships.

Arguably, what is polytheistic about the peoples' religion in believing in Gods' agents when Christianity has prophets and prophetesses, spiritual healers who equally foresee the future and who claim to intervene in spiritual matters and so on today? Even in the Catholic Tradition, the firm belief in the Saints, Angels and the Blessed Trinity [though with different understanding - the equality of the three persons in one God] indirectly alludes to the peoples' stand on *Chukwu* and his agents. The Christian Bible reveals this Trinitarian reality when it says: "Let us make man in our own image" (Gen. 1:26) and "let us go down and confuse their language" (Gen.11: 7). The expression "Let us" implies more than a person. Biblical Scholars may still disagree.

The famous and highly celebrated *Iri-Ji* Mbaise or *Iko-Oji* of the Igbo of Nigeria, which globally involves and attracts practically everybody, Christians and Traditionalists alike, originated from the peoples' culture and not from Christianity. For instance, most Igbo people in the entire western world today celebrate these Traditional festivities. Especially, the ritual of *Iri Ji* seems to have currently become an international practice among all sons and daughters of Igbo land living in all parts of the world, particularly America, London and Europe, as a mark of their solidarity and identity with their ancestral lineage. These were enriching activities and celebrations, which the missionaries would have explored to drum down their message; instead they classified and jumped over them as ungodly.

The Igbo Traditional shrines for sacrifices of the native doctors and traditional priests (*Ndi Ogo Mmuo*) are highly revered and dreaded by everybody including Christians as sacred places. For instance, one day, an intoxicated Christian forgot his new bicycle at the market shrine and went home. When he realized himself later, he went back to the market and happily collected his bicycle right from the shrine. Of course, nobody would ever dare to steal from a shrine. On the following Sunday, he went to his Church in thanksgiving to God for recovering his bicycle. But at the end of that thanksgiving celebration, when he came out to pick his bicycle to go home, lo and behold, the bike was gone, stolen. The story is true and a good example of how a camouflaged Christian message could affect the religious beliefs and consciousness of a people. Moreover, if the missionaries had presented the Christian places of worship in the respectful context as the Traditional shrines, cases of stealing could not have been recorded today in many Churches, let alone ministers embezzling Church funds. Moreover, a place of worship or shrine may not be 'sacred' when the chief priests or ministers do not reflect that sacredness in their lives. Among other rituals and symbols that are typical of the peoples' Traditional religion and culture, which Christians in Igbo land hypocritically neglect, include:

ii.   Symbol of Peace [Odo/Nzu] or clay

Traditionally, *odo* symbolizes peace and tranquility. There are nothing else that relationships need than these values - peace and tranquility. For an Ezinihitte man or woman, this peace, which is sought in every human relationship, is also life and salvation. Our ancestors gave this to them as a sign of love, unity and peace among the *Umunna* or community. *Odo* is made up of clay or *Uroo*. This is a product of *Ala* (land). The people believe that it protects and saves all that God has created. Most of the people prefer making use of pots and cups made of clay, because of its symbolic and therapeutic effects to those made of iron. We can now understand why many people in Ezinihitte of Igbo land use mortar and pestles, made of wood in preparing their food, especially *Fufu* than the modern facilities. Anything that has got to do with *Ala* or land has a serious reference to the ancestors who share in whatever the people do on earth. The significance and relevance of *Ala* (mother earth) in human nature is not limited to the Igbo of Nigeria alone. Globally, many people gladly aspire to be "close to nature", and any down-to-earth relationships last longest. Artificiality is not a true test of healthy relationship. Moreover, the use of symbols is not totally foreign in the life experiences of the western world. Among western cultures, for instance, white color denotes peace while red symbolizes danger. Similarly, in the context of the Igbo of Ezinihitte, *Odo,* which is yellowish, (*Nzu,* whitish) in color or earthborn peace, signifies and portrays peaceful ancestral and divine relationship with humanity. The *Dibia* [native doctors] particularly rob it across their eyes to enable them see into the spirit world of the ancestors. Also, when partners implant peace in their hearts, they will look beyond their common mistakes and experience the hidden blessings of love and posterity.

However, with the arrival of the missionaries and their attitudes to *odo,* conflicts were inevitable. They came and preached peace, tranquility and transformation of individual hearts. But, they failed to take note of the symbol of that peace, tranquility and its significance in the lives of the people without any replacement. Consequently, their evangelization bore no much fruit. Rather, it sounded shallow and meaningless to the point that many of the people have remained disgusted with, and suspicious of the Gospel message till now. They lost the opportunity they would have used to present the Eucharist and the Bible as the greatest symbols of peace, which Christians and society employ in their relationships. If they had properly done their fieldwork, it would have assisted the people to appreciate the Eucharist and the Bible as symbolic realities that could help them build strong and healthy relationships with God and society. Instead, the missionaries discarded *odo* as dirty, infectious, useless, pagan and barbaric. The greatest disorder and irony of the Christian message is that right now many of the Christians who read the Bible and receive the Eucharist equally value and keep *odo* in their homes. They normally present the *odo* to their visitors as gestures of peace and heart-felt welcome. More importantly, majority of the Igbo people of Nigeria apply this *odo* as powder on the bodies of their newborn babies because of its symbolic, medicinal and welcoming effects on the new life.

Similarly, the introduction of modern utensils into Igbo land through the missionaries or western civilization without paying any attention to the significance of the Traditional ones, indirectly violated the peoples' fundamental values, objects of peace and tranquility. All the same, some of the Igbo people of Nigeria, due to exposure to western civilizations and technologies, use and prefer modern utensils to the Traditional ones, thereby, consciously or unconsciously neglecting the moral and therapeutic values that protect their lives. Ironically, some of those who prefer modern utensils to the locally made ones still keep and make use of them in their homes, at times, in form of "decorations".

iii. Incantation

This was one of the media the people used in praying and invoking on their God or ancestors. This is not just a form of prayer. It goes with deep spiritual mark, force and absolute trust in God. In incantation, people and the spirits meet. The situation is better understood in relation to the present *Juju* or *Voodoo* priests, fortunetellers, diviners, or magicians. Incantation is a communal practice and major form of supplications that draw the human and the spirits together. Up to the present Igbo people of Nigeria, incantation has potently remained a means of prayer for individuals and the community. The attributes of god are recounted and enumerated during incantations, which easily and spiritually link up the supplicants to their God and ancestors. In a way, this prayer of deep trust joins the minds and hearts in solid relationships.

Abuses and confusions entered into this Traditional manner of prayer and invoking the spirits of ancestors especially at moments of need, sickness and misfortune with the presence of the missionaries. Instead of encouraging this positive way of approaching God, they regarded it as a lunatic display of ecstasy and introduced countless forms of prayers among the people without proper Catechesis. As long as the people did not understand prayer in the Traditional context, which meant power and life, many have entirely lost the sense of prayer. On the contrary, today, so many people, especially some Christian fanatics use prayers to dupe others. Deceptively, some of the Christians, especially the Pentecostals and born-again Christians who regard this Traditional medium of prayer as devilish, equally adopt it, not only as a pattern of prayer but also associate it with the gifts of the Holy Spirit and glossolalia - speaking in tongues. "Praise the Lord! Alleluia!" is a form of incantation and for some; it has become a way of hypnotizing people for selfish ends.

A born again is of two types: One to truth, another, deception

Right there, in Igbo land and so many other places on the planet, the phrase "born again" sounds strange and frightening. It is easier and very simple to say: "I am born again" in words than showing and proving what that means in practice. Spiritual psychology does not care about who is born again as who is truthful, just, honest, realistic and accommodating in his or her relationships with others. Among the Igbo people, that phrase mostly seems to be associated with dupes and violators of basic moral principles instead of a state of permanent righteousness, struggle towards perfection in virtue, et cetera. A born-again, assuming it is feasibly a call to change; who still tells lies and steals, has never wished to live in the first place. Why should a person who has received Jesus bracket his or her face with wrinkles of anger and animosity? Does one become holy by carrying long faces that seem contorted, marked and contoured by disappointments? For instance, what do we say of an Igbo Traditionalist who does not go to any Church but consistently remains truthful, just and keeps to sound moral living? Can we say that such a person is born again? In this light, spiritual psychology would want to know "where a 'born again' was before, is now, and wishes to be or from what state of life, he or she was born again?" Is this a physical or spiritual, instrumental or intrinsic reality, a change from one religious denomination to another, disassociation from friends or a transformation of one's unhealthy inner attitudes? The relationship one keeps says it all and not the Church one belongs. For instance, any Christian Church without the Bible or sound morality is just a social club and the Bible without a Church that effectively applies its principles in the lives of members, is an archeology. No wonder, most people in Igbo land, especially the youths generally see prayers, let alone incantation as burdensome. Whether we accept it or not, in any level of human relationship, elements of the cross, sacrifice and a Gethsemane is certainly inescapable. Christianity without the cross is false.

iv. Mourning [Igba Mkpe]

Mkpe is a ritual in Igbo land of Nigeria particularly in Ezinihitte whereby the bereaved families demonstrate solidarity and oneness with their dead. In a ritual such as this, relationship is celebrated and adorned. The living identify with the dead either by *Iku Isi* (shaving), disfiguring their hairs or putting on a piece of black cloth on their dresses. The ritual has a religious undertone and physically lasts for the period of one year. This is not purely done for sympathetic reasons because the people strongly believe in the reality of death and each person prepares for it by leading good lives. Thus, the people are obliged to mourn "their dead" relations as a mark of solidarity, appeasing their spirits and protecting themselves from shame and criticisms. Some believe that failure to observe this ritual; the dead person might attack them. As I noted in one of my writings, "out of the peoples' magnanimity, sympathy, love and concern also, the issue of shaving could be done at one's maternal home" (2002:148). The people say: "*Onye kwagha onye nwuruanwu, kwagha onwe ya*" – this means "he or she who mourns the dead equally mourns him or herself". Make others happy and be one.

On the contrary, abuses have crept into this ritual today. The missionaries overlooked this powerful means of human relationships and solidarity. Rather they emphasized the need for proper Christian burial, prayer requests, love and Mass offerings [especially in the Catholic Tradition] for the souls of the dead, thereby silencing the people's Traditional manner of mourning the dead. As a convinced Catholic, Igbo priest, I accept Mass offerings, requests and celebrate for people's good intentions and those who have nobody to pray for them, especially, counting and relying on the efficacy of the Eucharist to accomplish its work in their lives. The problem is that the missionaries failed to present the Eucharist within the context of what the people believed and practiced. The concepts of "prayer and burial" in the Christian context always remain vague in the minds of the people as long as they have not been told what went wrong with their Traditional manner of praying, burying and mourning their dead. Moreover, it sounds funny to note that despite the emphasis laid on Christian burials today, most people, especially titled men and women complete the Traditional rituals for burying their members before Church services. For instance, the body of a titled person must be received and honored at his or her market square by the community before proceeding for other burial arrangements. Again, most of the Christian fanatics who regard the ritual as evil, adopt various ways of identifying with their dead members like putting a piece of cloth on their dresses or staying with the bereaved family members on routine visits, for a couple of days or weeks. These hypocritical behaviors adversely affect the peoples' socio-religious consciousness and relationships.

v. Eating at a Husband's or Wife's Death. *[Iri ihe N'onwu Di or Nwunye]*

The chief mourner when a man dies in Igbo of Nigeria is his wife, and vice versa. The people always perceive the atmosphere of death as sadness and grief and not occasions for merriment or feasting. Among the people, death is a big threat to relationships. In real traditional Igbo set up, no food is cooked within the homes of those who lost their members. As such, when a woman loses her husband, she is not allowed to eat any food served there. Out of this great concern possibly for security reasons or otherwise, the chief mourners are not allowed to partake of such food items. To this effect, a special person is always employed to take care of the widow or widower. This practice has become part and parcel of "the life" of the people generally. Their ways of life, culture, religion, morality, psychology, politics and salvation are one, visibly and invisibly united.

However, since the advent of Christianity and western civilization in Igbo land, this ritual has been greeted with many abuses, animosity and ill feelings. The question is: "Why should the affected partner not eat of the food items?" For instance, the missionaries taught the people a message that made no distinctions between Jews and Greeks. Contradictorily, they turned their backs on such sensitive issues that entertained division and encouraged suspicion, disbelief and mistrust among family members. Where then lies the truth of the Christian message in this context? Besides, it is more confusing that while the chief mourner is not allowed to taste the food prepared in such occasions, whatever he or she has to eat equally comes from the same source mapped out for the burial. On a more serious note, many Christians in Igbo land single themselves out from participating at this ritual of communal solidarity with the dead by frowning against the rituals that forbid a partner from eating at his or her partner's death. For them, it is sinful and devilish not to allow a partner partake of such food items. Yet, when their own partners die, they consciously avoid eating any food that is prepared on such events and served to the public, thereby and indirectly affirming the same Traditional practices of the people in general.

vi. Funeral Oration *[Itu Aka N'Esse]* and Symbolic Music

Funeral rites take various forms among the Igbo of Nigeria. In this publication, we chose to present an aspect called Funeral Oration or *Itu Aka N'Esse.* This is where the first son heroically responds to the musical interrogation regarding the achievements and moral qualities and achievements of his dead father. Traditional music is the expression of the people's culture, morality, *Nladu* (salvation), and religion. Traditionally, it is a display of the beauty of creation, a total exposition of the people's inner selves, dispositions and relationships. It is disciplined, classified and follows a pattern and unites the body and soul, the physical and spirit world of the people. It is eternally the mark of the highest level of communal relationship. The wooden gong [*Ekwe*] or [*Uhie*] is always used with a special person that beats it. It is the sound of that gong, *Uhie* that the first son, [*Opara*] of the dead man responds to. Questions like: "What and what did your father achieve or do?" will be beaten on the wooden gong. Then the first son, [*Opara*], will respond orally, enumerating all that his father did on earth when he was alive. The sound of the gong represents the voice of the ancestors who, sitting on their judgment seat in the spirit world with God, interrogate and call on the first son of the dead man to bear witness to the life of his father. One can call this a form of eternal judgment. That is why Ezinihitte people instruct their first sons always to "grow after your fathers jaws" [*kwatakwa aba nna gi*], meaning that the son grows to morally behave as his father. This practice challenges all parents to leave behind them, some good examples for their children and society to follow. Similarly, when an elderly woman of proven character, dies at a very ripe old age, a type of dance or music called "*Uko*" will be played. The first daughter of the woman will carry the picture of her mother, announcing her achievements as she dances the music around the family circle or market area.

The wooden gong is often called *Ekwe Mmuo* [spirit gong]. Besides, every town in Igbo land particularly in Ezinihitte has the big wooden gong called *Uhie* or *Ikoro* positioned at their market squares. The sounds reach every cage and cave of the town and summon everybody to the common gathering ground called "*Mbara*, the community park". It is always beaten when a serious thing happens in the community or at the end of the ritual of *itu aka' esse* when the first son, *Opara*, cuts off the head of the "he goat" called *Ewu isi n'ama* as indicative of the dead person's life being fulfilled or reaching its fullness. It is a mark of dignity and respect shown to the dead, especially to a man who led sound moral life and has a son. In Igbo land, to celebrate the greatness of a father who lived well and had a male child, the first son on behalf of his father, gives lama or a cow to the community. Often, a man may die without fulfilling this ritual of giving lama or cow to honor his own father because of economic reasons. But the dead man's own son might eventually become rich and gives the lama to the community on behalf of his father. Serious problem arises here. It is a case of giving two lamas or cows to the community instead of one for his father. Customarily, this young son cannot give any lama or cow on behalf of his father unless he gives one, first of all, on behalf of his grand father. For instance, in a succession of first, second and third generations, the present third successor or first son cannot prestigiously perform this ritual for his immediate dead father unless he is ready to give the community three lamas or cows to honor his great grand father, grand father and his own father.

Moreover, a first son who has not given this lama or cow to honor his dead father cannot partake of any meat from other cows or lama given to the community for the same purpose. The rest of his brothers can. It is a thing of shame for a first son who, for economic reasons, cannot perform this ritual for his father. In many cases, his richer siblings can aid him do so. Unmistakably, almost all the Christians appreciate and celebrate this ritual and gladly struggle to honor their dead parents, fathers and mothers by giving lama or cow to the community on their behalf. The old question continues to rear its ugly head: "Where then lies the relevance of Christian burials among the people?" Due to the fact that in Igbo land, fortunately or unfortunately much premium is placed on male children, only the first sons perform the above rituals even if they are the babies of their families.

Besides the above symbolic music, that is, the wooden gong associated with *"Itu Aka N'Esse"*, and other serious events in the land, the people have other forms of Traditional music such as *Uko, Esse, Ekpe, Agborogwu, Abigbo, nkwa Ike.* Each of these forms of music is also symbolic in the sense that they have specific religious messages for the people. Traditionally, any form of music is packed with its own symbols and messages. For instance, *Uko* music is played at the death of an elderly woman who died at a very good old age and every one can dance it. *Esse* music, as already hinted, is of two types: The high one *(Esse-elu)* is played on an elevated height while the lower *(Esse ala)* is played on the level ground. Each is played when an elderly man dies. The *Esse elu* is comparable to the *Nkwa Ike* (tough music) as discussed below. The dancing of both *Esse elu* and *Nkwa Ike* is reserved for special "Traditional healers" or individuals who have been historically identified with tough, heroic or dreadful activities that are not common to everybody. *Agborogwu* music features at festivals, harvesting period, and Traditional marriage ceremonies et cetera, and mainly the adults dance it. *Abigbo* music is Traditional also. It is played at various occasions, Church and Traditional weddings, priestly ordinations, burials; child-naming ceremonies, age grade festivals et cetera and basically everybody can join in the dancing. *Nkwa Ike,* tough music is specifically played at the death of a native doctor or an elderly man who was known for one heroic act or another during his lifetime. Traditional music is different from

Pop, High life or other forms of music. Most of them indicate the inevitable bonds and identity the living share with the dead.

Traditionally, one person dances *Nkwa Ike*; the sole entertainer who symbolically demonstrates some sordid acts of the deceased person. If any other dancers accompany the sole entertainer such dancers must also have credible acts of valor in their own lives. It is believed that a person who has not excelled in powerful acts who dances *Nkwa Ike* shall die sooner after dancing it publicly. Dancing it is an act of claiming to valor, which must be investigated and confirmed by elders. In fact, people who did extra-ordinary things like killing or defeating the enemies of the community often celebrate their achievement by dancing *Ikwa Ike*. The word "*Nkwa*" in English simply means music. Music is a mark of solidarity, an expression of communal and ancestral relationships. In the context of *Ikwa Ike* [tough music, literally put], it does not feature ordinarily. On the same par, when partners take time to dance together, it underscores the road map to peace.

Unfortunately, with the influence of the Christian message, an atmosphere of disorientations and confusions began to blow around the land. Most Christians in Igbo land especially in Ezinihitte look at the symbolic music and the rite of *Itu Aka N' Esse* as devilish. Yet, the same Christians who attack it, consciously or unconsciously turn around to baptize the rite of *Itu Aka N'Esse* with another name called "Funeral Oration" where the family enumerates the achievements of their dead relations. Fortunately, the rites in both contexts aim at achieving the same purpose thereby creating confusions in building trust and reliable relationships in the practice of the true religion among the people.

vii. Second Burial *[Ikwa Ozu Nkwa Abuo]*

Generally the lgbo people of Nigeria believe that there is continuity of life after physical death. Due to this belief, for them, man does not die as reflected in their 'Theophoric' names. As noted above, a person of proven character, who lived sound moral life and died at old age is always and essentially given "befitting burial" to mark his or her inspiring qualities. Unlike today, many people associate befitting burial with physical displays of wealth and lavish ceremonies, even for a wealthy armed robber. Thus, Traditional "memorial service" or *Okwukwu* is a child of love and concern. First and foremost, it is a solidarity ritual. It is not necessarily done to quicken the journey of the dead to the spirit world or to avert any harm from the dead person against the living. For Ezinihitte people, there is no second burial. A person dies once in the flesh and is buried accordingly. In Onwubiko's view: "In traditional Igbo society there is no second burial'. None of the… aspects (interment, funeral ceremonies and festivities) are ever repeated for anyone (1990: 26).

However, the influence of the missionaries and western civilization in Igbo land challenged the above belief. As such, they introduced conflicting elements into the peoples' normal way of burying and remembering their dead. The people celebrated *Okwukwu*, a type of thanksgiving to God or ancestors to mark the anniversary of their dead members. The missionaries classified the ritual as devilish. Unfortunately, Christians quickly turned around and replaced the so-called evil ritual with 'memorial service' as a way of reverencing their dead. Virtually, it is not the Igbo of Nigeria who introduced the whole idea of "second burial" or that nickname, but the Christians themselves. Based on these erroneous pictures painted and presented here by the missionaries, regarding the peoples' rich culture, most Christians in Ezinihitte today regard the burial and memorial services of non-Christians as devilish. In this light, it becomes difficult if not impossible to understand how Christianity that condemned the peoples' Traditional way of celebrating or remembering their dead, *Okwukwu* as fetish, turned around and enthroned the same ritual, 'memorial service' as holy and heaven-oriented. These are practical problems and make this book interestingly a must-read. As we noted earlier, hypocrisy is number one killer in every level of human relationships and spiritual psychology out rightly condemns it.

9. Village Court *[Ala Di Mma]*

Ala Di Mma literally means, "May the land be good or peaceful". It is a mandatory village court where different cases of fighting, bribery, land disputes, embezzlement of pubic funds, religious violations, sexual abuses et cetera are justified and settled by the leaders and eldest of the land. This village court is in accord with the legacy bequeathed to the Igbo people of Nigeria especially to Ezinihitte by their ancestors. The village court has link with the village gatherings and some social group systems, like *Oku Umunna* (Community summon or gathering), *Iri mbata oke* (a mandatory provision of food items to qualify as a member in the women group), *nkwa ndomi* [women dance], *Igba mgba* [wrestling], *Otu ebiri* [Age grade systems] et cetera. These are important values that encourage healthy relationships among the Igbo people. These activities highlight the maintenance of peace and order in the community, which eventually attract blessings from the community representatives in the spirit world. Partners also need to engage in some exciting events that keep them together.

On the same par, confusions began to infect the community social group systems through the influence of the missionary activities. One wonders why the missionaries missed such wonderful values of unity, peace and love to press down their mission. For instance, there were nothing like local, divorce, high, judicial, federal or supreme courts besides the people's native court *"Ala Di Nma"* for settling cases of all sorts. Yet, such powerful media for peace and unity were dismissed by mere wave of hands as heathen. It is even worse to note that such nuances like wrestling and women dances in some parts of Ezinihitte of Igbo land seem consumed by modern influences. Today, many prefer civil law courts to "Ala Di Mma" where they can bribe their ways out. The worst aspect of the disorder in question is that most Christians in Ezinihitte, especially the born-again, have not only disassociated themselves from these practices, but also advanced and perpetuated hatred, deceit and sown seeds of discord and disunity in the land.

10. Presentation of Kola Nut *[Igo or Iko Oji]*

We have earlier on mentioned this rich heritage and practice of *"Iko Oji"* in Ezinihitte of Igbo land. Due to its unifying effects, there is every need to elaborate on it. *Iko Oji* simply means presentation of kola nut, a fruit harvested from kola nut tree. The importance of this event, *Iko Oji* in the life of Igbo people centers on the fact that kola nut is the first thing to be presented to any visitor and at public meetings or gatherings. There is a common belief among the people that if a person visits your house and you fail to present kola nut to him, it means the person is not welcomed. Traditionally, kola nut is never presented to women in Igbo land. In case one welcomes a woman in his or her home, a man must break the kola nut for her to eat. *Iko Oji* is a sign of love and trust. It guides, establishes and operates on both individual and communal relationships. The people also regard it as *Icho oji*, in which case, the presentation of kola nut formally assumes a ritualistic order. *Iko* or *igo oji* could simply mean to offer kola nut as a sign of hospitality to ones friends and visitors. This could mean a person-to-person affair. But, *icho oji* normally involves a big gathering. *Oji* Ezinihitte of Igbo land is a typical example of it. The religious value of this ritual principally lies in the fact that it teaches the young ones and society the need for unity, respect for the elderly and one's seniors and healthy relationships.

The Igbo Catholic Priests reacting to the above view noted that the "Igbo man values… its unity and solidarity… places high premium on community loyalty…respect for age and elders (2000:16). The order of *icho oji* generally is that, the younger person or town hands the kola nut to the elderly one, who hands it over to the eldest, et cetera. In the case of *Oji* Ezinihitte, it is the other way round, from the eldest town to the youngest. According to a Retired Vice Principal, Nwachukwu John Ubadinachi, in this capacity, "the handing over ceremony is done at the boundary of the town next to the host town" (1991:28). The entry of the *Okwa, Oba Oji or okwa Oji* (special wooden container or tray holding the kola nuts) is heralded with sixteen gun or canon salutes. If an ordinary piece of kola nut from a kola tree could generate such enormous attention, peace and celebration, why cannot a simple smile from parties solidify their relationships? After this, men from the host town who must be dressed in a traditionally dignified manner, like all the participants, carry the *Oba Oji* into the arena. Eventually, the kola nuts are presented in small-carved bowls called *Okwa*. Of course, only the native kola nuts according to Nwachukwu are used, and not "the ones known as *Gworo* or *Oji Awusa*" (1991:28-29).

In Ezinihitte of Igbo land, the seniority order in which kola nuts are presented to the constituent units is as follows: *Oboama na Umunama* [site of the ancestral shrine of Ezinihitte], *Ife, Chokoneze, Ihitte, Akpodim, Amumara, Eziudo I & II, Itu, Okpofe, Ezeagbogu, Udo, Obizi, Onicha.*

The kola nuts are then passed from *Oboama na Umunama,* the most senior town, to *Onicha Ezinihitte* the youngest town. This is the major annual festival, besides Christmas that brings all Ezinihitte citizens together. It has socio-religious, cultural and political implications marking them out as spirit-filled community with a common identity and objective. As noted earlier, relationships are celebrations of shared identity, peace, love and trust.

The problems here hinge on the failure of the missionaries to have integrated their activities on such terrific communal services that would have rallied different minds together to the love and appreciation of the Word of God, Eucharist and love of neighbor. Instead, the celebrations of *Iko Oji* or *Icho Oji* were dismissed as evil practices. Worse still, most of the Christians who count themselves off and condemn this celebration as against the Christian faith, grow kola nut trees in their homes, eat, and use them for various purposes, commercial, at meetings and to entertain their visitors. What a misrepresentation of the man Jesus in Igbo land of Nigeria? Even if your partner is bad, talk to him or her in his or her presence and avoid misrepresentations.

11. Customs/Traditional Laws *[Omenala or Omenani].*

The peoples' experiences of the natural bond within their families and extended relations oblige them to establish healthy relationships and work for the common good of the community as a whole. Their moral, socio-religious, political laws and obligations are defined and summarized as their *Omenala.* On this note, Meek says: "The primary functions of religion would seem to be the function of rites and standard of social behavior" (1943:20). These customary laws help to unite the people together in their religious, moral and political life. They are not only the expressions of the dynamic spirit of co-responsibility among the people (Mozia, 1987:221), but also their solidarity with one another, God and the ancestors. *Omenala* is primarily for the maintenance of the bond among members of the community. In Ezinihitte, no bond exists in a vacuum. It must have reference to the ancestors and God.

Literally speaking, *Omenala* for M.I. Mozia "means legitimate acts and reactions observed in the land" (1987:221). *Omenala* does not exclude westernization, civilization, and modernization. According to Osuji, it includes "all provisions and prohibitions, traditional beliefs and practices, which are contained in the written or unwritten laws and customs and brought down from the ancestors to posterity" (1977:25). In a real Igbo setting, particularly in Ezinihitte of Igbo land, *Omenala* is believed to represent those basic norms and principles that guide men and women in every age and place. *Omenala* has been handed down to humanity from one generation to the other as taught by the ancestors through the direct instrumentality of the elders and the *Opara* of each village. There exist various sanctions and punishment attached to *Omenala*. It simply demands a general conformity just as intended in every healthy relationship.

As a universal concept, any society that is devoid of a common identity, obligation, order or force that directs their socio-moral lives or conduct seems to be dead. In Igbo land for instance, *Omenala* forbids theft of yam (the principal Igbo Crop) from the barns, farms and other forms of stealing, adultery or fornication among blood relations, incest of any form, children fighting their parents et cetera. These are basic values that guide their relationships which people of every culture; especially teenage boys and girls need also. Reacting to these prohibitions, Baseden appears to be addressing Ezinihitte people of Igbo land when he remarked: "Cases are not unknown when infidelity on the part of the wife has been punished by torture and death of both offenders" (1966:34). The people of Ezinihitte see it as an abomination to beat or fight a priest of God or a minister. This is not necessarily because the Christian message taught it "do not touch my anointed ones, do my prophets no harm" (Ps. 105:15). Rather, it is simply because their *Omenala* forbids such acts and condemns them as *Aru* (crimes) against their ancestors and God.

On a more important note, *Omenala* helps to preserve the cultural and religious values of the people. It protects the moral principles, which are manifested in the customs of the people, and equally helps in the objective formation and application of conscience in concrete human situations. In supporting this purpose of Omenala, Ilogu observes: "Omenani, therefore becomes the means by which traditional Igbo society enforces conformity culturally speaking, Omenani is the means by which the ethos of the people is measured, the values of the society are contained from one generation to another...Because Omenani is derived from the guardian spirit of "Ala" and sanctified by the ancestors, it is religious in nature, although it fulfills social, moral and cultural sanctions" (1974:23). From this eschatological viewpoint, the Ezinihitte people regard their *Omenala* as a means of enjoying the beatific vision of their God and ancestors. To be candid, if Christianity had not succeeded in Ezinihitte soil today, it is practically due to the peoples' irrevocable attitudes to *Omenala*. Even, when certain aspects of the *Omenala* seem to go contrary to the Gospel message or sounds negatively conceived it has to be adhered to, since the people see it as a legacy bequeathed to man by God and the ancestors. In Igbo context, "*Omenala*" is inviolably, a personal perception and judgment of one's deeds and how they inform one's life. Any infringements on the customs [*Omenala*] of the people equally mean an annihilation of the community as a whole.

Fundamentally, for the general public and the people of Ezinihitte to achieve healthy relationships and interpersonal co-existence, I recommend that the following ills and problems that militate against their *Omenala* must be condemned in all aspects:

> *Various systems of apartheid, Godlessness, violence, racism, sexism, class dominations, discrimination, exploitation, 419, robbery, dehumanization, selfishness, greedy-driven aggressiveness, lack of self-control, sexual immorality, disrespect, and inhumanity to man, blindness to the injustices of political, economic structures, ideological oppressions, constitutional policies, social inequality, political maladjustment, cultural disparagement, marginalization, generalized debilitation of the very basis of human existence, total destitution, misery et cetera (1994:42-43).*

It seemed P. O. Kemdirim was also referring to Ezinihitte people of Igbo land when he noted that the "overwhelmed, suffering, oppression, poverty and socio-cultural injustices, racial and class discrimination... the agonizing problems of childless couple calls for salvation and liberation (1996:235). Continuing, Kemdirim noted that one of the disappointments of the African Synod (10 April – 8 May 1994) was: "Its post-synodal message made no substantial reference to any specific cultural heritage or social structures not yet fully transformed by the Gospel such as: patterns of marriage, traditional burial rites. Oath and title taking, widowhood practices, divination and fortune telling, caste system, etc. undermine people's integral salvation" (1996:237). The people of Ezinihitte are engaged in the process of liberation from socio-religious and politico-economic forces by the various things they religiously and materially do to achieve and assure peace and unity in their relationships.

In recent times, due to the influence of western civilization and missionary activities in Igbo land of Nigeria, the peoples' *Omenala* or customs have been abused. This violation of the people's identity constitutes a big problem. The *Omenala* would have overwhelmingly formed strong grounds for implanting the Gospel message right into the consciousness of the people. Gods' Ten Commandments, civil laws and principles would have been easily comprehended and appreciated within the contexts of the peoples' Traditional laws and customs. Such rare opportunities were blown to the whirlwind and dismissed with the wave of the hand. One can imagine what impact the Gospel message made on the people when their primary source of belief as reflected in their lives was neglected. Incredibly, a mention of *Omenala* or Tradition generally sounds repulsive to so many people today, especially among Christian fanatics and the youths.

In the Traditional laws and customs of the people, chief priests of various shrines were highly revered and feared. It was an abomination to challenge such priests. But today, cases of having Catholic and Protestant priests beaten, disgraced and killed abound in their thousands. Such obnoxious behaviors and taboos have terribly affected the basis of life and healthy relationships. Glaringly, it is very easy to note the nature of relationships aggrieved people are expected to keep with one another. On another note, the missionaries condemned Traditional Medicine men especially those who foresaw future events as fetish. But today, due primarily to the shallow implanting of the Gospel message, self acclaimed healing ministers, prophets and prophetess abound everywhere, proclaiming deceptive visionary exploit that reap friends, families and communities apart.

12. Oath-taking *[Idu-Isi, Iku-Ofo, Ikwa Ala or Isu-Ogwu Oriko]* and placating of the land after abominable offence has been committed

We had earlier on remarked that the Igbo of Nigeria have powerful channels for providing remedies to cases of misconducts in the community. Igbo people are community people who believe in community efforts and identity. For instance, if there is an abominable act like theft in the community, the people have two basic ways to deal with it. First of all, formal enquiries will be conducted as regards who might be responsible for the act. If after that initial enquiries and nobody owns up or agrees to have done it, then the matter will be resolved by *Iku Ofo or Idu-Isi,* that is, a public form of oath taking in which the entire community gets involved in the ritual without focusing on any individual person. The matter takes different shapes if there is an accusation. The rite of *Idu-Isi* and *Iku Ofo* belongs to the same family. Either of them takes place, only if an accused person denies the allegation. *Idu-Isi* or oath taking goes with a lot of taboos and curses from the ancestors and they work. *Idu-Isi* remarkably points to the accused person while *Iku Ofo* is the act of carrying out the ritual itself.

As soon as one has sworn publicly, especially on a serious issue as mentioned above like theft, the family members and the community as a whole disassociate with that person. False oaths on the part of the victim have always resulted to untimely deaths and terrible and incurable diseases. Actually, it is within this period that the community waits for a clue either in the affirmative or denial of the victim's innocence of the accusation. In the Traditional Igbo of Nigeria, hardly do people accuse anybody falsely. However, the rite of oath taking whether it is carried out for an individual, for a group, family members or the community is performed through *Iku-Ofo.* The ritual takes the form of "repeat and answer question". The oldest man or chief priest who is impeccably a symbol of truth, justice and honesty officiates at the ceremony. He asks the victim certain questions in which the answers must be either 'Yes' or 'No'. Of course, this ritual has never been a child's play. It works like magic. No offender has escaped instant punishment.

Again, if two compounds have disputes over a piece of land and none of the parties is ready to surrender it, the only way to bring peace in their relationships or settle them is through the same ritual, *Idu-Isi* or *Iku Ofo* - oath taking. Usually, during the process of investigation into the matter, one of the parties could emerge as accuser or the accused. This generally determines who takes the oath. In all circumstances, however, the community judges or arbitrates in the matter, determining who actually takes the oath. In many cases, a family may accept to take the oath for ownership of the said land. The guiding principle has always been: *"Onye eboro na-ago"* meaning; the principal accused person denies by taking the oath. In this case, only one compound takes the oath for the other compound. A period of one year is allowed by the community to give verdict on the ownership of the said land. Within this period, none of the members of the compounds or families that have the land disputes will relate, visit or talk to each other. It is a waiting period to ascertain whether the oath was falsely taken or not. If, at the end of one year, no member or members of the family that took the oath died, the land automatically belongs to them. The waiting period equally demonstrates the people's strong belief and trust in their God and ancestors and how they closely intervene in their problems. In cases involving murder, the safest option for victims of such grave offences is to be ostracized or banished from the community.

Undoubtedly, the Igbo regard and value relationships as sacred. For them, relationship is life. In fact, cases have abounded where a person who falsely took an oath, shortly came back to the community and owned up his or her responsibility for the crime that necessitated the oath. The same thing could equally happen to a person who was banished from the land. To welcome either of the parties, the ritual of *Ikwa Ala* and *Isu-Ogwu Oriko*, that is, placating the spirits of the land must be performed. The same chief priest or eldest man of unquestionable character performs the rite of welcoming the victims back on behalf of the community. For a victim to meet with the requirements for placating the spirits of the land is extremely difficult because of the nature of the items to be involved or provided.

Truthfulness (*Ofo*) as repeatedly sung in this book, has been part and parcel of the life of the Igbo people of Nigeria. Abuses emerged with the missionary influences that tend to fight these powerful means by which the community maintained peace and order in the land. The people absolutely trust *Idu-Isi* and *Ikwa-Ala*, that is, oath taking and rites of placating the spirits of the land. The missionaries did not see any ennobling value in these aspects of the peoples' lives. Such beliefs were out rightly condemned as superstitious. Yet, the missionaries centered the content of their Gospel message on truthfulness and sincerity. Society, at large, is witness today that the virtue of truthfulness has become more of a speculative reality than a practical one. The missionaries failed to convince the people of alternative ways of achieving truthfulness in the land besides *Idu-Isi* and *Ikwa-Ala*. Instead, they introduced the idea of confessions especially in the Catholic Tradition. Besides the Sacrament of Confession, which is a treasure in the Catholic Church, so many Christian fanatics satisfactorily claim to confess directly and solely to God. For the Igbo of Nigeria, and the Africans at large, any confession that does not instantly lead to restitutions and change of hearts is meaningless.

Here lies the greatest problem of the Christian message to the Africans: "Is it justifiable before God and man for a thief to rejoice that his offences have been forgiven after confessions when the victimized is still in pains?" The Sacrament of Confession was wrongly presented to the people. The people could not understand what went wrong with their Traditional and powerful manners of confession by which they reconciled with their God, ancestors and one another after the land had been violated. Traditionally, confession was not limited to one-on-one affair. As noted earlier, any sin committed against an individual is considered a communal affair. But with the missionaries, emphasis gradually shifted from the moral implications of the actual crimes that are committed against the community and the efforts to eradicate them, to individual interpretations and feelings. Eventually, some tend to look for good reasons to get out of trouble than say the truth. Most of the Christians, especially some Catholics who kick against the Traditional rite of confession - oath taking or placating the spirit of the land, either perpetuate evil in the community or receive the Eucharist without any Confessions. One can at this point imagine what effects the Word of God, Confession and the Eucharist have on the people.

This is a religious calamity. Pretence is incompatible with relationships. The question that faces us is: "*Idu-Isi* - oath taking or *Ikwa-Ala* - placating the spirit of the land and religious confessions in general, which one is more sacramental and powerful, and essential today for evangelization of the Igbo people? I think, God, from my personal encounter and experiences, seems to have been completely fooled by most people. How did the idea of God who searches human hearts, understands every step man or woman takes on earth in the African context become a foot mat where individuals clean their dirty feet? The God of the Africans is felt and revered in every relationship. Therefore, for individuals to fashion in their heads and claim that God is merciful is misleading. Definitely, God is merciful and praiseworthy for those who seek him with truthfulness and honesty and he remains so irrespective of whatever any one does or says of him. God is never limited by human tricks and actions. Making God an appendage to suit our whims and caprices is the worst and most dangerous track and lane any human relationship and being can take (CCC, 32092). For instance, my uncle, late Simeon Amaefule Ohakpougwu, the chief holder of the Traditional "*Ofo*" of Mbaise never went to Church or belonged to any other religion besides the Traditional. Everybody still wonders how he got a Christian name. He was well known among Mbaise people of Igbo land and beyond for presiding over serious land cases and disputes that the courts could not handle. He abhorred all forms of bribery and stood only for TJP – truth, justice and peace. Till his death, he settled cases for various Christian groups. The question then arises: If the missionaries actually succeeded in planting the values of the Gospel message among the people, why was the embodiment of truth and order hung on a Traditionalist who never went to Church? Today, one of his daughters is a Nun, Religious or Sister (DDL) of proven character, living in Chicago, USA.

13. Outcast/Free Born Controversy *[Osu/Diala]*

Outcast/Free born or *Osu/Diala* is a cultural institution among the Igbo of Nigeria, particularly in Ezinihitte that seems to have completely soiled all possible relationships and beliefs in the Christian message. Right there in Ezinihitte and most parts of Igbo land, *Osu* is an outcast, hated, dreaded and isolated. Of course, according to Kevin Njoku:

"No *Osu* may be allowed to hold the traditional *Ofo*...of any of the autonomous communities" (2/5/78). They are given all sorts of names as "*ndi mba ozo* [foreigners) *ndi aka ikpa* [leftists], *ndi oma* [flattered as the fine groups] et cetera.

In Ezinihitte of Igbo land of Nigeria, *Osu* means an "outcast". This is a person believed to have been dedicated to a spirit or god. Such a person is looked upon as a victim for sacrifice in order to maintain peace in the land or community. The shocking aspect of this belief and practice is that *Osu* is rationally a normal person with full human faculties, who has become an object for placating the anger of the spirit in case the spirit turns around to attack the community in question. In this case, the *Osu* or the person becomes "the property of the spirit" (Azorji, 1986:80). This was the point, for which Achebe lamented in the Arrow of God, saying:

> *A disease that has never been seen before cannot be cured with everyday herbs. When we want to make a charm we look for an animal whose blood can match its power; if a chicken cannot do it we look for a goat or a ram; if that is not sufficient we send for a bull. But sometimes even a bull does not suffice, then we must look for a human (1978:133).*

The choice of human beings in sacrifices was necessitated as the only way "to avoid future calamities in the community" (Uchendu, 1965:89). As noted already, there are no criteria for the choices because an honest person could be involved. This is where *Ohu* or slave is different from *Osu*. *Ohu* is a freeborn held in spiritual and material bondage. All the same, a freeborn could be forced to become *Osu* for obvious reasons - economic and immoral behaviors. This type of *Osu* is a special outcast known as *Osu Nwa* or a child who has been made to become an outcast. That was the case with slave trade. Those who were sold into slavery were considered less important or meant nothing for the community or family. But if a person is *Osu* by heredity or dedicated to the gods or spirits, automatically that person remains *Osu Arusi* or an outcast dedicated to the spirits.

On the other hand, *Diala* means a "free-born" of the land, the son of the soil. Because of the *Diala/Osu* dichotomy, every *Diala* fears *Osu* to avoid offending the gods or spirits. Worst still, no *Diala* or freeborn dares to marry from the *Osu* family or village. But the bad economy is forcing some Christians to marry from wealthy *Osu* families today. Besides, some convinced Christians are against this caste system and marry whoever they want. In this caste system, only the *Diala* or freeborn hold titled and leadership positions in the land.

The highest problem the missionaries created in Igbo land was their inability to resolve the *Osu/Diala* controversy. Their message was unmistakably clear on the issue of unity and healthy relationships. For instance, the Christian Bible specifically stated that: "When the Scripture says...it makes no distinction between Jew and Greek: all belong to the same Lord" (Rom. 10: 11-12). The situation is better elaborated in another version of St. Paul's letter, thus:

> *There is one Body, one Spirit, just as you were all called into one and the same hope when you were called. There is one Lord, one faith, one baptism, and one God who is Father of all, over all, through all and within all, Ephesians 4: 4-6 (Malachi 2: 10; Col. 3: 11-12).*

Contradictorily, the issue of 'outcast/freeborn' is a controversy that hits at the fabric and foundation of unity, peace, love and relationships. That the missionaries practically preached peace and unity among the people but ignored this fundamental issue of Christian unity was enough evidence to conclude how far the people understood, accepted and still practice the Gospel message vis-à-vis their Traditional beliefs today. Unfortunately, *Osu/Diala* controversy has resisted Christian principles even by staunch Christians. Conclusively, the institution of this ugly belief, according to Uchendu, has remained "a living anthropological reality" (1965:89). As luck would have it today, the issue of sacrificing humans seems to have officially disappeared from the Igbo of Nigeria, particularly in Ezinihitte, but the reality of treating *Osu* as an object for sacrifices still dominates the minds and souls of the people at this 21st Century Christianity.

To stop over stating the issue of violations, which the missionaries unconsciously created among the Igbo people of Nigeria, we cannot treat all the ritual observances here. For instance, in Ezinihitte of Igbo land, there are such religious values and rituals as *Isu Ogwu Oriko* (a reconciliatory rite after welcoming an ostracized person). *Isu Ogwu Oriko* can equally take place after one has committed incest and any other moral offence against the goddess of the land. Other religious values and rituals which the missionaries classified 'fetish', include *Ishi oshishi* (Traditional title taking), *Igba afa* (Divination which is equally observed and carried out in Christendom by some Healing Ministers) and *Iro-Nro* (Dreaming and interpretation). They equally throw some lights in addressing the problems confronting this book.

Nevertheless, the good news is that amidst all these seeming confusions, abuses, cultural multiplicities and diversities infiltrated by foreign cultures among the Igbo of Nigeria, majority of the people still maintain a common cultural identity both in their language, habits, beliefs, behaviors and relationships. So long as their culture remains their religion, they try to reflect them in their relationships. In other words, despite the discrepancies the western culture has created among the people; the African or Igbo values of hospitality, communality, generosity, oneness, eye-nose-blood-relatedness and the extended family systems et cetera uniquely single them out as models for human relationships.

All the same, the immeasurable advantages derived from the influences of the western culture on Igbo land of Nigeria cannot be overemphasized. The westerners, in a clear and profound manner, transformed the economic, social, and political lives of Africa as a whole. For instance, the same westerners, (though, more lives are being lost today through the introduction of artificial birth control), eradicated the issue of killing twins. Thanks to the westerners also, the banishing of mothers who gave birth to twins from the community received a mortal blow. Cannibalism, which posed a big threat to the life of the people in the pre-colonial periods, was equally brought to an abrupt end. Regrettably, these acts of inhumanity to man have differently resurfaced in the world today in which innocent souls are used for ritual purposes, kidnapped, murdered, maimed and trafficked as objects of commodity.

Consequently, the Igbo of Nigeria remain indebted to the westerners for so many reasons. It is the westerners that tremendously created powerful media for global relationship. In effect, the westerners succeeded in their mission in a variety of ways by introducing formal education, health facilities, hospitals, good roads and what have you. Today, the world has become a family, thanks to western science and technology. The seeming problems the westerners created in Igbo land of Nigeria were simply wrong application of individual dynamics and knowledge to the people's identity and meaning. By implication, every relationship should unequivocally seek understanding.

B. Purpose of the study

This undertaking is essentially based on investigating the issue of relationships in general, especially from psychological and ethical perspectives as the springboards for the realization of holistic personality and order in society. In one of his quotations, Tillich noted: "Man is asked to make himself what he is supposed to become to fulfill his destiny" (1886-1965, IFE). In the light of Tillich's observation, the basic concerns that face each individual are: "Who am I supposed to be, what is my destiny and how do I fulfill it? These are practical and anthropological problems that challenge individual relationships. For instance, if a person does not, first and foremost, realize, trust his or her nature, he or she cannot become who he or she is supposed to be and it will be impossible for him or her to fulfill his or her destiny. Eventually, from these backgrounds, spiritual psychology draws its strengths, not only to examine how far the individuals in question have realized themselves and their destinies, but also guides them towards achieving positive objectives and healthy relationships.

Moreover, spiritual psychology is on path with "low or smart power" – diplomacy as against "high power" – military. On her diplomatic address to students at Moscow State University, Russia, Wednesday, October 14, 2009, the US Secretary of State, Ms. Hillary Rodham Clinton, indirectly advocated the need for spiritual psychology in the pursuit of global peace and order. In her understanding, "smart power" calls for smart people who are, not only creative, but also take into considerations all the non-confrontational possibilities and approaches that allow flexibility in decisions and actions. This is in line with the main purpose of spiritual psychology in which a person has to be open to the possibilities that people can go wrong and also change. According to Clinton, there are problems in the world today especially in religious circles because some people think they have absolute truth in their positions. There is need to strike a balance and agreement on issues that create global peace and order, irrespective of each others' cherished belief systems. Peace is absolute and not relative. Therefore, the book specifically seeks the following:

1. To identify the nature and enormity of the immoral practices which create conflicts in the realization of human destinies in their relationships.

2. To investigate how individuals feel and react when confronted with moral obligations and how they apply the knowledge of common moral principles to their particular cases as recipes to understand and appreciate others in similar situations for global interpersonal relationships.

3. To extensively study and determine the sources (causes) of immoral behaviors, misconducts and conflicts which people encounter in their relationships.

4. To ascertain the opinions and experiences of other people through enlightened minds [Western and Traditional cultures] as a case study to understand and eradicate conflicts in human relationships in general.

5. To determine the best methods (measures, judgments, standards and instruments) that can be employed to control the negative effects of global village syndrome among teenagers, individuals and society.

6. More importantly, to demonstrate the need for Spiritual Psychology in the school system and in building healthy relationships in society. There is need to understand, identify and anticipate the magnitude of changes individuals make in their behaviors through a professional process. This is a process that disposes the individual to accommodate and accept what

is available at the moment, especially when the desirable is far fetched or not there. Uniquely, this process is designed to assist society and individuals to re-learn themselves in the light of having a new range of focus and ex-cogitate some of their nasty past, perceived ideas and impressions about themselves and other people. It is a retroactive process, an inward journey from one's characters to habit, actions, decisions, emotions or feelings, thoughts, impressions and stimuli (external world), the primordial cause of activity and one's state of life. The book, according to the Catholic Bishop's Conference of Nigeria, is aimed at:

> *A total transformation of primordial values, which shape the individual attitudes and judgments, decisions and choices, behaviors and relationships (2004:5).*

The changes spoken about here guide people to achieve their destinies and they basically begin from "self" and not from others. The love that exists between two people may only depend on one person at a time.

7. To demonstrate that spiritual Psychology is therapeutic and educational. As a counseling and educational psychology, it is strategically designed, not only to assist people in difficult moments within the areas of marriage, family, career, emotional instability, children of separated parents, but also revitalize the teaching profession, school children, seminarians, research students towards interior transformation and self-supervision.

C. The scope of the study

Relationship is a universal and global issue existing on different levels on the planet, corporate, economic, political, professional, religious, social, cultural, personal, interpersonal, groups, family, associations, various systems, et cetera. Healthy relationships have no limits. Today, most celebrities, both social and religious and political reporters have provided valuable resources for guiding human relationships. For instance, there are so many "Get it right" TV Shows all over the world today. Such TV Shows include Steve Wilkos.com, Jerrey Springertv.com, Linus Okwu/Home Media Friend and Foe, Oprahshow.com, Dr. Phil.com, Tyrashow.com, Tony Robbinson - Ultimate Edge.com, Larry King Live – CNN.com, Dr.OZ.com, Ellenshow.com, Harlemmothersave.com, Dominic Carter – Inside City Hall, NY1.com and Bonnie Hunt.show, Harvey Steve.shows, Comedians, Funny/Hilarious Shows, Family Feud Video Games, You are not smarter than a 3ʳᵈ Grader, WendyShow.com, et cetera. They are playing heroic and prophetic roles from different perspectives in America and beyond to keep human relationships together and lively. I am not bothered about their religions as their efforts to educate and enlighten society on vital issues that immensely affect individual and global relationships. Practically, in no less measures, they have professionally contributed and created healthy awareness and changes in the bad behaviors and attitudes of so many. Some are radical in their methods.

Therefore, in this book our discussion is limited to and concerned with the various human conditions that primarily affect individual, social, cultural, personal and interpersonal relationships from the perspectives of psychology, religion and ethics. We critically and necessarily considered Spiritual Psychology apt for bringing about the changes society needs today to move on the right direction. The book, however, did not claim to have exhausted all the issues that pertain to relationships. Rather, it is credited for creating the consciousness and awareness of those factors that militate against human relationships and the management strategies and skills, which individuals could apply to successfully achieve positive results.

The language of the book is carefully chosen and structured to fit all high or secondary school children, college students and the general public with average knowledge of the English language. The book is academic, historical, informative, instructive, inspirational, motivational, educational – formal and informal with emphasis on guiding each person to understand him or herself towards achieving healthy relationship. It is a compendium of moral instructions, authentic religious advocacy, an academic manual and a handbook of self-supervision.

The survey is conducted for global application and advancement of healthy human relationships. However, every book carries the cultural perspectives of the author. As it were, this book, to a great extent, is largely punctuated by the African and American worldviews. The objectivity, therefore, lies on one's ability to diligently interpret and apply cultural diversities and values within the framework and organization of one's own cultural milieu.

The book generally studies the causes and effects of conflicts in human relationships. The case study or fieldwork of this book as noted in the statement of problem is chiefly limited to the Christian religion, Western and Traditional cultures, particularly America and Igbo of Nigeria, with particular reference to the people of Ezinihitte Local Government Area of Imo State. Consequently, our population is largely drawn from the Questionnaires, which the teachers, physicians, engineers and Lawyers (The Middle Class) from America and Nigeria, precisely, Ezinihitte people of Igbo land furnished us regarding the factors that affect relationships in general.

D. The significance of the book/study

The significance of this work hinges on the question: "What contribution is this book going to offer to individuals in particular, to the reader and society at large in their various levels and types of relationships? The book becomes significant, if, after individuals and the general public have gone through or read it, the knowledge and skills they gained thereupon guide them to properly perceive or understand the complexity of human nature and assist them bring about the following changes and values:

1. Appreciation of the need to understand and self-supervise themselves in resolving misconceptions, conflicts and build solid relationships.

2. Respect of other peoples' values and feelings, allowing enough flexibility in every relationship.

3. Flexibility and tolerance in their decisions, [especially in the formation and judgment of conscience], choices and actions as marks of civilized relationships.

4. Inculcate the virtue and ideology that each person is part and parcel of the external environment of others. No person is an Island in relationships - No CP. A little help rendered to a partner in relationships may multiply in a geometrical ratio to form a community of relationships.

5. Paradoxically become more conscious and aware that no matter how careful an individual is in a given relationship, his or her partner may always act otherwise. For instance, despite the relevance of established, and accepted moral laws and norms in society, some people will always and naturally go against them. Each person behaves true to type. No one is completely predicted till one has shown one's stuff. The book therefore guides us to expect the unexpected in the behaviors of other people no matter how diligent and prudent we may tend to be with them. That is to say, relationships, at times, are clarion calls to accommodate the weaknesses and mistakes of others, because we live in a world that is not so perfect.

6. Understand that human natures, temperaments and personality traits differ. According to Henri Matisse:

   When we speak of nature, it is wrong to forget that we are ourselves a part of Nature. We ought to view ourselves with the same curiosity and openness with which we study a tree, the sky or a thought because we too are linked to the entire universe (IR).

7. Build capacity and skill in identifying, assessing and managing own emotions and impulses as well as those of others and groups, injecting self-motivation, social competence and empathy in interpersonal relationships.

At this point, we are constrained and challenged to review the thoughts and inputs of other scholars on the matter at hand.

Chapter Two

* * * *

Review of related literature

There exist some literatures on the nature and use of the term "relationship" as an indispensable value of human life. Many authors have attempted to give varying opinions and meanings on this matter. In the words of William J. Grace:

> *Before one embarks on a serious study of a subject, it is helpful to stand aside and get the long view of it, to see it in perspective-in its largest terms as well as in its details... The material out of which the human artist creates its experience of life (1965:5-6).*

This "experience of life" in one's relationship, dates to the creation of man. Amazingly, due to the seemingly unscientific and subjective nature of relationship, attention is gradually paid to it in the course of history as an academic issue. Thus, as already noted, the main thrust of the book is the study of relationship from psychological and ethical perspectives for interpersonal co-existence. This chapter is, therefore, aimed at putting various minds together as ways of assisting both individuals and society to appreciate the diversities in human behaviors for a common understanding that may lead to peace and harmony in relationships. Since a tree does not make a forest, we need the cooperation of each other to build a union of authentic relationships.

No author can completely claim self-knowledge of the true nature of human relationships. Constructive discussions on relationships from psychological, religious and ethical perspectives as the foundations of human life are rare. Therefore, we are going to review the opinions of various scholars that bear relevance to the realization of our set objectives. Though, due to the fact that literature on this "particular mission" - keeping human relationships together: self-guide to healthy relationships, is not as available as one would expect, this chapter seems to be the most voluminous and we beg to be obliged. The review and discussion of our related literature, particularly concerning all the factors that influence human relationships, are constrained by this situation and thereby treated under the following headings, numbered A to J:

A. The images of relationship

The book anchors on real human issues, values, situations, behaviors, characteristics, stories and reactions emerging from lived human experiences and relationships. It is essentially born out of deep and intensive fieldwork or survey, reflection, consideration and analysis of needs to keep human relationships healthy. The issue of keeping human relationships together may suggest either a pat on a person's shoulder, an encouragement to keep the ball rolling on the right direction or a presupposition of a nasty behavior, present or past that needs to be fixed. The emphasis here is not necessarily on what people do as how they ought to do it because there are thousands of things done under the sun that defile the eye. Spiritual psychology realistically attempts to equip individuals with the basic skills they need to live in the moment with themselves and each other in their relationships. It provides antidotes to those habits and misgivings that create conflicts and serves as guide to healthy living. Antoine de Saint Exupery in Coffey F, observed: "It is only with the heart that one can see rightly. What is essential is invisible to the eye" (1993: Dedication page). Human relationships have both agreements and disagreements because life itself is cyclical. Our lives reveal themselves in moments and need to be appreciated accordingly. The need to maintain certain equilibrium in relationships at various times, favorable and unfavorable is urgent and timely. There is time for everything (Eccl. 3:1-8).

Generally, human relationship tends to sing the same music in various tones and builds on the same universal ethical principles. Also, it incorporates certain images such as: origin, mission, name, language or sign [Dialogue], joyful noise, mindfulness practice and belief. There could be more images as revealed in individual characteristics and relationships than studied and presented in this book. These components have to be there to ensure proper alignments in relationships. Thus, we shall reflect on these images separately:

a. Origin: How does relationship generally begin?

Relationship is not a COMD business, that is, a commodity, an hourly, weekly, monthly or annual affair. As already noted, it is a life affair even when separation is evident. It has to exist first before it is capsulated into a healthy or unhealthy state. We tell others how to treat us and relationships begin from there. A stitch in time saves nine. For those who are interested in our campaign to keep human relationships together, there is need for them to meditate and recapitulate their knowledge on the following basic enquiries:

- ✓ How do I know you, have you had any previous relationship, or do you currently have one, and if you do, how far?
- ✓ What do you do for a living?
- ✓ Tell me more of your family history: Do you have relations, how?
- ✓ What do you think of this relationship, how do you feel about me right now?
- ✓ How are you sure this relationship will last or be possible?
- ✓ When did you begin to nurse the idea of this relationship in the first place, is it spontaneous because you saw my attire or out of some thoughtful considerations?
- ✓ Now, what are your main reasons and objectives for this relationship?
- ✓ Do you not think we give ourselves some time first for some deliberations?
- ✓ Do you have any faith tradition and to what extent are you involved in it?
- ✓ What are your hobbies and what do you love and hate in a relationship?

✓ Can we have some contact information to keep in touch, et cetera?

✓ On professional and work levels, issues of resume, work experiences, length of time needed, where, with which company, references, conditions of services, duration, and remunerations et cetera, come in too.

In his recently released book, entitled "Act like a lady and think like a man", Steve Harvey recommended 5 questions young girls need to ask before they engage in any friendly relationships:

1. What are your short-time goals or plans?
2. What are your longtime goals?
3. What are your relationships with your family, God and others?
4. What do you think of me?
5. How do you feel about me? (Harvey, Steve, Tyra show, September 2009).

In his analysis, girls should allow a period of 90 days for observation before they commence any relationship with men. Biologically, human relationship is congenital. It begins right from the moment a child is conceived in the womb. This aspect is basically true of babies. However, while our discussion on human relationship in this book is not limited to age or gender, the emphasis here is on the conscious, practical, life-fulfilling experiences, voluntary commitments, naturally aimed at nurturing life, creating, recreating and bringing about unity, peace, love, progress in the lives of individuals and society.

Marital relationship works better when partners close one eye

With reference to adult and marital relationships, a survey I conducted among the Nigerian Middle Class population in 2001 featured wonderful responses as contained and cited in my book entitled: The 50 Steps to Happy Marriage, 2001: vii. Among the few personalities interviewed, we have the following observations:

1. Dr. Festus Ngumah, "Marriage [Relationship] begins, first of all, with an agreement a man and woman make to each other, be it the Traditional or Ecclesiastical perspective" (Chairman, Pastoral Council, Ahiara Diocese and Chairman, Local Government Service Commission, Imo State).

2. Lady Julie Anyanwu, "No marriage can survive without prayer...and for any marriage to be successful, one partner must appear to be 'foolish' that is, close one eye, just to allow peace reign..." (Owerri Archdiocesan and Provincial President, C.W.O).

3. Ms. Victoria Ibe, "Only little, little things, just doing little things for each other, has kept our marriage journey smooth and moving. If my husband, Prof. Sylvester Ibe loves me today, or does anything for me, I am really instrumental to it and vice versa" (Staff, University of Agriculture, Umudike, Umuahia, Abia State).

4. Lady Otigbuo Mary, "Marriage for me is just tolerance, live and let live, allowing your partner to have his or her way and space, and avoid being greedy" (President, C. W.O. Aba Diocese).

5. Ms. Philo I. Ekanem, "I congratulate you, Fr. Anthony on your beautiful booklets just out, worthy son...Both booklets are very interesting and enriching, especially the statement you made, thus: 'The fault a partner always complains about the other may really be in him or her" (Former National President, N. C. C. W. O. N).

Examining closely the above remarks, it is easier to underline that individuals decide how best or worst their relationships can go. For instance, relationship should not be forced. It is an agreement freely consented to between individuals. Prayer is indispensable for healthy relationships. In this sense, partners should pray, trust, dispose themselves and love each other. Besides, individuals should avoid insisting on details of each other's behaviors. At times, it works out well when one eye is closed against each other's minor mistakes. Needless reiterating here the fact that little things count so much in relationships, like, "did you sleep well to night, how was your day", and "thank you for the other day" when actually the day in question has no specific time or date. To be wealthy is important in relationship, but it is not the deciding factor. Giffin Emily expressed it better:

> *Beyond the money, there was something else at play....It was a feeling of inadequacy ...a worry that, on some level, maybe I wasn't good enough. Maybe I didn't quite measure up to....* (*2008:235).*

In a special note, relationship is simply tolerance; allowing each other a breathing space and avoiding being greedy for anything, even in sexual matters. Rape should not be mentioned or practiced in any relationship because of a greedy partner. More importantly, before partners think of the faults of the other in relationships, it is necessary that they patiently and thoroughly examine themselves first. The Christian Bible beautifully summarized this issue in these words: "Why do you observe the splinter in your brother's (partner's-mine) eye and never notice the plank in your own? How dare you say to your brother, "Let me take the splinter out of your eye", when all the time there is a plank in your own. Hypocrite! Take the plank out of your own eye first, and then you will see clearly enough to take the splinter out of your brother's eye" (Mt. 7:3-5). Naturally, it is possible that we are primarily, many a time, the cause of the blames we apportion to others in our relationships.

More profoundly, the life of human relationships is nourished and essentially begins in the embryo of the individual mind before it reaches out to embrace the other. Relationship, just like 'religion', is natural to every human being and primarily the fulfillment of Gods' injunction to man to increase and multiply. Humanity can as well increase and multiply in love and kindness. In conjugal relationships, a man and woman multiply themselves into a litany of lively relationships. Therefore, relationships are ontologically linked to God or a Mighty Force, the source of human beings. Thus: "God created man in the image of himself, in the image of God he created him, male and female he created them. God blessed them, saying to them: Be fruitful, multiply, fill the earth and conquer it" (Gen. 1: 27-28). We are Gods' work of art. The Greek word used here is "poiema". It was the same word used at the creation account, describing when God created heaven and earth. As Gods' handiwork, the beauty of our relationships is reflected, not only on our own efforts as such, but on the strength of him who stands and knows the end of everything [our worries and concerns] from the beginning. He knows the solutions to our problems before we encounter them. For a person to doubt him or herself is sickness. Each person or life counts.

Each time we bless others, the air fills us with eternal blessedness – No miracles in relationships

Fundamentally, we are Gods' creation and unique part of the new creation through our cooperation with one another in his son, Jesus Christ. Life is as beautiful as creation itself especially when the various works of art and humanity admirably reflect themselves in an undivided unity in their relationships. According to Jeremy Taylor in Mead Frank: "Some friendships (Relationships-mine) are made by nature, some by contract, some by interest, and some by souls" (1965:157). In this light, a Track Star, Jackie Joyner-Kersee cited in Buckingham, Jamie, in support of our guiding principles in this book, made the following encouraging statements:

> *While athletics has consumed a big part of my life, I try not to let athletic accomplishments change who I am inside. I've gained a lot of material things from athletics, but I know that's not what matters long-term. It's my soul, my character, the God I stand for that means more to me than anything in the world. I hope the people I interact with see that in me (2000:21).*

Practically, it is of paramount importance for relationships to emanate from the life wire of each individual heart and soul. We offer such hearts purified in bodily penance, love and tolerance in order to show and share with those in need, the downtrodden, the goodness of God we celebrate in our lives and relationships. Jackie concludes her testimony for God's goodness in her life in these words: "God is the one who gave me my success - and He can take it away if I don't handle it well. Knowing where my true success and self-worth come from puts my life in the right perspective" (2000:21). We should seriously emulate the good seed and example Jackie has sown here, especially in a world where many people no longer care for the source of their being or success. Such self-acknowledgements generate tranquility of mind and guarantee a level of inner security in one's relationships with God and man. Each time or moment we give blessings to others, the air fills us with such fresh life that comes directly from the Supernatural Force or God who is the foundation of peace and joy.

Usually, we lavish our precious time speaking about others and forget ourselves. Naturally, we tend to analyze, praise or devalue the efforts of others based on what we think of them. We may lack the basic facts. There might be bias or prejudice in our judgments; at times, we do so subjectively. Whichever way, it does not matter. Whether we consider letting people naturally live their lives or not, is our own cup of tea. Paradoxically, people live their lives; make their choices irrespective of what we think or say of them. For instance, the lives we lead ourselves count more to us than what others do or say about us. Msgr. (Dr.) Nwaorgu Anselm, seems to be addressing this situation when he remarked:

> *The bottom line is that the behavior of others is unpredictable and to base your future and success (relationship-mine) on such unpredictability is to build on a foundation upon which the outcome of important things in your life is uncertain (2008:5).*

No matter how deeply we are connected with and love others or our partners and friends, we have our own lives to live. There are so many other lives; issues and relationships many people have that are not known to us. Therefore, according to Allison, E. Peers: "Let us strive, then, always to look at the virtues and the good qualities which we find in others, and to keep our own grievous sins before our eyes so that we may be blind to their defects" (1960:142). As a matter of fact, we have to first of all, begin to trust in our nature, our capacity to adapt, take care of ourselves, smile, face every life hurdle squarely and be responsible for the decisions and choices we make in our relationships. This is indubitable - 'kpom'. For instance, how can a person who has not mastered his or her own life be fitting for a successful relationship? Relationships grow as humanity and vegetation do. What is more important is to keep it alive by caring for it in love.

There is no miracle in a relationship one is careless about or cannot maintain. Our passions, characteristics, thoughts and actions form the basis and steps with which we climb the huddles of every relationship. We relate the ways we are, as we noted already. Expecting much from the world or any relationship may lead to disappointments. We cannot judge situations by their appearances because there could be more to that. Apparently, when some issues in our relationships seem unresolved and unsolvable, the best ways to handle them is to take a deep step towards a desert experience, active silence. Silence is active when we deliberately refuse to take notice of the various occasions for quarrel.

God is a friend of silence and not noise

In quiet moments, the self makes a journey, exhaling the bad airs of confusion, sadness and inhales the fresh airs of liberation, joy and forgiveness. Always be truthful to yourself and silently aspire to do that which is generally noble, phenomenal, awesome, inviolable, enviable, best and do not expect rewards or praises. Relationship can work better when partners, at times, simply sit down, lean on each other or **hold hands** without any talk for some time. God is a friend of silence. For instance, when Elijah sought God, he found him not in the mighty wind, earthquake or fire but in the gentle breeze, hearing the still small and comforting voice of God in silence "what are you doing here, Elijah?" (1 Kings 19: 9-13). Relationships thrive more in silence. No wonder the Bible noted that, for Christ to heal the deaf man that day: "He took him aside in private, away from the crowd" (Mk. 7:33). Why? He needed to avoid the noisy world as ours, for the healing to take effect, for a graduate student to pass his or her exams with an A.

Society is filled with all sorts of noise. There are noises everywhere, in the air, land, forest, water, sports, computer, music, kitchen, accidents, untimely deaths, natural disasters, terrorism, from material pursuits, powerful network system, movies, scrambling for money, genocide, political squabbles for power, various forms of marriage, sciences, friendships, religious advertisements, daily news, theological debates, media, electronics, crazy ambitions, and the boom of 'lovemaking' ventures etc. There is no end to the necessary and unnecessary noises in society, especially in individual lives. For instance, the unlimited noises of human choices and preferences are unimaginable. Many are already infected with insatiability, restlessness for various wants, unsatisfying urges for women, money, men, trial marriages. The resultant effects have led many to anxiety, various forms of depression, suicide, broken relationships, homicide, chronic sicknesses and untimely death. On a bitter note, Pellegrino Joseph, lamented:

> *Our world is full of noise, full of people telling us what we should say, do and think. The whole goal of our existence has been confused by agnostic or even atheistic media and a consumerism that has turned materialism into a new idolatry. And we work like dogs for food that we lap up in seconds then we go to work again. Is this life? (IR, 10/25/09*

Eventually, noise drives away most of our fortunes and healing opportunities. We succeed in relationships when we deal with our emotions and feelings [the life wires of relationships] in quietude. For instance, no student can succeed or achieve his or her educational objectives in noises, like, constantly, playing Video Games, writing love letters, text messaging and making phone calls, et cetera. Silence is concentration and noise is distraction. In silent moments, we establish priorities, boundaries and pace ourselves for the same inevitable question God asked Elijah: "What are you doing here"? In recollection and moments of great need, the voice will always be heard for us or a believer, now, not "Elijah", but "my friend, Anthony, --------, (fill in the blank space with your own name) why are you downcast, worried because of the loss of an unreliable friend, a job or politics of the ministers of the Gospel?" Even when we feel cheated, deceived, abused and hurt in our relationships, the same consoling and curious voice will always sound in our souls and show us the way out. But, we may not hear it because of our preoccupations with worldly worries and ambitions. The need for silence is validated in all forms of prayer and active engagements. Prayer, like relationship, is not based on the noises we make before God, but actively being in silence till God is heard. In noise, we hear ourselves but in silence we hear God speak to us. That was the point Johann Robert meant when referring to 'love' in these words: "Its sincerity can almost be measured by its speechlessness. Its very directness imposes silence" (1966:19). Love talks less.

Nobody is beyond the love and favor of God

There is no one, no culture, race or religion that is beyond or above the favor of God. For instance, Eldad and Medad were not among the 70 elders God initially gave the spirit of prophecy, yet they equally prophesied with the rest (Num. 11: 24-26). Similarly, when John complained to Christ against a lay man he saw casting out devils in his name, he replied: "You must not stop him: no one who works a miracle in my name is likely to speak evil of me" (Mk. 9: 38-39). Frankly, in line with the objectives of spiritual psychology, God does not lay any emphasis on who is a Minister, Priest, Catholic, Protestant, Jewish, Muslim, Buddhist, Non-denominational, Hindu, Utilitarian, an Atheist et cetera as who keeps his law of love for one another. Appearances are human but the heart is divine. Implicatively, to love God without loving one's neighbors with whom one interacts on daily basis is nonsensically more of an object of the mind. As the Christian Bible explains it: "Anyone who says, 'I love God', and hates his brother, is a liar" (1Jon. 4:20). That is, LG – LN = 0 or nil and LN – LG = LG, where 'G' stands for God, 'L', love and 'N', neighbor. Love seeks love and it is never vindictive or 'comes to an end' (1Cor.13: 4-8; Rom. 12:14-21).

When we seem to become victims of circumstances in our relationships, there should be no panic, because help might be on the way. The story of Abraham, his son, Isaac and Elijah (Gen. 22: 1-14; 1 Kings 19: 4-8) confirm our assertions here. In the case of Abraham and his son, Isaac, if it were today, Abraham would have failed that eternal test that universally made him the father in faith of those who believe. Most children of this age are smarter than their parents and teachers. If it were today, Isaac would have disappeared, noticing that his Daddy was ready for the sacrifice without a sacrificial lamb. In a sense, for Fulton Sheen in Marlin, "Love is the soul of sacrifice" (1989: 279) and that is what keeps relationships healthy. God does not overlook the least sacrifices individuals make on daily basis, their generosity, caring for the poor and love for one another.

Obviously, spiritual psychology suggests the various paths we can follow to keep our relationships on track. Nobody is a judge in his or her own case. "Live and let others live" is the first law of relationship in spiritual psychology. Healthy relationships start with the first singular personal pronoun "I" and not with the plural "we" or the other. According to the first century philosopher, Epictetus as reflected by Corey: "People are disturbed not by events, but the view which they take of them" (1996:319). We may hold different interpretations for the above position, but one fact is not debated. For instance, if you perceive your neighbor as a bad person that is the way you value, approach and relate with him or her. Focusing on the negative sides of others or one's partner, whether in the marriage state or other states in human relationships, stressfully frustrates progress. It is better we think of our own faults and stop being grumpy and cranky with other people's choices of living. We need to fix our own problems first before we blame others. We are all insufficient in every interpersonal relationship.

Kids may lack the words in adult conversations, but they interpret them & you can't expect your partner to be honest when you are selfish

As adults, we show others how to relate with us. But kids expect us to follow their lead. This aspect of our discussion has been handled in the book. Generally, it is bad to say negative things about others at their back or before kids and children. As already noted, these kids may not comprehend; understand or follow the conversation, but they can easily pick and react to the tones of the words spoken. The later effects of these emotional foundations will be awful and dangerous to society. For instance, as these kids continuously get oriented to bitter conversations and attitudes, by imitation and associations, a generation of terrorists and bandits are inevitably incubated. We cannot expect our partners and friends to be good and honest when we are selfish and greedy or hope to enjoy healthy relationships in dirty and filthy environments. Cleanness is next to Godliness and it is not limited to gender. Insatiability, the habit of Oliver Twist, "I want more, more and more" in relationships is the highest display of insecurity and selfishness. Too much of any particular thing in relationships is never going to be enough and it is a major problem. In relationship, extravagance is sickness too. Partners must optimize spending to eschew financial stress. In other words, if you want to avoid wastefulness in your relationship, simply start applying discretion in the way you spend and handle your resources. Living in the state of contentment and openness is self-rewarding. Adjustments to what one cannot change in relationships are very necessary. If you hate discrimination, stop being one. When we consciously give birth to healthy relationships, the world will always be there to praise and write our history.

b. Mission: Specific objectives and goals?

Life is purposeful. My field of research and studies at GTF in the area of Basic Psychology and Psychological Practice, especially the Spiritual, has forced me to raise concerns as regards how best human beings can relate with each other. Surprisingly, the enquiry has revealed various faces of human relationship. In this book, as noted already, it is our fervent desire to examine some of those faces of human relationships. By "faces" here, we refer to the different conditions, levels, stages and shapes we find in our relationships. However, whether the face of a particular relationship is bright, pleasing or nasty, it is 'one and the same thing'. Once, a 17th Century English Philosopher who lived in a time of upheaval and Turmoil in England [1588-1679], Thomas Hobbes, citing a popular Roman proverb by Plautus (184BC) noted that: "Man is a wolf to man –'*homo homini lupus*' and to outweigh the other is felicity" (Leviathan, xiii. 2-9). These sentiments as raised by Hobbes compounded my interests to dig out the best ways to handle the canker worms that attack the taproots of human relationships. Nobody doubts the reality of what Hobbes remarked judging from what is happening in our society, particularly in politics. We see it acted out in many relationships, even in religious circles also. The book is therefore encouraging individuals to embrace their differences as powerful tools to solidify their relationships. We must always agree to disagree. Allowing third parties such as drugs, alcohol, and bad habits in our relationships is destructive because a devil cannot fight itself. Relationship is a precious jewel at the hands of those who understand and treasure the value. A shameless person or partner does not know when the other is hurt or offended.

The 5th century Thinker, Socrates on the other hand, once remarked: "An unexamined life is not worth living" (IR). Naturally, he is right.

No one has all the answers to the exigencies of life. Living an undefined life is as deadly as not living at all and this is the problem we have with some of our teenagers. On the same par, Viktor Frankl cited by Morgan John in Baunoch Joseph remarked:

> *Ultimately, man should not ask what the meaning of his life is, but rather must recognize that it is he who is asked. And he can only answer to life by answering for his own life (2006:119).*

In line with Frankl and Tillich, we are answerable to our own lives. Each person holds his or her own life as an egg on a platter. Only the individual agent understands how delicate it is holding or losing it. The fact is that human life is never static. We are constantly engaged in one act or the other. We try to maximize our environments, (Okeke, 1989:34), mainly to make some progress, because we are essentially, ethical-minded beings.

To change society or the other, we must adjust our own lives first

Human beings are always occupied in a search for meaning, a mission and long-life process of decision-making. This mission or search for meaning involves the decision to act, either rightly or wrongly. Hence, Huxley cited by Morgan in Shaw J. and Morgan J. [eds.], remarked: "Moral development is the inevitable result of human behavior" (2006:25) towards survival because as Okoro Kieran would put it:

> *The human existence is more than a merely biological – psychic existence; the human person transcends matter…if a person therefore sees his life as meaningful, if he has the hope that his existence goes beyond temporal life, he is affirming his hope in his resurrection or eternity, and eternity here, again, is not an endless continuation of time but rather the ultimate and definitive value of the human person's existence which has been brought to a successful end and fulfilled in freedom (2000:61).*

In this way, the book invites each person to abhor judgments and avoid jumping into rash conclusions. Unfriendly habits greatly contribute to the various mishaps we encounter in our relationships today. When we listen to other voices and experts from different cultures or fields of academia, it prepares us to make up our minds and guide our relationships. In a situation, for instance, where an individual does not appreciate the sacrifices his or her partner makes to keep their relationship healthy, the said and reasonable partner must brighten up and move ahead. As for doing good, that is the sacred state of nature and the mission of healthy relationship. Often, we become sick of nothing but our bad life. Jamison was right when he remarked: "The times in my life when I feel the worst are those times when I've not been true to myself—have not said what I think, feel, believe. That's the time when I've betrayed myself, diminished my energy by confining my growth to keep myself small" (1989:18). The best way to change an individual else is not by intimidation, yelling, feeling disgusted, snubbing, keeping aloof or being angry with him or her, but by changing the tone of our responses to him or her. That is to say, to change others, we must first of all examine and change ourselves. In the words of Spring A. Janis:

> *The best way to change my partner's behavior is to change my own first. In essence, I' am advising you to create an environment in which your partner is most likely to fulfill your needs. If nothing comes out of it, at least you'll know you did your part (1996 :165).*

On no condition should one allow or rent a space to animosity in one's relationship. For instance, whenever your partner gets you angry and expects you to feel it, calmly feel as if nothing has happened. If he or she wants you to shout, simply relax and keep quiet. But if he or she wants you to sing and dance, even if you are so tired to join him or her, courtesy demands that you smile, stand if you can and shake your body a little in response to a peaceful invitation. Occasionally, it does not work out that way. For instance, how will you react or feel when you expect your partner to smile and brighten up but he or she refuses to do so? Surely, for some people, it is a let down and they may get upset over it. But for some others, this is an occasion for immediate, greater and deeper reflection and invitation to visit a partner's private

147

world, possibly to source ways to deal with the moment. Introspection is necessary in life. According to Stravinskas, Peter: "The devil and his angels…make a 'career' out of hatred for God and trying to lure people away from God" (1998:116). Little things emit strife in relationships. We need to get into ourselves and set times apart for self-examination and reflections to avoid relational temptations. Human relationship can only be possible when we provide some spiritual self-space to each other. In this light, we "provide spiritual self-space" when we physically refuse to respond and react to insults and yelling. Instead, we express sympathy for the other, because each of us has personal issues to deal with. It is pointless getting angry because some one else is annoyed with us for no just reason. After all, paranoid is a personality type. People are like that.

The heart to give opens an eternal account beyond the physical gifts

At times, to get things right, many people learn from their costly mistakes. Each person represents a face in the cluster of faces that build or destroy human relationships. Whatever gives meaning to our existence, not only, commands our attention but also defines our goal. This goal is often and relatively unlimited. It could be earthly or heavenly oriented depending on individual's value judgments and assessments. Each living experience is a mission. In his book entitled 'Cashing in your receipt with God: With each act of giving, a deposit is made to the believer's heavenly account', Oral Roberts said: "When you give, you have an account with God, make no mistake about it" (2006:53). The act of giving is not so much limited to the physical material thing that is given as to the hearts or love extended in it. Two or more people can experience and embark on the same mission and event differently. Our spiritual and social maps differ from one another. To establish lasting relationship, we must be disposed to listen to other peoples' stories. For instance, there can be 6 people in a car, but only one driver holds the steering at a time. When two partners talk and seem to be making serious points at the same time, if one of them does not listen, no matter how cogent or convincing his or her reasoning might be, no point has been made. Such attitudes also lead to a clash of interests. Individual stories teach and assist society move forward.

c. Name: Unity in diversity - our stories

Our Stories differ. Give your relationship a name that identifies your feelings and values. The faces of human relationship differ because each individual is unique. As Donze T. Mary, puts it: "You are the only one person like you that makes you special. And because everyone else is just himself or herself and nobody else, that makes everyone else special, too, but each in a different way" (1998:70). The fact is that every relationship is shaped by its own story. Our individual identities, personalities and stories differ because we are both our stories and values. Our lives are perceived as stories and every name is associated with a particular story. As Crites Steven has insightfully observed in Rabbi Goldberg and Jay:

> *A man's sense of his own identity seems largely determined by the kind of story which he understands himself to have been enacting through...the story of his life (1983:13).*

Inasmuch as our stories and values are different, we cannot be expected to behave the same way in any particular relationship. This is what constitutes major obstacles in human relationships. We clearly need to underline that point. It has been medically proved that each person's heart is distinctive from the other. That is to say, though, scientifically speaking "no two hearts are the same" but they perform the same functions. For instance, the three layers of the heart beautifully and harmoniously work and carry out their functions together to keep us alive. While the first or outer lining - Pericardium cooperates with the second, the flesh or muscles of the heart - Myocardium, the inner lining, the Endocardium simultaneously synchronizes with the other two to assure vitality, suitability and balance of the human person. Similarly, when socio-cultural, economic, religious, political, and individual stories complement; they equally bring about harmony in a relationship.

Therefore, in healthy relationships, partners should not care who gets the credit but the benefits. Just as the whole parts of our body are different but work together to keep us alive, we also need to relate as human families and beings, and benefit from our socio-cultural diversities and enjoy the uniqueness of each other. This is the surest way human beings can relate with each other. For instance, when we ascribe the quality "spiritual" to Mr. B, it does not mean that Mrs. B is "unspiritual" because the word "spiritual" does not mean the same thing in all situations, for a Christian, Muslim or an atheist. Besides, what does being spiritual mean in reference to others or in the pursuit of a common life goal? Again, does being religious mean the same thing as being spiritual? These questions are relevant in this book and each of them demands a response and not necessarily an answer. No person is completely useless. Every one has something unique to offer in relationships if well harnessed and directed, no matter how insignificant it might be. Aristotle once observed: "Virtue is its own reward", (Nic. Ethics 1-7). A good partner is the happier partner, because, according to Coffey, "the graceful heart does not depend on thanks to continue to love and serve" (1993: 141).

A delicious dish can equally kill

Consequently, spiritual psychology guides individuals to deeply appreciate how their worldviews, external impressions, thoughts, feelings, decisions; actions, habits (*ethos*) and characters (*Ithos*) dynamically shape their relationships. This is obvious because the impressions we have of the external world (stimulus), to a great extent, lead to the ways we approach, think, feel, decide, build attitudes towards them, and these are what eventually make us who we are as individuals. In spiritual psychology, we refer to this process of character formation and building (S = TAC, that is, Stimulus = Thought - Decision, Action - Habit and Character) as "A prodigal son's journey syndrome - PSJS." It is a 2-way-meeting points or axis of character building. Like most of us, a cherished child of his or her father can easily become prodigal because of his or her choice disorientations. Every reasonable person makes choices that might promote or demote him or her. We are projected as travelers on a taxi. The driver, like the human intellect, does most of the work, spots out passengers, stops to pick and assign seats to them just as the intellect interprets the beauty or ugliness of an object that is presented to it. The joy of traveling on this taxi is not solely dependent on the driver but the amenities and comfort of the car itself. The comfort (desire, will and appetite) equally determines whether we take the car to our destinations or stop and take another one. Each person is a driver of his or her own car of life. Teenage boys and girls have to be very careful in the choices they make. Entering into a friendship out of curiosity because others do it, is a costly mistake any rational young man or woman can make. A delicious dish or meal can equally kill. Frankly speaking, for instance, the few boys and girls I have come across in my life, especially in Nigeria who singled themselves out and never listened to anybody, have, either ended up being useless for life or died accidentally. Life teaches, at times, the least unexpected and sad lessons.

This is the problem most of us encounter in building healthy relationships. For instance, when our appetites or choices are not guided by strong will or desire in conjunction with the intellect to resist the beauty of what appeals good to us, irrespective of its effects, definitely we begin to feel, think of it and decide what to do with it. In this situation, if the will, which always seeks immediate gratification, succeeds in influencing the intellect, then the deed is done. The deed in question could be likened to that of the prodigal son. It could be harmful or beneficial. If, at the level of liminality, "the axis or meeting point", assuming a wrong choice has been made, the agent, like the Prodigal son, does not refrain from habituating or continuing in such a bad habit, he or she automatically forms a character. In the case of the Prodigal son, he stopped at the axis of his action and habit, and coming back to his senses, refrained from, either forming a bad habit or character. At the axis or meeting point of human choices, actions and habit, spiritual psychology guides the individual to listen to the voice of his or her inner self (conscience) and positively follow the paths to integrity and wholeness. Unfortunately, studies have revealed that it is easier to form bad characters than retract from them. Again, bad character once formed greatly constitutes the number one destroyer of individual relationships. For instance, most of the addicts to drugs and alcohol have their relationships too. Usually, they feel normal that their behaviors are the best ways to fully enjoy this life till bad habit pays them with the unwelcoming atmosphere of "had I known".

Therefore, the choices we make in our relationships shape our stories. In the words of Beecher Ward Henry: "Moral sense without common sense made an enormous amount of clashing in the world" (NY Times, 2/25/1886). When we avoid hurting others, we affirm the need to be peaceful ourselves. Life is principally relationship and the best mirror a person may have is a good partner or friend. A friend in this context is one who is able, amidst all odds, to tell us the ugly side of our lives. Moreover, only two groups of people can tell us the truth about the unpleasant sides of our lives. While our best friends approach the matter from positive perspectives, our enemies do the same, but from negative angles. This is evident of a cultural saying that "drunken children always tell the truth". As Henry Home in Mead F. would have it: "The difficulty is not so great to die for a friend, as to find a friend worth dying for" (1965:156). In Lauder Robert's words "Friendship is the greatest gift: in it what is given is the self" (1978:72). Elaborating more on the nature of "gift" he remarked:

> *What makes a gift so attractive is that the giver is not compelled to give it…Gifts are signs of the giver. That's probably why often it is difficult to pick a gift. The more special the person who will receive it, the more difficult the giver's task in choosing the gift (Ibid, 1978:72).*

In other words, the life of any relationship depends on the values we attach to it. These values equally determine the manner we approach our partners.

No matter what image a partner or friend may reflect in our individual mirrors, "our remembered wellness" (1996:25) or the very unique way we consistently and gladly get about accepting and living our lives depends on us. Hence, it is not proper for other people to decide the ways we feel about ourselves in any relationship. According to Kate Relling Garskot: "Advice is often a vote of no confidence in the ability of others to solve their own problems" (NYUMC, 2/11/09). Some people ask for advice, not that they do not have solutions to their problems, at times they do. That is why; every relationship demands common sense. In support of Garskot, Kennedy observed: "Every decision is a risky exposure of the self to all the things that can go wrong…. There is so much of ourselves to take into account in any particular situation that it is clear that no advisor no matter how shrewd can really make the decision for us. At this moment of choice, even after all possible information and advice have been gathered it is up to me. The mature person becomes increasingly sensitive to his own feelings" (1972:32). The pictures other people or friends may hold for us, may simply be an appendage and do not tell the whole story about us. In this light, Novak in Goldberg and Jay, made the following observations:

> *If our lives are, therefore, "a tangle of stories" (to use Michael Novak's phrase) which in turn entail a jumble of convictions, before we stand up to champion some particular moral position, [or engage in relationship-mine] we first better sit down and get our own story straight. We need to see if we can piece together the diverse story fragments in our lives in order to give our life-stories some coherence (1983:13).*

The Christian Bible as we saw earlier on, seems to be alluding to the same observations Novak made here when it stated that, it is pointless trying to take the splinter out of your neighbor's eye when all the time one has a plank in one's own eye (Mt. 7:3-4). In support of the foregoing remarks, Chenu, in Ware remarked: "Each individual is radically insufficient in realizing his or her own nature fully," (1995:29). Apportioning blames publicly over and over again on one's partner because of his or her mistakes indirectly exposes the level of one's undistinguished personality, stupidity in dealing with one's own issues. Generally, only stupid and creepy people talk ills of those they love in public. To complain is to limit or empty oneself and empower the other.

According to Jean-Paul Sartre in Zelinski, as noted at the introduction: "Everything has been figured out except how to live" (1997: ix). We said it already "to live" entails more of self-commitments, truth, justice, honesty, being sensitive to one's environments and willing to learn from and assist others, make sacrifices for the progress and improvement of the human condition here and now. Besides, in Bowker's view each behavior or "religion carries with it its own implicit anthropology - that is, its own account of what human nature is" (1988:21). To harmoniously live together or relate to others, we must always expect the unexpected and constantly be disposed to respond in humility. We can now understand why Goldberg and Jay made this clarion call:

> *Each of us carries within himself or herself fragments from many different narratives. Consequently, our lives are often fragmented morally as well, involving partial and even contradictory commitments, as we act on the basis of first one, and then another, of these story-pieces (1983:13).*

Patience is a significant value and key in listening and hearing the hidden implications of each other's stories. Each person has other issues to deal with besides the seeming pleasantries in relationships. Therefore, to succeed in any relationship, we necessarily need to study and understand a bit of other peoples' stories. To 'study' here is more of a disposition than academic sophistry or being smart in worldly standards. Rationalizing our roles in relationships is unhealthy.

d. Language and signs: Maintenance and appreciation [Dialogue]

In general terms, language is a powerful means of communication and cannot be overemphasized. Emotional language distinctively conveys a journey of no specific destinations but can easily be understood by everyone. Human relationship is not about the other, but knowledge of oneself as a person. We set the pace and shape the nature. It begins with, and ends with us. By signs here, we do not refer to the mathematical aspect that elicits equations and command. Rather, they are personal dispositions that oscillate the balance of relationships either positively or negatively. Once relationship is schooled or taught, it becomes ritualistic. Naturally, it is better controlled from within. As we jealously protect, provide for and comfort ourselves in matters of insecurity, relationships also call for a change of dynamics in the ways we approach and think about others. As an inward journey, it leads the individual to reach out and share his or her feelings, aspirations, hurts, and emotional wounds with the other. Normally, people care and feel more the sweetness and bitterness of what they cherish, long for, and work hard to build. We are our own relationships. For instance, no one else decides our relationship, even with God. Having been created in Gods' image, he judges us, not necessarily on the good things we do, but on the good ones we fail to do. In the words of Eamon: "God uses our willingness to do what we don't feel like doing in order to bless us"

(1993:30). For instance, being kind to our enemy is not always easy but it is a mark of spiritual growth and grace.

Relationships are all about the ways we have planned our lives, future and death. In this instance, the role a friend, relative, mother, father, brother and sister in-law may play in marital relationship has to be carefully, diligently and closely monitored to avoid conflict of partisan involvements. There is a limit to which an outsider or a third party can go in marital relationship. Moreover, such factors as workloads, financial resources, personal habits, staying late at nights outside one's home or long on the computer, on the phone, or listening to music or news at meal times, reading of news papers, addiction to photographing, frequently waking up at the middle of the night for no just reasons, et cetera, should seriously be controlled. Sexual engagement respectfully speaks it's own language and specifically observes a decorum that is appropriate for rational beings in every marital relationship.

Dictionaries may have many definitions for relationship. People talk of it on daily basis. But relationship itself, as an experience, is felt, lived and not defined. In this light, Allison P. observed:

> *Having gone through so much myself, I am sorry for those who begin with books alone, for it is extraordinary what a difference there is between understanding a thing and knowing it by experience (1960:145).*

Certain things are easily done in relationships than defined and promised. The true meaning is realized by deeds and not words. Relationship is so commonly used in every cranny and hook of society that practically everybody speaks of it in conversations. This makes it imperative to have some standards for measuring its success rate. These standards are realized in our ability to speak the non-verbal language of self-commitments in assisting one another. Relationship is not masqueraded. As already observed, in Wendy: "If we allow silence to open up within, we shall see the gate and be free to open it" (1998:12). The uniqueness of relationships demands openness, its own particular language and maintenance. For instance, according to the growth theory of Jamison: "This way of living works like a candle.

155

When you give away some of the light from the candle, by lighting another person's candle, there isn't less light because you've given some away-there is more. That works with love too…When everybody grows, there isn't less of anybody; there's more of-and-for–everybody (1989:3). More importantly, healthy relationships take more time and energy to maintain than the ones that are already soiled and crashed.

In the light of our target, "relationship is a connection by blood or family, kinship, friendship, a natural association" and 'relation' as "the relationship between people by marriage or blood lines" (Dict. Def). New Webster's Dictionary on the other hand describes it as referring to "dealings between persons or nations; connection between two things; kindred; connection by consanguinity or affinity" - the natural attraction or feeling of kinship. "Feeling" here, points to "an emotional state or disposition". In this instance, relationship is a state of connectedness between people, especially an emotional connection.

The American Heritage Dictionary presents relation as "a logical or natural association between two or more things, the connection of people by blood or marriage; kinship" and 'relations' as "mutual dealings or connections as among persons, groups or nations or sexual intercourse". From this very point of view Haughey John noted:

> *What are to be related, then, are not two static entities, nor two abstract concepts, but two histories, that of the community journeying toward the kingdom and human history in the broadest sense of the word (1877:47-48).*

In a broader sense, "relationship is an interaction between two or more things or one thing and another, an affiliation, agreement, integration into, a link, relating to business, boss and employee, between objects, entities, nations, as in sciences, mathematics, marriage, ancestors, partnership, financial communities". The word 'relationship' can be defined or approached from social, economic, religious, political points of view. However, due mainly to our audience targets and focus in this survey, we approached it from psychological and ethical perspectives. We also studied and presented relationship here as an incorporation of values, a marriage of feelings, a realization of oneself in the other.

In the language of spiritual psychology, relationship is a decision, a commitment to love and share one's thoughts, feelings, and trusts with others for the achievement of common goals within truth, justice and peace. There are still as many definitions as there are Dictionaries and Encyclopedias. Nominally, it is one thing to define what relationship is all about, but another for those who are actively involved in it, to narrate their stories and tell us what relationship is not all about.

Every person on the planet has some broken suitcases

Everybody came into the world naked like any other animal. Our dresses or wears cover only the body and not the heart. Thus, relationship is a precious union of ideas, aspirations, hopes, warmth, feelings, and goals, both on the cognitive, speculative, affective and emotional levels. Constantly, it calls for self-supervision and evaluation. There cannot be any trustworthy relationships besides the decisions and efforts individuals possibly make about them. Yet, there may not be such perfect or trustworthy relationship in the world because, generally life is both beautiful and chaotic. In her own words, Sheffield noted: "No successful relationship has foundered on exorbitant declarations of cherishment…Do not expect your mate to change dramatically overnight" (2003:227). By implication, every person has some broken suitcases.

As it were, healthy relationships can be the synthesis of order and self-esteem. In this light also, Wiener remarked: "In a very real sense we are shipwrecked passengers on a doomed planet. Yet even in a shipwreck, human decencies and human values do not necessarily vanish. And we must make the most use of them" (1950:40). That is to say, only the individual knows the weight and content of his own particular suitcases. For relationship to thrive, every party in the play has to be non-judgmental, carrying empty portfolios, phenomenally allowing the reality of the relation to naturally manifest itself without any egoistic push. Relationship, in our context, is more of a moral reality, how each person evaluates his or her life than a legal matter. Law is indispensable in some relationships but not inclusively expedient. Healthy relationships are not born out of what we say "no" to, but what we say, "yes" to. The only thing worse than being called a bad person or a cheat in relationship is being cognitively aware that the accusation is true.

The process to build healthy relationship is always clear and understandable. The language is always "w-a-w! " - whole and whole" and not 'half and half'. Strictly speaking, relationship does not require a particular degree. Pomposity is a threat to human relationships. Just as air and water are important in the life of every living thing, so is the use of language essential in any human communication and relationship. Language in this sense takes different shapes, spoken, written, body language or movement, nonverbal, preverbal communications or sincerity of heart et cetera. According to Sue Wing Derald and Sue David:

> *There is a common saying among Black Americans, "If you really want to know what White folks are thinking and feeling, don't listen to what they say, but how they say it"* *(1990:60).*

That is why some people perceive healthy relationship as an open-ended and necessary community of love and institution of feelings. It is basically and essentially there for the benefits of all, irrespective of race, language, gender and religious affiliations. The fruit of healthy relationship is enormous and often realized in acknowledgment of one's weaknesses. Every culture under the sun has it's own nuances that enhance and affect communications and relationships. A simple wave of hand culturally means different things for different people. For instance, when an American waves "bye" to a person, it means, "come" for an African. The 'sigh' sound, "che-ie!" for an African indicates a disappointment, sympathy or means that something very serious, like an accident or death has occurred. The word "joke" entirely means different things for both an American and an African. What is considered a joke in Africa might be taken seriously in the Western world. For instance, an African has no specific time frame, level or degree designated for jokes. An African might appear so infuriated when he or she is only joking, or laughing when he or she is terribly hurt.

Therefore, a rapt knowledge of "paralanguage...other vocal cues that individuals use to communicate" (Op.cit 1990:56) and body movements is so important to keep relationships out of the sand. Again, when an Igbo person says: "Who dash monkey banana", it is just a metaphorical allusion to an important issue that conveys what is not there. In this sense, the person is resolutely affirming his or her autonomy as against the power of the other person to achieve and realize his or her own claims. Literally, the force of this phrase or slang lies on the fact that monkeys feed on bananas, and once it is impossible for them to have some, it means they die. Undecipherable impressions and phrases create problems in communication, relationships and work best with the "body - door" typology. Ambiguous attitudes create tension and chaos in relationships too. It is even possible that some of the words employed in this book may be interpreted differently and culturally, and I beg to be obliged. The Igbo of Nigeria hold that the manner in which an ugly impression is conferred or presented to a person creates the likely problem and not the impression itself. Proper use of language is essential in communication and relationships. However, in such moments, we recall the words of Bluestein and Katz:

> *Everybody feels nervous and tense sometimes, but when this makes it almost impossible to pay attention, think straight, sit still or just feel comfortable in your own skin, you may be experiencing anxiety or a panic (2005:159).*

Therefore, when a relationship becomes nervous, tense, and thorny, watch patiently and pray over it because, at times, the darkest time of the night is before dawn.

What prayer is not in spiritual psychology

We pray not to add anything to or change God. One of the Catholic Weekday Prefaces, IV reads: "Our prayer of thanksgiving adds nothing to your greatness, but makes us grow in your grace". For me, in the light of spiritual psychology, to pray means putting reasons ahead of the things hoped for in that prayer session and resolving to be a better person. We pray in acknowledgment of our loopholes that God may assist us fill them or the lacuna created by our inadequacies, change our evil ways, our deplorable economic conditions, secure our relationships, insecurity, sickness, keep to his ordinances and be better people in the ways we perceive others. According to Kierkegaard in Mead: "Prayer does not change God, but changes him who prays" (1965:342). God is good, truth, justice, love and peace. These are the basic values we share with him and the 'prayer points and requests' we expect in our prayers. Eventually, these values determine whether our petitions are consented to or not. We are our own prayer points. It is baseless praying for economic prosperity when we are irresponsible and dishonest in our jobs and ministries or for security when we lack moral virtues and discipline. Prayer is a reenactment and reliving of belief, solidarity and identity with both the living and dead in keeping to the moral standards, values and societal expectations we share together in general. In active spiritual meditations and reflections, prayer means, one, listening to and looking at God while God listens to and looks at one. Prayer is to call the attention of Eternity.

In Tillichian idea, when a person requests the attention of God to grant his or her petitions, it implies some elements of fear and insecurity with regard to his or her status quo. To pray is to acknowledge a lack or express a favor. When we offend each other and ask for forgiveness, it is also a form of prayer. Prayer can also be a sign of deep dissatisfaction with oneself, society and feeling of complete abandonment. Mindfulness of these situations is important. Asking God for a favor or to pardon one's weaknesses and sins is an insult to God when one is not prepared to acknowledge and fight against one's bad behaviors. Prayer is an act of humility and solidarity with God and neighbor. In the African context, prayer is always an acknowledgment of one's helplessness and affirmation of God's infinite goodness and abounding love to control the supplicant and his world. An African does not present prayer in the context of doubts of what God or their Ancestors could or not do in their lives. It is a talking - to, one-on-one encounter with the one who does not disappoint or fail in his duties to identify with his people. Objectively, prayer is neither an expression or admission that one is not ready to live up to one's moral standards nor an escapist way of dodging responsibilities or fear and insecurity to instantly face one's challenges in life. Rather, it is an empowerment to be good to oneself and society.

God's grace, forgiveness and mercy only abound when one respects other people, leads honest lives and appreciates each other as a member of the same eternal family. These are universal and eternal values sought in prayer and they uplift or dehumanize the human condition. In the light of spiritual psychology, prayer is "doing what one ought to do" in manners that promote love, unity, peace, truth, justice and bring progress in the human family. Paradoxically, there is no gulf between sin and grace, love and hatred, joy and sadness, life and death, heaven and earth, et cetera, depending on one's choice levels. In a nutshell, prayer is relatively scientific, systematic and positive-oriented. It touches the soul and heart of individuals, sows the permanent seed of integrity, probity and accountability and accomplishes in the agent, the change necessary for healthy living. Prayer essentially employs sound moral life as the main instrument for testing individual souls and hearts. Praying for an opportunity to kill one's enemy is outside the realm of prayer and a sign of an unrepentant heart that is doomed to eternal loss. It is on this basis that the Christian Bible says: "When you stand up in prayer, forgive whatever you have against anybody; so that your Father in heaven may forgive your failings too" (Mk.11: 25). Therefore, prayer is consequential in building moral stability in relationships. Moreover, God sees beyond the words spoken or silence observed in prayer to the innermost heart of the supplicant. A student who does not study can never pray to pass any exams.

When a relationship persists to sink –
flush it out and wash your hands

All the same, where a given relationship persists to sink, defiling all honest efforts, prayers to heal, and metamorphoses into a-kill-and-die affair, even in the case of a validly celebrated marriage, calmly take a big breath, "flush it out", wash your hands and gladly move forward. Moving forward here is understood within the following biblical injunctions:

> *If your brother does something wrong, go and have it out with him alone, between your two selves. If he listens to you, you have won back your brother. But if he does not listen, take one or two others along with you...report to the community.... treat him like the tax collector (Mt.18: 15-17).*

We must fight at all cost to win peace in our relationships. According to Faith Forsyte: "Peace in Mead, like every other rare and precious thing, doesn't come to you. You have to go and get it" (1965:326). Therefore, to treat our partners as 'tax collectors' does not mean physical separation but a way of flushing out the conflicting bad air and feelings. We do this by adopting a stronger attitude to contend and cope with the situation in the moment. Some seek annulment in some marital relationships to allow peace reign in society or through Dialogue, others prefer to be single in order to breathe fresh air. It is always better to be alive than die in an unfriendly, unreliable and incompatible relationship. Thanks to the canon law of the Catholic Church, for the Catholics, once enough reasons are established for incompatibility in the previously and validly contracted marriage, annulment might be granted. As a judge, once, in the marriage tribunal of the Catholic Diocese of Ahiara, I discovered that very little thing could lead to divorce or mistrust and I succeeded more in bringing many couples together than approving annulments. God does not wish to nurse and encourage disharmony in relationships. On no condition should relationship be regarded as an object under one's shoe that can easily be removed once one takes out one's foot from it. While partners must make meaningful sacrifices to ensure peace in their relationships, they also need to be alive first. The loss of relationship is painful because it is not an "agency theory" where a third party is delegated.

The importance of dialogue is treated in this book under the section "opinion". In dialogue, sensible parities resolve their conflicts. As Hawkins would have it: "Self-honesty requires examining the ego's ulterior motives that are concerned with vainglorious image…because the ego loves to get on a soapbox" (2006:216). The most effective and positive evaluations we can give to others must begin from self. For instance, if something is bothering you, talk about it. There is nothing worse in life or relationship than hiding something one feels bad about or that is good. When there are mixed signals and feelings in any relationship, parties should endeavor to find out reasons to avoid hurting others. No partner or team in a given relationship is above the individual player. There is nothing in human relationship that cannot be changed if one processes and guides one's life properly. A stereotyped kind of relationship should be discouraged out rightly.

It is fatal to be sad in a relationship. Unhealthy relationships can be infectious, acute diseases that gradually corrode the peace of society.

When a relationship ceases to be enriching, creating and recreating, all embracing, holistic, inclusive, it can become a 'relation to shame'. Dr. Wayne W. Dyer in one of his TV Shows insisted that: "When your cup is full, stop pouring" because there is need to create balance in every relationship. If you are tired of a particular relationship, it is better you say it than frustrate your partner for no just cause. Feelings have no banks but expressed. Relationship is simply life shared. It gladdens the heart. The only ingredient that propels a given relationship is emotional intelligence, having a good listening ear, readiness to consider the values of others and to own one's mistakes. These are the purifiers of the hearts in our relationships.

More importantly, the gracing privilege that opens wide the hearts and horizons of relationship is the ability to speak the language and say: "W-a-w! Wait a moment, what is going on here, let's view it this way, why not allow me do it this way, I hope it is okay with you, the world is not going to break down because of this, look-look-look-look, please calm down, be patient, I will fix it, I am sorry". Life physically becomes a stage in the heavenly theatre once it is actively and constantly nourished in virginal and dedicated love. This is mainly the language of human relationship, the only language that makes it holistic. At times, animals like Dogs bark to attract attention or assert their autonomy. That does not mean they are always going to attack anybody. To quarrel in one's relationship is normal and should be expected as part of its healing process.

Anger, though, a positive value: Women are exciting and need soft voices

To be angry, some times, in relationships is normal. Anger is a positive and powerful way through which individuals express their feelings to their neighbors. We feel angry over what we value in life. But, getting angry constantly in our relationships instinctively makes us primitive, uncultured, uncivilized and brings us to the level of brute animals. In this instance, anger management therapy becomes necessary. First of all, the victim has to patiently find out the major causes of his or her bitter feelings and irritations, write them down and privately ask him or herself some hard questions such as: "Who am I in relation to others, am I better than everybody else, do I feel so proud or full of myself that I cannot even listen to and consider the feelings of others, am I really correct upstairs, is this habit natural or caused by events, can I do anything about it, etc?" For instance, women are generally verbal. They want communication and exciting stories in their relationships. If you love them, you have got to prove or show it in action. Naturally, women are the most vulnerable, trustworthy and protective human beings on the planet. They can also be very heartless and deadly if their wonderful dispositions and feelings are completely neglected, ignored and trampled upon. Their level of patience is unimaginable. Most often, when they lack this communication and a bit of reassurance of their selfless sacrifices in their relationship, they begin to nag and men generally hate nagging or complaining. In this way, if care is not taken, suspicion, which is the sign of insecurity and jealousy, creeps up.

Anyone who hates complaining should not be instrumental to it. On a very general note, men and women have some qualities by which we tend to describe them. But it is corrosively wrong for a person to approach his or her partner from these unhealthy general impressions, preconceived ideas or prejudices. Each man or woman is unique. To draw or make a particular conclusion or judgment from such a faulty universal premise, like, "men are unfaithful and women are very suspicious" is always counterproductive in relationships. We can patiently discover what makes each person unique and find the best ways to relate with him or her. "Good will" must not be abused or taken for granted in relationship. For instance, if your partner always wakes up early to wash the dishes, once in a while, it does not hurt, wake up with him or her and join in the exercise. This is most applicable in the Nigerian context. Mere standing around might send a powerful message of reinforcement that touches, not only the individual heart, but positively shapes the future of that relationship.

A human being relates according to his or her nature and not as brutes. Watching out for a bad look from your partner's face is, not only, an indication of mental deficiency and rudeness, but also, it does not encourage any healthy relationship. Rather, we should approach each relationship differently as a participation in the divine nature as St. Paul recorded it: "Treat everyone with equal kindness". (Rom.

12:16). Every look from a partner is pregnant with meanings. If you have nothing to say or share, try and get yourself busy with something that eventually may or may not attract the attention of your partner. Focusing your two eyes on your partner, at each movement he or she makes in the house, unless to admire or share some light mood like smiling, is a sign of emptiness and idle mindedness. Worse still, it sounds devilish for a person to feel envious over his or her partner's progress, fame and status. Being envious of another person's progress is an internal and irresistible acknowledgment of one's own failures and inefficiencies in life. Naturally, one can be jealous for the sake of learning and improvement. But, when it aims at the good or to hurt the feelings of others, it becomes sinful.

This is where the second law of a given relationship vividly comes out: "The law of harvest" - Whatever you sow in relationship is what you get, consciously or unconsciously. According to Innocent Onuoha of Obetiti Nguru in his Family instruction of March 9, 2009, he stated: "He is never happy who hates" because he or she has nothing pleasurable to share with others. Fr. Joseph Pellegrino seems to be supporting Onuoha when he remarks: "When we allow ourselves to be so overcome by hurt and hatred that we refuse to (love and forgive-mine) extend the healing hand of the Lord to others, we take upon ourselves the sickness of the other person. Hatred kills. When we allow hatred to be part of our lives, we commit suicide" (IR, 2/15/09) and face eternal judgment. The above assertion is in line with our position in this book. Forgiveness is about us, and not the other person. Our lives are about us just as we are our relationships. Forgiveness and un-forgiveness in relationships need maintenance. For instance, if I know I have hurt somebody and I don't forgive, the punishment is mine and not that person's. Most often we carry heavy and depressing grudges against people who mean well for us and at times they are not even aware of our headaches, heartaches and burdens. In this instance, MacNutt Francis lamented:

> *When I think of how much junk and chaos was inside me;*
> *I was weighed down by my sins and ready to blow my mind*
> *away... The hypocrisy of my life was getting to me---smiling*
> *on the outside, pretending that everything was O.K., while*
> *deep inside I was hurting (1992:224).*

We must not give the devil any position in our relationship. Naturally, we tend to draw conclusions of others' behaviors from our sense perceptions because we are so shortsighted to see beyond our own limitations. Mere sense knowledge should not be the basis for healthy relationships. A sound reasoning that is positively controlled and channeled in the right direction is indispensable. We said it already, the greatest and precious gifts we can give others are our forgiving hearts, listening ears and our readiness to be reflected and represented in our gifts.

e. Joyful noise: Appreciating relationships in music

The Christian Bible is explicit on the need to make a joyful noise or use of music in human relationships. The Psalmist remarkably made the following remarks: "Come, let us praise Yahweh joyfully, acclaiming the Rock of our safety; let us come into his presence with thanksgiving, acclaiming him with music (Ps. 95:1-2; 100). This "coming together" primarily pertains to our relationships. We acknowledge our presence to each other before we extend same to God. In one of his quotes, a German novelist, Auerback, B noted: "Music washes away from the soul the dust of everyday life" (1812-1882). In music, the dust of anger, hatred and unforgiving hearts disappear. We can understand why St. Augustine once noted: "He who sings once, prays twice" because, singing publicly and immediately attracts both human and the divine. The importance of music in human relationships cannot be overlooked. Music is an indispensable echo of joy and gratitude that is dramatized in human actions. "In other words" according to Rev. William G. Lamont in his 'Hidenwood': *Let us Worship*, observed: "The hymns we offer up to God are actually musical prayers or upbeat hymns" (IR). The differences in music tastes should not constitute obstacles in our relationships. Rather, they should lead us to accept our differences and each other. According to Sidonie Gabrielle quotes: "Music is love in search of a word". For instance, when one prefers a Pop music to Classical or vice versa, it is a declaration of one's innermost heart, love and joy, which one invites others to share. We must always allow our partners enjoy their own taste of music.

Daily experiences show that individual styles of music build relationships beyond the limits of physical contact. Music, at times, spiritually carries with it some unworldly tones and voices. Personally, I would not have loved music if I had not perceived therein some spiritual connections that are beyond human imaginations and interpretations. Human ears hear some musical instruments but some cannot exactly be represented in words. They directly invite the soul to timeless jubilations. Hardly does any music intend to hurt others. For instance, whenever a person feels disgusted to watch his or her partner dance or smile, it clearly indicates a red flag of a relationship that is on the verge of collapsing. However, some people are not lovers of music and should accordingly be respected and not feared. In a practical sense, "Music produces a kind of pleasure which human nature cannot do without" (551-479BC). I recommend that partners momentarily withhold the play of music when there are burning issues to be settled in the house or one partner is in great pain. In this light, one of Serqei Rachmaninov quotes noted: "Music is enough for a lifetime, but a lifetime is not enough for music" (IR). Even as one takes one's last breath, music has the capacity to accompany and introduce one to the world of spirits. Music is therapeutic, medicinal, healing, inclusive, friendly and trans-cultural. Most often, according to a French Romantic Poet, Hugo V: "Music expresses that which cannot be put into words and cannot remain silent" (1802-1885). No wonder then Monet held: "Those who danced were thought to be quite insane by those who could not hear the music" (Ibid. IR).

Music is divine and boundless - It hears all languages and has no enemy

Music soothes the mind and heals the heart of all infirmities and hatred. In the words of American Editor, Edgar Watson: "When people hear good music, it makes them homesick for something they never had, and never will have" (1853-1937). This does not mean that some people cannot thrive in their relationship without music. It hears all languages and magically challenges its hearers with a common knowledge of oneness, love and unity. The deaf also enjoy bodily movements of music and dancers. When music is at the foundation of relationship, it becomes life itself. In support of the irreversible nature of music in human life, a German Philosopher remarked: "Without music life would be an error" (1844 -1900). On the same par, an ancient Greek Philosopher said: "Music is a moral law. It gives soul to the universe, wings to the mind, flight to the imagination, and charm and gaiety to life and to everything" (428BC-348BC). Musical sound goes beyond physical appearances to the deepest depth of human consciousness. It is an inevitable call to order and wonder. Music revolutionizes, creates and recreates. As a Musician, I wholeheartedly share the view of E. Y. Harburg that: "Words make you think a thought. Music makes you feel a feeling. A song makes you feel a thought" (1896-1981).

Undoubtedly, most people are unconsciously addicted to music because of the joy it brings to their souls. For instance, the excitements that accompany the commencement of music are practical examples of its formidable and transforming nature. Peoples' reactions when a famous musician dies are equally expressions of solidarity with music in general and evident; not only of the power of music but also the healthiest, glorious and joyful relationships music could build among people of all nationalities. The issue of music is not about a musician, but the relationship he or she has built in the music world and industry. It is amazing to see how God could use an individual talent in music, celebrities, and sports to bring humanity together in a remarkable and lasting relationship. The magic of music lies on the fact that, in it, ethnic, religious, political, language barriers are instantly healed, giving birth to love, peace and unity. It is divine and boundless. In music, there are no differences between ugliness and beauty, sinners and the righteous. Its unifying effect is enormous and eternal.

f. Conscious reflected actions: Mindfulness practice [Conscience]

Relationships demand self-consciousness and reflection. Can there be any human relationship without moral obligations? This is where human conscience plays an important role in building healthy relationship. As it were, the pattern of life we lead announces to us the worth and meaning of our actions. No action or decision is taken in a vacuum, unless it is in the case of a psychotic or akratic person. Even at that, there is reason for anti-social disorders. Most often, as Burdette observed: "It is not the experience of today that drives men mad. It is the remorse for something that happened yesterday" (1997:147). Every kind of decision to act or not, to relate with Mr. A or B, is made under the patronage of an active principle of the soul. And "each of us, according to Neiberg in Doniger carries within him a definition of those laws (principles-mine) that are good and those laws that are bad" (1967:16). For instance, in the face of two alternatives, either to continue or discontinue a particular relationship, this active principle guides us to select the one that is in conformity with the created order, moral and natural law. This "awareness" by which we judge our decisions and actions to face the challenges in relationships has attracted the attention of various fields of study - theology, philosophy and psychology et cetera. Unanimously, these disciplines describe this awareness or self-consciousness as conscience. This "internal awareness or conscientia" is as old as humanity itself. According to Soloveychik: "As language, conscience is individual in each person and it is common to all" (IFE, 2007). In other words, we are our own consciences, the way we act, evaluate, react and relate to others.

Therefore, we extensively studied this inherent and essential part of the individual person, his or her conscience. Renard H expressed it as "an act by which we apply our knowledge of the moral principles in the practical intellect to what we do, did in the past or will do in future" (1948:132). These unique human quality and facts, as stated above, are based on the premise that every human being has knowledge of these moral principles, which guide relationships. For instance, any human being who is not guided by moral obligations and principles is more of a wild animal. Conscience makes humans different from brute animals. This makes the study of conscience expedient in this book. Today, a moral principle may say: "Do not kill or tell lies against the other". Undeniably some people kill and tell lies against others because they lack self-conscious consideration in their actions, organizations, schools, and families and thereby exhibit animalistic and frustrating aspects of human relationships.

What happens - when the good behavior we expect from others turns otherwise or in a relationship where nobody takes any responsibility?

Eventually, the need to understand why people behave differently from a universally accepted moral or natural law that guides society becomes urgent and timely. Any human relationship that is not in conformity with the moral, eternal, positive and natural laws must be misleading and dangerous. For instance, can man or woman be human if he or she has no conscience or moral obligation of any sort? Any relationship, ministry, company, organization, establishment that has no moral order normally collapses. That is to say, what could have become the consequences of relationships or society where the parties and inhabitants have no obligation and moral principles guiding them? Is it feasible to have such a relationship or society where nobody takes responsibility for his or her actions? This is why our schools, individuals and society need spiritual psychology today more than anything else. This has to do with our behaviors and their implications in our lives and those around us. Each person precisely behaves true to type. The term "type" is used to identify a certain collection of traits "characteristic pattern of behavior or conscious motive which can be self-assessed or assessed by peers that make up a broad, general personality classification" (Sonderegger, 1998:124). It is natural. This "true to type" culturally and emotionally makes a world of difference in our behaviors, opinions, and the ways we understand, perceive and relate with others. A partner who fails to take note of this human quality has something up his or her sleeves.

Generally, there should be a consensus of opinions regarding certain behaviors and mannerisms that identify, define and characterize a human society as different from that of other animals. There is a difference between "actus humanus" - human act and "actus humanis"- act of man, typical of brutes. Thus, our studies and presentations of conscience here become compulsory for each person, because, as I indicated it in one of my books: "The very thing or behavior a person may hate in others may be in him or her" (2001: 12-13). As noted already, both our physical and spiritual worlds are different. Getting offended or angry over other peoples' attitudes may not change their situation rather it compels us to "an inward process' of self-examination to change our own perceptions that may be creating those some-what nasty differences. Put differently, what happens when the good behavior we expect from others in relationships turns out otherwise? In situations like this, flexibility is unavoidable.

It is necessary that people cautiously behave the way they are. We can now appreciate why Sigmund Freud made this remark: "Conscience requires the capacity to see ourselves from the point of view of another person, ourselves and some others as being in social relationship and between…nature as a whole" (IFE). Therefore, it is a sine qua non for us to note that we share certain basic and fundamental values together, even when we disagree, especially today that technology seems to have made the world a family. We have to live and interact within a given community; call it the Church, public offices, school and belief systems, the governments, sports, ideological values and our family circles. Barack Obama, the President of the United States of America, in his address at the University of Notre Dame remarked:

> *We must find a way to live together as one human family,*
> *in the spirit of the Gospel until we touch each other's hearts.*
> *Each of us is called to love, serve and stand as lighthouse,*
> *aiming at the law that binds all people irrespective of religious*
> *affiliations, gender, color and race et cetera (5/17/09).*

In the words of the Catholic Bishop's Conference of Nigeria (CBCN): "Community life means, not merely living physically together, but sharing on the spiritual, pastoral, and human levels" (21, EIA, No. 97). These human levels may include unity in diversity, our failures and progresses. Imperatively, it becomes inevitable and urgent to investigate the various and possible ways of bringing common understanding in our relationships and among nations and cultures of the world.

g. Belief: Levels of convictions - better be alone than forgotten or die relating

Relationship demands certain faith levels as we noted in the introduction of this book. We have to believe in our relationships. The faith and trust we employ in any relationship cannot go beyond the level of our convictions. For instance, if a woman believes that her alcoholic husband can change one day, she patiently follows him in that spirit, tolerating him with a firm belief that nothing is permanent under the sun. If the man dies drinking, the wife must have done her best and goes ahead to accord him a burial befitting for a drunkard. One can be addicted to a habit, favorable or unfavorable, but to become a slave to one's own choice is idiotic and silly. We either, believe in others and relate with them or we do not. The thought of being successful in life, rich and having friendships, competition, anger, rivalry or enemy, et cetera, are meaningless when we do not have relationship and people to challenge and evaluate us in the process.

A person can only be rich in the midst of poor people. Practical life events and challenges shape most of our decisions and actions. To be happy is to do things right. To be safe is to avoid trouble. To live is to die to sins and unhealthy attitudes. To learn is to avoid ignorance. To succeed is to work hard. Therefore, to relate is to sacrifice part of self. In a nutshell, relationship is the basis for industry, progress and organizations. It sets the standard for measuring success rates, accomplishments, achievements and rewards. Relationship must anchor on something that gives hope and joy at the same time. Eventually, this compels us to weigh the implications of Benson's words in the following statements:

> *More and more, I became convinced that our bodies are wired to benefit from exercising not only our muscles but our rich inner, human core - our beliefs, values, thoughts and feelings …again and again, my patients' progress and recoveries often seemed to hinge upon their spirit and will to live…and the beliefs we so often associate with the human soul-had physical manifestations (1997:17).*

These "our rich inner, human core - our beliefs, values… spirit and will to live" can invariably be concretized in human relationships. They are indispensable assets for keeping our relationships alive. This spirit or belief, which does not easily affect a person's relationship with others despite internal and external pressures, is what Benson calls "remembered wellness". Basically, every human being should discover and cultivate this 'remembered wellness' or something in his or her relationship that goes beyond the ephemeral and transient world of matter. As such, relationships can still grow stronger and stronger even when the parties are physically incapacitated due to sickness or death. Moreover, relationship is not limited by age as already noted. It is like an old book with old ideas that remain relevant and valid for ages.

Similarly, it is possible for a person to be alone and actively engaged in relationship. Preferably, it is better to be alone than forgotten in relationship. Somebody can be alone in relationship for a lot of reasons, situational, psychological and circumstantial. According to the *AudioEnglish.net, Online Dictionary,* loneliness (noun) has three senses:

> ➢ The state of being alone in solitary isolation
> ➢ Sadness resulting from being forsaken or abandoned
> ➢ A disposition toward being alone.

The question that faces us at this point is whether it is better to be alone than languish in relationship? This, again, boils down to the issue of commitment and non-commitment in relationships. Being alone and loneliness are two different realities and exits from healthy relationships. Physically, it is possible for a person to be present in a relationship, crowded audience or company and still remains alone because of lack of attentive listening partner or personal reasons. Loneliness in this context can be a conscious activity. Most people experience this in their relationships. Relationship has to be communicated and shared.

Put differently, some people have physically been lonely in their relationships because of greedy and selfish partners. Even if a person has a large family, as long as he or she has no one to listen to him or her, care for the ways he or she feels or someone to confide in, he or she is lonely. The above situations summarize the state and condition in which a person is said to be lonely but not alone. That is to say, a person can actually have a partner and at the same time remain lonely due to his or her self-centeredness and busy schedules. Wikipedia observes: "Loneliness is an emotional state in which a person experiences a powerful feeling of emptiness and isolation - a feeling of being cut off, disconnected and alienated from other people in which having meaningful human contact is impossible" (IFE). To avoid loneliness, people can decide to be alone as their own choice. Generally, such choices often destabilize progress in society and interpersonal relationships. Therefore, spiritual psychology encourages people to fully enjoy their lives as a community of rational beings. We need to come together because loneliness is anti-natural. For instance, an orphan amidst family members still experiences loneliness due to his or her disconnection from parental warmth and company. That is normal, but hard, because blood is always thicker than water.

On a different note, V. Pomnyun Publisher observes that: "It is not because we are alone that we are lonely, but rather, it is because we are wrapped up in the thought of being alone" (IR, 2009). For Pomnyum, loneliness does not exist. He emphatically observed:

> *People assume that being lonely means that each of us is alone, but that cannot be. The saying: "I am alone" signifies that we are consumed by the illusion of being alone. If we let go of these illusions and understand that all things are interconnected, not even being alone in a field can stop us from dancing or taking delight in nature (IR).*

The Ven Pomnyun Publisher has presented a beautiful analysis and picture of what being alone means in her understanding. I am positive that a lot of people buy these ideas that, as long as all things are interconnected, it is hard for some people to practically experience loneliness in their relationships. Moreover, that something is beautiful or sounds objective does not make it relevant. Life is larger than logic and every life experience is unique and teaches something new. By juxtaposing V. Pomnyun's notion of loneliness and the main thrust of spiritual psychology, we may land at something that is entirely different from our focus. This book is concerned, not so much with what brings people to lonely states of life as how those already condemned to loneliness due to individual differences and selfishness can eventually come together. It is sickness to be lonely or in the state of solitude for no justifiable reasons. While I agree with Ven Pomnyun Publisher that humanity is biologically interconnected in various ways, I do not believe or agree that "to be alone" or that "loneliness" is an illusion. The scenario Ven Pomnyun has presented here is misleading, especially when we analyze and take a closer or second view on these words: "…. not even being alone in a field can stop us from dancing or taking delight in nature". If we were to pause for a moment and re-examine the above statement, the following concerns and questions will necessarily emerge:

1. Do such sayings of Ven Pomnyun suggest a dream world where everything is okay with everybody, when in actual fact; people physically experience excruciating pains in their relationships due to loneliness? How did we come to the picture of the imaginary field mentioned here in the first place, was it voluntary or under duress? Loneliness is real. Situations in which people are alone abound in thousands. To be alone or loneliness is neither an illusion nor a fantasy.

2. Again, of what reasons should our situation in such an unclassified imaginary field warrant or lead us into dancing and taking delight in nature? What image does the field stand for in Ven Pomnyun's view?

3. Besides, what could "dancing or taking delight in nature" mean in Ven Pomnyun's understanding when the person or people pictured at the field appear to be held in bondage? Naturally, people do not; because they are alone or lonely begin to dance. Loneliness or being alone, whether it is by choice or forced, has never been associated with a sense of great joy and merriment, unless it is a personal choice. Even, at that, something is wrong somewhere.

4. Therefore, the mere fact that we are pictured alone in a field, not to meditate and reflect on our broken relationships but just to dance and take delight in nature, for no other specific purpose, contradicts the very idea of interconnectedness with the rest of humanity. Also, the images of 'dancing and taking delight in nature' are phenomenal. These are physical realities that characterize individual behaviors. Yet, there are people who do not like to dance. In other words, whether one chooses to dance or not, take delight in nature or not, is irrelevant here. Importantly, individuals decide and choose to be alone and dance and these activities are not brought about by any illusions? There are various levels of loneliness people pass through in their relationships.

Most often, being alone and loneliness are dispositions of the mind that are practically translated in concrete human situations and not fallacious images or illusions as Ven Pomnyun would want us to believe. At times, they are physical. None of them encourages healthy relationships. In the final analysis, they are obstacles to interpersonal relationships and have torn society apart today.

Besides, some people choose to be alone or 'lonely' due to atrocious behaviors, religious reasons, idleness, laziness, sickness and the unwillingness to share with other people. When 'being alone' or 'loneliness' is necessitated by unavoidable circumstances, it remains compatible with relationships. Being alone and loneliness, whether they are physical, emotional, a decision or choice affects relationships in noticeable ways. But Ven Pomnyun specifically seems to be referring to loneliness or being alone as an object of the mind or a fictio mentis, that has no foundation in reality. Many people prefer to be alone or relate only to themselves not for delusional reasons or illusions, but "as a way of life" in Dumm's view (2008).

Being alone, when viewed from the perspective of choice and decision takes us back to the need for healthy relationships. Each person shares in one relationship or the other. Like Ven Pomnyun's view, even when we are alone or isolated from the physical world, we are still conscious of and related to others and ourselves in certain degrees. Unlike Ven's view, the state of being alone or lonely whether it is sad or joyous is a cognitive activity. We meaningfully and consciously relate to ourselves first and then to our environments, which equally play active roles in our overall relationships. For instance, one's first charity, concern, love, forgiveness et cetera should be given to oneself before it reaches out to others. In the same plight, we should claim responsibility for the first misunderstanding that springs from our relationships before we accuse others. That is the only way we can naturally succeed in relating with others amidst confusions, misconducts and suspicions that are unexpectedly bound to happen.

In order to maintain bounds in relationships, it is important each person takes note of a few categories. There is a popular aphorism among the Igbo of Nigeria that says: "Every shoe has its own size". Birds of the same feather flock together. In other words, there are levels in relationships. Each person knows with whom to relate. For instance, that an idiot dresses like and claims to be a Professor or an Engineer does not make him one. Life is metrically ordered in a way that every living being directly or indirectly, conscious or unconsciously relates to its own level and kind. Just as human beings have their specific modes of operation, *modi operandi*, communications and relationships, so do other living creatures. As far as each being is part and parcel of the created order, all living things enjoy a symbiotic relationship for mutual benefits. This undeniable fact does not mean that other living beings like animals relate to humans on equal level. Human relationship is the yardstick, apogee, summary description and high water mark of all relationships. Relationships exist, not only, in human circles, families, and clubs, Churches, marriages, on professional levels, among friends, academic, corporate, personal et cetera, but also in animal kingdoms, sexual levels and among all living things. The interrelatedness and connectedness of relationships are unique and phenomenal. The need for each other in relationships goes a long way to evaluate our progresses and failures as rational beings. Having discussed some of the images of human relationships, its differences from those of other creatures, it becomes important to study, at length, that essential aspect of a person that greatly influences and makes his or her actions and relationships meaningful as a rational being.

B. The role of conscience in human relationships:

Every person is his or her own conscience as we noted earlier on. Our studies on conscience reveal that man is principally a moral and rational being. A deviation from this natural state devalues the dignity of the human person as a rational being as such. Unavoidably human conscience is the individual playing vital roles in his or her relationship. It is synonymous with the human agent who decides and acts on the basis of his or her choices. The usefulness and importance of conscience lie in its ability to guide relationships. By the time we examine the various kinds of conscience and their relevance, we would have come to the conclusion that there is healthy relationship in some quarters today because some people identify and obey their consciences. The individual's judgment of conscience, to a great extent, is responsible for the shape and nature of the relationship he or she keeps. Fundamentally speaking, conscience marks us out from the rest of all other living beings. It is typically human and not predicated to brute animals. Few questions may arise here. What is brutal about a pet that loves unconditionally and a human being that deceives his or her partner? Why are some pets like dogs and cats more reliable in relationships than 'human beings'? Events occur in which dogs, for instance, save their owners and run errands for them. It is always easy to notice when these pets are angry and the best ways to respond to them. On the contrary, some people appear saintly with evil intentions in their minds and kill those who trust them as their best friends.

Pets are not created in Gods' image. Yet, their behaviors instinctively seem to outweigh those of some human beings in many steps. For instance, on Thursday, September 10, 2009, in New York City, I saw a dog owner order her dog to pray, and instantly, the dog stooping, joined its hands together and raised them up. It baffled me to watch a dog behave in a disciplinary, convincing manner and responded to a universal need for prayer while most humans do not have the word "prayer" in their vocabulary. Wild animals move as herds to protect themselves against predators but most humans choose to move alone. Certain animals are more intelligent than some humans. They only lack rationality. Could God have made animals in place of human beings to ensure peace, unity and healthy relationships on earth? Of what use are such human values as reason, intelligence and conscience any more? Despite the fact that many pets love their owners, in the animal kingdom, there is still chaos and madness just as in ours. That is to say, in society we also have many honest and good-spirited people in their relationships. Relationships are about the individuals who conscientiously share their feelings and values together. The application of conscience in whatever we do is imperative. One may, at this point, ask: "What is conscience?"

The term "conscience" is certainly an undeniable and inevitable fact in human nature and moral life. Though, it is frequently used in everyday language, a thorough elucidation of its true meaning is important for sincere and healthy relationships. In fact, the issue of conscience is as old as humanity itself. It is never procured in advance, but assumes an independent role as soon as one becomes aware of one's differences in life. Two famous psychologists, Hilgard and Atkinson support this view in these words:

*As a child comes to seek approval and to avoid disapproval,
he begins to see himself as a responsible agent. He develops a
conscience whereby he judges his own conduct according to
the ideas he has acquired (1967: 645).*

In this capacity, the environment in which a child grows has much
influence in the formation of his or her conscience and the nature of
relationships he or she might likely keep. This is because conscience
always refers to the attitudinal displays of a common knowledge of
reality and moral order to individual deeds. According to Whewell:
"As science means knowledge, conscience etymologically means self-
knowledge…It is the reason employed about questions of right and
wrong, and accompanied with the sentiments of approbation and
condemnation" (IR, 2007). By implication, any relationship that is
built on deception and immoral practices easily backfires. Truthfulness
and honesty are basic ingredients and values of life and must form the
basis of all healthy relationships. These values place us apart from other
animals but not when we behave like them, yelling and calling names.

Rational beings do not need to belong to any faith Tradition, religion
or Church to imbibe and practice moral values in their lives. The
truth that is naturally told lasts for a moment but the truth that is
discovered significantly remains forever. For instance, if Mr. or Mrs.
B has told his or her partner that he or she was gay or lesbian, they
would have figured out a way to easily deal with it. That, this truth
or fact was revealed to them from an outsider is going to affect their
relationship for life. Conscience assists individuals to discover the truth
of their lives and make amends. For instance, when a drunkard realizes
and discovers the damage he or she has done to his or her life and
quits excessive drinking, this truth forms part of his or her growing
edges. At this axis or liminal stage of bad character formation, he or
she may not remember the useful advices given him or her by friends
and acquaintances. The reality of conscience is always self-explanatory
in accord with the ideas one has acquired which may be in direct
conflict with the universal or particular moral standards. As it were,
any conflicting ideas that are not straightened on time, adversely affects
relationships. That means we must fix our shoes to avoid stepping on the
toes of other people. According to Bourke: "Only the individual agent

is capable of knowing his own intentions, the peculiar circumstances of his particular actions... no other human being can do this for the moral agent" (1951:197). To always expect what we need and how we want it in relationship naturally constitutes serious obstacles in relationships.

The manifestation and application of conscience in every moral decision is explicitly personal. No wonder, Wikipedia, Internet Free Encyclopedia - Internet Resources on conscience observed: "Conscience can prompt different people in quite different directions depending on their beliefs". This boils down to our earlier assertion that every person behaves true to type due mainly to his or her personality traits and developments. Despite the efforts partners make on personal levels, there is no uniformity of judgments, decisions and actions in human nature and relationships. In the Heraclitian and Tillichian paradoxical co-existence of the good and evil, there is always a "despite of or a probability" that generally guides human relationships in the right direction. As a consequence, different people perceive conscience to mean one or all of the following:

- ❖ The silent voice of God or Gods' presence in a person,
- ❖ The voice of the soul
- ❖ An individual silent adviser and companion,
- ❖ That still small controlling voice,
- ❖ Moral faculty, perfect interpreter of life
- ❖ Inward power or the voice within,
- ❖ Moral sense, a good whisperer
- ❖ Spiritual life alert,
- ❖ The real person
- ❖ Virtue,
- ❖ Independent fearless judge,
- ❖ A cultural stamp in the heart of every person,
- ❖ The most secret core and sanctuary of man and woman,
- ❖ Self-knowledge
- ❖ Seat of consciousness and wisdom,
- ❖ Synderesis, et cetera.

Any person who lacks one of these fundamental values has a serious problem in his or her life. Conscience is not only a private affair of an individual person but also a public and socially relevant phenomenon in human interactions and relationships. That is why; as we guide the effects of our behaviors on others we must curiously examine the feedback we receive from them. As Swani observed, conscience is:

> *Light of the soul that burns within the chambers of your heart…voice of the self which says "yes" or "no" when you are involved in a moral struggle. It is a call from within to do an act or to avoid it. It is the internal monitor…a form of truth, which is the knowledge of our own acts and feelings as right or wrong. It is the sensitive balance (scales) to weigh actions. As a silent teacher, it is the soundless inner voice that shows you the path of virtue and godliness. It is above reason and discussion. It is sudden, dictatory command to plunge deep into the depths of virtue, or rise high above the levels of vice. It is a needle that points steadily to the Pole Star "Do this action, it is right" or "Avoid this action, it is wrong" (IR, 2008).*

Adhering to one's soundless inner voice and weighing the consequences of one's actions, can go a long way to assist individuals build, maintain healthy relationships and college students to choose wisely. This is an application of one's emotional intelligence. For instance, if a person knows what annoys his or her partner, he or she is bound to avoid doing it. Again, if the college student knows that failing his or her exams will not lead to his or her life aspirations, then, he or she is challenged to work hard and avoid distractions. In the words of Mackenzie, conscience is "a feeling of pain accompanying and resulting from our non-conformity to principles" (3rd ed., Bk. 111, Ch. 1, Sect. 14). The Catechism of the Catholic Church presents conscience as: "A judgment of reason whereby the human person recognizes the moral quality of a concrete act he is going to perform, is in the process of performing, or has already completed" (CCC, 1778). It is a fact seriously reckoned with in every social life and an irreplaceable factor in human relationship. Murray expressed the view, thus: "None will deny that conscience is ever present and always legislating for us, blaming us, approving us. It fears nothing from us, and delivers its judgment unsympathetically, we may disobey it, but we know that we ought not to do so" (1960:392).

Etymologically, the word conscience is Latin, a transliteration of the word "conscientia" used in the Vulgate as the translation of the Greek word, "Synderesis". But, the New Bible Dictionary noted: "The Old Testament has no word for conscience...calls it "Synderesis" (2nd Ed. 1992:226). It is derived from the Latin verb root 'SCIRE' meaning "to know". And when 'Scire' and 'con' are joined or put together, they give conscientia, which means awareness, a sense of discernment. To lack conscience is to lack knowledge. Therefore, any human knowledge that excludes conscience is disastrous. The Scholastics appropriate synderesis to mean "the general moral principle or primarily moral truth, which demands no process of reasoning or efforts of the intellect or mind to recognize them". Synderesis is "an innate awareness of good and evil that cannot be mistaken" (Aquinas, IR. 2009). Yet most humans, especially the young ones and some politicians, seem to ignore and pretend as if to say it is not there. To shun conscience is to invite indiscipline and to be disciplined is to be orderly.

Therefore conscience becomes the conclusion from premises ultimately derived from this Synderesis or knowledge of the general moral principles. For instance, a partner in business or marriage does not need to be told that cheating, carelessness, grouchy countenance can always constitute squabbles in their relationships. Not many people consciously hate themselves. As such, what the broad metaphysical principles of contradiction, sufficient reason and causality are to theoretical, speculative judgment and reasoning, the principles of synderesis such as "do as you would be done by", are to practical moral reasoning. For instance, to preserve the dignity of human life is generally a metaphysical principle and value which some people, mainly, teenage boys and girls may or may not adhere to. Practically, in human relationships, conscience constantly reminds individuals of their moral obligations in respecting each other's values and boundaries. This confirms that relationships are more of deeds than words. Again, the English Language translates synderesis as conscience, a guide to future actions. Any relationship that is devoid of this self-knowledge of moral principles and practical moral reasoning is bound to fail.

On a different note, every culture has its own name for the word conscience. For instance, it sounds so interesting that the Igbo of Nigeria that prominently featured in our statement of problem do not actually have a word that corresponds to the English translation of "conscience". However, the people have a general Igbo usage "*Ako N'Uche*", meaning wisdom and intellect or simply put, 'the marriage of wisdom and reason for any course of action'. They use different expressions, idioms, and proverbs to describe various situations and instances where a person makes or fails to make use of his or her conscience or out of alignment with the moral and created order. It is vital to note that every reasonable human behavior should be guided by certain degree of wisdom and rationality. Therefore, the word "conscience" as studied and presented in this book, enjoys a wide panorama of meanings among different cultures, especially the Igbo of Nigeria where their socio-religious lives are highly interwoven with practical moral principles. Conscience is not utilized by definition but in action and good example.

As a universal value, there are few definitions of conscience as there are individual actions and relationships. Conscience is central in the study and practice of spiritual psychology. In human activities and relationships, conscience can be approached from various perspectives, religious, cultural, philosophical and secular. The importance of this value is generally studied in all fields of human knowledge, anthropological, cultural, socio-religious, philosophical, ethical, psychological, scientific et cetera. However, in this survey, we studied conscience in spiritual psychology not only as an essential asset in achieving healthy human relationships but as man or woman, him or herself. We did so from the following perspectives:

1. Theological Perspective:

In the Scriptures, conscience is perceived as the voice of God speaking within an individual. This is the voice that peacefully restrains, encourages and guides interpersonal relationships. In this light, the Second Vatican Council presents conscience as "the most secret core and sanctuary of man. There, he is alone with God, whose voice echoes in his depths" (GS, no. 16). In St. Paul's words: "You must obey, therefore, not because you are afraid of being punished, but also for conscience's sake" (Rom. 13:5). Obeying the law to avoid punishment contradicts the basis of human integrity and rationality.

That is why the Psalmist calls conscience "blameless heart" (Ps. 101:2). We obey the laws, respect each other and morally aim at the best, not to satisfy the government or religious faith Tradition, but as living true to type, rational beings, and the individual differences notwithstanding.

However, the theological perspective involves the religious, ethics, science of morality, and 'psychology' as powerful ways of guiding human relationships. In this light, spiritual psychology challenges society for a big change that encourages practical and positive moral reasoning and life. The best way to get started is by 'cultivating blameless' hearts in one's cultures, attitudes, utterances, prudential judgments and relationships.

2. Cultural perspective:

Conscience, as a cultural phenomenon, is a kind of indelible mark and stamp on the personality of the members of society that no one can escape. The perspective thus presented here is best understood in the context of collectivistic and multicultural environments. Definitely, cultural stamps and maps affect individual relationships. It "originates" according to Freud, "in the superego, taking its cue from our parents during childhood" (IR, 2007). To the fundamental concern, "Need man or woman be reasonably so if he or she has no conscience?" Haring promptly responds in these words: "Nobody would like to be labeled as being unscrupulous or without conscience, because all kinds of decision (even in relationships – mine) are made in the name and under the patronage of conscience" (1964: 92), including the decisions to live or die.

3. Philosophical perspective:

Broadly speaking, philosophy (Philos + Sophia – love of wisdom) incorporates practically all branches of human knowledge, ethics, psychology, anthropology, religion, theology et cetera. All the same, our main concern in studying conscience within the context of philosophy is to appreciate the tremendous impacts it has on individual relationships. We shall do so in the following order:

i. Gnoseology:

This is the science of knowledge in general. It states that man possesses some knowledge of the natural law and moral principles. Each rational person applies this knowledge of moral principles, reasoning and judgment to his or her own particular actions and relationships. The principal agent equally judges the implication which his or her actions [wrongness and rightness] have on others. At times, this is not always the case with those individuals who willfully violate the basic moral principles that guide society. In the same way, they create problems in their relationships. As Renard noted earlier, conscience is that very act (we do) by which each person applies his or her knowledge of the moral principles, (doing good is self-rewarding and doing bad damages), which are already in the practical intellect to what he or she does or did in the past or will do in future. It is "a faculty or moral sense that leads to feelings of remorse when we do things that go against moral values" or our relationships (IFE, 2007). Claiming ignorance of one's responsibilities is not only a sign of cowardice and weakness but also deception that generally affects interpersonal relationships.

ii. Ethics:

Ethics is particularly the science and study of morality. Morality is necessarily the basis for all human relationships. Etymologically, ethics is from the Greek word "ethike". It means that which concerns ethos. The plural form, "ta ethea" was found in the works of Homer, translated as "the abode or habitual places for animals, or a place of pasture... but in the works of Hesoid, ethos designates the dwelling place and habitation of men, (Ekennia, N. Justin, 2003:1). Undoubtedly, this "dwelling place and habitation of men" implies a state and condition for possible human relationships. Today this concept "ethos" has undergone some transformations, from the basic sense of a dwelling place to designate the actual involvement of a human being at home in certain situations. In other words, ethos points to the way and manner in which individuals can relate or be at home with one another and in the world. In a sense, 'being at home in the world' entails a permanent condition that relaxingly guarantees the person's safety, peace of mind and progress. This is what relationship is all about, a state of openness, peace, trust and harmony. Relationship is to be at home with the other.

Consequently, the safest way individuals can be at home in their relationships or in the world is by consciously obeying their consciences. These are the inner guiding principles each person has towards him or herself, others and the world. Untill society, especially our young children, comes to terms with the reality and value of conscience, cases of indiscipline, social and domestic violence will never stop. Therefore, ethos, ethics or habit (conscience) means the way each person acts and conducts him or herself before other people. It is the science and knowledge of that quality in human behavior by which an act is said to be right or wrong. Thus, "if any detail of thought has a vital bearing on man's destiny or helps to shape his life, that detail of thought is suggested by ethics, and morality is that study" (Owen, 1928:1). Ethics is a branch of philosophy that studies the principles of right and wrong in human conduct. On the other hand, conscience is that silent voice that urges us to accomplish whatever is good and true in our relationships and to avoid evil. Systematically, it studies and analyzes all we ought to do and how we ought to do them. One of the modern philosophers and theologians, Pope John Paul 11, defined ethics as:

> *The science of human actions from the point of their moral value, of the good or evil contained in them. Every human action involves a particular lived experience that goes by the name ethical experience... This whole lived experience has a thoroughly empirical character...(Wojtyla's Lectures, 1993:23).*

Ethics is fundamentally normative in John Paul's philosophy. It is rooted in experience guided by healthy principles. As it were, healthy relationships are offshoots of lived experiences and practices. Ethics addresses people in their personal experiences for more fruitful and meaningful relationships. It equally helps them to avoid obstacles that create chaos in relationships. To banish personal experiences from ethical life or one's relationship for Aristotle, points to stripping it of its very essence. Aristotle believes that virtuous acts, not only, bring joy and happiness to the person, but also, are their own rewards. Any good work accomplished in relationship guarantees the joy that binds and keeps it healthy. No wonder, Thomas Aquinas, the disciple of Aristotle maintained that: "Nothing is in the intellect that was not first in the senses" [*Nihil est in intelletu quod non prius fuerit in sensu*]. That is, whatever junk or healthy food one buys at the supermarket is what one takes home. This is where spiritual psychology guides individuals to make the right choices in order to avoid blames and enjoy brighter future. This position is unique in spiritual psychology and important in all levels and types of human relationships because any spirituality that has no physical foundation is meaningless.

Unlike Aristotle and Thomas, Kant seems to have separated ethical experiences from the act or reduced ethics to rational agreement to norms. The implication seems to suggest that all forms of relationship have to be subjected to the book of law. That is, keeping healthy relationships becomes a way of fulfilling the law. Subjecting relationships to legal compliance and order is an admission that humanity has almost lost its rational capabilities and conscience. This ideology cannot lead to any healthy relationship. In such a situation, trusting one's neighbor in a given relationship serves as a condition to avoid violating or being punished by law instead of doing so as a way of life. Plato in his own position seems to have presented ethics outside the realm of human practice and management. In Tillichian analysis, the separation of reality from the physical world is an expression of one's disappointments in dealing with the moment.

Postponement, at times, is fear and laziness to face the challenges of the moment. The taste of the pudding is in the eating and that is how it works with relationships. Only the individual person understands the nature of his or her relationship. At times, we have the tendency to blame others based on our limited knowledge of the cause of their actions. Until the real story is told, which often is not, some may stop at nothing criticizing and blaming them. As earlier noted, it is not always proper to judge situations by the manners in which they are presented to us. Moreover, it is bad to speak of somebody you do not know or judge him or her based on what others told you. Each person knows him or herself better than any one else. There might be more facts that meet the eye. For instance, Ms. A. quarreled with her husband the previous night. In the following morning, because Mr. B. did not understand why the wife failed to respond to his greetings, left in anger and refused to return home that day.

The scenario just cited may sound nonsensical and funny. But, it is not. How could Mr. B draw conclusions from what happened the previous night to judge the present? This is the problem with many relationships. Mr. B. failed to give his wife the benefit of doubt or "the despite of" and probability that it was possible that his wife did not even see him at that moment or could be trying to deal with some other personal issues also. On the other hand, it was possible that Mr. B did not hear when his wife responded or was not expecting a greeting because of the magnitude of the misunderstanding. It was even possible that Mrs. B was figuring out the best way to approach her husband and say "sorry" for what transpired previously. Again, the human mind does not stay in the same state for a long time. Instead of Mr. B to calmly weigh the situation from a wider perspective, he jumped into conclusions that his wife was looking for more trouble. Such behaviors as that of Mr. B are akin to men and women who lack confidence in each other. These are also signs of insufficiencies in human personality developments. For instance, why couldn't Mr. B initiate a peace movement by greeting his wife the second time? Erratic decisions and judgments portray the animalistic tendencies in human nature that were never resolved through the reality principles. These, to a great extent, have ruined many relationships today.

We can now understand why Socrates, Plato, Aristotle and Kant hold that ethics involves a system of mental activities that aids man assess the degree of goodness or badness in any given situation. In Kant's own view, "conscience is autonomously supreme…. Every duty must be brought home to the individual by his own individual conscience" (The Catholic Ency., Vol. IV, 1908). In Singer and Kuhse's points of view, conscience is "essentially reflective, dealing with reason, giving solid justification for positions held" (1999 in 1997:63-89). Ethics provides the criteria for the formation and judgment of conscience and of knowing whether an action or judgment is right or wrong, morally good or morally bad in any given situation or relationship.

However, there is no consensus in ethics regarding these criteria because a variety of opinions exist regarding what constitutes morally right or wrong actions. That is to say, there are certain behaviors that are being celebrated in other countries like America as part of their culture that are taboos in other cultures like the Igbo of Nigeria and vice versa. In this understanding, that popular saying becomes necessary here: "When in Rome behave like the Romans". Universal ethics or bioethics significantly incorporates those principles, religious and traditional values that defend the dignity and sacredness of the human person, right and life. In this light, one may ask: What is morality then?

iii. Morality:

The word morality comes from the word 'mores' meaning morals and manner, which embody the principles of human conduct. Morality is the quality in human acts by which we say 'they are right or wrong, good or evil'. In judging the morality of any human action or relationship, we concentrate on the subjective peculiarities of the agent, and look at the act as conditioned by his background knowledge (gnoseological), emotional (psychological), stability, socio-religious (faith traditions) and other personal traits. Individuals need to know that circumstances can negatively affect their relationships, hence the need to understand and be ready to pardon.

Morality in its completeness is both subjective and objective. Ethics generally stresses the objective aspect of morality, [in Kant's view] as condition for society to live peacefully and avoid conflicts. Morality, on the other hand, points to the subjective phase of ethics, with emphasis on what has to be done to eradicate conflicts and bring peace among human relationships here and now. To this effect, Higgins noted that morality, which is synonymous with conscience, involves "all intellectual acts which discern the goodness or badness of a concrete act...the last practical judgment concerning the moral goodness or badness of a human act here and now to be performed" (1948:125).

Eventually, this awareness to conventionally apply moral principles in our individual decisions and behaviors is an indispensable condition for interpersonal relationships and co-existence. In effect, moral conscience considers the nature of moral obligations that bind on everybody. It analyzes and describes the values, obligations, finality and freedom of moral actions of the individual within any given society and relationships. This awareness of the obligation to do the good and avoid evil deeply points to the ability of the individual to weigh the consequences of his or her particular action. We call this 'intellectual or moral virtue' because it perfects the intellect to reason correctly about particular actions to be done or avoided. This "intellectual virtue" or emotional intelligence is highly recommended in relationships. Thus, conscience is a unique and practical judgment and the conclusions we arrive at, through the process of prudent reasoning concerning what is to be done here and now or to be avoided. This ability to reason correctly equips the individuals with those values they need in other to achieve harmony in their relationships. There is need to note that the "ability to reason correctly" at certain moments gets vitiated by circumstances and can adversely affect relationships as already noted.

The mind is a playground in which positive and negative thoughts interplay. Therefore, education of the mind is generally important. This eagerly assists and teaches individuals to pursue ideal perfections of citizenship and how to rightly relate well with others. For instance, human beings are essentially "moral agents" who have the capacity to meditate and differentiate between the good and the bad. Depriving children of this fundamental training and value equals to extinction of their healthy future. As moral beings, we have no option than to act accordingly, educate our children to apply right judgments in their decisions and choices. To deviate from this primary and natural state makes them and us incomplete human beings. For a government, especially run by Christians, to sign into law any bill that goes against morality is the highest display of disbelief in oneself and God. That a transient human government can rule against the permanent Government of Eternity, indicates the extent society has been messed up. The education of the mind involves the transmission and inculcation of values of right behaviors. The process, as such, will help to raise up generations of people who can always think for themselves, respect the views and feelings of others, live and relate as good citizens of society. As a medical professional, Benson puts it:

Learned in childhood, the act of pleasing others often has its own rewards, including health benefits, as is suggested by the word "placebo", from a Latin root meaning "I shall be pleasing or acceptable (1996:35).

Benson has noted a striking point here. Once relationships are built on the very act of making peace as a way of life and pleasing others and one's partner irrespective of the ways they take them, the one who is making the sacrifice will always be happier and healthier. Even though it is a big cross to continually please somebody who is not appreciative, I strongly believe that nemesis will always catch up with an ingrate. This is where we are challenged. If life is worth living, then, there is need to live it peacefully and happily.

iv. Psychology:

Psychology is also a branch of philosophy. Nonetheless, relationships are basically psychological in nature. The ways we feel and interact with one another determine the nature of our relationship. We do this in a variety of ways. Psychology "is a very diverse field because human behavior is highly varied." There are as many branches of psychology as there are human behaviors and interactions. Again, these diversities in human behavior cum their psychologies are big signals to prepare people to face the upheavals that might spring up in their relationships. For instance, if the traveler knew it was going to rain, he or she would have made provisions for an umbrella. Every relationship needs "this provisional umbrella" to avoid getting stuck or agitated should the unexpected and conventional rain falls.

Generally, psychology is all about human behaviors and it appears to be of two kinds: basic and applied. The applied type incorporates research within the areas of psychological practice. For Romero and Kemp, it refers to the use of "the knowledge derived from scientific psychology to change the world" and guide society as that of ours (2007:xxv-xxvi). This is basically the function of spiritual psychology, to bring a radical change in the negative ways of perceiving the world. Consequently, we appropriated psychology as the science, which studies consciousness and the behaviors (experiences) of people. For instance, daily experiences of life show that the knowledge of anything is accompanied by its own psychology and particular reaction.

v. Spiritual psychology (SP) and the marketing of religious practices in human relationship:

Spiritual psychology (SP) belongs to the category of psychological practice, which is an applied type. It concretely studies and examines the human person from the perspectives of his or her behaviors, actions, dynamics, characteristics, histories, relationships, belief systems, knowledge, educational aspirations, progresses, losses, fears and hopes et cetera and how these values holistically inform his or her life. What the human brain is to human cognitive activities and actions, spiritual psychology is to human social and moral consciousness and behaviors. As a social-religious and ethical oriented discipline, it is radical, confrontational, revolutionary, educative, transforming, informative and deeply aims at getting things right. It employs attentive listening technique as one of its basic tools.

SP is naturally analytic, interpretative, systematic, consistent, inductive and deductive, experiential, experimental, existential, practical, challenging, therapeutic [counseling], dialogical and inviting et cetera. In a nutshell, spiritual psychology is "man" – the special one, in his completeness, fearless of the uncertainties of nature, and with the optimism of the moment, faces the future with greater hopes, strides and fortitude. It incorporates both the basic and applied psychology in its pursuit for a holistic personality. In the field of basic psychology, spiritual psychology critically examines and utilizes the following values and areas culled from Romero and Kemp as noted here:

> Social psychology - the study of the effects of social interaction on behavior,
>
> Developmental psychology - the study of the changes in behavior due to age …
>
> personality psychology - study of individual differences in behavior…

psychology of consciousness - the study of our experiences of ourselves,

psychology of emotion - the study of the feelings that color our experience,

psychology of motivation - the study of why we do what we do, psychology of learning - study of how experience changes us to be more capable in the world,

psycholinguistics - study of how people communicate using language,

cognitive psychology - study of thinking. It is closely related to the study of the senses and of perceiving the world,

psychophysics - study of how the physical world creates the sensory world (2007:xxv).

However, besides the basic psychology, SP appropriates some applied research in psychology such as:

educational psychology - study of the psychology of teaching..

psychotherapy - study of ways of treating people with mental disorders ...

Health psychology - study of the interaction between behaviors and health and the areas of psychological practice that includes...

school psychologists - work in schools to help school children with behavioral problems and learning disabilities...

counseling psychologists – help people with difficulties in various areas of life, such as marriage, family and career (2007:xxvi).

Generally, basic knowledge of psychology is important in building healthy relationships. Practically speaking, there is nothing human beings do that is not psychological, including religious practices. There can be psychology without religion but it is inconceivable to practice religion without psychology. Therefore, due principally to the fact that religion claims to provide harmony, peace, love and salvation to the world, spiritual psychology is critically curious and anxious to examine and evaluate how far these claims are being justified. SP is not aimed at conversion, in favor of or against any religion. Rather it enjoins the human person to maximize all the various fields of his or her study, science, humanities and belief systems for the enhancement of his or her condition in general. Thus, the basic principle of spiritual psychology is: "The progress, peace and unity of the world begins from self".

While SP is not against any religion, or field of study, it is skeptical of those religious practices, sciences, mannerisms and studies that pose threat to the safety and peace of the human person. By "human person" in this context, SP refers to the person, the individual agent at the moment, on the spot, actively engaged in one act or the other. For instance, the person that is involved in writing and reading this book, experimenting, taking a walk, working, sleeping, or resting, eating, listening, in the office, air, sea, and watching events of life unfold et cetera, and who equally expects to be encouraged, protected and saved, either from physical, spiritual, psychological, economic or religious needs. Human relationships only thrive when the individuals are recognized and cherished for who they really are and not for selfish gains. Spirituality is inclusive of one's neighbor, friends and enemies. In line with the Christian Bible: "...a man who does not love the brother that he sees cannot love God whom he has never seen" (1Jn. 4:20).

Spiritual psychology is holistic and all embracing in content and scope. Basically, it aims at tapping the various human resources and values, economic, political, socio-religious, ethical, spiritual and anthropological, for the well being of the individual person. It cuts across all fields of learning and culture as a means to study and understand the human person and his or her behaviors in the light of his or her spiritual typology as exemplified in those three (ABC) belief systems. SP is meaningfully, an integration and application of human resources and values to the areas of need, for total realization and appreciation of the dignity of human life. This type of applied psychology is completely new in the field of psychology. Hence, it urgently calls for application in human interactions, school systems, government quarters and relationships with God and neighbor. Resourcefully, it requires the ability for an individual to integrate all aspects of his or her living experiences, learning, evident-based practices, and personal values that accommodate cultural diversities in his or her relationships. SP is revolutionary in the sense that it focuses on bringing positive and radical changes and effects on human dynamics and actions.

Feasibly, the moral value, 'conscience' is irreplaceable in this field of study because it arms and witnesses to the individuals the qualities and traits of their behaviors especially when they put veils over their ugly sides. For instance, frustration levels tend to be unbearably high in relationships where and when partners claim to be right and just in whatever they do. Holier-than-thou attitude is a display of inferiority complex that demands a psychological attention. Hiding in the hood of a monk is fear and one of the greatest disservices any person can do to him or herself. In this light, the Encyclopedia Britannica affirms that: "Conscience ... the active principle in the soul which in the face of two alternatives tells a man that he ought to select one which is in conformity with moral law" (Vol. 6, 1972:367). Moreover, due to the increasing fact that most people play down on these active principles in their souls, we necessarily and briefly juxtaposed the knowledge of psychology and spirituality for a broader understanding and justification of our study on spiritual psychology. This approach is necessitated due mainly to the formation, judgment and application of conscience in human decision, action and practice, be it socio-religious, political or educational.

Spiritual psychology is more of the science of religion in general. It is better understood in the context of psychology of religion, which "is the psychological study of religious experiences, beliefs and activities" (Web def.) and the hypocritical tendencies that are typical of some practices of religion in the world today. These tendencies have adversely affected interpersonal relationships, especially when truth and justice are relatively sacrificed at the altar of religious indifferentism. Notably, due to the fact that religion is at the forefront of human salvation, order and harmony in society, spiritual psychology analytically examines those religious claims in the light of what is happening in real human situations today. Therefore, spiritual psychology condemns the "cafeteria type and practice of religion" – where individuals decisively pick and choose what aspect of religion and the Gospel to practice and share with the public. Searching the Scriptures for some versions that might support your dirty habits is just like unconsciously inviting the devil to come to Church. In this instance, spiritual psychology objectively differs from psychology of religion. While psychology of religion seems to be concerned with religion in its instrumental and intrinsic levels, spiritual psychology intrinsically and instrumentally includes all aspects of learning, preoccupations, religion and religious dynamics evident in the life of the individual. Spiritual psychology emphasizes the practice and integration of values, personal, socio-religious, cultural, economic and political into one's life.

The word "spirituality":

This means different things in different contexts. When a person says: "I have no religion, I am spiritual", what actually does he or she mean? Our survey reveals that those people who claim to be spiritual simply refer to their belief in God. Any person whose belief in God is not concretized and evident in his or her daily activities is not spiritual. Spirituality employs the whole cognitive and affective faculties of the person at work. Therefore, "Spirituality" in this book is better understood in the words of Svoboda:

> *Our spirituality is expressed in the little daily decisions and choices we make, what kind of food we eat, how we talk to the clerk in the store, how much time (if any) we devote in prayer. Our spirituality also includes the big choices we make: whom we decide to marry or befriend, the kind of home we live in, the type of work we choose to do. When life presents us with few options, our spirituality influences the way we accept and work within the confines of such restrictions (1996:5).*

According to Au: "Spirituality is holistic when it acknowledges that all aspects of a person's life must be subjected to the transforming influence of the Incarnation" (1989:219). However, in Smith's own words: "Spirituality is an elusive term and has as many definitions as people who write about it" (Vision Vol. 17 No. 9, NACC, Oct. 2007:5). When we say that "humans are spiritual beings", at times, it is difficult to explain and understand because there is spirituality from both positive and negative perspectives. One can spiritually be a nuisance or an asset to society. Spiritual psychology, therefore, tries to throw light on the mysteries that surround individuals in their interpersonal relationships. In support of our studies on "spiritual psychology", Thayer remarks: "In the most general sense, spirituality has to do with how we experience ourselves in relation to what we designate as the source of the ultimate power and meaning in life, and how we live out that relationship. Spirituality is not merely feelings; it has to do with the integration and coherence of ourselves as experiencing and acting persons" (Vision, NACC, Oct. 2007:5). As Thayer noted, it is important that each person understands that spiritual psychology "has to do with the integration and coherence of each of us as experiencing and acting persons".

These 'experiencing' and 'acting' aspects of human life provide the backgrounds and bones on which spiritual psychology anchors and builds its analysis and operations. These operations include how a child strives and imbibes societal values in its personality developmental stage and how these values later shape and inform its character in life. It is of paramount importance to note that no one is born a criminal, terrorist, President or Bishop. One gradually becomes aware of one's spirituality or the sense of morality once one is able to interact with society and make decisions. To a great extent, the environment in which one is raised influences the concept of one's spirituality and morality. In Dallas words, "spiritualities abound on all sides, and we are fast coming to the point where we have a spirituality of practically everything" (JPT 2000:255 & Obiora, F. 2002). Emphatically, Dallas has this to say: "The spiritual side of the human being, Christian and non-Christian alike, develop into the reality which it becomes, for good or ill…. Spiritual formation may be thought of as the shaping of the inner life, the spirit, or spiritual side of the human being. The formation of the heart or will…of the individual, along with the emotions and intellect, is therefore the primary focus, regardless of what overt practices may or may not be involved" (2000:254).

Only ordinary human beings become Saints, not Angels

Spiritual psychology looks at those religious, material and spiritual values that may actually guide individuals or distract and destroy them from their desired goals in life. Speaking to priests as men of prayer, Pope Benedict XVI reiterated the importance of spirituality in these words:

> *The priest ... is a man of charity, lived and practiced, thus all the simple acts, conversation, encounter, everything that needs to be done, become spiritual acts in communion with Christ (2009:26).*

In the light of what Pope Benedict observed, nobody has become a Saint in the Catholic Church because he or she spent longer hours in the Church praying or reading the Holy Bible or had no weaknesses, faults, sins, or incapable of sinning. Any person can become a saint by integrating his or her spiritual aspects and parts such as, kindness, truth, honesty, peace, etc, into his or her physical realities like being there for others, sensitive to his or her environments, assisting the needy and hopeless of society. Thus, sainthood involves "simple acts, conversation, encounter, everything that needs to be done" our dressing and eating habits, our appointments, dispositions, vocations, vacations, marriage, sickness, success and the manner in which we interact with others, use of the trains, buses, school and office property, kitchen and restrooms etc. Sainthood is synonymous with spirituality. Saints are not plastic or preternatural beings whose powers are beyond human capabilities. Rather, these were human beings who tried to do ordinary things in extra-ordinary manners, identifying with the helpless, the dejected and 'no bodies' of society. For example, Mother Teresa of Calcutta has achieved her sainthood by identifying with the sick, those in prison and the sufferers of society. What of St. Theresa of the Child Jesus, who was known for spending her life doing little things that sounded funny in worldly standards? She lived a cloistered life of obscurity to save souls and pray for priests and ministers. Saints were the anawim of society. Poverty is the highest ideal of sainthood.

Paradoxically, the saints were not poor people in human standards. Rather, for the heavenly race, they abandoned wealth entirely. This is the same wealth that has driven most people crazy today. Just like Christ, they offered their energies, wealth, time, talents and lives for the good of society. We lived with most of them and knew their family backgrounds. Some became saints through martyrdom like Ss. Paul and Ignatius of Antioch, to mention but these two. In the face of death, St. Ignatius declared: "I am God's wheat and shall be ground by the teeth of wild animals" (IR) and so it was. Their heroic sacrifices did not mean that they were never offended and misunderstood. History still holds St. Paul as one of the most hot-tempered of the disciples. What of St. Augustine who nearly got lost in promiscuity but later climbed the mountain of grace to be a priest, Bishop and now a Saint, thanks to the intervention of his mother, St. Monica? The selfless life of Pope John Paul 11 is a glaring example of how one becomes a saint. If a personality of that magnitude, with the highest function in the Church, the President of the Vatican City, could aspire and choose the way to poverty, then, we can imagine the reasons and joy for such costly choices. Goodness has no boundaries. Canonization is never an obstacle for aspiring to sainthood. No wonder Lillie remarked: "If outward show of religious practice is no more than a cover for internal lack of upright character, then religion becomes a travesty" (IR, 09/23/07). Again, according to William, Barry: "If religion is the root of all evils in the world, religion's role is the overcoming of fear. But the overcoming of fear cannot be illusory. Religion must not become the opium of the people" (1992:61) as Max would want us believe.

Sequentially, religion must not be narcotic, an appendage, but a way of life that largely builds strong relationship with one's faith in oneself, neighbor and Supreme Being. In this sense, many religious groups are challenged today to positively live up to the ideals of their message and radiate the moral principles of truth and openness in their relationships with society. Ultimately, spiritual psychology capitalizes on the hypocrisy of some religious groups as a way to holistically sanitize and move the individual and society in the right direction. According to the Psychologist, Gordon:

> *There are two kinds of religion: Instrumental - which serves God for what you can get out of it; and the Intrinsic religion- which serves God regardless of what the consequences of that might be (1974:29-30).*

Relationships operate more on the intrinsic level of religion than the instrumental. Instrumentally, spiritual psychology emphasizes that while people pray for their personal needs, they should intrinsically and selflessly pray for the good of others and assist them realize that goodness. That is why the relegation of moral instructions, particularly in the school system, families, human behaviors and industries has mostly led to the chaotic experiences students and people encounter today. The danger is proximate when people become parasites and seek personal gains in relationships. On a more serious note, Raab, in full support of our survey in this book, alarmingly observes:

> *One study reports that 80% of members of religious groups indicate they are more concerned about comfortable life on earth than other-worldly considerations, and 54% admit that their religious beliefs do not have any effect on the way they conduct their daily affairs (1964:15).*

Wow! Without asking Raab which religious groups he meant here, I think that, his observation is revealing, frightening and indicative of why many relationships are already in shambles. As a spiritual psychologist and counselor, I strongly believe that "religious groups" here include world religions as recorded in my book:

> *Basic, of pre-historic peoples, Hinduism, Jainism, Buddhism, Sikhism [originating from Indiana], Taoism, Confucianism and Shinto [originating from China and Japan], and Zoroastrianism, Judaism, Christianity and Islam [originating from the Middle Ages] (2002:57-59).*

Spiritual psychology is not against those who found Churches, ministries or originate religions as how their basic belief systems have meaningfully assisted society move forward on the path to peace and unity. Further more, I fervently believe that religious groups Raab mentioned here equally include their leaders, ministers, their belief systems and practices. Besides, it is necessary, at this point, to have a general and etymological knowledge of the actual meaning of the word 'religion' in our survey.

b. The etymology of the word "religion":

According to the New Bible Dictionary: "The word "religion" came into the English from the Vulgate, where "religio" is in a 13th century paraphrase of James1: 26f. In acts 26:5, it denotes Judaism" (cf Gal. 1:3f) (2nd Ed.1992: 1017). Etymologically, the word "religio", according to Iwuchukwu came from three Latin verb roots, namely: "Religare: to read again and again, to study closely and then to observe conscientiously. It signifies attentive and deep study of matters pertaining to God. Religere: 2nd verb means to choose once more. Here religion means that one chooses once more, God whom he has lost through sins. Ligere: meaning to unite oneself and to bind oneself to something. In religion we bind ourselves fast to God in worship and adoration" (1998:2). Nonetheless, there seems to be a common consensus that the word "religion" is of Latin origin. According to Harring:

> 'Religion' derives from three Latin words as its roots, namely, 'Ligere' (meaning to bind), 'Religere' (meaning to unite, or liken) and 'Religio' (meaning relationship)" (1964:119).

For Harring, when religion is translated into action, respecting God and man, it is equal to relationship. In his "Comparative Religion", A. C. Bouquet examines the etymological meaning of the word "religion". According to him: "Religion is a European word, and it is a European convention to embrace certain human interests all over the world" (1933:4). For Alfred E. Garvie "Religion is ambiguous and implies that it is necessary for the scholar to know as he approaches this baffling and elusively delicate subject" (1933:88). The meaning of religion in Bouquet and Garvie has a lot of lessons for the present day religious practices. For instance, the "human interests" implied in religion is as ambiguous and delicate as people who assign different meanings to it. These problems seem to create most of the hypocritical tendencies we encounter in religious practices today.

In his own words, Cardinal Arinze objectively documented that: "Religion has three elements; truths to be believed (dogma), worship to be carried out (cult), and rules for guidance of conduct (morals)" (1970:31-32). These are the living expressions of the souls of vast group of people and all religious systems should be guided by these elements. From what Arinze has noted, spiritual psychology can effectively deduce the following values: Firstly, truth is not relative. Therefore, religion must always tell the truth that guides her adherents in their relationships with society. Secondly, the manner in which religious practices are carried out must respectfully be acceptable, consistent and represent the moral ideals of its belief systems. Thirdly, there must be certain moral principles that are inevitably in compliance with order, truth and justice or compatible with general public expectations and values that conform, guide and unify each adherent or member. According to Fr. Lawrence Lucas: "Remember, no justice, no peace" (2/6/09). Unless, according to The American people's Encyclopedia, religion is no longer "the relation between man and the supernatural …in whom he believes" (Editor, 1963:15 & 502). Can any one who does not believe in oneself ever believe somebody else, let alone in the Supernatural?

Though, according to Omoregbe "religion means one thing to the theologian, another to anthropologist or sociologist, another thing to psychologists…" (1999: 1), it consists of the existence of a being who is the 'primum movens' of all things, the unmoved mover, the ageless, causa in causata, the uncaused cause, the unchanged changer. Bouquet on his part conceives religion as "a fixed relationship between the human self and some non-existent, the sacred, the supernatural, the self-existent, the absolute or simply, God" (1941:16). To describe this relationship between the absolute and man, the Christian Bible informs us that God created man in his own image as already noted in this book. Therefore, man or woman is not only a "homo religiosus", a religious entity, a moral being but also has a religious bond between him or herself and God. This bond is meaningfully tested and validated in human relationships. In a simple language, religion is spiritually 'earth-bound'. The heavenly examinations begin and end on earth; each person only awaits his or her result in eternity.

For the Africans, attentive listening to the voice of elders, parents, teachers, seniors and ancestors is the epitome and apogee of human relationship and salvific work of God. In a more elaborate observation, Arinze maintained that religion also consists of the following:

> *'Objective' - body of truths, laws and rites by which man was*
> *sub – ordinated to the transcendent being and 'subjective' –*
> *the consciousness of ones dependence on transcendent being*
> *and the tendency to worship him (1970:8).*

To isolate any form of religion from Raab's survey is a serious limitation on the part of the researcher. Again, for any religion to go contrary to these values presents some lapses. Either, these religious groups have no leaders or their leaders have failed in their primary functions and duties to assist their members integrate religious values in their lives. Or, is it possible in Raab's fieldwork and analysis that religious groups here only refer to blind leaders? There are no two ways about this disturbing revelation. His observations are acutely insightful to what is going on in society today. In support of Raab's remarks, Holland G. Josiah in Mead, particularizing on Christianity alone, lamented:

> *A man may carry the whole scheme of Christian truth in*
> *his mind from boyhood to old age without the slightest effect*
> *upon his character and aims. It has less influence than the*
> *multiplication table (1965: 64).*

With these human attitudes, the need for spiritual psychology becomes consequential. For instance, how can an unworldly-oriented life of relationships be easily measured and based on perishable values of individual calculations? Of what significance are religious beliefs, practices, services; concepts of Church, heaven and the efforts millions make to worship God if religious practices have no effects in individual lives? Spiritual psychology is playing similar role as Joshua of the Old Testament, thus: "Joshua gathered all the tribes of Israel together…. And said to all the people: 'If you will not serve the Lord, choose today whom you wish to serve…. As for me and my house, we will serve the Lord" (Joshua. 24:1 & 15). Any service rendered to God that excludes neighbor is baseless. Both God and his worship, whether it is "latria – by virtue of being a creator, dulia – by virtue of the position he placed his saints, or hyperdulia – by his choice of Mary to be the mother of his son, et cetera, are only possible and realized in human relationships.

Humanity is the basis for all heavenly journeys. Jumping across the needy, the afflicted and such values as truth, honesty, love and unity which are the constituents and components of heaven to climb the ladder of faith is like carrying a heavy cross that is devoid of the man Jesus. To act otherwise, raises such concerns as where then lie the Christian hope of resurrection and the meaning of life itself? Raab and Holland seem to have caught most of us in our own traps. The unhealthy sentiments they raised confirm why the Traditional and religious values of the Igbo people of Nigeria mean more to them than Christianity. As noted already, the problem is not with Christianity or religion but individual agents. Rear-Admiral Richard Byrd in Mead is fully in support of this view:

> *Christianity has not failed. It is simply that nations have failed to try it. There would be no war in a God-directed world (1965:62).*

Knitter Paul, on his own side, argues that things are the way they are today because of the failure of religious leaders to perform their tasks. Thanks to Enculturation, Ecumenical Councils, Interfaith Debates and Religious Conferences that have attempted to establish relationships on a global level. But for many people some of these important bodies merely appear somewhat academic and doctrinal and do not functionally and immediately address the basic needs of Mr. A and Mrs. B. in their relationships. Religion is more of life-oriented than theoretical. Knitter Paul, in unmistaken terms, lamented:

> *I would suggest that one of the major reasons why there is so much disunity and lack of peace in today's world is because the religions of the world have not done their job (1992: 283).*

Similarly, as if Blaise Pascal in Mead is in support of Knitter, writes: "The Christian religion teaches me two points-that there is a God whom men can know, and that their nature is so corrupt that they are unworthy of Him" (1965:66). So, in Blaise's view, men and women are capable of knowing God. To the question, "why do they not know him?" Sweany in Mead, provides answers in these words: "Christians are found almost everywhere…sometimes they are found in the church, but not all persons in churches are Christians…" because "what persons do outside the Churches is the test" (1965:67). Christianity and many relationships, thus appear artificial because they have refused to pass the test for healthy living.

vi. The spiritual boom of prophets/God's or ghosts' ministers, religion and society: Who is fooling whom?

The matter of healthy relationships has become more urgent in our time and among individuals, irrespective of religious affiliations than in the past. Is it not scandalous, heretical and misleading for people who claim to be the torchbearers of sound and healthy relationship to say one thing and do another? As a consequence, hypocrisy rapidly spreads like an epidemic in society. It is on these bases that Karl Rahner condemned heresy as:

> *The distortion of the word of God preached by the Church into human error, by a Christian who makes his own fancy and his own standard a measure of the word of God, and suits it to himself instead of himself to it, and so sets up his own Christianity against the Church's (1964:64).*

The fact that some ministers have selfishly set up their own Christianity against the very way of life Christ preached is the beginning of Pseudo religious entities and failures. Is it better then to forget Christianity, religious principles and God who chose and commissioned human beings as his representatives? These are problems for spiritual psychology. Considering what Raab has said here and as observed among many Church goers and their ministers, it is totally a denial, if not a mockery of self, neighbor and God when religious beliefs and values can no longer influence the ways believers in God or individuals think, feel, act and relate to others. What else could be more valuable, precious in human relationships and life than leading righteous lives and peacefully relating with one another? This is where many relationships hang on a balance, becoming more of jungle-oriented, brutes in human appearances and clothing.

Basically, two things stand out from what Raab and Holland have pointed out here as regards religious groups. Therefore, as Christians, we are equally bound to accept one of these options to evaluate our relationships with God and man, either:

1. To admit the truth of their costly remarks; that we know what those Gospel truths are, carry them in our minds and not allow them to have the slightest effects on our actions, characters, aims in life, the ways we conduct our daily affairs and relate to others OR;
2. To deny that we are aware of the Christian and religious truths they are talking about and choose to remain adamant to the way of healthy living.

The disturbing remarks Raab and Holland made here, have constrained me to recapitulate and raise more concerns with regard to the manner and ways the Gospel message I preach to other people has shaped my relationships with them and fellow ministers. In support of this disturbing air of religious mismanagement, Castrovilla noted:

> *If one is concerned only with external manifestations in a religious career, then that person is making more difficult the acquisition of a deep and inner sense of fulfillment and personal growth to be found in the pursuit of such a career.... External touches are generally on the demonstrative; it manifests the character of a religious career, but this is not enough....When one makes an external manifestation the essence of a religious career, the essence is simply too shallow to subsist (2000:4).*

The Christian values are non denominational. Jesus Christ himself is one as his central message. As already noted, all the differences amplified in his name today are sheer products of human selfishness - the "id" of Sigmund Freud. Of course, in Pellegrino's words "selfishness is never a factor in the divine equation" (5/3/09). Beyond the diversified versions of the Christian message announced today, strongly stand the unchangeable man Jesus Christ, his person and values and only a few find him. In this understanding, Castrovilla added: "There is an important pivotal point from which all other elements spring and in which they are resolved...For it is ultimately the Almighty who consecrates and invests a person in a religious career" (2004:4-5). That is the same point the Letter to the Hebrews recorded in these words: "No one takes this honor on himself, but each one is called by God, as Aaron was" (Heb. 5: 4) In the light of what Sweaney rightly pointed out, I believe the test for Christianity is based on accomplishments, being Christ-like, in emulating his footsteps, listening to the heartbroken, wearied, coming to the assistance of the poor, providing physical healing to the sick, forgiving debtors, and more importantly, being available in loving relationships with all those who seek Christ in our company.

As a matter of urgency, we must seriously consider the timely warning of Sandford:

> *The Christian prophet's power is to humble the mighty and to raise the destitute. When others are laughing, he weeps in his spirit, and when they weep, his spirit rejoices. For, he is one step ahead in vision, and the burden on his spirit (1977:19).*

No minister can be "one step ahead in vision" when his or her emphasis and aim are centered on material possessions. Standford has alerted the ministers to sit up and imbibe the 3 basic values and Trinitarian formula of spiritual psychology (SP), namely: TJP (Truth, Justice and Peace). Just as the devil never goes on vacation, the minister must be awake at all times to lead society, especially our youths out of dangerous zones. By implication, the minister weeps most of the time, when others laugh because he or she "is one step ahead in vision" and understands the tricks of the devil more than other people. For instance, "as it was in Noah's day" as noted already, (Mat. 24:37) without any notice, the flood came and swept people away amidst festivities. Those warning signs have begun again in our time and many people do not seem to be listening.

Spiritual psychology does not want history to adversely repeat itself. The evil one or the devil does not wish an honest person well. He will relentlessly fight to rob him or her of all moments that bring joy and smiles in his or her relationships and lives. That is understandable because a wicked person or devil knows no peace and cannot be expected to generate and give it to others. On the other hand, when people weep in their relationships due to disappointments, hardships, temptations, sickness, et cetera, a genuine minister rejoices because these are moments of transformations, God's interventions and manifestations. God is always able to transform miserable relationships into joyous ones once his presence is felt, acknowledged and identified. Any spiritual rejuvenation or encounter re-energizes the mind to physically deal with fears and concerns.

Based on the above criteria, it is easier for each minister to evaluate how much of Jesus Christ, God, Yahweh, Light, Truth or Allah he or she has in his or her ministry. Preaching could be an art. Beautiful homilies and sermons are even published in journals. Preaching, in the Christian context, becomes an exercise simply lavished in futility if devoid of content, legacy and the experience of the man Jesus Christ and his values.

According to "the principles of quantum physics in Restak's view, the observer cannot be meaningfully separated from the experiment that he or she is conducting" (1991:11). A minister must preach and relate to others solely by examples. To separate our preaching from our life style is a mockery of God. Why must we not lead society through the narrow gate that leads to peace and life? (Mt.7: 13). The Lord, God has appointed us "as covenant of the people and light of the nations, to open the eyes of the blind, to free captives from prison and those who live in darkness from the dungeon" (Is. 42:6-7). Our functions as ministers are enormous. Science and technology seem to have fulfilled this aspect of our function by providing the handicapped of society with some modern facilities that aid them in one way or other. But on the other hand, the Gospel message seems to have produced little effects in the lives of many people. For instance, those who have their eyes, close them against truth, justice and peace, thereby becoming spiritually blind. While our captives are being released from the physical prisons, many people are continuously held captives by their evil deeds and lack of morality. Again, how can the present society be freed from living in darkness when sound moral principles and discipline have directly been ignored in our schools, families, establishments, politics and in many churches et cetera?

The Christian Bible enumerated the signs that would accompany our beliefs in ministry (Mk.16: 17-20). Out of these five assignments, how many have we exercised today? For instance, "In my name they will cast out devils". The question is: "Have we identified the devils in society in order to fight or cast them out?" "In my name, they will have the gifts of tongues". Let us be frank, can a minister or priest who tells lies ever have such gifts of tongues? "In my name, they will pick up snakes in their hands". Is it possible for a minister or believer who consciously avoids the cross of Jesus in his or her life, pick up any snake of any size, identifying with his or her enemies and trying to assist them, the dejected of society, trusting, sacrificing his or her time, energy, resources for and relying on people who may not even believe in any religion? "In my name, they will be unharmed should they drink deadly poison" Is there any deadly poison in the course of this ministry than the insults, abuses and ingratitude people generally show to religion and her ministers? Then, how many priests or ministers are ready to stomach them without complaining to their Bishops or Authorities? Finally, "in my name, they will lay their hands on the sick, who will recover". This is where I am really concerned. Based on the funny attitudes of many ministers today, especially towards money and fame, which hands are we going to lay to the sick? I strongly believe that any hand that is already soiled in materialism may not have positive effect on the sick, rather, may help to bring them to untimely death. As the Scriptures expressed it: "Can one blind man guide another? Surely both will fall into a pit" (Lk. 6:39). We need self-supervisions.

Nonetheless, a serious critique of how our ministries as priests and ministers impact and inform our relationships with fellow ministers, our immediate faith members and society urgently call for attention. We are the various organs of the Church and spiritual foundation of society. While the Church of Christ and her mission have inviolably remained the same, the ministers are accountable for the various scandals experienced in the churches today. Of course, to fight the Church or a particular Church leader is basically to fight Christ himself. It is high time, individual ministers and leaders convincingly sat up and looked into themselves for a change in the right direction. This concern is more urgent today considering the magnitude and level to which society has infectiously been influenced by modernity and technology. Moreover, whenever I reflect on Jesus Christ's farewell discourse to his disciples, one point continues to ring bells on my ears. Christ maintained wonderful relationship with his disciples and did everything to unify them with his father. Based on that singular fact, I wonder how far the following injunctions to his disciples have actually been implemented in our ministries today:

> *I give you a new commandment: love one another: just as I love you, you also must love one another, By this love you have for another, everyone will know that you are my disciples (Jn. 13:34-35).*

It is no longer news that by our religious activities the world has known us. That Christ emptied himself of his divine glory and accepted crucifixion at the hands of those he came to save were enough evidence that he really left the tomb empty and fulfilled his words. Let us take a moment and ask: "What actually precipitated the new commandment in the first place and what happened to the old one? These are concerns for deeper reflections. The new commandment generally reveals two major assignments, particularly for his ministers, namely: "Love one another...you must love one another" and "By this love...everyone will know that you are my disciples". As to whether we love one another, is an issue each person or minister has to answer. As on the second section, reflecting on the antagonistic attitudes and materialistic ambitions of most ministers today, I wonder how far our ministries and relationships have convinced society that we are one and Christ's ambassadors. Even though, Jesus Christ, naturally did not find it easy with his innermost companions or society, I fervently believe that the unselfish, other-regarding, kind, sympathetic, and healing love he recommended are enough guiding principles for ministers to come together, preach and live out the same Crucified Jesus in their relationships.

Therefore, there is no other time in the history of this age that our services, as ministers are needed than now. From all indications, the world is urgently in serious need for redemption from religious, economic and political distortions. Society, through this inquiry on spiritual psychology (SP), wants to know and see something that is unique and different in us, the ministers of the Gospel that marks us out from the rest of humanity. Today, most ministers are no longer identified with their actions but their churches and names. This ministerial identity is necessary and dimensional. It is very simple to put on the ministerial wears, carry the Bible and manipulate the message for personal gains but very difficult to represent Christ in words and deed. The hood does not make a monk. The manner in which each minister consistently conducts and carries out his or her ministry definitively provides and indicates the source of his or her identity. Obviously, each minister personally knows the identity – Truth, Justice and Peace (TJP), we are talking about here. Ministers are not expected to do extra-ordinary things or perform miracles. Yet, within the context of simple, sincere, honest and selfless ministerial services, extra-ordinary things and miracles occur.

As a matter of great concern, the role of those who represent Christ and his mission on earth cannot submerge or swim in the ocean of ignorance. The powerful message of Christ, which vitalizes and breathes new hope and visions to peoples' relationships, must be the yardstick of today's ministries. The cross and sacrifice, which form the LCM of all human relationships, should not be negligible or swept under the carpet of personal interests. Definitely, after rain must come sun. Playing jokes with our primary function as ministers and representatives of Christ is the most costly and highest mistake any of us can dream of. Within the "choice of focal options", the churches or religious ministers must transparently lead the world in equity, justice and truth. By 'choice of focal options', we mean the various possibilities, actual events, happenings and options available to ministers from where they can freely base the emphasis and choice of their ministries today. One of these events points to the negative influence of science on our teenagers. It does not matter who owns or claims to found a Church, society expects ministers to lead by examples, period. "If you have a meaningful religion, show it by your actions". Deception has paralyzed many relationships and it is time for spiritual psychology to put religion back on track.

That Jesus came for sinners did not mean there were no righteous men and women on earth or in Israel by that time. The book, therefore, encourages ministers of the Gospel to hold firm to the objective truths of the Gospel. These are critically the moments in history when revival, transformation of hearts, hope, radical change of faith commitments and restoration are irreplaceably needed in every level of human relationship. Despite the fact that the Church, the human face of Christ, experiences and faces numerous oppositions today, to maintain identical oneness in TJP with the person of her Founder, Jesus Christ is indisputable. Historically, referring to the unshakable nature of the Church, Whalen William expressed: "Shortly after the discovery of America, the unity of Western Christendom was shattered by the Protestant Reformation. That bond of common faith, which had cemented the brotherhood of European Christians for a millennium, was broken and altar was set against altar. Christians remained brothers in the grace of baptism and in loyalty to the person of Jesus Christ but they became separated brethren" (1979:9).

Therefore, the big efforts some ministers make today to keep relationships in alignment cannot be allowed to submerge into materialistic tendencies. When one finger gets soiled, it affects the rest, and that is the situation with many honest ministers of our time. That is, as society seems to polarize its message of selfishness, those who are called to announce the good news of righteousness, unity, peace, love and healthy relationships should leave no stone unturned or get discouraged in doing so. As it stands, our worry here is not about the rest of the affected fingers but primarily the soiled one to stop its contaminating and infectious mission from spreading. There are no reasons for ministers, the spiritual pilots of eternal airplanes to play jokes with their lives and those of their passengers. Ministers at the hospital settings, Directors, Supervisors and Chaplains of Pastoral Care should always be mindful that they represent the spiritual arms of their Institutions and should remain truthful, compassionate, dedicated and caring. More importantly, seminarians in training must examine their consciences and be truthful to their calling. The way of the cross is no easy anywhere, either as a seminarian or priest. Anything short of these, suggests that the Gospel has fancifully lost its sacred qualities for personal gains. This is where ministers need prayers to change from worldly distractions and live up to the standards and the right things society expects of them now as true and faithful reflections of the Gospel. Healthy relationships on earth are the prerequisites for admittance into the heavenly banquet.

Moreover, heaven consists only of righteousness and (TJP) – Truth, Justice and Peace. And it begins right here in our actions. By the way, who knows with certitude what God expects from us and who is actually righteous before him? As Paul recorded it: "Who has known the mind of the Lord? Or who has been his counselor?" (Rom. 11: 34). Does the God who "deals with death and life" (Dt. 2:39) really need our prayers in the first place and for what? Is he insufficient of anything? Belonging to a faith Tradition is encouraged, but it is not as important as making a personal decision to represent Christ and his principles, by being a shining example and upright life model to others. For instance, in the judgment of some people, an atheist, who does not believe in God, is damned. Yet, it is possible that the same atheist, as we saw earlier, might love him or herself, his or her environment, creation, relationship, family, neighbor, society, honesty, justice and meaningfully demonstrates a high level of appreciation and belief in the sacredness of life. Who is an atheist then in the light of truth, justice and peace?

The Christian Bible informs us that "God is love and anyone who lives in love, lives in God, and God lives in him" or her (1Jn. 4: 16). Bible scholars may have their interpretations. We must not belong to a Church or have religion to live in love. In this instance, it is hard to decipher how "an atheist who lives in love" can be excluded from living in God and God living in him or her. In a simple language, 'religion' per se, is not the yardstick for lively relationship or going to heaven but how meaningfully one demonstrates and puts religious values into actions. Any religion that lacks discipline and morality is gibberish. Practically, our destinies are in our actions (Jam. 2:17). In a sense, religion is like the gate that leads to a football, or baseball field. It does not matter how important or beautiful the field or gate is being decorated, emphasis is centered on the performances of the athletes. Moreover, people can still watch the game from various locations without coming into the field. Yet, two things stand out: without opening the gate, the game will not hold and without aiming at a win or defeat, the game is of no use. Therefore, our performances in interpersonal relationships to win the favor of God and neighbor through the good works we do on daily basis are more significant than the gate, field or one's own religion.

In this sense, to become a minister of the Gospel in the Lord's vineyard is not just a favor or privilege but also an additional call to sacrifices in carrying the cross. Any ministry that is empty or devoid of meaningful and truthful applications of moral principles that promote solid relationship with the rest of humanity has missed the mark. Our education, degrees, personalities and roles as ministers of the Gospel should humbly form an integral part of a whole body of relationships that reflect peace, honesty, unity and harmony in society. A relationship healthily lived out in thanksgiving to one another and God can serve as the most powerful prayer God expects of society. It is the good things we do and the trustworthy manner we relate with one another that count. According to Pope Benedict XVI in his "The priesthood, Spiritual Thoughts Series":

> *The priest ... should make his spiritual life his highest priority.*
> *He is called to seek God tirelessly, while remaining attuned to*
> *the concerns of his brothers and sisters (2009:22).*

In this light, relationships are essentially about our honest lives and the good things we do for others as priests and ministers. Most often, we know when we are doing the right or wrong thing. The question is: "Why do some people choose to do evil when there are valid reasons to do good? To choose evil is to reject peace and to breathe health is to exhale sickness. Let us choose life to death.

A person, who secretly chooses to indulge in wrong actions instead of the right ones and goes about deceiving and misleading others in their relationships, is simply an impostor. The Bible equally observed it while protecting innocent ministers who toil day-in-day-out to devote themselves to God's service: "You are well aware, then, that anybody who tries to live in devotion to Christ is certain to be attacked; while these wicked impostors will go from bad to worse, in deceiving others and deceived themselves" (2Tim. 3:12). Because of unaccomplished life objectives and goals, some people may internally, not only feel guilty of their failures in life but also physically claim to be of great service to the public. They show this tendency in different forms. Such people always try to appear neat, friendly, quiet, unassuming. They do not like to remain in a particular group or same environment for a long time because they have no peaceful stories to share. Besides, any one who does not have trust in oneself normally feels insecure and seeks satisfaction somewhere else. All the same, whatever way we live our lives, whether as ministers or not, our actions are the eternal tests that fundamentally bring our lives and hopes to meaningless or meaningful ends. Our goodness speaks beyond earthly bounds. Any person who is constantly the first to attend a meeting, a Church service, a ceremony and the last to leave may have some issues with his or her family or home. Ministers must be consistent.

As a consequence, it is expedient that ministers of the Gospel reflect on the viruses that, not only plague their primary missions as Christ's Ambassadors, but also, block effective relationships, particularly with themselves and society at large. Our functions in society are irreplaceable and unique. As St. James stated:

> *No body must imagine that he is religious [minister-mine]*
> *while he still goes on deceiving himself …any one who does*
> *this has the wrong idea of religion" (1: 26-27).*

It is only reasonable that ministers preach to others from the wealth and riches of their beliefs, convictions and relationships with the one they represent, Jesus Christ. But, based on lived experiences and various surveys carried out in this book, some of the ministers, world champions of truth, trust, accountability and honesty et cetera, seem to have scandalized and polluted the Gospel mission in a very large proportion. For instance, what is the aim and outcome of advertising prayer requests and healing opportunities to the public? What becomes of the Gospel message when churches engage in high competitions and rivalries for salvation programs? Competitions, often, lead to strife, rancor and acrimony. The same spirit of rivalries operates within some religious communities and among ministers who live together in the Lord's vineyards. How plausible does it sound to call a place of rancor the Lord's vineyard? The Lord's vineyards are never mistaken. The untamed, primitive and unconverted egos of some ministers are the infections that contaminate God's words and create problems for healthy interpersonal relationships in religion. Why can't the ministers build on their internal strengths, reality principles and the enormous power of the Gospel message and become brothers in the light of the Psalmist? Thus, "Ecce quam bonum et quam jucundum habitare fraters in unum" meaning, 'Behold how good and joyous for all (brothers and sisters - mine) to dwell in unity (Ps. 133; 1).

Certainly, the book sounds pedantic here or like preaching to the choir. But, it will terribly be a disservice to the general public and spiritual psychology not to reflect the concerns, though, comparatively insignificant, our respondents raised in this work as regards the ministers of the Gospel. Therefore, we are necessarily obliged to invite and assist the ministers to build disciplined and convincing relationship that reflects the standards of the Christian message. From the survey, some concerned Christians are wondering whether the ministers who represent God in the world today are genuinely and faithfully the salt and light of the world as Christ enjoined them in these words:

> *You are the salt of the earth. But if salt becomes tasteless, what can make it salty again? It is good for nothing, and can only be thrown out to be trampled underfoot by men. You are the light of the world. A city built on the hilltop cannot be hidden…. In the same way your light must shine in the sight of men, so that seeing your good works, they may give the praise to your Father in heaven (Mt. 5:13-16).*

These are special privileges that should constantly put smiles on the face of every minister or priest. Only the individual minister knows how far he or she has been the salt and light to a world that luxuriates in all kinds of atrocities and evil practices. Practically, every living creature under the sun has the same natural tendency towards a happy end. Undeniably, the ministers of the Gospel, though some married and others unmarried, are basically not different from the rest of humanity in matters relating to sin, self-protection, preservation, esteem, sexual urges, having money, eating, driving, housing, resting, studying, et cetera. Even though the way each person or creature gets about it differs, is it not incumbent upon the ministers to prove themselves as the embodiment of TJP, order and discipline that control the egocentric forces of society and life? For instance, it is evident to our senses today that society has terribly been polluted by immoral behaviors and various kinds of horrible life patterns; must the ministers be included in such messy attitudes? We must be ministers to ourselves first before we can minister to others. It was on this basis that Pope Benedict XVI observed:

> *The faithful expect only one thing from priests: that they be specialists in promoting the encounter between man and God. The priest is not asked to be an expert in economics, construction or politics. He is expected to be an expert in the spiritual life (2009:22).*

In the light of the Pope's exhortation, why cannot the priests and ministers be proud and boast of one thing they have as "the salt and light of the world" and spiritual experts which others do not, especially, "Truth and Trust"? We must make real in our own lives the Gospel Jesus taught with his life. This is not to encourage religious indifferentism. For instance, in the Biblical quotation (Num. 11:27-29; Mk. 9:38-39), already cited in this book, Moses neither told Johusa to leave him or the meeting tent and join Eldad and Medad, nor did Jesus ask his disciples to abandon him and follow the man casting demons. Christ even allowed both the good seed and weed to grow till harvest time (Mt. 13:30). Judgment is not ours. According to Dr. Amadi-Azuogu: "Tolerance towards other Christian denominations is also part of the Christian message of love" (9/17/09). From the example just cited, though, the three men – Eldad, Medad and the one in the Gospel, were carrying out the same ministry; they were doing so, from different perspectives. While there are no differences in moral principles, there are in doctrines. For instance, Holy Communion or the Eucharist does not mean the same thing for Protestants and Catholics. Spiritual psychology does not lay any emphasis on who receives the Eucharist or reads the Bible as how far the Eucharist and Bible have assisted the person become a changed agent in him or herself and society. A 'sinful' priest or pastor still holds the embodiment of eternity.

Self-assessment test - For ministers of the Gospel message

To the question, Archbishop Timothy Dolan asked: "What are priests to do" (Catholic NY, 1/14/2010) in the face of criticism, Most Rev.

Bishop William F. Murphy of Rockville Center Diocese, in his 2011 Lenten Pastoral Letter, insisted that the Faithful must "belong deeply" to Christ's sheepfold in words and deed. To do this, we must equip ourselves properly. There should be no basis or justification for ministers to compete within them or with the rest of the world as regards the prime target of Christ's mission. These concerns are agonizingly presented here in the form of open-ended questions, designed to elicit self-responses, interior conversion of hearts, evaluations and reflections among the ministers themselves. I am also involved.

- Can a minister of the Gospel tell lies at all, whether against fellow ministers or others, be envious and greedy of their promotions & success?

- Does a minister or priest who uses his or her "position" to create problems for fellow ministers and priests, hopes to be saved or doing God's work?

- Or, is it possible that a person who functions as a minister can simulate truth, even when it is obvious? Categorically, when a pastor, priest, minister or religious cannot say the simple truth and shame the devil, (it does not matter what he or she gains by lying), he or she has eternally condemned him or herself and denied Christ and his ministry. How can we add eternal death onto our daily mistakes and shortcomings as ministers? Where then lie our consciences and the hope for everlasting life?

- Is it possible that certain degrees of partiality, inhumanity to one's folks, racism, favoritism, injustice, application of dead consciences to judgments and actions, et cetera, are also possible among the priests and ministers of the Gospel? Already, Raab has noted that most religious people personally place much premium on earthly security and conveniences.

- Is it possible then that a highly positioned minister of the Gospel can equally, financially at times, be occupied and be busier with his or her personal commitments than what God or society expects of him or her? Who do such ministers actually take God to be and what impressions do they really have of him? It is true, while society has tremendously changed from what it was at the time of Jesus, the word of God and the missionary targets have essentially remained the same. What then brought about the play down and falsifications of Gods' words in many quarters today when he is constantly at work irrespective of any person, minister or not?

- Can a minister of the Gospel be less Christ-like, less Godly, less loving, less prayerful and less caring in his interpersonal relationships? Unfortunately my previous book, "The Devil has come to Church" (1999), seems to have actually come to the limelight here. I wrote the book when the devil simply walked across the Church. But today the devil and his angels appear to have taken seats in some churches and their ministers.

- Worse still, is it a platitude that some ministers of the Gospel no longer perceive their roles as services and functions but as political positions?

- Surely, in human history, God has never handed over his Omnipotence to anyone. Therefore, it is baseless to believe he is responsible for empowering some of today's ministers to carry out anti-Christian ministries of hate and envy in the world as such when most of our people love us.

- Moreover, is it true that some priests and ministers play partisan politics in the Church and the honest ones are victimized on account of that?

- Has humility, the sign of Christ's presence in the world, which characterized his ministry, been replaced by inordinate desires for gluttony, fame and affluence, pointing to the same three items with which Jesus was tempted by the devil? Or, could it be possible that when "the devil left Jesus", he turned at the appointed time" to face his ministers? (Lk. 4:1-13). Acting the big man or woman as a minister of the Gospel is a misnomer and sign of disappointment with self and the ministry too.

- Can a minister be frustrated and traumatized by fellow ministers?

- Has, according to Obiora, "marketing God become a top bracket business" (Obiora, F. K. 1998:57), mainly for material comfort? Here lies the urgency of the book. Naturally, when the forefinger points at others, the rest of the four fingers equally point back to the pointer. Today, homeland security in the USA has almost suspended and suspiciously been embarrassed as regards the issuance of R-1 visas to genuine ministers due to the nasty attitudes of some foreign ghost ministers who operate in the name of one fictitious church or the other. What a big scandal? Has God any place in deception? After amassing wealth and economic prosperity through deceptive means, what happens next? Raab is right. Religion does not influence the ways some people live their lives today.

- Is it possible that some ministers seem to have become groups of evil forces, critics, cliques, powerfully engaged in endless competitions, rivalries, gossips, struggling, castigating one another and fighting for everything humanly and materially possible except holy and upright lives? Wow! It is no longer a guess; personal conveniences as observed by Raab seem to have, not only, corrosively dominated the minds of most ministers, but also, become the standard and measurement of present day evangelization. Tufiakwa (Shame)! Are we no longer the light of the world?

- Is it conceivable that some of the ministers of the Gospel who willingly accepted this ministry, of the heavenly program for caring and saving souls, consciously and unconsciously turned their backs to attack Christ and his ministry by their actions? We are free to agree or disagree.

- Can we physically have satanic ministers in the world today who executively operate in Christ's name, considering mainly the magnitude of scandals, intensity of hatred and envy among some ministers and priests?

- In the Catholic Tradition, for instance, if the Sacraments I celebrate and the word of God I preach to others have no more impacts or effects in my life and in my relationships with the rest of the world, other priests or ministers, can I still claim to be a priest or true minister? Even though the Sacraments function "Ex opere operato", that is, irrespective of my wonderful dispositions, pious actions, holiness, sins et cetera. But why must one choose to deceive oneself and others assuming the Sacraments work "Ex opere operantis" that is, by virtue of one's ordination or calling? Who called whom? Does a person who claims to be a minister of God in this context not constitute the highest level of hypocrisy and deception?

- Is it possible that some religious houses, Pastoral Care Departments and rectories have become war zones and semi-battle fields where survival of the fittest is rampant?

- If the worst enemies some ministers of the Gospel have today are within their own folks and religion, is something not seriously wrong with the whole program of salvation, which Christ mandated them to announce?

- Can a minister have or command more powers and authority than those of Christ or can there be another standard for this ministry besides the one Jesus laid down? Ineluctably, every day is Lent for a Christian. Easter remains eternally glorious for those who follow in the footsteps of Christ.

- Is it not a danger signal for those ministers for whatsoever reasons, who, through their actions, have created the impressions that the present day ministry has either partially or completely and spiritually lost bearing with the Founder? We must continue to serve gladly but avoid some criticisms.

- Are the unfriendly and anti-Christian practices of some ministers today not signs of the world's waning spiritual values and religious fervor or warmth being replaced by materialism and self-entailment or are they, the effects of a minister's personal fall towards evil and corruption?

- Please, fellow Catholic Priests, Evangelists, all Ministers of Christian Religion, Religious and Lay People, (Society in general), "Let us belong more deeply" - be more committed, realistic and convinced of the Presence of Christ in our lives by what we say and do.

Furthermore, if water is generally used to clean dirty things, what happens when water becomes dirty? Ministers are meant to counsel and soften the hearts of stones of the world. For ministers to turn cruel to themselves is incredibly serious. How do we reconcile our belief in one God, when his ministry has seemingly and selfishly been divided and isolated from its primary objective - the love of God and neighbor? Again, does discrimination, particularly among the clergy, not contradict the Christian message? In this light, the book is compelled to ask: Has this universal disease, discrimination based on race, color, national origin, religion, sex, family status, mannerism and disability, accent which seems to exist in all strata and levels of human relationships also been endorsed, practiced and perpetuated by some ministers? Our survey reveals that discrimination is natural to human beings but practiced by only few individuals. It is not limited to any particular race or culture. It is even worst in the western world among many immigrant folks. To underscore the importance of sound moral life, the Christian Bible warned:

> *If your right eye should cause you to sin, tear it out and throw it away; for it will do you less harm to loss one part of you than to have your whole body thrown into hell (Mt. 5: 30).*

In a simple language, we either minister in Christ's name and get our heads out of trouble by accepting his cross in our relationships or in our names and seek earthly pleasures and their consequences and stop embarrassing and deceiving ourselves and society in general. There are so many trustworthy men and women in society who strive on daily basis to live upright lives. For, "God does not see as man sees; man looks at appearances but Yahweh looks at the heart" (1Sam.16: 7). A lot of people have become ministers without any divine mandate.

The Christian Bible observed: "Be aware of false prophets who come to you disguised as sheep but underneath are ravenous wolves" (Mt. 7: 15). The big question that faces each of us today is: "Who are these ravenous wolves" in the Lord's vineyard when we have all appeared in sheep clothing? For instance, Paul acknowledged his own weakness in these words: "About this thing, I have pleaded with the Lord three times for it to leave me" (2Cor. 12:8). Whatever that thing is, he did not say. What a perfect example of encouragement and perseverance in ministry has Paul shown us in those words? He equally prayed for strengths to fight against obstacles or "that thing" in his own ministry. In the depth of his heart, Christ spoke and reassured him: "My grace is enough for you: my power is at its best in weakness" (2Cor. 12:9). Yet, based on the hypocrisy of religious practices in our time, I wonder if any of us ever admits of any form of weakness that affects or impacts on his or her ministry. Certainly, when blind leaders claim to be objective in their decisions and actions; the general public suffers at large. Imperatively, no minister should be a blind leader.

Actually, the enormity and magnitude of religious politics, bigotry, hatred, rancor and acrimony among most ministers are more of unrealistic agenda signed and approved only by evil forces. Our studies have also shown that any priest or minister, especially the single, who is free with women and men or engages in illicit relationships with them, hardly represents his fellow ministers in a friendly light. Such ministers will always find faults and castigate their colleagues within and outside the Lord's vineyards. This is sad. We cannot be an African watermelon that is whitish inside and greenish outside. How can a minister of the Gospel lead others or the world faithfully to healthy relationships when he or she has not gathered him or herself together? It has to be noted that our bodies and actions are the beautiful pieces of engines that energize and hold the faith of most people in society together. Sadly, this is not the story. In his own words, a Catholic Prelate, Bishop Ezeonyia noted: "Religion is sold in the market place like everything else these days" (1998:1). Who are these spiritual traders? How can the profit made from selling Gods' words be quantified or classified? Could Ekweh be referring to the same preachers of the word when he cried aloud in these words: "A lot of people are so much concerned about personality, status, qualifications, without considering the wisdom of God in their lives (2002:6-7). Yet, when we seek this wisdom of God in our own standards, plights and fail, we blame God or fellow ministers or those in charge of us. There are so many powerful preachers everywhere. Society expects and is in dire need of powerful doers of the word. Any religion, especially Christianity that focuses more on physical healing and wealth than interior transformation lacks its basic foundation. Unconsciously, most of the healing ministers of today are physically sick without taking notice of it. I am also a healer.

Absolutely, there is no success in deceit. For instance, when we tend to be sailing smoothly on a high sea of materialism without any reference to God for assistance, it will be late and futile calling on him when our ship hits the tempest that sinks it. Alleluia! The Gospel of prosperity! This is contradictorily a manifestation of selfish ambitions and failures of identity with the political world. Peter, an Apostle of Christ asked him a theological question that has never been answered in our time and ministry. Thus: "What of us? We have left everything and followed you" (Mt. 10:28). While Peter might be objectively truthful in his concern, "what actually have we left" in the course of this ministry when material pursuits are the prime targets of some of us? A minister, who always preaches material prosperity, has indirectly admitted his or her spiritual hollowness.

It sounds crazy for a minister to evaluate the success rate of his or her ministry by material standards. When James compared those who live in selfish luxury with calves fattened for the slaughter, (Jam. 5:1-6), he did not exclude the ministers. Only "the pagan" according to Fulton Sheen in Marlin, "fears the loss of his body and his wealth; the faithful fears the loss of his soul" (1989:217). "Our God is not a poor God", in the midst of hungry people and economic crunch, is not true. There is no poverty, in worldly terms, among God's children because, according to Benny Hinn: "When God's Word invades your heart, prosperity is the result" (IR, 10/24/09). God has already made himself poor in his son that mankind might spiritually be rich in his grace; equitably using his material gifts to build egalitarian society and relationships of oneness and love (Eph. 2:7; 2Cor. 12:9). While we need money in our ministries, there is no selfishness in God. Again, greedy people are never certain of their future, settled or satisfied to enjoy peace and the presence of God in the poor. Therefore, let us heed to the warning of Berger, cited by Dr. Imo Cletus Chukwudi in Morgan John in these words:

> *Theologians especially, must not allow themselves to become conceptually or methodologically blinded to signals of transcendence.... This is like an invitation to all of us involved in religious ministry - theologians, canonists and Church leaders...(2009:52).*

Ministers of the word should not allow the spirit of wants or secularization get in the way of their primary needs, to lead themselves and others in the heavenly race. Heaven reflects itself in the good work people do on earth.

vii. Religion is not an option for heavenly rewards:

Regrettably, in the light of spiritual psychology (SP), heavenly rewards should not be the concern of any one besides aspiring for sound moral living and good work. As already noted, heaven consists of upright lives and getting things rightly done here on earth. In one of her annotations, St. Theresa of the Child Jesus said: "I want to spend my heaven doing good on earth" (IR). It was in the course of "doing good" that she has become a saint today. Doing good extends to the classroom, hospital block, Market Square, football field, airport, in whatever we do and wherever we find ourselves. Senior Rabbi and Chaplain, David Rabhan (NYUMC), once asked me: "Anthony, is it possible for one to be good without believing in God?" It is the same thing as asking if an atheist who has excelled in good work, practiced it in his or her life can go to heaven. These questions are not merely sentimental. They demand answers and not responses. Biblical scholars and Theologians may have their arguments and opinions. But, in the context of spiritual psychology, it is impossible to understand how an atheist who has not confessed any belief in God but represented him, willingly or unwillingly, in goodness and sound moral life will be disqualified before God. That an atheist does not believe in God is not the same thing as not knowing that God exists, at least, if not for him or her, but for others. Experiences have revealed that some children deny their parents and vice versa. But, hardly does a parent abandon his or her child because of his or her recalcitrance. No one is insignificant to God. This issue has been given serious attention in this book. By the way, who has ever paused and cared about the driving, energizing and motivational forces behind the good qualities of many atheists. An atheist is not a terrorist but a human being who equally falls short of the grace of God in his or her beliefs and actions like most of us. As a rational person, his or her level of spiritual connections might be higher than some of those who play tricks with religion. In this sense, his or her situation is a matter of serious concern, sympathy, and not condemnation. We know that our up bringing, association, environment and life situations, to a large proportion, shape our lives, and at times, our belief systems. The practical questions that inevitably face us in this regard are:

a. Who is God to a person who has no knowledge of him? OR

b. What does God signify or mean for a Christian or Jewish, who has no regard for him in his or her decisions and actions as Raab indicated?

The Christian Bible rightly observes: "It is not those who say to me, 'Lord, Lord', who will enter the kingdom of heaven, but the person who does the will of my father" (Mt.7: 21). Believing and confessing one's faith in God, as one's creator and savior, is not debated. Practically speaking, we must choose between these options: Who is more acceptable to God, the person who does his will or the one who believes in him? This is where some believers are caught in their own traps. From the above biblical quotation, the "will of my father" is inclusive and not exclusive as recorded in these words: "Now the will of him who sent me is that I should not lose nothing of all that he has given to me" (Jn. 6:39), "for the laborer deserves his wages" (Lk. 10:7). Belief in God only works in good deeds.

The meaninglessness of God

Nothing is meaningful to a person who does not appreciate good things. The Preacher or the OT Qoheleth said: "Vanity of vanities. All is vanity. For all his toil, his toil under sun, what does man gain by it. A generation goes, a generation comes, yet the earth stands firm forever" (Eccl. 1:1-4). Of course, the earth stands firm forever irrespective of the generation that occupies it at a time. Is our generation going to make a difference in the created order? Yes! If we identify with the source of our own earth, who is meaningful, definitely our toiling under sun will transform into a reality that challenges all vanities. We identify with God in action. A denial of this primary source plunges us into the uncertainties of everlasting darkness because every moment holds its own message of success or failure. To affirm success is to negate failure and vice versa. According to Fr. Joseph Pellegrino: "There is nothing normal for a person created in the image and likeness of God to reject his or her spiritual essence for the sake of momentary and monetary gain" (IR. 11/22/09).

There is no gainsaying that a world that rejects its creator and source of being is already dead. For instance, a child who is not cognizant and appreciative of the sacrifices his or her parent or guardian makes for him or her, hardly succeeds in life. Life is meaningless for a living dead or a person who seeks comfort in materialism and self-pleasures. Consequently, spiritual psychology calls each person to stand against all unethical business practices of society. Our actions testify to our belief systems. Nobody takes God by surprise. He knows what he is doing.

The fact that he revealed his name as "I Am who I Am" (Ehyeh asher ehyeh) is enough indication of how to approach him (Ex. 3:14). It does not matter what impressions individuals hold about him, he is "I Am", always present in human history and endeavors. Different people and cultures call him whatever works for them. For instance, there are people who name God in view of the various favors they have received from him, like "my Provider, Healer, Protector, Supporter, Only Hope and so on. There are no restrictions, humanly speaking, to what names individuals have to give God. What is important is the position they have for him in their hearts, actions and one another.

The manner in which we represent him in our behaviors determines what name we give him and our relationship with him. Just like in human relationships, the attitude of a partner shows his or her level of concern, love and involvement. As noted earlier, so many people call on God, but only himself knows those who are sincere or his own. In a way, must God be identified by only one name for him to be known and worshipped? Or must a person belong to a Christian denomination to have a religion? Already, he has situated his name in the moment. It is left to individuals to discover and embrace him in their daily activities and lives. Even, when we are sick, downcast, lose our friendship, job, et cetera, he is still there "AM", for us. There can be as many conflicting opinions as there are religions. But there are no ambiguities and confusions in being truthful, honest, just, disciplined, practical and morally supportive of others. God is meaningless to any person, Christian, atheist or believer who fails to represent him in concrete terms. Any belief in God that is not translated into one's action and does not have effect in one's relationship with others is meaningless. No wonder, Tim Hughes expressed: "I will never know how much it cost to see my sins upon that cross" (IR). Hughes, by that singular statement, has challenged society, particularly Christians to appreciate themselves and model their relationships after the cross of their master, Jesus Christ. The little help we render to others in God's name reduces the debt we owe by our wrong doings and opens the door of his grace to society. A heaven or life that is exclusive of others is not of God.

The Christian Bible vehemently specifies what heaven consists of in the context of spiritual psychology:

> *Then the King will say to those on his right hand, "Come,*
> *you whom my Father has blessed, take for your heritage the*
> *kingdom prepared for you since the foundation of the world.*
> *For I was hungry and you gave me food; I was thirsty and you*
> *gave me drink; I was a stranger and you made me welcome;*
> *naked and you clothed me, sick and you visited me, in prison*
> *and you came to see me. Then the virtuous will say…when*
> *did we see you etc. (Mat. 25: 31-46).*

The qualifying criteria for heavenly rewards in the above citation are based on being practical and sensitive to the minutest needs of the least of society, the helpless, and those hidden poor stricken individuals in our streets who have nobody to care for them. This is spirituality. Heaven demands truth, justice, equity and spiritual prosperity. Religion is never a choice of chance. We can now understand why Pastor Benny Hinn made the following remarks: "We are in the most amazing season of harvest in our history" (IR, 9/26/09). Yet, according to Paul's letter to the Galatians, we read: "Don't delude yourself into thinking God can be deceived: where a man sows, there he reaps: if he sows in the field of self-indulgence he will get a harvest of corruption out of it; if he sows in the field of the Spirit he will get from it a harvest of eternal life" (Gal. 6:7-9; Mtt. 25: 24).

As it were, this means: "Religion plus good work is equal to eternal success, and good work minus religion is still equal to eternal success. But religion minus good work equals to eternal loss (R + GW = ES, GW – R = ES but R – GW = EL). For instance, many different religious sects today, in appealing manners, promise society of one redemptive opportunity or another, with hidden agenda behind them. In the light of these pseudo-religious paraphernalia and appearances, Bishop Vincent Ezeonyia frowningly seemed to be referring to them when he described the various Christian sects in these words: "The Pentecostal type of religion seems to draw people who are highly emotional and long for spiritual "highs". The Liturgical types of religions appeal more to people who love order and drama. The Intellectual types of religions attract people who are looking for a cerebral faith. The Prosperity-religion has great appeal to those who seek wealth and health and power. The Fellowship type of religions draw people from who are looking for an experience of community" (1998: 34).

Definition of religion in spiritual psychology

Playing on the intelligence and psychology of people in the name of religion or ministry is deceptively not right. It is sinful. Sin is categorical. A lie or deception is the worst. There has never been a long lasting prosperity in material possession than graciously in one's good name. The negative influence of science and technology and global village syndrome have blown up the wind of inordinate desires for some individual ministers. Such ministers scramble to be rich and famous, and in that process typify another branch of heaven-on-earth liberation that affects global trust. Ultimately, a spiritual psychologist is constrained to ask: "What actually is religion and how can it be felt and realized in human relationships?" In this book, religion has been adequately studied, presented and explicated in different capacities. Yet, that living and uplifting experiences expected from religious practices appear subtle and confusing in many quarters.

Therefore, in the light of this religious dilemma, Spiritual Psychology attempts to give a broad definition of religion as:

> *A conscious awareness, integration and use of one's situations, health, music, suffering, sickness, death, sports, food, wears, environments, dispositions, achievements, failures, struggles, destinies, education, status, neighbors, friends, enemies, name them, in endless, timeless and perpetual adoration, devotion, thanksgiving and appreciations to one's source of being and life.*

Contextually, whoever this Mighty Force or Source is, spiritual psychology (SP) has no specific name for him. However, SP strongly believes that this piece of beauty and construction, the human person, the apogee of existence, the summary and climax of all living things and life, is purposeful and meaningful. This meaning goes beyond any human imagination and ultimately traceable to a source whose existence is permanence and beauty itself. Most religious adherents and individuals call this source God. As an African Christian, I firmly and wholeheartedly believe that God is the source of life. The way each person accepts, invites and experiences him in his or her life is quite different in SP.

Today, it is no longer news, particularly in Nigeria that some armed robbers disguise themselves and operate as Rev. Gentlemen. Greed is the foundation of unhealthy relationships. Reacting to this ugly situation, Joseph I. Omoregbe remarkably stated:

> *If a person believes very strongly in making money, then money is his religion, if another person believes strongly in Marxism, then, Marxism is his religion and so on"* (1996: 1).

The Christian religion cannot be subjected to the whims and caprices of individual ministers and evaluations. In the light of these unhealthy religious atmosphere and leaders, George Emeka Ekwuru appeared to have supported Raab in these words: "They have lost the sense of respect and reverence for the divine and the sacred. Thus, religion has lost its compelling sacred aura. People have been known to put on the sacred masks of religion, to commit all kinds of virtual atrocities for material purposes and with these masquerade fiesta of religious exhibitions" (1999:101). These hypocritical activities that are being carried out in the name of religion today soil human relationships with God and one another. Some hold, "it is a human factor, we live in a free world". Yes, it is. Yet, there are so many honest ministers up there. No one can maintain honest relationship with the one he or she deceives. How can trusted groups of ministers call on the name of God with ulterior motives? According to Obiora Fidelis, such earth bound, end-time or reward-on earth evangelists: "Dish out intriguing half-truths.... exaggerations, inarticulate premises, insinuations, distortion of facts, false testimonies...all geared towards the accumulation of wealth (1998:79). Most of these "new ways" ministers claim to have the spiritual powers to cure all ailments, yet, from daily experiences more people are dying today than in the time of Jesus Christ. There is no kind of trick some priests and ministers have not introduced in society in the name of one religious practice or the other.

It is timely to reflect and heed the words of Archbishop Okogie cited in Obiora that "carrying the Bible is one of the quickest means of getting money today" (1998:109) and for Obiora, "the Bible has become a deceptive tool" (1998: 191). What else can bring various relationships together than the Bible? How can "religion" be "blown out of proportion"

(Op.cit. 1998:119) because of greedy ministers? Based on this "imitation evangelism" of the present day ministry, it is hard if not impossible to decipher the authenticity of relationships these ministers keep with society, families and themselves. In Ekwuru's understanding:

> *The center of religious belief and practice has been variously tagged with commercial values.... The religious vision and mentality is obviously earth bound and totally mundane (1999:105)*

On the contrary, as recorded in the Igbo Catholic Priest, "the Igbo man values...its unity and solidarity...places high premium on community loyalty...respect for age and elders" (2000:16).

Unequivocally, the Traditional priests of the Igbo of Nigeria are role models. They lead by examples. Every minister knows where his or her strength in ministry anchors. I vividly insist that we keep Jesus Christ or religion out of the picture now for the moment because most of the present day ministries have no bearing with his legacies, principles and discipline. Let us face it. For instance, that I am priest today, is not a mistake. It is just a gift of God, a privilege I have no right to, as observed earlier because "no one takes this honor on himself" (Heb. 5:4). It may sound strange to some people if I observe here that my impeccable belief in the unquestionable power of God to bring humanity together grew first, from my Traditional religion and values and not from Christianity. Substantially, for the Igbo Christians like myself, who welcome and accept Christianity in the spirit of the African Traditional beliefs and values, God has no comparison, no equals and unmistakably compromised in any form or shape. He is cherished, worshipped and revered as a 'great biological visible father', creator of the universe in charge of his household. He is perceived as no nonsense, but caring and loving person, practically alive and not as an object of the mind or a subject for philosophical and theological debates, theoretically hiding in the sky, as an amputee of history. Among the Igbo, God or *Chi-Ukwu*, is actively Omnipresence in all the adventures of their lives.

The Igbo man's belief in God is far from being Pantheistic that identifies him with everything in the universe or Unitarian ideology that denies the Trinitarian reality of God. Rather, they see him as the only power that confronts, calms, and directs the uncertainties and unforeseen forces of their lives. As equally noted in the Christian Bible, Jesus said to the storm: "Quiet now! Be calm! And the wind dropped, and all was calm again" (Mk. 4:39). Our society seems to be constantly in turmoil today because we have not asked the only expert on this area of science of nature [storm] to assist us as the Apostles did in their own plight (Mk. 4: 35-59). We can now understand why the Psalmist once said: "The One whose throne is in heaven sits laughing" (Ps. 2:4) and laughing at society and individuals who think they are in control of the world to scorn. Why will not God laugh at us when we claim to be more intelligent than Intelligence itself? Many families raise their children without any fear of God because of materialism. An atheist who has refused to believe in God once shouted "Oh my God" when an armed robber pointed gun at his face. We are all children of God, no doubts. From the paradoxical context of spiritual psychology, why cannot the human person open his or her eyes, think, humbly take this once-in-a-life-time "risk" and accept the forces that challenge and prove us wrong on daily basis despite of our science and technology, and believe in God and ask for spiritual directions? The bell for radical change for unbelieving hearts is constantly ringing and "had I known" will always come at last.

In a sense, Christianity nourishes my Traditional beliefs and values in a being who is, his own authority and power. He never deceives or is deceived. In the context of spiritual psychology (SP), being a priest or minister is no option for going to heaven or obtaining the Eternal Identification number - the EIDN. Personally, the joy I have today for being a Christian is not necessarily because I am a priest, but the ransom Christ paid that has made me traditionally *"Katholikos"* – towards being all-inclusive, embracing and indebted to others in humility and love. We need to live and travel together in truth and justice. For instance, I could not have become a Christian let alone a priest, if I did not encounter Jesus within the context of community, in my family, parish priest and tradition. Thus, it may sound exaggerated and strange to say that my life is more important to me than the sacred priesthood because my being a priest does not mean I cannot face eternal loss. Each person has a life to live and save, especially for the one who cares, whether he or she is a minister, a president or politician. A lot of people can still debate on this issue as they once did when I was in the major Seminary. Why should not our individual lives, created in the image of God, be more important to us than any state else we find ourselves in life? The priesthood can actually assist me climb the ladder of faith, only when I embrace it as such. For instance, when dishonest people join politics they have only indicated their aspirations to fight against truth, justice and peace. Similarly, when a young man or girl stubbornly takes to the road to addictions and global village syndrome, he or she has equally shown his or her preparedness to constitute a nuisance and problem to society. Thus, a person with unreliable character and ambiguous life pattern who finds his or her way to the priesthood or ministry is not going to change over night. Ministry is a decision and choice.

It is very possible and easier for one to act the priest or minister than being one. This is why religion has been misrepresented today. For instance, in response to Martha's concern over the death of her brother, Lazarus, Christ said: "I am the resurrection. If anyone believes in me, even though he dies he will live, and whoever lives and believes in me will not die. Do you believe this?" (Jn.11: 25-26). The emphasis here is on the "living" in gratitude and appreciations for this special privilege, precious consciousness and life and "believing" that its giver will absolutely bring it to fulfillment and happy ends. Definitely, the priesthood or ministry is a blessing. The blessing is not realized by the wears or hood we put on, but actions, practically and freely carried out in the spirit of the cross, sacrifices, sufferings for the sake of truth, justice and love. This is because, a minister who languishes in jail for breaking the law of the state is also suffering and carrying, may be, a heavier cross. A question may arise here as whether such a cross is ministerial and meritoriously being carried in the name of Christ or in vain? A person, priest or minister who does not identify with and assist the needy or poor is carrying an empty cross, at least, within the Christian context.

This is where a lot of people grievously go wrong. Many tend to forget themselves, their source or God when they feel so highly elevated, favored and positioned in the government, profession and business. This is catastrophic. For instance, the priesthood is a call to service with its ups and downs and there lies the joy of ministry. One can answer the call without any commitment to the service. While the ministers or priests, for instance, are set apart and called to perform a particular ministry in the name of Jesus Christ, an individual minister can decide to set him or herself apart for other personal goals substantially unrelated to the ministry. Experience has shown this. By virtue of the power invested on our ministry and vocation, each minister ought to adequately represent Christ in words and actions. Yet, no minister or priest can take the position of Christ. The priesthood or ministry is perceived differently. Our studies in spiritual psychology have indicated that the intention, which motivates an action, equally controls it. Experiences also show that the interest most young men and women have today in becoming ministers, priests, evangelizers and religious primarily springs from societal influences and associations. For instance, a person who is attracted to become a minister because he or she has seen that ministers feed sumptuously, ride good cars, and own comfortable houses et cetera, may eventually succeed in becoming one, but not of Christ. Definitely, the ministry or priesthood of Christ is one, but the intentions for aspiring to be ministers, for many, differ, especially in our time. The seminary training can be the same in one's denomination, but the learning process impacts differently. These are facts and the criteria for evaluating individual ministries.

Eventually, a person may hide his or her identity till he or she becomes a priest or minister. Paradoxically, a person who opens up and behaves true to bad type may not have a chance to learn, change or complete the training, let alone becoming a minister or priest. Simulation to Christ's ministry is a crime. Each person needs to put up his or her best, the wedding and trustworthy garment. This is why the Bible made it clear that "many are called but few are chosen" (Mt. 22:14) and that "many who are first be last, and the last, first (Mt.19: 30). Unfortunately, many people have forced themselves into the ministry today for various agenda, without caring about what happens at last. For instance, some of the ministers who hold important offices in their churches today or that appear more saintly may not be the right ones or realistic. This absolutely points to God's prerogative and gratuitous gifts to make the choice of his minister, irrespective of one's holiness or state. In the final analysis, it is the individual minister or priest who knows him or herself better than anybody else. In the "choice of focal options" people follow what is consistent, meaningful, endless and reassuring to them. But Christ's ministry is specific and targeted. Therefore, our ministries should holistically reflect the person and image of Christ and not the subjective impressions each individual minister holds in his or her heart.

Most unfortunately, the greatest problem spiritual psychology faces today is to ascertain to what extent the Gospel message has influenced individual actions and relationships. The joy of God is the key success to life, which every person should emulate and fight for. What actually is the ultimate goal for the sacred priesthood, ministry, Church, the Gospel message, the Bible, World Religions besides honest life? This is the main concern of spiritual psychology.

The personality of the humble of hearts always poses great threat and riddle to the pompous. Jesus Christ is the gentlest personality on earth who moves society, not by force of material possessions but humility and love. This picture is most ad rem in the African context for global religious practices. As a priest and African, I strongly believe in those values of TJP – Truth, Justice and Peace, which God and the ancestors bequeathed to humanity or the Africans. These are universal values that should guide the belief, character and personality of each minister or priest. Honesty and sound moral lives are traceable, only to him who practiced and gave them in the first place, and to preserve them, is personally more important to me than anything else. For instance, all the efforts I make today to relate with society, and to effectively minister to the spiritual needs of others as a Catholic priest are simply, demonstrations of appreciations and gratitude to God and humanity for this special privilege of-one-life-opportunity.

In this light, whether one is rich or poor, a minister or not, holding an important office or being a homeless on the street, the way one accepts one's life, preserves, protects and guides it, matters more than silver and gold. As Paul would put it: "That is how I run, intent on winning; that is how I fight…. For, having been an announcer myself, I should not want to be disqualified" (1Cor. 9:27). We might belong to different religious groups or be ministers of the same denominations, but the "winning" Paul speaks about here, is on personal note. It does not depend on the privileges we enjoy in the Church, the fraternity of oneness and love shared together. Individual salvation lies in his or her hands.

viii. Deliberating on personal encounter and religious dynamism:

As a matter of fact, I have frightening, baffling, incredible and shocking testimonies and stories to justify my convictions and unshakeable belief in God. At a point in my faith journey, I carried out religious functions as obligations. But today, 'brothers and sisters', there is real life in God and neighbor. My stories and testimonies in this book are historically fact based. They are not fairy tales, made up stories, fictions or dreams. They are, despite my unworthiness and sinfulness, concretely and personally dimensional experiences I made in my life journey, especially during my early childhood, many years of training in the junior and senior seminaries, ministries in the parishes, seminaries, secular colleges, official and national services as a registered healing minister in the Catholic Church etc. God's favor is unlimited and any convinced priest, believer, person, or repentant sinner could be a healer. Of course, nobody heals but God. The story of my priesthood began as a toddler or kid. For instance, how many people will ever believe me, if I begin to narrate how I plainly, distinctively and clearly heard "strange voices" that commanded me just like in the case of Peter to "kill and eat" (Acts 11:6-7)? I have seen different and dreadful sights, visions, witnessed many uncountable and real miracles, not magic, heard the spirits of the dead or the dead themselves physically operating and marketing around 1 a.m. at 'Eke Nguru' in Imo State, Nigeria while I was on my way to Owerri Capital in 1969, during the Biafra/Nigeria war, et cetera? There are so many unforeseen and indescribable forces operating in this physical world. I talk of what I have seen, perceived and experienced. They are beyond personal feelings, doubts and debates.

My encounter and experiences with the supernatural are inexplicably historical and fact-based. They give me much joy and confidence in my position as an African Christian. In citing Jung in Morgan, Dr. C. Mayer remarked: "Mystery can be experienced deeply and represented vividly, but never known completely" (2009:119). The summary of my story is just as Christ said to his disciples: "There were many rooms in my Father's house; if there were not, I should have told you" (Jn. 14: 1-2). Theologians can still argue and debate on the dimension of the said "rooms". Nature does not look at faces to take its course. Agnosticism is also a powerful philosophical system. While life teaches, experience is relative.

Therefore, I sincerely and humbly urge every one, to do all it takes, to please secure an EIDN – Eternal Identification Number especially now that it is on sale and absolutely believe in the following: "God, call him whatever you like, exists. Christ is alive. The Holy Spirit is ever present. Mary, the mother of Jesus, historically remains a model of faith. The African ancestors realistically play their vital roles. The spirits, spiritual world, angels, the devil and his angels, heaven and hell are patently and profoundly realistic. Physical death is never an end. Life is endless, the spirit of the dead still operates in the physical world". For a person to deny his or her source because of money, comfort, sex, riches, education, status, science or technology is to admit that he or she is not worthy of this life to begin with. I might sound so funny here. I am not. While Theologians spend endless days and nights describing what heaven and hell look like and how God's judgment is going to be, God and his judgment are constantly at work in our every day life, at times, unrecognized. Besides, nobody has absolute knowledge of these heavenly realities except the certainty that is guaranteed in sound moral lives and behaviors here and now. The world is absolutely a mystery that no man or woman, religious or not, can fully comprehend or divulge. Every human life is just and singly "in a flux" (Heraclitus) swiftly hurrying to an inevitable end that awaits all created order. Failure to utilize and optimize one's own life drastically plunges one into a state of perpetual and everlasting regret. I refer to this as hell. After all, eternity extends to hell and God also controls it. Obviously, heaven, hell and the EIDN are within our decisions and choices, because as noted earlier on, the heavenly or eternal examinations have already started right here in our actions. I may be afraid to die but very sure of where I will be going, simple. This is the time to book the flight to the eternity of good life.

I fervidly accept the Christian religion and values because of personal inexplicable encounters with supernatural forces and the fact that they are in strong alignment with my cherished Traditional values and convictions. Religion runs in the blood of every African. Their mistakes in the Pre-historical and Stone Ages were made honestly and religiously. Times for vindication are almost on the corner and those who refuse to believe, either in God, live upright and just lives or love their neighbors will definitely have themselves to blame at last. For instance, I am no longer under any inducements and obligations to believe in the Sacraments of the Catholic Church or in Jesus Christ as a Personal Savior, his Words, Successor, the Pope, and in my fellow clergy, Catholic or Protestant, as embodiments of love and Sacraments whose presence also needs to be celebrated at sight. I do not celebrate the Eucharist to avoid breaking any obligation or law of the Church as noted earlier on. These have become cherished historical facts, meaningful life events and experiences that guide and give meaning to my life. My solid convictions in religion and in this "once-in-a-lifetime opportunity" to share the beauty of creation with the rest of humanity are based on these lived experiences with him who has blessed my life journey with his unmatchable presence, even, in the most excruciating, suffering and painful moments of my life. In this light, I try to integrate my religion, destiny, priesthood, prayers, sufferings, progresses and relationships into my life. They have entirely and inseparably become part and parcel of my daily activities and life pattern. Religious practices face extinction once people separate their feelings from life events. This is the major problem with teenagers for which SP invites each person to represent his or her values in manners that enhance progress and peace. We need to be in touch with our feelings and how they affect others.

Therefore, as a Catholic priest, I marvel at some Catholics who pray the Rosary or Stations of the Cross while the celebration of the Mass is in session. While I pray twenty decades of the Rosary (the heavenly phone number, with so many extensions, that never lack service) on daily basis because of its therapeutic and unifying results and effects, to pray it when the Eucharist is being celebrated, is not proper. I believe that each Eucharistic experience is unique and a Trinitarian distant and self-rewarding journey that begins and ends with the embodiment of love and acknowledgment of the Father, and of the Son and of the Holy Spirit. In every Eucharistic meeting, participants enter into a mysterious encounter with the Word made flesh, in the visible realities that challenge them to act and radiate the same unconditional love and divine hypostatic union to others. It is a heavenly banquet made manifest through the death of

Christ who offered his body as food, a "meal within a meal" for the sake of love. Therefore, for any Catholic to engage in other forms of devotion or praying the Rosary during Mass is totally a display of ignorance of what the Eucharist and prayer mean or dichotomy of knowledge of who Mary and her Savior, Jesus Christ are. In Christ, Grace (Mary) is in full. For instance, little or nothing else is normally done while we are eating food, why the Eucharist? To receive the Eucharist is to eat Food within food - Jesus Himself and to become Sacramental or the Person we eat to ourselves and to others. Absolute time should be given to Him, period.

Here lies the mystery of the incarnation: Jesus Christ is the son of Mary and at the same time, her God and Savior. Mary is the mother of Jesus Christ by divine privilege and through her personal efforts, her absolute trust and total resignation to the will of God, fidelity, acceptance and unique role as mother. As noted earlier, Mary is not God, but just one of us. Comparatively, as the first Christian mother and the mother of the life President of Christianity, Christ, her position outweighs all human imaginations, as how and why this unique privilege was given to a poor girl of her time. Was it by election or appointment? In amazements to God's works, the situation consequently compels most believers, even non-Catholics to respect and honor her with an equal magnitude and undivided devotion deserving only of such immeasurable personality and status. In like manner, human relationships cannot exist when the hard work of a partner and his or her concerns and feelings are not respected and felt. Trying to be busy or praying when one's attention is urgently sought and needed in relationship is not only demonic, pharisaical but also a sign of self-mistrust and rudeness.

Indescribably, my understanding of religion today is unique because my convictions in the absolute are beyond religious comprehensions in the sense of organizational and denominational debates. In practical terms, I hardly refer to my religion and its debates to live my life and relate with others. Just as the air we all breathe unconsciously, so do I feel, smell and touch prayer and religious values in others as we relate together. Basically, I tend to regard the world, religion, the sciences, priesthood, especially fellow human beings as important, precious gifts and human documents, to be respected, handled and treasured with uttermost care and love. A child who wakes up in the morning and greets his or her parents "good morning", in a sense has fulfilled a religious function without going to any Church. Every human face or living creature should give us joy and instantly remind us of the ransom and enormous sacrifice Christ made at Calvary, and this his unmatchable love irrevocably leads us to reciprocate same in others. As a matter of necessity, each person should endeavor to travel to Calvary, either through the Airplane, Train, Car or Bus of sound moral principles and healthy relationships to obtain his or her own EIDN – Eternal Identification Number.

Interestingly, from the scope of spiritual psychology - SP, both those who believe in God without religion, have religion without practice, or have religion and practice, and the atheists are all loving children of God.

Circumstantially, no one is completely bad or good. We are all in the process of becoming a better or worse person. There is urgent need for moral instructions and spiritual psychology in human organizations, establishments, particularly in the school systems and families. Each person can always obtain his or her eternal visa and identification numbers through human relationships that are totally based on truth, justice and fairness. Life is meaningful, and purposeful and it has to be fulfilled. Imperatively, we repeat, no life is more precious than the other. Respect is reciprocal. Being elevated in any position, whether by personal merits, achievements, appointments or just gratis, does not make any difference. These are opportunities and stages that need to be shared with others and appreciated in healthy relationships. One's level of humility determines one's greatness and spirituality growth. Despite the efforts individuals make, some will always be low achievers while others, high achievers. Appreciating oneself and others as gifts and in the spirit of love and care is eschatological and a practical display of religious belief, practice and insurance of one's EIDN.

In the light of the African belief and eschatology, a famous Nigerian writer, Onwubiko, observes that: "Religion and religious belief and their effects on the African community are the key to understanding the African world and ideology" (1999:23). Undoubtedly, religion is synonymous with family life in Africa and that constituted a great problem for the early missionaries in that part of the world. Bishop Chikwe Adebe Victor, citing Mbiti in his paternal address to Igbo Catholic Community and their friends in Baltimore, USA, remarked:

> *Mbiti rightly puts it that the Igbo are scrupulously religious in whatever they do. They eat, work, play, dance, and even sleep religiously" (6/28/09).*

In this context, religion is not only a belief in the absolute but also life carried out in practical terms and deeds. Thus, religion can totally be embraced as an aspect of spiritual psychology. This is religion in the true sense of the word - a movement that changes, challenges and encourages the individual to quit hypocrisy and holistically and intrinsically embrace oneself and others as fellow pilgrims on the same eternal journey of life.

Repeatedly, the point has been hammered in this book that the people's entire religious beliefs, their culture and cosmological worldviews are inseparably one and the same thing. In Anacletus Odoemene's own words:

> *Religion does not only serve the interest of the society but also of the individual, in that religion provides answers to the questions and the search for meaning, leads him into loving confrontation with the source of his being and integrates him into the society to enable him participate in the religious rituals of the community and values (1993:54).*

Inevitably, writing about the role of human conscience in religious practices, interpersonal relationships and society, Davis K. noted: "Religion serves to compensate people for the frustration they invariably experience in striving to reach socially valuable ends" (1948:526). The fact is: "What brought about the frustration in question and what are those socially valuable ends?" Again, this is where spiritual psychology challenges each person to respond to his or her internal energy in the pursuit of sound moral lives. That means, while religion seems to provide hope and compensate society for the injustices, frustrations, lack of Truth, Justice and Peace - TJP she suffers because of bad government, politicians, citizens, spiritual psychology assists her and individuals to realize the need to faithfully avoid behaviors that lead to such frustrations. In this sense, religion can meaningfully guide and resuscitate relationships particularly in moments of hopelessness and confusion just as spiritual psychology does itself.

That was why Vincent Odikanoro, citing Capuzzi & Gross in his Ph.D. work, noted: "Indeed, spirituality and religion have been a source of stability and hope for minority groups for many generations and are part of their socialization" (2008:19). The big question that comes to mind is: "Why is religion not for majority groups of society?" This is basically because it serves as a source of stability for the minority and the few that understand and accept its moral implications in their lives. Therefore, any religious belief that has no practical application to individual concerns and problems on the moment is misleading. Then, if religion and spiritual psychology have such unique and enormous roles in the life of the individual, how can the situation be described when some of the politicians and ministers who are meant to facilitate these healing opportunities to society turn around to perpetuate the frustration by false policies and Gospel?

According to Idowu: "Religion is very much and always with us. It is with us at the very moment of life" (1976:1). People are free to accept or refuse it in their lives. In Bouquet's own words: "Religion cannot wisely or safely be ignored or neglected" (1941:23) because, according to Bishop Ezeonyia, a "person's real religion lies in that something that has taken possession of his life" (1998:30). The "something" meant here has nothing to do with acquisition of material wealth, education or social status but God. Personally, I am not against material possessions that people honestly achieve through hard work and accountability. To be rich implies poverty or an escape from it. As such, any little help rendered to the poor as a way of solidarity, matters a lot. However, for some one to use his or her wealth to punish or terrorize the vulnerable of society is sickness and death. Thus, Fulton Sheen in Marlin noted: "Religion is popular only when it ceases to be truly religious. Religion by its very nature is unpopular---certainly unpopular with the ego" (1989:263). Therefore, for a minister to strive for popularity in the world contradicts the essence of the Christian mission.

Eventually, I firmly believe that the axe is now laid at the foot of every tree (Mt. 3:10); call it ministry, any believer, politician; minister found wanting or in wolves clothing faces the danger of eternal loss of identity. Christianity cannot be swept under the carpet as mere cosmetic, decorated entity for material gains. Possibly, for some people, it appears that a line of battle has sharply and unconsciously been drawn between the focus of religion and the practice. For instance, Jesus was easily and exceptionally accessible to the public, thanks to the Pope, most Bishops and Religious Leaders and Ministers who try to keep this flag flying. In this plight, the rich, the less fortunate, the sick, the dejected, the alienated of society, the homeless, the poor, and people were not in doubt about the class he belonged to, due to his clear-spelt humility. "Power corrupts" some people say. But if a minister of the Gospel of salvation neglects selflessness, love and begins to usurp and exercise powers that are comparable to worldly and political standards, it means that such a minister has completely and spiritually missed the inherent sacrificial marks of Christ and the wedding garment of the heavenly banquet. Again, when a minister of the Gospel is no longer accessible to the people for whom his office and function are distinctively defined, it equally means that such a minister is out of alignment with religious, Christian and moral values and eventually an enemy to Christ, his Gospel and society.

Worse still, for those people who do not care about religion and her ministers, this book is an invitation for them to rethink and reevaluate their relationships with God and man. Luckily, the result we obtained from our survey analysis seemed to exonerate ministers and priests from the ills of society today. Most people today use their political positions, academic professions, social status, affluence, time and energy to attack religion, the Church and her ministers for no just reasons. This is clearly underlined and shown in the removal of Moral Instructions from public schools and most parents support it. Yet, the same groups of people have religion, attend religious services, ask and send for ministers, the chaplains to visit them for one reason or the other. Humanity really claims to be in charge. Jesus and his ways have always been in the minority. But, through his love and humility, he controls the majority. The level at which anti-clericalism seems to have advanced or being nurtured and encouraged by some Christians and ministers is frighteningly astronomical. These Christians and ministers have, in a serious manner, watered down the only irreversible and life wire and source of unity in relationships.

Besides, for all the heaven-on-earth ministers, there is need to heed the warning of Burdette in Zelinski: "The only thing wealth does for some people is to make them worry about losing it" (1997:147). Therefore, if a minister of the Gospel begins to worry about losing his or her material possessions, it is indicative that such a minister has not functioned and labored in the Lord's vineyard. Our individual relationships with Christ provide unfailing guide to our relationships with ourselves, with one another and the world at large. This one-on-one relationship with God remains personal irrespective of one's religious affiliations and involvements. Consequently, spiritual psychology - SP calls for the right attitude for a change of heart. In this capacity, our hearts have to be broken or crushed (Ps. 51:17) and the stony hearts changed to those of flesh (Ezekiel 44:7). That is why Mangis made this clarion call: "The Church certainly needs a call beyond spirituality focused on comfort and self-fulfillment" (JPT, 2000:259). It is time we began to heed the warning of Comstock cited in Dossey, in these words: "Seek not abroad; turn back into thyself for in the inner man dwells the truth" (1993:57), the "indwelling Christ presence" (USC, 2000:6). According to Mangis:

> *This emphasis on outward behavior over the inward qualities of the heart is partly where the Church has lost its role in fostering spiritual formation. This is what Dallas Willard calls 'gospels of sin management' (2000:260).*

These "gospels of sin management" or the emphasis on outward behavior and religious piety that lack inward bases, seem to have destroyed Christianity.

Today, emphasis is centered more on preaching the word than doing what the word says, (good deeds), and to avoid breaking the law than ideally living up to the spirit and reasons for the law. Some ministers of the word are anxious and busy preparing wonderful homilies to dish out to others but hardly make efforts to preach to themselves and live by examples. This is a problem that unconsciously affects the global relationships and community. Therefore, in the words of Zundel: "Listening to one's soul, by becoming attentive to what one thinks, to what one wants, to what one really loves, every being can thus confirm the words of St. Paul: "In Him, we have life, movement and being" (1993:23).

Again, according to Whitson: "The inner deepening of life in Christ does not turn us in upon ourselves in a holy isolation" (1995:102) but it leads us to openness. Ward cited in Shaw and Morgan, in his own contribution noted: "Religious faith itself, however, lies in a realm of experience outside the reach of the natural sciences, experience of a personal dimension to reality" (2006:46). Of course, while religious experiences are practical, they are beyond scientific analysis.

By necessity, ministers of the Gospel are called to wear their wedding garments in their hearts as they carry out Christ's mandate. They do not deserve any human sympathy but respect. The Lord who calls them into his ministry is their portion and strength (Chr. 16:22; Ps. 105:15). Despite the trials and abuses the ministers of the Gospel seem to have suffered at the hands of those they serve, society generally counts on them for spiritual growth and edification. This expectation is a must. I often wonder at the level of humility that lies within the regalia of most of our senior ministers and Church leaders. In actuality, most ministers or shepherds of Gods' people assiduously and tenaciously carry out the divine mandate in all honesty, sacrificially guiding the faith of society. They really need our support and prayers.

Oblige me to say that the Catholic Church has for centuries encouraged celibacy among her priests and the women religious. Reasonably, the conclusion is reached not because marriage is evil or against the Gospel. Rather, the denominational aim is to allow the priests give enough and undivided attention in dedicating themselves to God and to the people for whom they are called to serve (Mt. 19:12; I Cor. 7:26-27, 32). The theological backing for celibacy is not as important in the area of spiritual psychology, as realistically embracing and living up to it. That some priests and ministers get involved in one sex scandal or the other is regrettably part of the human story and factor that needs to be given mortal blows by prayer and personal orientations. It must be noted that celibacy is unnatural and out of the ordinary. But it is not impossible. Celibate life is not a problem for a person who voluntarily embraced it with love and devotion. This is what makes it unique and a model for fulfilled life. It is a formidable and free sacrifice only comparable to the virginal sacrifice Jesus Christ made for the salvation and well being of humanity. Some are celebrates today, not necessarily for religious reasons, but personal choices. Sexual urge, as noted earlier, in the life of any healthy person is undeniably forceful, normal and natural. It is never sinful, but tempting. Therefore, it should be acknowledged and sublimated for more effective practice of the individual celibate, to freely live and carry out his or her vocation. However, when a celibate begins to question and argue about the theology and legitimacy of celibate life, he or she has simply demonstrated his or her unwillingness and hypocrisy for being one or accepting it.

ix. Tapping strengths in yourself as in "the remembered wellness" of Benson:

Truth is self-evident and our consciences and relationships draw their strengths from there. Whatever a person sows, he or she reaps. If he or she sows in the field of self-indulgence, he or she reaps corruption, but if he or she sows in the spirit, eternal life (Gal. 6:7) as noted earlier on. The strength in sound moral life is unlimited. The law of harvest equally states that bountiful sowing leads to bountiful harvesting. The true meaning of life is goodness. What is good for one person is also good for everybody because it is a universal value. The Psalmist joyfully echoed the goodness of God in these words: "Taste and see that the Lord is Good" (Ps. 34:8). Tasting the "goodness of God" is a unique experience and encounter. Figuratively, it is a process of initiation into the life and value of the other. It is a call to radical self-supervision and transformation. One can only taste the goodness of the other if one is in touch with one's own goodness or has dispositions towards it. The whole emphasis on technology, religion, and economy today are geared towards making human life more meaningful. Every one wants to breathe fresh air of goodness, joy and life. All the same, only few people succeed in this regard because of human wickedness and evil inclinations. Bad life is both corrosive and infectious and there is no glimpse of goodness or joy in it. Yet, the human mind has the capacity to heal itself whenever it aspires for the good. However, for Aquinas, borrowing from Aristotle, the ultimate end of life and goal is the "summum bonum" – the highest or supreme good (happiness) from which all others are derived (IR). The problem is that "happiness" can relatively be derived from illicit means and sources. For instance, an armed robber who escapes gunshots feels happy for his or her being alive. Ultimately, goodness is the basis for true happiness.

Eventually, Benson's work becomes a vital tool at these days of verbal, physical, emotional, mental and spiritual abuses and tortures. According to him:

> *In my 30 years of practicing medicine, I've found no healing force more impressive or more universally accessible than the power of the individual to care for and cure him or herself"* *(1997:22).*

Alleluia! This is consoling and essentially confirms the objective of spiritual psychology - SP. The engines of healthy relationships are within each individual. Healings do not come by accidents or without reasons. This "power of the individual to care for and cure him or herself" primarily comes from his or her positive memories, energized by sound moral life and good works and not from remorsefulness. Therefore, the earlier individuals realize how important it is to lead good lives and how precious their lives are and the need to appreciate the lives of others, the better for healthy relationships. This is precisely why spiritual psychology aims at the holistic fulfillment and realization of individual persons and leads them to authentic living and a broader way of viewing the beauty of the world singularly in human relationships. According to Benson: "This visceral truth is, something we can count on, something that remains the same despite the dramatic changes we often experience in our public and private lives" (1997:24).

That "something" we can count on, that "something", which remains the same irrespective of the emotional pains, difficulties and changes in our lives and relationships, differs from one individual to another. That something, which does not easily affect our relationships despite poverty, individual sicknesses, mistakes and weaknesses must be terrific and explendid. Some may call it love, personal convictions, others hope, but Benson calls it "remembered wellness" as already noted. For me, it is "sound moral life" guided by Truth, Justice and Peace - TJP. We need this remembered wellness or what "we can count on" in every relationship. Each person should have and radiate one of these qualities in his or her relationship. Ironically, nobody gives this quality or value to another person. It is not transferable. It has to be part of the individual's spiritual mark, goodness and identity, exclusively within his or her soul. Those who are constantly in the same runway with their God know what I am talking about here. Has it ever occurred to anybody to ask or wonder why some people always look cheerful in their misery, hardship and abject poverty? Sound moral life is divine. That was the goodness the Psalmist was talking about in the above quotation. The case of King Hezekiah, is also glaring here, especially when Yahweh sent Isaiah to say to him: "Put your affairs in order, for you are going to die, you will not live'. Hezekiah turned his face to the wall and addressed this prayer to Yahweh: "Ah, Yahweh, remember I beg you, how I have behaved faithfully and with sincerity of heart in your presence and done what is right in your eyes" (2Kings 20: 1-3). Amazingly, because of Hezekiah's remembered wellness or his "faithfulness and sincerity of heart" Yahweh said: "I will add fifteen years to your life" (2Kings 20:6). Remembered wellness is one's power manifestation. This is not dependent on one's affluence, education, science, religion or being conditioned by any external force or the ways others think of one. This is an individual system memory or conscience that internally records whatever he or she does, knowingly or unknowingly. Preciously, it is a conscious awareness of one's good or bad life in relation to the world around and beyond one.

Relationship is not dependent on material things – Oprah's perspective

The success story of Tereral Trent of Zimbabwe as narrated at Oprah's Show on Thursday, October 1, 2009 is enough evidence of how personal determination, will power; inner strength and energy can lead somebody from ground zero to the Ph.D status. Moreover, listen and read about the Queen of Media, Oprah and her life or success story.

Self-determination is the key. There are no limits on how thankful souls can be to mother nature in the midst of the exigencies of life. The sky is always the limit for whoever is disciplined and respects God and society in his or her actions. Therefore, if material things alone cannot guarantee that which is permanent in our lives and relationships, then the only option must be something that is immaterial and eternal. Though, healthy human relationships are seemingly experiential and physical, they go beyond worldly influences and individual weaknesses. They elevate partners to a higher spiritual level. That is why we noted that; to be religious is not the same thing as being spiritual, because spirituality is intrinsically an ordinary way of life that incorporates the person's values, strengths and limitations that may not emphasize a belief in any religious system. In Hawkins's words: "Acceleration of spiritual energy is facilitated by relinquishment of narcissistic, egoistic self-interests, such as seeking of personal gain" (2006:258). He elaborately remarked:

> *The source of joy stems from the inner subjective experience of the innate source of one's existence itself, unimpeded by the limitation of presuming the personal self to be a causal or primary agent. By humility and surrender, the imaginary control is relinquished to God and Divine Will (2006:259).*

In this context, spirituality is a struggle for the best; call it a state of blessedness that takes into account the little details of a person's life, his environment, relationships with God, others, thoughts, actions, and so on. According to Broccolo in Svoboda: "Spirituality...involves a way of viewing and experiencing God, self, others, and the world" (1996:5). The effects of personal experiences, whether they are positive or negative determine how we feel about God, others, society and ourselves.

To be spiritual is to take a middle course, distancing and breaking from those forces that create uneasiness and restlessness in one's relationships, like craving for wealth and fame. It is within the context of spirituality that a person discovers his "remembered wellness". In other words, coming to terms with ourselves in relation to the world that surrounds us is a way to spirituality. Spirituality is not exclusive of religion but it is not limited to anything. Rather, spirituality is holistic and inclusive.

Religion, most often, provides the energy for climbing the spirituality ladder and vice versa. Whether religion is "ideal" by deduction (what it should be) or "real" by induction (how it influences life experiences) "the faculties of mind, heart and will must be brought to bear in discernment" (Op.cit. 1990:18-19). For instance, many partners gladly strive in their relationships amidst extreme difficulties and economic setbacks. The key lies on the spirituality contents and "remembered wellness" of each individual relationship and not necessarily on material wealth. History has recently presented a religious zealot and fanatic, Garrido Philip, here in America as a rapist, who hid an innocent girl of 11, Jaycee Lee Dugard for 18 good years in his backyard and selfishly forced her into an unprepared motherhood of 2 children. We thank God that the victim miraculously survived the ordeal. Yet, why do humans operate in forms of animals? These are questions that confront the field of spiritual psychology - SP. Good life is an inspiration and success requires perseverance and courage.

x. Mary, the mother of Christ: A model, permanent in all relationships:

As a follow up from Benson's "remembered wellness" and personal experiences, I always radiate Mary, the mystery of mercy, God's Master Piece of Truth, Care, Purity and Sincerity, the Full of Grace, the mother of Christ as my 'remembered wellness" in all my life goals, aspirations and relationships. From my early childhood, the person and presence of Mary, the mother of the Lord has been a big source of confidence, strength, safety and courage to me in the face of uncertainties and my sufferings. My relationship with her is unique. Generally speaking, the love of a mother and child is inseparable and that we know. Relationship is recognition. To recognize is "to know again, to identify, to acknowledge, to treat as valid" (Dict. Def.). We hardly relate with people who do not recognize and acknowledge us as such. Recognizing a person's worth, importance, position, status, personality, feelings and aspirations is an asset in building healthy relationship with him or her. Incidentally, Mary is historically the only person on the planet who perfectly knows the mind of God as exemplified by the Scriptures when she advised the disciples: "Do whatever he tells you to do" (Jn. 2:5) because your hour of liberation from evil and restoration has arrived.

Let us join Mary and make Jesus' 'hour', our own: A motherless Society is in trouble

Naturally, every request has elements of approval or disapproval. This is typical of the human experience and relationship. But in the case of the request Mary made of the disciples, something very unique and mysterious happened. Now the question is: "Who told Mary, except God himself, what she had expected Jesus to do for the disciples?" As it were, Christ had apparently turned down her request of "they have no wine" [Jn. 2:3] in these words: "Woman, why turn to me? My hour has not come yet" [Jn. 2:4]. After Christ had warned and made it clear to her regarding the hour his father gave for his public ministries or to start performing miracles, why did Mary persist? Definitely, it was Mary alone who knew, released and launched Christ into the said 'hour' to embark on his father's mission and subsequently accomplished his father's will that day, his first sign or miracle of changing water into wine [Jn. 2:11]. By "hour" here, we do not specifically refer to the time of the day when we expect something to happen. It is deeper than that. This is the hour of radical and complete change, transformation and revolution which spiritual psychology is bringing about to society through this book. Mary launched Jesus into the "hour" and that central moment and point in human history when relationships would take different shapes, an hour when humanity would live in peace thereby transforming into the image of its creator. This is the hour to love one another; the hour college students must face their studies and shun bad companies. It is the hour to deliver society from injustices.

Delightfully, today, spiritual psychology, religion, morality, science et cetera, is calling individuals to make Jesus' "hour" their own hour, the hour of love, unity, peace and togetherness. Every day is another day. Years and lives, progress one day at a time. Buoyantly, healthy relationships operate on the level of Jesus' "hour" and not on the uncertain hours of material gains, sufferings and insatiability. No wonder, Jesus had no option to change "my food is to do the will of my father" [John 4:34] and "I came to do my father's will" [John 6:38] into "I now do the will of my mother" because he did not doubt that "hour" and the clarity of his father's voice, re-echoing in that of his mother. No relationship thrives in the absence of trust. Therefore, I proudly and absolutely claim Mary, the changeless, unalterable and permanent 'hour' of blessedness, truth, good luck, sound moral life and safety as that 'something' in my life that does not change despite the trials and temptations of this changing world. In this light, I made the following remarks about Mary in one of my publications:

> *Chances are, that those who tend to play down Mary in their families or relationships end up creating a vacuum that can only be filled by immorality, frustration, laziness, Godlessness, even divorce. This is very serious, because to have a motherless family, community, or nation is dangerous. We need to have mothers after the motherhood of Mary, a symbol of peace and love we seek in every relationship (1995: 56).*

No wonder, Muller, in the Bulletin Dei Verbum, of the Catholic Biblical Federation, entitled "Mary: Model of Evangelization" rightly noted: "Mary is distinguished, above all, by the fact that she, throughout her life, was totally dedicated to God" (1992, Jan. – Mach: 20). Dedication in relationships is self-rewarding too. That was precisely why, in one of my books, I observed:

> *Mary's unique place in the economy of our salvation is unquestionable, indisputable, unchallengeable, irreversible, and irrevocable. It has happened. No living creature was, and will ever be consulted for this singular role or function (1995:17).*

Thence, I recommend Mary as an indispensable presence and gift in all human relationships. For instance, Mary was absolutely obedient, not only to her husband Joseph, but also to Jesus Christ, her son and savior. Even the request she made, "they have no wine" was a practical demonstration of her caring attitude in her relationship with humanity. Mary successfully played an enormous role in her relationship with God and man. Today, she is a historical figure, worthy of emulation for those who care in their relationships.

In the Holy Quran, the Muslims have this to say about Mary: "Vowed a fast to (God) Most gracious, And this day will I enter into no talk with Any human being" (Surah XIX 26). The ball is now in our court and she has not ceased to feature in the scenes of human relationships. According to the Koranic Commentary No. 2479, it is stated: "The passage means abstinence from the ordinary household meals, and indeed from human sexual intercourse generally". Moreover, other instances in the Koran, testify, not only the fact that Mary was preserved from Original sin, but also had no other child after Christ as the above Surah pointed out. In another passage, the Koranic Commentary reads: "God had destined her to be the Mother of the holy prophet Jesus Christ, and now had come the time when this should be announced to her" (Surah XIX 19), alluding to that hour.

Besides all these, common sense does not contradict the fact of giving honor to whom it is due. We have to get it right that devotion is part and parcel of human nature. Any relationship that lacks devotion does not last. Speaking about the irreplaceable nature of devotion in general, Karl Rahnar noted: "We mean something to one another, not only in everyday things of life, not because (since we exist), we have parents" (1963:26). In other words, when we honor Mary, we are at the same time honoring ourselves because we are constantly engaged in one form of devotion to someone else. Explaining further, Rahner said: "Devotion to Mary is something that by the very root from which it springs has something to do with love of one's neighbor" (Op.cit. 31). That is why devotion to Mary – hyperdulia, is both Imitatory or exemplary, Intercessory and Laudatory or Reverential. In our context, any devotion whereby a person is honored in view of his or her exemplary qualities or sound moral life, hard work, humility, fervent faith, truth, honesty, and love et cetera is not limited to Mary or any particular individual. Devotion is a universal value that can be applied to anybody. By Christological implication, there can be Jesus Christ, without Mary, but we cannot speak of Mary without Christ. The borderline is, Mary will always be and remain for all ages and generations to come, the mother of Christ.

Generally, people, Christians alike, can speak of themselves and others without any reference to Christ. On the contrary, if there is a person on earth who may speak or claim to have Christ as his or her personal savior, then, Mary should be remembered and honored for the primary position she is already occupying. That was the point Pope Paul VI meant when he said: "It is natural that in true devotion to the Blessed Virgin, the son should be duly known, loved and glorified…when the Mother (be it any person's mother) is honored" (LG. no.67), such devotion is an approach to Christ, the source and center of ecclesiastical communion" (Nov. 21, 1964). Even if one does not need the Catholic Church or religion for anything, Mary's qualities are very important in interpersonal relationships. Our teenagers need her qualities for their educational achievements. As a guide to what we are saying here, St. Germanus in Shepherds of Christ, once observed: "As breathing is not only a sign but even a cause of life, so the name of Mary, which is constantly found on the lips of God's servants, both prove that they are truly alive, and at the same time causes and preserves their life, and gives them every succor" (2007 Issue No. 5, pg. 2). St. Ambrose, as if he was referring to Mary's role in our relationships, noted: "Mary was such that her life alone was a model for all…. Thence learn how to live, what to correct, what to avoid, what to retain" (Op.cit. 5, Page 4).

To make Mary a model in our relationships does not imply she is God or an invitation to religion. Every relationship needs the good qualities and values of people who are role models like Mary. Notwithstanding the fruit of Mary's womb, Jesus Christ, she is just like any human being, mother, and an ordinary woman of her day. Characteristically, through sound moral upbringing and selfless commitment for the course of truth and justice, anybody can be a model for others in their relationships. Mary is neither Catholic nor Protestant, but a Mother per excellence. In this understanding, Pope Benedict XVI in his homily, 12/31/06, cited in "A Moment with Mary" makes the following inviting remarks:

> *Let us entrust to Mary, who is Mother of Mercy Incarnate, particularly those situations to which the Lord's grace alone can bring peace, comfort, and justice" in our relationships (6/ 27/09).*

These clarion calls, Pope Benedict XVI, St. Ambrose, Benson and I have made here are urgent, especially today that some relationships "are in crisis: a crisis in which the traditional bonds of affection [and relationships-mine] have been breached, theological differences [points of views-mine] have become public quarrels" (Strudwick in Baunoch [ed], 2006:208).

As I remarked in one of my books, there are mindfully "three warlords fighting in each person" (1994:32) and they affect our relationships. These are the intellect, which weighs the 'pros' and 'cons' of any course of action, the desire or will, which focuses on the beauties of this world or object and the appetite or choice, which seeks momentary and immediate gratifications. These three warlords constantly fight for supremacy over the other in every relationship. In situations like this, it is only the spiritual psychologists who can assist individuals develop the fourth spiritual self. This fourth spiritual self is so essential to calm and keep these warlords and drives on hold for the individual agent [in any particular relationship] to plan and have enough deliberations to justify his or her decision and course of action. When the "p' in a partner becomes capital "P", relationship wobbles away from its track. Discretion, self-trust, confidence and prudence are parts of this fourth spiritual self. To die in the presence of one's enemy is painful and the worse enemy an individual has is bad life or lack of good memory.

Objectively, spiritual psychology is the practical application of conscience to individual actions for a realistic utilization of personal, religious and moral values in the building of healthy relationship. From our discussion on the Prodigal son episode, as recorded in Luke 15:11, spiritual psychology is calling everybody to stop at the axis of wrong decision, action, and return from his or her distant journeys of selfishness, avarice, sin and insatiability to practically embrace the love and warmth of God and neighbor in the healthy relationships of the family. Spiritual psychology challenges society particularly the ministers of the word of God to be conscious of their responsibility as practical examples and models of the Christian life because to whom more is given, more is expected (Lk.12: 48). The need to live the Gospel message in our relationships urgently and inevitably calls for personal decision, involvement, commitment and courage to identify with the Cross and crucified Christ. The sacred priesthood or ministry, in many cases, is not merely an appendage or a substitute for politics or marriage as earlier on observed. It is a Sacrament, gloriously realized and fulfilled in personal sacrifices within the Ecclesial Community of relationships and must jealously be guided through sound moral lives.

Priests or ministers are individually part of one another. Their gifts of service differ according to the grace God gives them. Personally, "I did not become a priest to avoid marriage or women. Rather, my priesthood, in this context, is a choice that helps me appreciate the uniqueness and beauty of womanhood, divinely raised to an admirable height in the sight of God, through Mary the mother of Jesus. Therefore, any priesthood or ministry that relegates or is devoid of the services and love of women is not of Christ. In more concrete terms, fieldworks and experiences have even shown that the spiritual balance, stability and continuity of the faith of most churches of civilized cultures, like Nigeria today, tremendously hang on the supportive presence of women. They are generally part and parcel of the foundation stones of the Church that is built on the "Yes" of a woman, Mary. Billy in Baunoch, speaking about the need of this functional theology in the growth of faith, remarked:

> *The matrix of God-human-world activity becomes the underlying principle guiding all theological reflections. When seen in this light, "faith seeking understanding" (fides quaerens intellectum), however it is conceived, becomes a process by which each of these realities is probed more deeply both in itself and in its relationship to the others (2006:11).*

Vivaciously, if there is God, spiritual psychologists want his adherents to prove it in their relationships. If we accept that humility is a sign of Christ's presence, then spiritual psychology is a catalyst for such a realization in the lives of rational beings. If religion is important in the lives of believers, spiritual psychology wants to see its positive influences and effects in the lives of ministers and society. In the light of Koran philosophy in Mead: "Every child is born into the religion of nature; its parents make it a Jew, a Christian, or a Magian" (1965:370). Similarly, every child is born into the beauty of creation, its parents fundamentally shape how he or she behaves and perceives the world at large. This, again, calls for the need to respect our consciences.

xi. Deontology:

This deals with, and studies the duties of individuals in their various states of life, gender, age, status and functions. It is from here that ethics, which is the study of right or wrong living, derives its intrinsic meanings. Thence, deontology, morality and conscience are so interwoven that we cannot speak of one without the other. The implication is that, faithfulness to one's duties is important in any given relationship. Couples, for instance, share duties and responsibilities to keep their relationships moving. Failure to comply with their duties complicates the trust that binds their minds together. Individuals equally know when the moral order of their relationships is complied to or broken. Eventually, conscience plays the role of judging the rightness and wrongness of such individual actions and makes them known to the principal agents or partners. The secular or socio-religious perspective of conscience is a response to the moral standard of society. In this light, spiritual psychology emphasizes the application of the same moral standards to individual actions to keep society safe and sound.

However, each individual is a product of his or her own age and history. The issue of age and history in human nature plays an important role in human relationships. Therefore, to keep this book focused, we shall briefly and interestingly study the role of conscience in human relationships in the various epochs of history as a guide to the present society.

C. Human relationships and conscience in the history of mankind

Conscience has intrinsically and always been a guide to human relationships. Basically, it has been associated with 'man and woman' as an object of study by the Greek, medieval, modern and contemporary philosophers as the most fundamental characteristic that is peculiarly and typically human. God Himself, the author of life, in the creation account unfolded the necessity of conscience in these words when humanity soiled her relationship with him: "I will never again curse the ground because of man neither will I ever again destroy every living creature as I have done". (Gen. 8:21). The above biblical passage displays a rational judgment in God's decision and action on that creation account. But, while it is not a contradiction to say that God is not rational in human standards, we must admit that he is Rationality himself. He has set an example for us to follow in case we make mistakes. A theological problem of evil may arise here. If God is all Omniscience and Omnipotence, why did he not create human beings who would not make mistakes but always act rightly? Then, we could as well ask, if God created such beings who would not sin at all, could we still call them humans? These are revelations that empower us exercise our freedom within the limitations of our nature.

On the other hand, we are constrained to ask: "Does God have conscience himself because both rationality and conscience imply an imperfection? Or, could God still be infinitely perfect if he possesses these qualities? Obviously, to speak of God in these terms in relation to man and woman, may create problems because he outweighs creation in every respect. Therefore, when we say that man or woman has conscience or knowledge, it means God is conscience or knowledge himself. In the same way, if a man or woman is kind and generous, then God is kindness and generosity et cetera. But if man or woman is sinful, God is Holiness. As it were, a study of conscience in most of the major periods in the history of human relationships becomes consequential here.

a. Ancient period/antiquity

The Greeks dominated this age. In this period, the issue of conscience and its application in human actions and relationships were never raised but taken for granted. In Iwuchukwu, everything was seen in the light of matter and "reduced to a single primal principle of cosmocentricism - the cause of things in the world" (1993:1-2). The period looked to revelation as the only source of their religious authority, supporting those in our group C of the spiritual typology. By this time, the human spirit was seen as an orientation towards the great beyond and relationships were revered and kept sacred. The science of nature and other disciplines were studied in so far as they were means to this great beyond. The situation is better understood in the context of the Igbo of Nigeria where human lives and relationships are under the control of the Great God and interventions of the ancestors. The attitudes of the age were more like the Negro Spiritual: "I am going to tell God all my trouble when I get home" (Russell, 1979: 41). In the light of the Negro Spiritual, once individual partners have played their own parts as responsible people and handed their relationships over to God, there will be little or nothing to quarrel about. It is only from these traditional and cultural contexts that we understand the content and role of conscience in human relationships of the epoch.

In this epoch of history, for instance, conscience was essentially the voice of God and an "inward power...passing judgment on one's self" (Dict. Def.). As it were, through this power, God directs human relationships to their destinies. Based on the understanding of the age, Fagothey remarked: "Conscience is sometimes called the voice of God... an inner voice, a still small voice, telling us what to do or to avoid" (1963:45). A Roman philosopher, Cicero cited in my work also noted: "I do not set much store by what others think of me; my own conscience counts for me than the verdict of all other people" (1982: Preface). Accordingly, Cicero has equipped each partner with the skills that meaningfully guide relationships. This is an encouragement, a form of motivation to keep on playing positive roles in our relationships irrespective of what others might be doing. In the spirit of spiritual psychology, the mentality of this epoch regarded God as the supreme judge, in which material things; human relationships and the absolute were considered eternal and assets to one's EIDN – Eternal Identification Number.

Eventually, the mentality of this Age influenced the Christian philosophers or Apologetics (Patristic Age) who presented creation as the product of the absolute in which cheating and dishonesty in relationships are punishable by God alone. The situation just described, equally suits the Igbo of Nigeria. Both epochs arrived at the idea of transcendence and the belief in a supernatural power. Anaximander, a product of this age, as mentioned in our introduction, once remarked in William: "All things must in equity again decline into that whence they have their origin, for they must give satisfaction and atonement for injustice, each in order of time" (1929:35). What a beautiful picture and model has Anaximander set here for healthy relationships? He had, in a sense, implied the eschatological dimensions of human relationships.

That is to say, the role each person plays in any relationship must have its consequent rewards or punishments either here on earth or hereafter.

b. Medieval [Middle] period

This period was very much influenced by the work of the Christian Apologists. Much attention was given to reason in relation to faith. By the influence of Scholars like Thomas Aquinas, a distinction was made between philosophy and theology. With this intervention, religious and moral issues like conscience remained true irrespective of reason. For instance, there was no justification for individuals to cheat one another in their relationships. This was equally the time when philosophy was conceived as the handmaid of theology -*Philosophia ancilla theologiae* because relationships thrive whenever reason is guided by some moral principles.

c. Modern period

The modern age originated with the renaissance, a period of Cultural Revolution unlike the one this book is bringing about. The revolution in spiritual psychology is holistic, inclusive and antithetical to that of the modern age. Unlike the periods just ended, this age led to various philosophical schools of thought as we have them today in some cultures that seem to have destroyed both religious practices and relationships. The modern period was characterized by an atmosphere of Immanentism in which all emphasis shifted from theocentricism, transcendence and cosmocentricism to egocentricism. At this period, relationships became self-centered and anthropocentric. We can easily imagine what happens to relationships that have no bearing with religion, God, and moral values. The values of the period were more of aesthetic than religious or moral. It was in this spirit that a subjective idealist, Berkeley noted that: "The existence of things consists solely in their being perceived... esse est percipi... to be is to be perceived" (1975:30). Thus, human relationship becomes an insurance policy only reviewed and revisited when the need arises. In this way, the idea of sacrifices, personal commitments, beliefs in the Supernatural and application of conscience in relationship becomes a matter of choice. Unfortunately, this period greatly influences the present day relationships, especially in the area of trust.

In the spirit of the age, man or woman intellectually feels he is the builder of the world in which he or she lives. Thereby, each feels he or she has the power to liberate him or herself from all ecclesiastical authority and traditional patterns of thought and interpret reality that way. It is because reality has been interpreted wrongly today that a child can fight his or her parents and even get involved with drug addictions, and any form of atrocity and gets away with it, if not caught. In this capacity, Engels observes: "We wish to remove from our path all that appear to us under the banner of superhuman and the supernatural" (1965:371). In this sense, he represented the belief system of those in our group "A" of the spirituality typology. Ego-centered relationships are always exclusive than inclusive. Eventually, in this era, conscience, as Wolaman would put it "is the individual's set of moral values which was thought to be innate by medieval writers, but is now believed to be acquired" (1973:76). While we do not doubt that certain consciences can be formed by external factors like one's environment, upbringing and training, moral principles are not limited to any body of knowledge. Unfortunately, it was in the light of this age that Bochenski noted:

> *Conscience cannot be explained as biological function, nor should it be regarded as the voice of an alien power (God), the call comes from anxiety, from human existence, which is being "Thrown down" becomes anxious about its possibility of being (1966: 168).*

Again, when a relationship becomes a matter of survival-of-the fittest, obviously, the aim and objective get frustrated and cease to be healthy.

d. Contemporary period

This age is nominally concerned with the history of our time. Every relationship or development in life dynamically goes with some radical modifications and the peculiar situation people find themselves at the time. The modern period in history seemed to have failed humanity due to rationalizations and much ideology that still plague society today. On the other hand, the contemporary era focuses on the need for authentic living, dismantling man from metaphysical world to that of phenomenon, hence the relevance of this book. That is, while the modern period conceives human relationship as an end, the contemporary presents it as a living experience, constantly in search for meaning. The contemporary mentality reasonably enjoins people to listen and put aside prejudices, shameful attitudes and preoccupations that might create conflicts in their relationships and encourage one another to build a stable society.

Healthy relationships are necessary in every strata of human development, be it in religion, government, education et cetera. In reference to the failed system of education in this era, Okechukwu remarked:

> *Education is collapsing as a result of the shameful attitudes of some lecturers and students. Students are expected to face their studies. Let us restore the dignity of education", (2001:12).*

Thus, Okechukwu is implying that people should live up to their responsibilities and obey their consciences for a brighter and healthier cohesion, not only in their relationships but also in the school systems as a whole. This is the central message of this epoch.

That was why Stumpf once observed: "Whoever evades his responsibility through [mouvaise foi - bad faith] self-deception will not be at ease in his conscience" (1977:483). Uneasiness in relationships kills. The contemporary is an epoch where conscience is identified with the whole personality, inseparable from his or her values. In this sense, one of the fathers of contemporary schools of psychology, Allport in Limdesmith and Straussk, noted: "Personality is the dynamic organization within the individual of those psychological systems that determine his unique adjustments to his environment" (1956: 484). Therefore, healthy relationships flexibly call for continued readjustments of personal idiosyncrasies, thoughts, feelings and actions. The nucleus of this system calls for self-supervision, conscious awareness and evaluation. Invariably, this self-evaluation is important in all human relationships.

D. Human relationships vis-à-vis types of conscience

Generally, conscience is classified according to its operations and it also corresponds to, and represents the behavior and relationship of each individual. Most scholars like Murray and Fagothey seem to agree that different kinds of conscience can be reduced to two basic types, namely; correct and erroneous, hence we talk of healthy and unhealthy relationships. In view of our focus, we considered the following kinds of conscience, culled from many sources as acknowledged in this book in order to determine how each affects and influences human relationships:

i. Correct or true conscience

When conscience judges as good what is really good and as evil what is really evil, its resultant dictate is said to be correct or true. It is conformity to a valid moral law and application of that law to a concrete case. That is, when individuals feel they have done their best and that which guarantees peace and harmony in their relationships, they have less to worry about. This is what St. Paul calls an "inner power", even for the lawless, that is, anomoi and pagans who never heard of the law; they have conscience, (Rom. 2:14-15). These inner powers and energies are the guiding principles of healthy relationships.

ii. Certain conscience

When our consciences judge us without any fear of contradictions, they are said to be certain. Parties need to avoid fears in their relationships. According to William Barry:

> *The dominance of fear not only affects our relationships with God and other people but also affects inter-group and international relations and our relations with the environment (1990:20).*

Logically, something can be certain without being correct. This calls for serious caution in our relationships. For instance, if a man accuses his wife of cheating because he saw her talking with her ex-boy friend, the accusation may be certain but not correct. It is possible that at the very moment both ex-friends met the only exchange of words was the following:

Ex-Girl: "Hi! My husband told me you are now the manager of his company"

Ex-Boy: "Yes! I think your man is great. He is a professional in that field".

It is sad to note that simple wave of the hands; eye contacts, false accusations, unfair minded words and actions have ruined so many healthy relationships. Conscience is certain when the deed matches with the blame or praise, especially when the mind so adheres to the judgment excluding all probabilities and prudent fears of the opposite judgments. In this sense, we say that clear conscience fears no accusation. Any one who always and easily finds faults in others, practically in all their behaviors is sick and urgently needs medical attention. Suspicion is a sign of insecure mind. Partners in business and marital lives should study and understand bit of the characters of those they relate with and disabuse their minds from unnecessary misgivings. We need peaceful environment and trust in our relationships. Paulin, in his own words, calls this a "good conscience", (1992: 168). We experience this "good conscience" when we sincerely allow honest thoughts and feelings guide our relationships.

iii. Erroneous conscience

Strange things often happen in our relationships and at times we are at sea as how to figure them out. Erroneous judgment of conscience leads to some of the misgivings that create problems in our relationships. Conscience is erroneous when it is not correct or goes contrary to truth. There abounds in human actions when what the individual apprehends as a fact or moral law is not. In such cases, the honest efforts people make to keep their relationships healthy can be misinterpreted and receive wrong application or interpretation. Or, there are times when the judgment of individual actions is objectively not in accord with the pertinent fact. Error becomes harmful in relationships when it sounds intentional and constantly repeated. For instance, that a partner erroneously and mistakenly shut the door of the house before realizing that all the keys were inside should not constitute any ill feelings in relationships. This also distinguishes between truth and untruth. Every person has right to truth in normal circumstances. For instance, a partner who is careless with money has no right to the truth of the income of the house. When truth is told and eventually it turns out to be false because of inadequate knowledge of the matter being otherwise, it is untruth and not a lie. But when a fact is communicated with the intent to deceive, it is lie. For instance, that I told a parishioner that the Secretary was in the office when I was actually leaving the house, if the parishioner reached there and found nobody, it was untruth and not a lie. A person can phone his or her partner to come home and have his or her lunch, if he or she arrives home and does not find any food at the table, may be, because their little kid ate it up; it is not a lie but untruth.

iv. Doubtful conscience

This is where a person either hesitates to make any judgment at all or makes one with some doubts that the opposite may be true. Based on this apparent dilemma or probable reasons for and against a course of action, the person may withdraw or suspend decision, unable to favor either side of his judgment. This equally calls for flexibility in condemning the behaviors of other people in any given relationship. For instance, a caring wife may, because her sick husband does not normally eat in the afternoon refuse to make provisions for such meals including the very day her husband is so hungry and anxiously needs one in the afternoon. Doubts can only be ruled out in relationships when individuals are open to themselves. In the words of Ellis and Harper: "If you strongly believe, "I'd better do perfectly on my job, else I'll probably get fired, you will tend to feel somewhat anxious and insecure" (1975: 203). Whatever creates that sense of insecurity springs from doubtful mind as generally encountered in the state of human mind. Insecurity is a sign of fear and at times, immaturity. This is also dangerous in relationships. According to Ms. Victoria Ibe as earlier on noted, "little things, very little, little things" matter so much in healthy relationships. In situations as Victoria described above, where both parties trust and care for each other, doubts will drastically be minimized if not completely dealt with.

v. Perplexed conscience

Perplexity is a threat to relationship. When the mind is in a confused state, hardly do individuals act reasonably. In a state of indecision, where two alternatives are proposed and both seem evil, an individual may fear he or she will be wrong whichever alternative he or she chooses. For instance, a couple that is not sure of the best way to approach his or her difficult partner often ends up in separation. Therefore, it is important that each person adopts a healthy problem solving formula, management strategy or "a remembered wellness" to deal with pressures in relationships. Higgins seems to have summed up a solution in these words:

> *One is never obliged to do evil (tell lies). Tell the truth and shame the devil, if duties seem to conflict, and one cannot obtain advice, he should choose what seems most reasonable in the circumstance that is farthest removed from evil. Every rational intelligent person follows the maxim, 'I do the best I can' (1949:131).*

The maxim: "Let me do the best I can" is necessary and goes a long way to guide bewildered minds in relationships.

vi. Scrupulous conscience

Scrupulosity is a psychological case that can stigmatize relationships. It is the habit of the mind that inclines an individual to judge for the slightest reasons that moral evils exist where, in actual fact, they do not. This tendency particularly concerns those who play hide and seek games and lead inauthentic lives in their relationships. As a consequence, scrupulous people refrain from many innocent acts. At times, they are so troubled and haunted over their (nasty) past deeds and constant thoughts of wrong doings that they suffer torments and loss of tranquility of the mind. Fagothey summarized this fact in a long but beautiful passage when he stated:

> *A scrupulous conscience torments its owner by rehearsing over and over again doubts that were once settled, finding now*

source of guilt in old deeds that were best forgotten, striving
for a kind of certainty about one's state of soul that is beyond
our power in this life... it leads to a serious form of spiritual
self-torture, mounting to neurotic anxiety (1963: 47).

This state of scrupulous mind affects relationships in various ways. For instance, some partners engage in a lot of "trial-and-love" approach by the kind of questions they pose in their relationships such as: "Do you really love me? Do you think I am a nice person? Am I beautiful or handsome? Are you suspicious of the way I chat with people? Which person were you dating before me? Why do you put on these wears? Is your ex still disturbing you? Are you sure of this or that, what are you doing now et cetera". There are so many important issues to discuss and address in relationships than being scrupulous about them. Too many questions in relationships require no answers and responses and they create problems. The ability to trust oneself guides one to trust others. Partners must trust themselves in order to accomplish their set objectives. Building healthy relationship is a teamwork in which each party assists the other to achieve some balance and stability. The need to imbibe such images as common belief system, ideology, steadfastness, consistency, is necessary in relationships. To relate is to shift one's position and share part of self.

vii. Antecedent conscience.

Relationship has to be dynamic and progressive. Antecedent conscience, like synderesis, [moral consciousness or awareness] is basically a guide to future actions. Society needs this emotional intelligence, particularly in the school systems today. This is the practical judgment that instigates us to execute or avoid a course of action at a particular time. Every moment or minute counts in relationship and that is the only way to guarantee its healthy future. As a guide, it is not concerned with our past, present acts or remote future, which may never present themselves for practical decisions in relationships. Rather, antecedent conscience guides us to those acts whose consequences we often foresee on daily basis. For instance, the fact that one is unexpectedly laid off from one's job serves as a warning signal for one to be more economically careful and conscious of the way one manages one's financial affairs. According to Paulin, this is: "The process of making judgment of conscience before performing moral act" (1992:142). No relationship thrives in a vacuum. It has to be built on what works, taking into consideration the various immediate steps that help individuals move forward. When a lazy person is envious of the progress of others, he or she hardly succeeds in anything.

viii. Consequent conscience

This is the opposite of antecedent conscience or state of the mind in judgment. Morally, the judgment here concerns both our past and present actions. This precaution is also vital in relationships. For instance, that an employee failed to greet his or her boss should not constitute any ethical problem. What goes wrong if the employer greets his or her employee first? If there is an omission in a person's intended good action, the only way to deal with it is to try and guide against it from repeating. As a result of past judgments and actions, there may be a feeling of remorse, grief, or exaltation. These feelings are mere sensitivities. They cannot be conceived as conscience. This is what we often refer to as "prick of conscience" especially when our conscience hurts us for failing to accomplish a particular task. For instance, a person's failure to play the very number his or her partner suggested, which eventually won the lottery should raise no dust in relationship; but he or she, as the participant may feel disappointed. Every move in our relationships should be weighed and measured from its overall target success or goal and not on the accidentals.

ix. Objective conscience

Every relationship reflects the morals and ethics of society. This is subjectively and individually experienced. No particular relationship is exclusive of the larger community. Generally, all relationships are objectively evaluated by certain universal moral standards. The valid conclusion and agreement that each partner arrives at in any relationship are based on his or her judgment of conscience, which normally derives from a major proposition of universal moral order. This is an application of personal moral knowledge to concrete moral situations, which do not pertain to particular cases, but the generality of humanity. For instance, partners may refrain from telling lies against each other, not necessarily to maintain their relationships, but because lies are morally bad, sinful, harmful, destructive and effervescent to self and society as a whole. In the Nigerian context, a liar is regarded as a thief.

x. Subjective conscience

In a way, this is contrasted with the objective. This is where parties apply their knowledge of the universal moral principles individually to particular moral situations. In relationships, each party is expected to behave and act in a manner that respects personal feelings. According to Paulin, this is described as "actual conscience" (1992:139). This is the frame of mind that personally guides an individual to stick to what pleases his or her neighbor here and now. For instance, a person tells the truth because it is the only way to explain his or her action in this particular case, whether it is offensive or commendable.

xi. Tender conscience

Some people often confuse this conscience with the scrupulous. Every relationship needs to be tender-oriented. Tender conscience as a guide, is an inclination to be aware of the smallest elements of moral evil. Once parties consciously and positively take cognizance of the smallest moral evil in their relationships, they can easily guide against offending each other. For instance, by being early at one's work place, rules out the possibility of being punished for lateness. While a tender conscience is exact and true, the scrupulous one is not.

xii. Lax conscience

Laxity can always create problems in relationships. Frivolous attitudes towards life and relationship often result to lax conscience. Most laws are broken today because some people want to have it in their own way. A lax person sees whatever he does as natural and right. Sadly, this is the situation with most of our politicians and teenage boys and girls of today. Most of them do not care about the consequences of their actions, and many have destroyed, not only themselves in the process but society at large. Relationships are jeopardized when the voice of conscience is stifled to the point that an individual can no longer perceive where it hurts the other. This type of attitude gives us some clues regarding why there are conflicts in society today. In ordinary language, lax conscience is referred to as "Dead conscience". It seems Kennedy is proffering a solution to this ugly inclination in human relationships in these words:

> *The first thing a person must do is to make some effort to redeem himself from his troubles, rather than waiting for some deliverance from the outside. A good beginning is to listen to what is really going on inside ourselves (1974:85).*

If each person is his or her own conscience, there is need to understand the manner it generally functions in every relationship, to avoid hurting others.

E. The function of conscience in human relationships

This section creates the awareness and informs us of how conscience influences our relationships. This awareness is more of a guide to individual behaviors in any particular relationship. Actually, conscience is autocratic in nature as some individual behaviors are. It generally performs its function of applying moral laws to our particular actions and relationships in three fold manners:

a. Conscience forbids and binds certain behaviors in relationships

As a clear slighted force, conscience restrains us, breaks our hearts, initiates, holds, rescues, instigates, and saves us from the most powerful passions that surface in our relationships. For instance, an individual may be so infuriated as to plan to poison his partner. At this ugly moment, the same person, in the midst of aggravation, may feel so guilty and sorry for him or herself for such evil thoughts and begin to forgive all hurts and accept his or her partner with greater concern, compassion and respect. This is synderesis, moral consciousness and awareness in action. As Murray presents it:

Conscience brings our faults before us and rebukes and
scolds us about them and passes sentence upon us coldly and
impartially without fear or favor, as if it were not part of us
or had no dependence on us at all (1960:301).

The negligence of this grave human factor in the upbringing of a human person, in learning, communication, and interpersonal relationships and school system is deadly. Some of us are like a person who says: "I hate flying the air planes" but constantly engages and takes delight in traveling around the world. We all know how crucial and paramount safety and peace are to human life. Yet, most of us consciously and unconsciously block the very curriculum or channel through which those values are guaranteed in our lives.

b. Conscience executes and commends

The earlier the human person develops the spirit of appreciating the efforts of others, the better society enjoys healthier relationships. Conscience is the force from the depths of our social and spiritual lives that commends what is right and urges us forward irresistibly towards Truth, Justice and Peace -TJP. Remarkably, Aristotle noted: "Virtue is its own reward" (Nic. Ethics, X-8). The more we put up our best selves in relationships, whether others appreciate us or not, the more we peacefully enjoy the fruits of healthy living.

c. Conscience blames and disapproves

Certainly, most people know when they have done what they ought not to do. In this case, our conscience forcefully arouses, outrages and rises up in us and will not be silenced till the wrong is corrected. At times, it vibrates in us and cries out despite all efforts to stifle and put the wrong to sleep. Openness is the key. Pretending to be a caring partner in a relationship when one, is actually not, is superstitious. The Encyclopedia Britannica observes this ugly tendency in these words:

Conscience is generally understood as that which gives
intuitively authoritative decisions as regards the moral quality
of single actions...this usage implicitly assumed that every

> *action has objective or intrinsic goodness or badness (Vol. 6, 1972:367).*

Evidently, conscience is an unavoidable force in every rational human relationship. As a guiding force in our relationships, conscience primarily performs these two basic functions. Firstly, it reminds us and remembers whether our responsibilities and promises have been carried out and fulfilled or not. This is where conscience performs a memory function. Sometimes, it is regarded as psychological conscience. Secondly, it judges whether our past, present or future actions and behaviors conform to moral principles or not. In this light, the Christian Bible conceives conscience as a witness in these words: "Your own heart knows how often you have reviled others" (Eccl. 7:23). Obviously, conscience is an inescapable element in our relationships. The more we try to avoid it, the more active it becomes in its legislation regarding what we do, privately and publicly, leaving the person either sicker or healthier. It is imperative, therefore, that we study the formation and the judgment of conscience and how it influences our relationships.

F. The logic and judgment of human conscience in relationships

As rational beings, there are certain things that happen in relationships whose ignorance we cannot claim. Naturally, we acquire knowledge through various processes, principally by reasoning. Through the intuition of the natural law and other rules of conduct we come to the knowledge and implication of an individual act. The same reasoning process or syllogism by which we arrive at the judgment of conscience resembles the one that is applied in any other logical deductive arguments. The same reasoning process guides each relationship to certain extent. A 'deductive reasoning' presupposes a major premise of a general principle that is applicable to a particular case, and the conclusion that necessarily follows from it. To draw conclusions for any course of action that is based on a faulty premise, prejudice or bias, creates conflicts in relationships.

However, it is important to note that generally, the syllogism of logic in civil laws and the one employed in the formation of conscience follow the same process. They derive their conclusion from universal principles and laws and apply them to the nature and knowledge of the particular case. That is why our intellect mediates on what is to be done and accomplished in any relationship. Whenever our intellect gets satisfied with the matter, it always employs a syllogism or reasoning process whose conclusion is an act of judgment. The judgment could be an act of choice to play more active roles in one's relationships or dodge them. That is why in our individual choices, we normally and naturally prefer certain "values" to others.

These values according to Gruber "reside in the objects" (1834:261). That is precisely why some people say: "Beauty is in the eye of the beholder". But some other times, beauty is not only in the eye of the observer but also in his or her head and heart. Some people make wrong choices in their relationships due to the judgment presented to them by the intellect. All the same, the judgment of conscience, though, subjectively influenced by the act of the will, does not depend on the act or judgment of choices before it performs its function. In the words of Aquinas, conscience means "the concrete determination of the general principles, which the synderesis furnishes" (IR). The judgment of conscience is based more on the universal principles than on the particulars. For instance, a partner cannot, because, he or she loves to listen to music at nights, ignore the need to allow others sleep. Referring to judgment of choice, For Murray:

> *The judgment of choice is an act of the practical reason made in conjunction with the act of choice of the will. This judgment is an act, which flows from both the intellect and the will for it is made under the influence of appetite (1960:308).*

Choice (appetite) in relationships must be guided by enough deliberations because all that glitters is not gold. For instance, a student who is mad at his or her Dad because he failed to buy him or her a video game when he or she has no textbooks has indicated his or her willingness to quit schooling.

Every single conclusion we arrive at in our judgment, emanates from a universal proposition through the medium of that particular one.

The reasoning of the practical intellect must have a particular action for its conclusion. For instance, a person who is wishing to buy a car should not worry about losing it when he or she has not got any or the resources. For an act to be morally evil means it has already been performed. Until an act is set for execution, whether it is moral or not, the intellect remains a *"tabula rasa"*, a plain slate in which nothing has been written. This is where spiritual psychology and our conscience play vital role in guiding us to avoid any act that constitutes moral evil. In this perspective, partners should engage in positive and enriching thoughts and behaviors whose conclusions will always bring them healthy relationships. It is particularly on this plight, as we saw earlier, that Aquinas maintains: *"Nihil est intellectu quod non prius fuerit in sensu"*, that, 'there is nothing in the intellect that was not first in the senses' (IR). For any judgment of conscience to be meaningful, those universal principles (of good and evil) and our knowledge of them, which are primarily in our practical intellect, must be applied to our individual situations and relationships.

A major premise is the universal moral standards through which either a principle of synderesis [an innate, moral consciousness, or conscious awareness], a conclusion or judgment of conscience has derived from. For instance, "cheating is evil" and this is a major premise or principle of synderesis because of the destructions it causes, not only in individual relationships, but also in various quarters of human involvements. Such conscious awareness or value judgments need to be upheld by individuals as a general rule of conduct. Thus, "I will never cheat anybody". Getting involved in social or domestic violence is evil; therefore, "I will refrain from it and face my studies". The minor premise brings the particular act here and now to be done under the scope of the general principle enunciated in the major. For instance, "Mr. B. cheated his wife" and therefore has committed evil. As it were, "conscience acts on the information given by synderesis - the application of knowledge to activity.

This is where the virtue of prudence and application of emotional intelligence, intellectual or moral virtue is needed to reason out the "knowledge of synderesis" (IFE 2007) or the correct knowledge with which the intellect is fed. This illustrates our earlier assertion that conscience belongs exclusively to rational beings. Therefore, for people to doubt or play jokes with the dictates of conscience in their lives, interpersonal relationships, in the government quarters, school systems, is simply, to risk the essential values of rational beings and identity. According to Benson: "Doubts or negative beliefs, translated into actions help to determine whether we live or die" (1996:44), whether a relationship prospers or scatters. As an illustration of the logical formation of conscience, confer the observations of Murray:

> Major premise: Justice demands that debts be paid.
> [This is immediate universal rule of conduct]
>
> Minor Premise: This $50 or #50 is a debt.
> [The particular judgment]
>
> Conclusion: This $50 or #50 debt must be paid.
>   [The judgment of conscience],
>   (1960:308).

Similarly, in our earlier example, "cheating is evil" [Major Premise] and "Mr. B. cheated his wife" [Minor Premise], therefore, "Mr. B. has committed evil" [The judgment of conscience]. The logic or judgment of conscience and the decisions we make in our relationships determine the intensity of its progress or failure.

Murray equally illustrated a pseudo judgment of conscience, that is, knowledge derived from a faulty syllogism or reasoning. The conclusion may be logically sound in reasoning (as normally required in some legal practices that involve the sequence of argument, regardless of truth or falsity of the matter) but false in fact. Generally, conscience, just as human relationship, aims at the simple truth. According to Murray, for instance:

> Major: Gambling is unjust.
>   [Mediate universal rule of conduct derived
>   from a misconception of the law of justice].
> Minor: This game of cards is gambling.
>   [Particular judgment]

Conclusion: This game of cards is unjust.
[The judgment of conscience],
(1960: 328).

As a matter of fact, the above two examples differ in their gnoseological perspectives. However, they share in the same syllogistic process. This calls for caution and serious deliberations in evaluating other people's reasoning processes to avoid drawing undue conclusions and confrontation. Misconception or faulty judgment of other peoples' ideas and behaviors can easily lead to conflicts in relationships. Evidently, it is clear that the judgment each person makes as regards his or her own obligation here and now in a given relationship, is not only derived from general moral principles but also how he or she judges the situation. The implication and manner in which an action is performed is one thing and the interpretation or judgment that is passed on it is another. In the light of the examples Murray offered, it is still left to the debtor to pay his debts, play the game of cards or not. Regrettably, for William Rutler, "self-justification never works with God" (1995:77) and it is also wrong in relationships. For instance, a partner who always recommends the best things to be done, improved or provided in the house but never raises a finger to actualize or fund them, not only plays a joke, shows how lazy, irresponsible he or she is, but also takes a big risk of losing that relationship.

Eventually, spiritual psychology gives sight to society that seems darkened by immoral behaviors and challenges those in leadership positions and individuals to listen to the voice of their consciences and incorporate right judgments for interpersonal relationships and unity in the world at large. Anything short of these moral and social values leads one to inward uncleanness, surface spirituality and external piety that corrode religious practices and relationships.

From our studies on the judgment and formation of conscience, the intellect (conscience) is totally "will free" because the will does not directly enter into the reasoning process. However, the will can also influence the judgments of the intellect for its own advantage. Partners should be aware of this quality in matters of choice, decision and action. For instance, an individual can make a wrong choice based on emotional needs of a particular good. It may happen that, while partner A understands the implication of such a choice, partner B may not. Therefore, there is need for two of them to arrive at a compromise as why the act or choice should be made in the first place or not. The intellect objectively and always keeps us abreast with the reality and implication of things. People should always weigh the consequences of their actions to avoid quarrels over rash decisions. It is normal for quarrels to take place in relationships. But to quarrel over fantasies, like wrong choices made under unforeseen circumstances is unreasonable.

Moreover, when the judgment of the intellect (conscience) is under the influence of appetite (choice) as noted above, it includes the "intellect and will". That is to say, there are certain animalistic choices we make with full approval of reason, especially when what is presented to us sounds good and irresistible. Hence, it is always necessary to be spiritually mature to enter into friendship and marital relationships. That was the point Dr. Nwachukwu Udaku made as regards the attitudes of our young ones trying to play the adult game at teenage stage. Generally, these appetites or choices are formidable forces that easily influence relationships. For instance, it is sheer immaturity for a couple to buy a car just for leisure when they can hardly feed their family or pay their house mortgage and bills. When a person willingly deceives or fears to confront his or her partner in important issues that could affect their relationships, he or she has only succeeded in displaying his or her immaturity.

Practically, the human will or desire plays a vital role in decision-making. The will is stampeded or attracted to action by its object through the faculty of the soul (intellect) via sense perception that has pictured and magnified the beauty of the said object. When the will operates, it performs only one act – the act of freedom to its end "this is what I want, period". Our teenage boys and girls should take note of this part of human nature that has damaged most of them today. This is the freedom to enjoy a peaceful relationship or cranky one. For instance, individuals are free to move their hands around in relationships, but none is free to use them to hurt and harm others. Thus, the will enjoys three types of freedom with regard to its objects, namely: Specification, Exercise and Contrariety.

1. Specification: The will is not in doubt of its object or what attracts it.
2. Exercise: It knows how to get to its object without any limitations because it enjoys multiplicity of means to its end.
3. Contrariety: It enjoys multiplicity of choices between alternatives, which is the reason for or against that choice or course of action.

Paradoxically, individuals know that contraries, the good and evil, do co-exist. Only the right choice of actions we make brings progress in our future, educational goals and relationships. The human will has the freedom and capacity to choose between these moral good and evils depending on what appeals to it. Therefore, spiritual psychology - SP makes important calls for each person to guide his or her will, particularly the school children. Elaborating on the above three steps of every free will, Donceel remarked:

> *There are three steps in every free decision to be taken; firstly, being attracted by the object., secondly, the examination of the object, and thirdly, determination in which the reason for and against a course of action is examined by the intellect, (1961: 249:251).*

That we get attracted to an object, examine and decide to have or leave it does not necessarily guarantee that we are on the right track. In this light, SP offers society and partners some Action Alert Vitamins, "PP" - Patience and Prudence.

Consequently, there is need to study and examine the state of the mind in knowledge especially as it concerns the moral judgments individuals make in their relationships. The study of this aspect of human behavioral dynamics, the state of the mind in knowledge, is of immense assistance in establishing lasting relationships among individuals.

G. The state of the human mind in relationships

The state of the human minds in knowledge plays vital roles in every day life. It features, practically, in every aspect of human life, in conscience, religion, ethics, defense mechanisms, personality structures and developments, et cetera as studied in this book. Unless the distinction is fully explicated here, it will be difficult to understand why people behave differently on a matter that sounds obvious in their relationships. We are supposed to have certain knowledge about our environments. But the major concern that faces us here boils down to understanding the extent these cognitive acts; objectively claim responsibility for such awareness and knowledge. An example comes to mind. Most of the 'hit-and-run-away' drivers do not imagine that they would ever be caught. There are a lot of dirty things people do under different covers even in their relationships, especially when a partner plays a hit-and-run-away game. To hit and run is a sign of being 'an empty gong' and being afraid to face reality as it is. Straightforwardness is important in relationships.

The human brain, according to Agwulonu is the "organ that presides over cognitive activity and the center of all actions, mental, intellectual, sensitive and in fact the integral bodily functions" (2001:12). On the other hand, "the mind is the manifestation of the brain.... without the brain, there is no mind. Within the brain, in Spencer's view, lies the potential for self awareness, (*consciousness-mine)* and purposeful activity" (1989:61). The human "brain enjoys plasticity, that is, the ability to change and be molded under the influence of the external environment" (Op. cit. 2001:30). This is a confirmation of the judgment of the intellect under the influence of appetite. Besides, we earlier noted that the impression we make of others [the external stimulus], determines the manner we approach them. For instance, when an individual has the conception that his or her partner is mannered, handsome or beautiful, often times, that is the way he or she relates to him or her. Just as the brain does not rest, relationships should not be static. The silent mood of a partner might be pregnant with issues that can destroy or reinforce a relationship. Relationship should be alive just as the brain continually utilizes its resources whether one is at sleep or involved in active mental work.

As we claim knowledge of many things, even in our relationships, there are others we are totally ignorant of, due mainly to the state of our minds. The awareness of these limitations is important because they reflect and affect our mental attitude towards others in every relationship.

Many psychoanalysts and psychotherapists like Dr. Alexis Carrel in Nwachukwu, observed that: "Every normal person has some percentage of madness in him" (1994:13). This boils down to an important aspect of interpersonal relationships. Now, if a normal person or partner has some percentage of madness in him or her, is it not extremely necessary to avoid conflicts in relationships? For instance, an individual may get so furious, irritated and infuriated with his or her partner over an issue, to a point that, if discretions are not taken, the anger may turn into an uncontrollable and unanticipated madness.

There is need for individuals or partners to note that in such moments as described above, all memories of "I love you – you are the best" are gone in a twinkling of an eye. It is no fault of the outraged partner to behave like that. It is normal. Therefore, the best attitude, for those whose lives are vital to them, is not to stand there to retaliate or challenge back, but to silently leave the scene with your two hands crossed over your mouth. This is why the Igbo people say that the life and death of two individuals lie at the hands of one person. Generally, to live alone for the Igbo of Nigeria is unnatural and dreadful. We can now understand why some individuals have regrettably and unintentionally destroyed the relationships they cherished so much. Temptations easily spring up from what we admire and value most in our lives and the devil always succeeds more when he operates through them and our best friends than those we regard as our enemies. Little humor in relationships can be medicinal.

Genuine laughter can heal the 'wounds' of broken relationships

According to White Philip, in his article entitled "Laughter: A Holy Paradox" he noted: "One can be quickly released from the prison of pain [madness-mine] or grief if you will sing and praise and pray" (2000:24). Experiences and studies have revealed that "laughter" is not only medicinal, therapeutic and healing but also the essential music of life. According to Finkelestein Martin, a Doctor of Medicine in an exclusive interview on the issue at hand, observed:

> *The most important thing in life is not always beautiful. One has got to enjoy one's Life. There are 4 levels of the letter "L"*

namely: Living, Learning, Loving and laughing (NYU, 10/ 21/09).

Accordingly, any laughter that is released from the heart accomplishes four things - AAEL (Affirmation, Acknowledgment, Expression of self and Life), meaning:

1. Personal affirmation that one's life is precious, beautiful and enjoyable;
2. An acknowledgment of the communal dimension of ones life - a value shared with others. To always laugh alone is psychotic and mental.
3. An expression of contentment that ones life is not dependent on any material object, but a gift that gratuitously needs to be unconsciously appreciated, nourished and celebrated for its own sake.
4. Living along unity, grace, happiness or health, togetherness, <u>and</u> eternally reassured - LAUGHTER.

People should often laugh away some of their worries and misgivings in relationship. Life generally goes with unpredictable ups and downs. Dr. Alexis Carrel, in one of his masterpieces, "Man the Unknown" observed:

> *You have in your head right now, 12,000,000,000, yes, twelve billion brain cells. And in every one of these brain cells, there is on going continually that agitation of small particles around the nucleus in the center (1935:17).*

These brain cells, irrespective of their number, which are continually in agitation, equally reflect in our moods, and at times, create problems in our relationships. As Agwulonu pointed out: "The brain…continuously carries out the following programs: sensory, to - SHTT (feeling), motor, to - WCRL, cognitive, to - RWU and emotional to - IE and Intensify feelings" (2001:27). That is:

> *Sensory - to smell, hear, taste and touch (feeling), Motor - to walk, climb, run and lift loads, Cognitive programs - to read,*

> *write and understand languages, Emotional - to interpret,*
> *express and intensify feelings*

Again, Hamlyn deserves our credits in the field of the theories of knowledge. According to him our mind undergoes the following states in knowledge, "Doubt, ignorance, opinion and certitude" (1970: 225-232). This is a confirmation that the mind is a playground as noted earlier, occupied by so many athletes trying to compete with one another and gain stronger grounds. Yet, only one team plays at a time. That is, the states of our minds in knowledge prepare us to see beyond common mistakes, shortcomings, bad feelings, wrong doings in our relationships and reach out to embrace others with open arms. They can equally create problems if they are not properly analyzed. Hence, it is of immeasurable importance to understand how each of them affects human relationships in general. Reviewing each of the states, we have:

a. Doubt

Every doubtful situation, as noted in conscience, raises questions, as whether any of the alternative courses of action is the case or not. It is the state of the mind in which individuals and parties suspend judgment in their relationships due to the mind's inability to decide the truth and falsity of the matter. In a doubtful state, each partner definitely needs that action alert Vitamins "PP" - patience and prudence to avoid jumping into conclusions that might lead to unpleasant and ugly situations.

b. Ignorance

This is important in relationships because it can also lead to strife and rancor. Generally, in this state of the mind, questions are not raised. In the empiricist's language, the mind at this state is said to be a "tabula rasa in qua nihil scriptum est", that is, "a clean slate on which nothing has been written". Most of the misunderstanding and errors individuals encounter in their relationships come from ignorance. Again, ignorance, often, comes about due to some faulty judgments of the mind as regards the knowledge of the truth. The dilemma of ignorance is that it can generate blames when no offence is intended or committed. In this light, partners have to be careful in the ways they pilot their affairs. However, Ignorance involved in error can be of two kinds: vincible or invincible.

i. Vincible

Ignorance is vincible when it is voluntary. In this sense, the partner or individual actually wills to err. Vincible is of three types:

Simple:

This is where ignorance is indirectly voluntary, because the individual agent neglects to think prudently, diligently, cautiously and rightly. A teenage girl who tried sexual act because her friend lured her into it has indicated how foolish and immature she is. Not to think properly implies that the person actually desires to err. This is the mentality of "I can do it all" attitude in relationships. When a caring husband sheepishly decides to join bad associations as ways of life, instead of reasoning along with his family, the ignorance is simple. This tendency has brought about cultism in most school systems.

Crass:

Parties in any relationship should always make enough efforts to imbibe and grasp healthy knowledge of the general moral principles. Ignorance is crass when a partner makes less effort to tackle the problems of the family. This is the mentality of "I know it all" type of ignorance. Such people willingly, in playful manners, indulge in immoral and careless acts that can damage relationships. When a partner freely engages in atrocious acts like drug addictions, alcoholism, cheating, rape and defamation of the other's character without any remorse, ignorance is crass. Nobody is an island. Always allow your partner make his or her contributions in planning. That American slang "one team one dream" works better in relationships.

Affected:

Ignorance is affected as it adversely affects relationships. This is the type of ignorance that leads to unhealthy defense mechanisms. It creates conflicts in relationships. When a person or an individual makes extra efforts to avoid listening and finding out relevant facts regarding the issues his or her partner often raises in their relationship, ignorance is affected. For instance, a bad or careless husband will always complain for the least thing his wife does in the house, at times, to avoid being reminded of his responsibilities. This is typical of the "heaven-on-earth" people in our group "A" of our spiritual typology who are materially focused and oriented. What else is relationship when parties cannot accommodate each other's feelings and unconditionally share their values together?

ii. Invincible

It is necessary for partners to realize that despite their efforts, diligence and prudence employed to maintain their relationships, mistakes will always occur. In other words, invincible ignorance does not bring about any conflicts in society as such because to err is only human but persistence in error is diabolical.

c. Opinion.

Parties have to place some premium in the opinions of one another in relationships. This state of the mind is important because it allows for flexibility in deciding the truth of a judgment in any matter. For instance, when a husband tells his wife, "why don't we go to the movies tomorrow?" The statement implicitly involves "despite of" or fears the possibility "I have an appointment with my doctor tomorrow". In the above example, while the mind inclines more to one alternative – going to the movie, than the other – the probability [that is, the man not being sure of the response of his wife], he still suspects that the reverse could be the case, [that is, it is still open to his wife to accept or decline]. Opinions always invite relationships to a meaningful dialogue. In dialogue, parties resolve their differences and keep their relationships on board. For opinions to be meaningful, they have to be fact-based, because a person may be entitled to his or her opinions but not the facts. It is necessary to note also that there is no capital "P" in dialogue. In humility, and without any force, parties remain loyal to common issues that encourage and favor healthy relationships. There is need to understand the meaning of dialogue as an important image in relationship. A situation where a person always supports whatever his or her partner does or says, even when serious mistakes are obvious, indicates a red flag that something is wrong with either of them.

d. Meaning of "dialogue" in relationship:

From its etymology, "dialogue" comes from the Greek word 'dialogos' meaning conversation between two or more persons. According to the American Peoples' Encyclopedia: "Dialogue, from the Greek word 'dialogos' means the process of clarification of problems in the conversation between two or more people; its essence is that participants alternately speak and listen" (Vol. 7, 1962:7-42). Gracefully, once parties in dialogue collaborate in a search for a common meaning, in its historical, concrete situation, there could be total self-understanding and radical change of mind and acceptance of one another. In this way, Mozia remarked:

> *Dialogue becomes an expression of the reciprocity of consciences which are united in the search for truth and valid solutions to problems that continually arise in the individual and in the communitarian life of the faithful (1987:160).*

This is where education becomes consequential. It leads to a meaningful dialogical relationship by which the individuals become inter-dependent and co-responsible within the same mystery [divine-orientated] of human relationships. They can now appreciate the limit and ability of one another and be best disposed to listen and respond adequately to the truth presented to each of them in that dialogue. In this perspective, there can be different forms of education. But the ones that take the culture, values, feelings, and belief systems into consideration count much in dialogical relationships. Dialogue is a lubricating factor in any situation of doubts, confusions and divergent opinions. Through dialogue, people discover more areas of progress in their relationships and easily eradicate and resolve conflicts and disagreements. Thus, when a person tells his or her partner, "let us talk", it means there is a problem or something to be addressed and fixed, which every partner is bound to get involved.

e. Certitude

This is a state where the mind gives a firm assent to a judgment for a course of action without fearing the possibility of error. In such a situation, parties confidently execute and carry out their duties in respect to each other's values. The Bible said it all: "If we cannot be condemned by our own conscience, we need not be afraid in God's presence" (1 Jn: 3: 21). There are three kinds of certitude in relationship and every person needs to take note of them:

i. Moral certitude

Relationships thrive more when the individual boundaries, values and feelings are respected. No one is free to infringe upon this fundamental foundation. That is the only way to maintain peace and order in relationship and society. The implication is that individuals, under certain circumstances, morally and uniformly act and react in the same way. However, uniformity is not the same thing as unity as we noted at the introduction of this book. There can be uniformity in relationship without unity. Besides, "exactitude is not always the truth" (Henri Matisse, IR). Naturally, moral certitude demands unity of purpose and actions in all relationships.

ii. Physical certitude

Parties physically feel certain when their judgments and actions truly and reasonably correspond to their choices. They achieve this level of certitude through discipline and obedience to moral principles. Hardly do drunkards and individuals under the influence of drugs make valid judgments, decisions and choices. For instance, an object, a body whose weight or specific gravity is less than water will definitely float on it. Likewise, all kind gestures in relationships that are not appreciated, normally and naturally die away.

iii. Metaphysical certitude

There are certain forces, truths and realities about our lives we cannot control. Such realities affect our relationships irrespective of the efforts we make. Metaphysical certitude is based on metaphysical laws, whose denials and exceptions are intrinsically impossible and contradictory. For instance, greedy partners always seek self-interests. In physics, "a part will always be smaller than the whole". Such truths and axioms as "1+1 being 2" or that every living creature dies, are indisputable. Therefore, parties are cautioned, to avoid blaming others for such events that are bound to happen in their relationships. One cannot be blamed for an event that is totally beyond one's control. For an example, there are certain times a person may feel reserved or uncomfortable to say anything when his or her partner demands audience. It does not mean that the person has bad will or intends to be rude. Naturally, life is that way, at times. In the light of the foregoing states of the mind and the need for individuals to keep their relationships together, application of ethical principles is studied here as guide to healthy living.

H. Application of ethical principles in human behaviors and relationships

We have already touched the areas of ethical and moral principles in this book. The application of eternal, natural moral and positive laws in our relationships are so necessary. An in-depth knowledge of these laws will assist individuals, college students and society to easily adapt to the forces that influence human lives in general. Eventually, we separately treated them in this order:

a. The Eternal law

Eternal law is the will of God or Divine Wisdom which obligates parties to follow the essential and moral standards of life. This is the law by which nature takes its course. The Christian Bible presented it in this way:

> *From the beginning till now the entire creation, as we know, has been groaning in one great act of giving birth.... we too groan inwardly as we wait for our bodies to be set free...it is something we must wait for with patience (Rom. 8:22-25).*

By the principle of finality, for instance, 'every being acts for an end' (*Omne agens agit propter finem*). Certainly, for individuals to patiently act towards this end; it has to be in an ordered manner. It was on this basis that Oprah noted: "Everything is in divine order" (12/11/09) and we only need to cooperate. Eternal law points to the creator's everlasting order and plan by which he purposefully sets parties free from groaning and directs them to their ends. Generally speaking, this law applies to everything in the universe without exception, both organic and inorganic matters. Species incline to their own nature and equally respond to the law of gravity. Eternal laws bind on individuals and parties to work hard for the benefits of their systems. Playing a parasitic role in relationship is both a sign of weakness, psychotic, neurotic and also an inauthentic existence.

However, there seems to be a problem when we strictly reflect on the eternal laws. That is, if everything, including our actions is eternally ordered, to what extent is humanity to blame for non-compliance to moral order? This again boils down to the superiority of humans over all other created beings. Errors in human reasoning notwithstanding, it is only human beings that can, in a strict sense, obey or disobey the laws. All the same, such errors are quite relative because "ali alia faciunt" 'different people do somewhat entirely different things'. Just as each person is unique, individual relationships are different. Therefore, it is wrong to judge a particular relationship on the basis of others. Many have already obeyed these laws from various ages and enjoyed the fruits of happy lives.

Nevertheless, reasoning is a sine qua non for individuals to attain and meet their targets and objectives in their relationships. To maintain peace in relationships, parties ought to weigh the consequences of their actions before they carry them out. Aquinas took cognizance of the inevitability of reason when he remarked: "The voluntary act, which is out of harmony with reason whether reason be right or erroneous is always evil... therefore the will is good even when it abides by erring reason" (1949: Art. 1). Aquinas' views are on par with those of Murray in these words: "Even though our conscience be involuntarily erroneous, it must be followed" (1960:328). That is to say, compliance with those actions, which are morally compatible with parties in any relationship need to be encouraged.

Cases abound in relationships when partners differ with regard to the choices they make. It is wrong for a particular item to become a taboo in the house or office, simply because one of them hates it. For instance, if a partner loves to keep pets in the house, the other should accept that as part of his or her sacrifices for love. Again, to make sure individual choices and preferences do not break relationships, one partner should always be ready to go extra miles. Bourke in his own capacity observed: "The insufficiency of the ordinary man's knowledge of the natural moral law, in view of the supernatural end to which his moral actions are directed is the chief reason why man needs the guidance of divine positive law" (1951: 210). What Bourke suggested here can only be possible when parties try to act for the same end and objective.

Each person needs to understand his limitations and potentialities in a given relationship. Most often, partners fight for frivolous matters they have no control over. For instance, when eternal law enjoins us to respect and regard human life as sacred, issues of abortion and euthanasia face challenges in our relationships. In such situations, parties must reason together, agree and disagree. At times, they do so intentionally, and some other times, they act under certain psychological pressures. These are the pressures that create chaos in our relationships, which this book has addressed. No wonder Aquinas summarily put it this way:

> *The eternal law cannot err but human reason can. Consequently, the will that abides by human reason is not always right, nor is it always in accord with the eternal law (1949: q.6).*

This aspect of human reality or nature needs immediate attention. Deductively, it is implied in the act of creation also. Historically speaking, humanity is designed in such a way that "natures act in harmony with themselves and with the natures with which they are essentially related". Thus, relationships are, at their best, with creatures of their own kind. Therefore, it becomes more of a calamity when parties of the same kind, family, school children, system and group cannot harmoniously live together. Instead, we find people, according to the annotation of Thomas Hobbes's writing in Molesworth, totally fight to limit and bring the joy of others to annihilation (1997, IR).

Eventually, once individuals begin to fight themselves, they encounter qualitative jump between their natures and their source and maker. As earlier hinted, the presence of God or meaningful guide in relationships demystifies and creates balance in human understanding. The fact that the creator is Omnipotent and man or woman, a finite being, remains a guiding beacon in our relationships. This fact sets limits to each relationship. Ware, in her two spirituality poles, spoke of the "apophatic or non-concretized way of thinking and experiencing God and the 'Kataphatic way' that is, approaching God as revealed, knowable ... and in concrete terms" (1995:32). In this light, apophatic vision of God in relationship corresponds to those in our group C who intrinsically worship and approach God solely as their final point of reference, the source, last resort and guide of their relationships on earth. The kataphatic way of approaching God is more of the traditional, whereby adherents seek him through ritual worships, by offering sacrifices, praises and presenting themselves before him for one favor or the other.

Besides, relationships are echoes, patterns and shapes of life. It does not concern each of us to know everything. However, our own particular lives, relationships and destinies are already committed to our care. There might be no second chances to embrace them. Therefore, every person is bound to listen beyond the mere words spoken in his or her individual relationship and appreciate the underlying feelings of intimacy, sympathy and care, inherent in them. As a consequence, the error in our reasoning lies concealed within the mystery of our intellect and freedom. In support of this view, Murray said: "A moral act is an act which is performed with knowledge and freedom" (1960:328). In this sense, parties have no excuses for perpetuating those habits that constitute offenses and destructions in their relationships.

Moreover, reason is not the only norm for all moral actions but a means to its actualization. For instance, any judgment based on faulty reasoning naturally leads to conflicts in relationships. To this, Murray once upheld that:

> *We must affirm that conscience even though it be mistaken, is a means to the end of man and if man with good will follows an erroneous conscience he will attain his end (1960:330).*

Similarly, healthy relationships are the fruits of those parties with good will. For instance, both parties should accept mistakes resulting from ignorance or heart-felt behaviors as parts of the system building. It is on this ground that Paulin described conscience as the "source of moral wisdom" (1992:138).

From all indications so far, two things clearly stand out. Firstly, the eternal law does attain absolute perfection in human relationships. Secondly, disciplinary behaviors and relationships are in conformity with eternal law and the essential order of things. As Murray puts it: "For in creating human beings liable to err, God willed that the practical judgment of man is to be the proximate measure of his moral action" (1960:331). Relationships tend to crash when parties approach these created order and eternal laws differently or disobey them.

In a strict sense, eternal laws, in many writings, refer to the voice of God. For instance, to forgive an erring husband or wife is naturally and always not easy. Again, we err most often and need forgiveness. Therefore, to forgive others becomes a must. In this light, Murray furnished us with this important passage: "Even though conscience commands what is objectively wrong, being ignorant of the truth, it commands with an authority which is sacred and inviolate and in so doing participates in the eternal law, the source of all authority" (1960:332). It is obligatory that parties comply with each other in moral matters even when their choices of actions differ. They are morally evil, if they act against the desire to do good, relate and live in peace. Bourke seemed to be describing this situation when he noted:

> *For man to know without any doubt what he is to do and what to avoid it was necessary that he be directed in his own acts by a law, which is divinely given, of which it will continually be true that no error is possible (1951: 210).*

Good will is essential in all levels of relationships. The "will" employed in a relationship establishes and determines its nature, emotional and moral suitability.

b. The natural moral law

The eternal and natural laws fall within the descriptive division of law. For instance, when the laws say: "Cheating is evil" they state what is to be done and thereby guide the individuals to healthy relationships and right behaviors. Generally, the importance of laws in the guidance of the consciousness 'of society' in general cannot be overemphasized. However, we did not treat all aspects of the law in this book such as criminal, civil, public, substantial, procedural, International and family laws. Basing relationships primarily on the letter of the law has not always advanced interpersonal relations. All the same, natural moral law is part of the eternal law, which specially applies to our free acts. Bourke, in support of the above point noted: "The natural moral law is participation in the eternal law" (1951:209). Natural moral law expresses the fundamental inclination of the human nature in a universal form. In obeying our consciences, we equally apply the eternal law into our relationships.

We necessarily come to the knowledge of the practical precepts of the natural order: "The good must always be willed, preferred, done and evil avoided at all times in human relationships" through the light of understanding [synderesis or awareness]. Therefore, it is necessary for individuals to note that the natural moral law is not of human origin or dependent on human reasoning. It is naturally there, imprinted in the reason of man and it is inescapable for any one. For instance, in a marital relationship, a caring husband does not need to be told that his wife is angry or sick and vice versa. The evidence is just there, awaiting urgent attention. Bourke in affirmation of this value, remarked:

> Both the eternal and natural moral laws are made known to man through the natural tendency of his intellect to know self-evident truths either speculative or practical (1951:209).

The natural law always remains valid in every age. It is never invalidated, interpreted or legislated. Fortunately, it binds on all relationships irrespective of creed, color or race. Humanity is unavoidably immersed in it whether she likes it or not. Though, to obey this law is an up hill task, yet the natural law or natural moral law has one master, one ruler, one interpreter, who is also the author of existence. In this understanding, William noted: "Obedience to the supernatural order, of which this natural order is a faint code, requires humility that only grace can give" (1995:77). Imperatively, individuals should humbly respect these laws for their own advantages. However, each person is at liberty to obey them or do otherwise and naturally face the consequences. For instance, a student who refuses to listen to his or her teacher normally fails his or her exams. We are all witnesses to such self-evident truths whereby teenagers kill themselves in the process of lovemaking. Unfortunately, none of them has ever wished to die in what appears to be a friendly venture. Yet it happens, even with blind peers like drugs and alcohol. Therefore, each of our teenagers must be cautious and realize that 'love of oneself' is basic and it determines with whom they move with.

Most relationships, school systems and society are in shambles today because they arrogate to themselves the natural powers and forces and look askant to these laws of nature. This is where spiritual psychology -SP strongly takes up its task of economic, socio-religions, political, personal and cultural redemption in human history by insisting that people listen to the voice of their inner selves. Besides, none of us denies our willed objection to these obligations that lead to healthy or unhealthy living. As a consequence, a lot of relationships are physically sick. Thanks to nature, our inner persons bear witnesses to our actions. They hunt and reveal to us even to death, most of our hidden thoughts and deeds in all the relationships we keep. Our external pieties and behaviors should lead us to inward cleanness and not to pharisaical living. These inner attitudes are the energies that save or drive us crazy in our relationships.

Painfully, Dedewo commenting on the future leaders of society, stated:

> *Children of today are tomorrow's leaders. What we make of our children today will determine what they will be tomorrow"* (1993:5), *the nature of relationships they keep now is indicative of whether they will live or die (mine).*

In a serious note, Anyagwa citing Egbulefu in Odenigbo 2001, lamented: "Lack of co-ordination between the family, school and church has been identified as the root sense of immorality among youths of today" (2002:4). Immorality has gone global and most of us have fallen victims to its dangerous effects because of our negligence of moral order. There is no gainsaying that the family, school and Church can play vital roles in building healthy relationships among individuals in particular and society at large. Unless the families, schools and the churches pass on to the young generation the legacy of applying the values of both natural moral and eternal laws in their lives, human relationship will always remain a game of chance. In her own reactions too, Okonkwo identified immorality among secondary and high school children as a result of divisions in the individuals that are responsible to mould them (2002:4). Who are the individuals meant here, except the Church, parents, ministers, environments, schools and associations et cetera? There can be no time to heal these divisions than now. It is appalling that these agencies and factors, the family, school and Church do not seem to agree on what their responsibilities are towards building a healthy and egalitarian society where human relationships will be highly and equally respected. The future of our young generation hangs on a balance due to lack of adequate directions and education. The net result is that, once a person bites the finger that feeds and is going to feed him or her, he or she is likely to die of starvation. These are the situations with those who tend to violate the natural moral and eternal laws in their lives and relationships.

c. The positive or man-made law

Every healthy relationship is a united effort. A single person does not make a society. A lawless society, institution or relationship is not attainable. It is merely an object of the mind. 'Laws' equally guide the behaviors of the human family. Some sort of eternal design promulgated some laws. For instance, the "Ecclesiastical" or "Church" laws are those that consistently direct the life of the Church and people of God in their entirety. The expression "people of God" is inclusive, involving everybody under the sun. Mere intellectual process does not invent the positive laws. They are said to be positive because they conclusively derive from the natural moral laws. They are to the moral laws what conclusions are to principles. In all standards, these laws are meant to guide human society and relationships. There are no exceptions about them.

When a positive law states: "avoid murder", it points to the conclusion of the practical reason derived from a more general and obvious principle of the natural moral law, "murder is evil". In this light, Nwankwo seems to be referring to this deplorable condition of certain relationships when he made the following observations regarding what he considered an abnormal situation at a time in Imo State University:

> *At long last, a Daniel has come to judge. Imo State University was desperately in need of redemption when Prof. Anwuka arrived to clear the stable so badly messed up by his predecessors. What happened to IMSU before the advent of his administration looked like a great conspiracy against the people (2001:17).*

The situations just described are akin to some interpersonal relationships. In marital relationships, like so many others, for instance, cases have equally abounded in great numbers where a despised and divorced woman turns out to become a model in her second relationship. This situation raises fundamental questions as who has fooled whom in the foiled relationship.

The bad names some partners give to others in their relationships do not actually change their wonderful personalities. Beauty remains so irrespective of the impression of the beholder. At times, good manners alone positively bring about changes in a given relationship. In our own context, therefore, whatever force, law or manner the said Anwuka employed in IMSU to bring sanity and order in the said University at that period as Nwankwo observed is a good example of a positive law. Whether Nwankwo's statement was politically motivated or the said Anwuka was actually the Daniel and redeemed the University, are questions left to Nwankwo to address. Our interest here is that whatever brings about orderliness in any relationship, organization, community, school system must have been based on a general natural moral principles that encourage peace, justice, discipline, harmony, order and progress.

In this capacity, Bourke vividly expressed: "Positive laws are of great value to the moral agent since they express precisely the universal rules of good behavior which he must follow in order to live a good life" (1951: 209). To live a good life does not come by accident. Goodness is a universal value, to embrace it, is relatively a decision. Universal rules of good conduct include respecting the values of each other in a given relationship. On a wider and global level, for instance, the Principal of a school can say: "Any student that steals will be expelled". This is a positive law that has its bearing on the universal natural moral law that forbids stealing. Thus, compliance to such laws has to be enforced mainly for the interest of the entire students and for the achievements and enhancements of order and educational goals in general. College students need to have this piece of information. This is where many governments seem to have failed. How can the government expect discipline at schools where there are no role models and reference points like spiritual psychologists or moral instructors? Healthy relationships, whether in marital or other levels, will always have everlasting and positive effects on individual lives and society.

The circumstances under which concrete human acts are performed vary much with time, place and other contingent conditions. For instance, a man cannot complain of starvation in his home or blame his wife for same, when he rarely contributes to the feeding. If you, no longer love your partner for no reasons at all, be courageous enough to question yourself and consult a counselor for assistance. That is precisely why other positive laws spring from the natural moral law by way of determination. Therefore, there must be reasons for positive laws. Both single parents, the married, young ones and individuals and organizations demand openness and trust in their relationships. Again, as a positive way to bring a rude partner to order, especially the one that always finds faults basically in everything, dialogical and confrontational approach may help here. Some may prefer silence to dialogue as the best option. In this sense, silence serves as preventive and therapeutic to the scandals that would have erupted in responding to a partner with anti-social personality disorder or ADHD – Attention Deficit Hyper Activity Disorder. Silence in this context does not mean inactivity but acquiescence.

Therefore, the ability for an individual to always apply natural moral principles to his or her actions is, not only, the summary description of all personal and healthy relationships but also the apogee of interpersonal co-existence. In this light, Bourke noted: "Conscience involves the application of positive law to the human acts which come under it (1951:209). These positive laws are enacted for the maintenance of the common good and order in society. Psychologically, we refer to this as "public goods dilemma" or free-rider problems in which the combined efforts of a group, in turn, assist each member for equal and maximal benefits (Colman, 2003:604). That popular Latin aphorism: "*age quod agis*", as noted earlier on, meaning, "do that which you are doing, well" perfectly describes the situation here. Embodiment of truthfulness and honesty is the star that guides human relationship.

Eventually, we briefly studied certain personality structures, temperaments and stages of development here as to ascertain how they affect every relationship. In one of my books, I made it clear in these words: "The greatest problem of the human race today is to believe that God does not exist, but if he does, he is insufficient to guide our relationships", (1997:43). We need to repeat that, no aspect of relationship is Catholic, Hindu, Jewish, Christian, religious or meaningfully realistic which fails to reflect the love of God and neighbor in others. It is pointless carrying the burdens of yesterday and tomorrow when we have not fully utilized the opportunities of today. Definitely, once the devil capitalizes on our today, we will be left with confusion and chaos in our relationship. God can use set backs to move us forward. Individuals can make their plans but God has all the plans and times at his hands. The moment we turn our troubles, mistakes, weaknesses, and failures to him, nothing will be left to worry about in our relationship. We relate our beliefs, feelings, values, health, illnesses, lives and deaths to each other too.

I. Human personality in relationships

According to Romero and Kemp: "The psychodynamic theories of personality development are based on the work of Sigmund Freud, but have been modified by others over the decades" (2007:89) as I have tried to do here. Based on our earlier assertion that the mind is a play ground, Freud argued that the events and forces within a person's mind that motivate behavior are the core of personality. Individual relationships reflect their personalities and vice versa. Expediently, there is need to briefly examine the components of human personality and why each person behaves true to type in his or her relationship.

According to William J. Grace:

> *One can easily distinguish, for example, between the truly cultured person, the person who renders his life harmonious with his thoughts, and that person who is informed but not cultured, whose life is unrelated to his thought, whose life does not embody the fruits of thinking (1965:7).*

Therefore, it is essential to be aware of these basic differences in our nature and personalities. They equally prepare the individuals to respect boundaries, accommodate and incorporate right judgments, flexibility and respond appropriately in their relationships with others. More often than not, we speak of this person or the other. There is more to that. In ordinary man's knowledge, personality is often described in terms of one's structures and appearances; how tall, short, beautiful and ugly a person looks. In our context, personality means more than those physical presentations. Personality essentially has to do with the inner psychological qualities of an individual especially through the impressions he or she makes on the outside world through his or her behaviors. According to Romero and Kemp, "First, personality is the tendency to behave, think, and feel consistently over time and across situations" (2007:87). It is the characteristic behavior of an individual or "an individual's characteristic pattern of feeling, thinking and acting" (Op. cit. 1998:121). In other words, a person's character is, and shapes, his or her personality. As we hinted in our introduction, "character" is the boss that controls, builds or destroys healthy relationships. It determines personalities and relationships.

The determinants of personality, according to Ekeagba, include any of the following: "environment, individual constitution, (biological and psychological aspects), culture, sex typing or role, family, group membership and unique experience" (1994:10). Each of these personality determinants equally defines the level of a person's relationships with others and patiently calls for understanding. For instance, the same sex marriages, legalization of abortion, atheistic tendencies, sexism, 'selfism', selfishness and non-communitarian mentality, 'personalism' or self-centeredness, communism, capitalism, et cetera, are characteristic and products of their own age and culture. Such cultures determine personalities whose judgments of conscience and relationships are based on standards and principles that are completely informed by those same cultural and ethnic value systems. That is to say, a child that is raised from rough and nasty environments will have a personality or relationship that is characteristically consumed by the gloomy darkness of indifferentism, apathy and insensitivity. When personality is interested and culturally oriented, it tends to create problems for anthropology and in relationships. For instance, individuals born and bred in America absolutely see the world differently from those born and raised in Africa. These cultural-environmental differences equally influence and affect their relationships, hence the need for them to study one another.

According to Ekeagba, we have the following types of personality: "General instability or psychopathic, timid, sensitive, anxious, obsessional, hysterical, schizothymic (introverted), cyclothymic and paranoid" (1994:13). Generally, we elucidated these personality types and temperaments in this book because every human relationship reflects its own personality.

1. The role of personality types and temperaments in human relationships

Everybody has a temperament that equally influences and reflects his or her relationship. To properly understand the personality types, it is necessary to understand what temperament is all about, because a person's temperament, relationship and personality are one and the same thing. We are our own temperaments. They are our inborn personality traits and characteristics. Parties easily tend to get along when they are conscious of each other's temperaments. The temperaments reveal individuals' strengths, weaknesses and growing edges. They are the ways we are and naturally nothing can easily be done to change them. However, once individuals are cognizant of their temperaments, the application of management techniques and strategies becomes feasible. According to Agwulonu:

> *Temperament is the combination of genes and chromosomes of our parents and grandparents at conception. Temperament is not the only influence upon our behavior. …Prenatal, postnatal…influences are there to make us what we are, especially training, education, and motivation. Temperament, however, is the primary influence on a person's life, not because it is the first thing that affects us, but because, like body structure, color of eyes, and other physical characteristics, it escorts us through life. (2001:73).*

Just as our relationships are differently based on individual idiosyncrasies and life formation, so are our temperaments. Parental influences, one's upbringing, education, genes, and associations have big roles in our temperaments and personality types. In Tim LaHaye's words, we read: "Temperament sets broad guidelines on everyone's behavior-pattern that influences a person as long as he lives…. The primary advantage of learning about the four basic temperaments is to discover your most pronounced strengths and weaknesses" (1988:22). This awareness is important for healthy relationship. We are better shaped at this time to examine the following personality types and some of the corresponding temperaments. This is primarily carried out here to prepare and assist individuals prefigure what they would expect in their relationships. The issue is addressed in this order:

i. A general or psychopathic personality refers to those who are emotionally immature. For instance, such people tend to jump into arguments in which they have practically nothing to offer and deny their contributions once squabbles emerge. These are people who hardly tell an offender his faults in his face. Slowing down, at times, helps partners to remain focused on the issues at hand, in order to make meaningful contributions. Emotional immaturity is a psychological case resulting from poor development of the person's "super ego" because "emotions are critically important decision-makers in our minds and bodies" (Op. cit. 1996:251). In a relationship where one of the parties is immature, only God knows how it works out or becomes healthy. In such a situation, the mature partner needs to put up with a lot of difficulties to move the relationship forward.

ii. A timid personality fears offending anybody. He feels assertive and apologizes for the least mistake and may not easily show anger when he is really angry. Timidity may be mistaken for humility or being unintelligent. A timid partner needs to sit up and squarely face the challenges of daily life. It could lead to harmony if well harnessed. Many a time, timid people maintain healthier relationships in their marriages and in public quarters. The ability to readily apologize for one's mistakes is necessary in relationships.

iii. A sensitive personality refers to a serious minded person who may have the tendency to take offence for the least provocation. He or she restrains from cracking jokes to avoid being hurt or upset. Sensitive people easily get embarrassed when confronted with their ugly behaviors. Sensitivity in this sense is a sign of fear to be realistic with oneself. The world has not got to collapse because of a person. To relate well with such people, we need to read their lips and faces. While it is important to be sensitive in a relationship, it is wrong to get angry at the least provocation. Unnecessary ride, at times, disables relationships.

iv. An anxious personality is apprehensive, tense, always worried over trivial matters and constantly looking for reassurance. This mentality is a sign of insecurity. The habit to seek reassurance, as noted earlier, creates problems in relationships. This personality seems to correspond to what Agwulonu refers to as a person of choleric temperament such as:

> ...*a strong-willed, self-sufficient and very independent. He is quite domineering and self-opinionated, even deciding for others. An old poetical work describes a choleric as a man who fiercely kicks a stone, which lies in his way. In reality, the more intense movements of these individuals begin early in childhood where they lack a feeling of this power and must demonstrate it constantly to be convinced that it exists (2001:75).*

Such people could be impetuous, unforgiving, presumptuous et cetera in their relationship with others and create problems in married state and ministries. It does not matter how anxious and rich our partners might be, they need our care and love. The best approach to these people in relationships is to be less argumentative with them. Being anxious and insecure over things does not change their situation rather it complicates them.

v. An obsess-ional personality is meticulous and over-conscientious as regards a habit, paying attention to details and resentment if his plans are interfered with. A person can be obsessive over a particular habit, feeding or dress. It has to be "that way all the time attitude". It may lead to rigidity. Encountering such people in relationship is a "HAH" half and half and a problem. For instance, a husband of an obsessional personality may not understand why his wife goes to shopping on daily bases, even if she has to buy perishable materials. People in this group hardly keep to appointments on time. One has to make extra sacrifices to maintain and put up with them. Obsessional attitude is equally a sign of insatiability and inordinate life. It does not advance healthy relationships, especially in marital state.

vi. A hysterical personality is excessively commanding, demanding attention and trying to dominate with some superficial type of emotions. This type corresponds to "sanguine" temperament. "The sanguine", taken from the Latin word 'sanguis' meaning blood, is the warm type of person, buoyant, lively, so out-going that he could be called super extrovert" (Op.cit. 2001:74). According to LaHaye:

> *A sanguine always enters a room mouth first. His noisy blustering, friendly ways make him appear more confident than he really is but his energy and loveable disposition get him by the rough spot of life. People have a way of excusing his weakness by saying: "That's just the way he is (1988:26-27).*

Even though a hysterical personality is responsive, and seems to relate well with everybody, compassionate, enthusiastic, a talkative and a friend of all, may, at times be unreliably forgetful, egocentric and exaggerative. For instance, a hysterical personality is easily spotted out as being generous even when his family is economically on fire. There are lapses to be fixed herein for healthy relationships to grow. However, it is better to have a partner who is hysterical in personality than a stingy one. Being hysterical can also lead to a hide of one's real identity. That is to say, no one is perfect in his or her personality and temperament as to claim a capital "P" in relationship.

vii. A schizothymic (Introverted) personality loves solitary life, has difficulty to make social contacts, reserved, at times intelligent, sounds shy, calm and unexcited. This corresponds to "phlegmatic" temperament. In Agwulonu's view:

> *The phlegmatic is calm, quiet, easygoing, dependable, objective, diplomatic, efficient, organized, practical and humorous. For his weakness, he is unmotivated, procrastinator, selfish, stingy, self-protected, indecisive and fearful (2001:76).*

Relationships may experience some BS, Bomb Shells or emotional tensions when the extroverted live with introverted partners. Parties have to study themselves and share common values and those moments they find enriching and progressive in their relationships. Introversion can also be a sign of deliberate irresponsibility in relationships. Partners need to guide this too.

viii. A cyclothymic (extroverted) personality, like the hysterical, is an outgoing and outspoken person, warm and friendly. But such people can be boastful and flamboyant many a time to the point that they may not have enough resources to meet up with their actual needs and pledges. The extroverted need to be cautious of what they say and do in their relationships because "virtus est stat", that is; virtue stands in the middle.

ix. A paranoid personality is always suspicious of others, very careful in the choice of friends. This corresponds to "melancholic" temperament. According to Aqwulonu, a person with melancholic temperament is:

> *Analytical, self-sacrificing, 'industrious', gifted, 'aesthetic', perfectionist type and are very sensitive to situations, faithful to given tasks and friendships. Given easily to contemplation and introspection, careful in his choice of friends, clothes, and all...neat to a fault and seldom welcome criticisms...for*

> *his weakness, he is moody, self-centered, persecution- prone,*
> *revengeful, touchy, theoretical, unsocial, critical, negative*
> *and scrupulous (2001:75-76).*

For instance, in marital relationships, a paranoid personality can always provide enough money for the house, but lacks the patience to listen to the feelings of his or her family. The irony of this situation is that the paranoid is already suspicious of being blamed for lapses when he or she has not been accused. A paranoid personality needs self-supervision, to trust in him or herself and believe that nothing is permanent under the sun and that no life is perfect or more important than the other in any relationship. Partners of these kinds of relationships must develop more hard skins, positive attitudes and pay less attention to side comments in order to cope with their situations and lots.

After our brief study of personality types and temperaments, the need to examine personality structures, which equally influence and affect interpersonal relationships, is indispensable.

2. Personality structures in human relationships

Sigmund Freud (1856-1939), an Austrian Psychiatrist as earlier mentioned extensively studied human personality and arrived at the conclusion that: "Every personality has three aspects - the structures, the development as well as a system of dynamic interactions" (Op. cit. 1994:5). The personality structure, to a great extent, determines the personality endowment of the child right from birth. Adults also fall victims to the animalistic level of personality structure as presented in this book. Such structures adversely affect relationships. It is common and a psychological case to see adults behave like kids. Such partners create problems in relationships. According to Freud "personality has three structures: the id, the ego and the superego" ...(Op.cit. 1998:122) as against the "ego" of Erik Erikson. In our study of the judgment of conscience, we came across the role of the intellect, will [seat of freedom] and appetite [choices] in decision making. We also mentioned the three warlords, the intellect, desire, the appetite and the need for spiritual psychology to provide the fourth spiritual self (the moral virtue) that controls the other three.

Each of these forces and powers represents a personality structure that influences human relationships. According to Freud:

> *The id, a reservoir of unconscious psychic energy, operating on the pleasure principle, seeks immediate gratification, and is not restrained by reality. ...The ego, which develops in early childhood, operates through the reality principle, which seeks to gratify impulses of the id realistically and to bring long-term pleasure without pain. The ego operates at both the conscious and pre-conscious levels. The superego, a third structure, emerges as children reach 4 or 5 and internalize the morals of parents and society. The superego acts as the voice of conscience and operates mostly at the preconscious level of awareness. People also possess and are driven by a psychological (sex-mine) energy called the libido (Ibid.).*

It has to be understood that these three parts of personality structures are different but work together to shape the entire relationship. Interestingly, everybody or relationship represents each of them. However, according to Freud, each person has inborn instincts and drives that seem to be tension systems which are created by the organs of the body. These inborn instincts and drives are the energy sources of each person and they represent the id. It is the matrix and center upon which the other two structures perform their functions. The id is unconscious, illogical, primitive, irrational, selfish, subjective, fantasy-oriented, always seeking its own pleasure and avoiding any changes that might limit its comfort. Most teenage boys and girls today operate on this structure level. It does not even consider whether or not what is desired is realistically and reasonably feasible, socially, culturally, morally acceptable and desirable. The id is like an adult in his or her "infancy" stage. Hence, in our relationships, these are parties and individuals of psychopathic personalities who are emotionally immature and slow to listen and learn. Hardly does any partner put up with them and that is why most of them die young.

We can now appreciate the enormity and magnitude of the forces that create conflicts and misconducts in relationships in particular and society at large. But as soon as these energy sources are activated and tamed, they give birth to the ego. This is reality-based. Ego represents the person's view of the environment; social reality, conscious beliefs, the causes and consequences of his or her behaviors on other people et cetera. The superego is the moral consciousness (synderesis, awareness) of the individual person and can be expressed in different ways. In support of the above views, Romero and Kemp noted: "For example, the sex drive can be expressed directly through sexual activity or indirectly through jokes or art. Freud argued that there are two primary drives. First, self-preservation is the drive to meet with the needs of hunger and thirst. Second, eros is the driving force related to sexual urges and preservation of the species" (2007:89). At times, some of our thoughts, feelings and actions can unconsciously be determined and carried out. This calls for vigilance in judging others in our relationships. In the Freudian analysis, human behaviors are, most often, motivated by drives that we are not consciously aware of. According to Romero and Kemp:

> *We may act without knowing why or without direct access to the true cause of our actions. This is illustrated in Freud's notion of the structure of personality. He believes that personality differences arise from the different ways in which people deal with the urges that stem from their fundamental drives (2007:90).*

The ego controls the id instincts for reasonable behaviors to take place. We have to note that there is always a constant conflict and war between the id and the superego. It is the ego that mediates the conflict. For instance, the id always wishes to grab and satisfy itself, but the superego continues to remind it of the moral implication of its selfish choices, while the ego presents the need for that item in question. Spiritual psychology plays the role of the superego in human structures. Any teenage boy or girl who does not want good direction and discipline will always but ignorantly feel betrayed and find trouble with it.

Eventually, this is where spiritual psychology - SP challenges the individual and society to put on their thinking caps again and save our young generation from moral decadence. In this personality structures, the introduction of SP or Moral Instructions in our school systems have tremendous roles to play. For instance, when the "id" of the students takes the upper hand and overshadows their "superegos", what type of society shall we expect in the future? Mismanagement of the economy of any society has never been traced to the spirits. There are no solutions to human problems that neglect sound moral principles. The id wants immediate gratification and so do the present age. But the ego, as a reality principle, delays the impulses from the id and objectively assists the individual to listen and accomplish tasks with appropriate decisions and actions. According to Ekeagba, "Some people describe ego as the voice of God", (1994:6).

The superego is the last of the structures to develop and begins from the age of 4 to 5 [3 to 4] years. This is the internal representation of the traditional values and norms of society as interpreted to the child by the parents and teachers. As Erikson puts it, "at birth…the child's interaction with the world…is preverbal in nature…and its needs… totally depends on the mother" (1950, in 1967:20). For instance, as noted by Ekeagba, "when you tell your child 'don't steal', you are helping him to develop superego" (1994:6) or conscience because superego is the moral arm of the personality. As Dr. Nwachukwu Udaku would have it:

> *Children and teenagers are very receptive as far as learning is concerned. Little wonder, parents and reasonable adults are very cautious of their actions before them. Their sensitivity is higher than that of our modern day recording devices, and their senses and memories are quick to note, grasp and properly save whatever they observe. These, whether good or bad, later begin to play out in the course of their growth (2009:65)*

Man being a "homo religiousus", awakes and arrivals at the early morning of religious consciousness at this period, super ego. According to the Koran perspective as cited earlier, religion is natural to every child, its parents determine for it which one it belongs. No wonder Massignon in Zundel maintains that "God is not an invention, he is a discovery" (1993:26). We discover and experience him through sound moral life. But human beings are invented and created by God; only few of them realize this favor, discover and appreciate him in worship.

Consequently, in all human relationships, parties and individuals are enjoined to discover the God who holds everything in being. In a sense, each of the human structures is designed by the creator to pass from one stage of development to the other, from one school grade to the other as many scholars like Freud and Erik have attempted to analyze. Human structures are divine.

3. The effects of Freudian stages of human development in relationships

The importance of human developments lies in the fact that each of the stages represents a particular behavior or an individual in a given relationship. Freud as noted in Romero and Kemp specifically believed that: "Experience in infancy and early childhood had the most profound impact on personality formation and adult behavior patterns. He assumed a continuity of personality development from 'the womb to the tomb" (2007:98). These infancy and early childhood experiences have tremendous influences on human relationships in general. These are issues each person should guide against in any given relationship. Therefore, our salient reasons and aims for studying and presenting these stages of human developments here are to assist individuals understand themselves and the factors that unexpectedly affect their relationships. Generally, Freud called this "Psychosexual Personality Development". According to him, there are five stages as noted by Sonderegger and Ekeagba:

a. Oral phase 0-1.1/2 yrs. – (Mouth/sucking, biting, chewing stage)

Not allowing a child chew its hands or whatever it can grab at this stage is not helpful. Every stage of the child's development is as important as the other in any given relationship. This is a phase where the whole activity of the child centers on the mouth, holding and putting every object to the mouth, eating, sucking, and crying to draw attention and gratification. This is the id structure at work. When any child encounters difficulty in passing through a particular stage, or does not pass through the stages of psychosexual development, a psychopathology results and such a child becomes fixated, attached or "attach oneself to a person or thing in an immature or neurotic fashion" (Dict. Def.). This is the core of our treatment of the psychosexual development in this book. For instance, Fixation at this oral stage may lead adults, college students, or some married couples into funny behaviors like wearing apparels of the opposite sexes, becoming talkative, drunkards, heavy smokers, sex maniacs, walking naked and frequently chewing their gums as a means of getting gratification from the mouth. Such selfish people may have much wealth, be attractive looking, but they hardly play active roles in building healthy relationships. At the middle of this stage the child develops teeth and can begin to bite the mother's nipples. The child knows he or she can inflict pain to the mother or society. At this stage, mothers should not allow their kids to enjoy this aspect of biting, because, once they are fixated here, it may adversely affect their relationships with others later in life. Mothers should let them know that they feel the pain from the bite.

Moreover, allowing the child to have whatever he or she wants without some guidance, leads him to selfishness and nonchalant attitudes towards other people. We are all witnesses to how some husbands sit back and expect their wives to work hard, make money and do everything for them. This attitude does not begin in a day and has never advanced any relationship. No wonder today, we have so many atrocious behaviors, evils and childish inclinations of people who are fixated at this stage of their early developments. As it were, spiritual psychology guides individuals to get prepared for the unexpected behaviors and occurrences in their relationships, in case your partner is a victim of fixation.

b. Anal phase 1.1/2 to 3yrs. – Anus/bowel and bladder control (Infancy stage)

The child's interest at this stage is centered on the anal region and activities. Toilet training by the mother, baby sitters or the nursery school teachers at this stage is vital as it guides the child to normal behaviors. By constantly and gently instructing the child on the right attitude to adopt here, either "do it in this POW or that one" equally goes into the child's ego principle and may lead him or her to be loyal and generous in life. Children, for Kelcourse, who fail to utilize this stage well "may never live up to their intellectual potentials as a result of inadequate care in these critical early months" (2004:66). For Onwubiko Augustus, "This period can make a person obssessionally clean or defiantly messy" (2007:59). Whatever attitude the child adopts at this stage is instrumental in creating the feeling of hate or love for the mother. The feeling is first showed to itself, then to the mother. But the same attitude will guide his or her future relationships with the world. Thence, relationships are both personal and inter-relational. This is why those fixated at this stage of their lives, may either be generous or parsimonious (stingy) later in their relationships with themselves and society.

c. Phallic phase 3-6 Yrs. – genitals masturbation (childhood stage)

Again, this is a period in a child's development when SP and Moral Instructions are fundamentally irreplaceable. Moreover, parents should play vital roles here as their children's First Teachers. The attention of the child at this stage is gradually turning into the genital region, where either the boy or girl's erotic feelings are directed to the opposite sex. The good examples parents show their children at this stage eventually shape their future relationships and those of society. Sex education is essential at this stage. Based on this issue, Dr. Nwachukwu Udaku remarked:

> *Sometimes, these negative impacts from movies and television can be immediately noticed, for example, when your child sees movies that are heavily laced with violence or pornographic and indecent scenes, expresses or experiments what he had seen during play and association with peers. Other times also the impact may be remote though not so immediate or obvious, it occurs slowly as the child keeps such images over and over again, especially when for example, smoking and hard drugs, sexual irresponsibility are shown and rewarding without showing at the same time the consequences arising from each of these habits (2009:66-67).*

It is scandalous for parents to engage in carnal activities in the presence of their children as part of sex education or to make them sexually active. This must be condemned. Sex education and orientation are basic and so important in the life of any child or individual. The lack of this fundamental knowledge has, not only destroyed many lives, but also society and healthy relationships. Sex is central in nature, divinely designed to ensure God's creation and continuity of the human race. For an individual to mess up with it is to play with the very basis of life itself.

Sex has no Religion

The urge and act of having carnal knowledge with the opposite sex are not taught. They are naturally circumstantial. Just like death, it will come when it will. Studies in spiritual psychology have indicated that inquisitiveness and early engagements to sexual relations have critical and mental effects on the physical and spiritual growth of the child. Besides, research has equally shown that pornography is the major contributor to prostitutions and sex addictions. Sex without love is either rape, theft, stealing or brutal. For sexual acts to be reasonable, maturity has to be there, else it remains at the level of the id – selfishness, which has destroyed many relationships today. For instance, the increasing divorce and infidelity rate and instances in our time, are parts of the story. SP has revealed that only those who have divorced before are more likely to divorce again than those who have not. Since sex is natural, having it indiscriminately with different people diminishes the urge for its primary function and to have it with one's partner alone – worst still, for one who goes for a 2nd rib (Gen.2:22).

Spiritual psychology has also revealed that sex has no religion. It does not wish to belong or go to any Church. It is un-baptized and enjoys its own autonomy, self-government, kingdom and independence. Sex is a highway of life and death. Those who take it must avoid rush, think first and know their destinations because there is no U-Turn from it. It is adamant and does not listen. It hears and speaks only one language and that is, "let's go!" It does not matter where an individual wishes to go, sex can land him or her into a place and situation he or she has avoided for life. God made it that way to differentiate the humans from all other living creatures. That is why it is part of and not totally human. It is so forceful and domineering that only those who are self conscious, rational, spiritual and reasonable can control it. Even at that, one needs divine interventions and self-efforts at every moment in human interaction, by constantly praying and reminding oneself that even a Bishop could unexpectedly fall victim to sex.

By its very nature, it is uncontrollable and unbending in its demands. Sex has no timetable or schedule. It is such a secret visitor that the host can only realize its presence when it is already gone. We make it to obey us and, not only assign a religion to it, but also, teach it the basic language and values of life. Sex, the forbidden apple, created for a specific purpose, is a priceless jewel at the hands of those who appreciate and respect it for what it really is. This makes the study and need of spiritual psychology so relevant in our time. For instance, if a teenage boy or girl, ab initio knew that he or she was not going to achieve his or her life aspirations or going to be useless and die early because of excessive drinking and careless life styles, he or she would have self-supervised, avoided bad peer groups, companies, habits and lived. For instance, when death is imminent, especially for a person who lived bad life, a day significantly becomes an eternity while his or her entire life sounds like a dream or it never existed.

Sex occupies an important role in the life of any human being. Therefore, the earlier we take cognizance of its uniqueness and presence in our lives, and apply prudence and maturity in the ways we approach it, the better for society and healthy relationships. Sex is life and death. We live with sex. We are 'products' of sex. God made it so for an inevitable end and purpose, and not to use it for self-destruction or fight our relationships and selves. As sexual agents, we must not allow sex to distract and hinder our future progress, education, control our religion, our faith in God and in each other. While there will be no sex in eternity, it can equally decide whether we passed or failed the eternal examinations here on earth. Our children need sound moral upbringing, education and good examples and not early sex. Modern science and technology may say otherwise, that sex is medicinal and that without it, one shortens one's span of life. This is not a platitude because sex is not invented by science and most of the young ones who die on daily basis are not inaccessible to it. While I agree on its therapeutic effects in healthy relationships, any human sex without sound morality and reason is equivalent to death itself. All school children and graduate students must understand what it means to live first and properly behave before they enter into "sex industry". There is a problem here especially with some parents who claim: "This is my child, and nobody can decide for me how to train him or her". It is generally understood that parents educate and train their children. Yet, in the education of children, no parent, teacher or society has it all.

Moreover, no child lives and dies only for his or her parents, no matter which country, culture, ethnic group, race he or she is brought up. Globally, the problem is, when the same child raised by a careless parent grows to become an armed robber, an assassin, a terrorist, due principally to such unhealthy upbringing and background, his or her actions will terribly affect the entire world. Hence, the proverbs: "One good turn deserves another and once one finger gets soiled it spoils the rest". Therefore, in the words of Sonderegger:

> *Fixation at the phallic stage may create an <u>Oedipus complex</u> for the boy [jealousy of a son toward his father in competing for his mother's attention] or an <u>Electra complex</u> for a girl [who competes with her mother for her father' attention]. Children resolve these conflicts by identifying with the parent of the same gender (1998:122).*

This is a delicate stage in the life of the child especially regarding how he or she feels about his father or mother respectively. Such feelings are later transferred to the outside world. For instance, some girls whose love for their fathers is so strong hardly stay or last in marital state. Parents are advised to learn how to deal with this situation because the foundations of future heterosexual relationships and sex orientations are laid here. The "effects of childhood experience", according to Onwubiko, A. "does not end with childhood, it extends to adulthood even to old age" (2007:78) and one's relationships. The old adage goes, "however a tree stands so does it fall". Partners who show equal cares to their children are accordingly, reciprocated.

d. Latency phase 6Yrs. to puberty – puberty/repression of sexual feelings (school age stage)

Nothing specifically happens at this stage but physical. There is growth in height and weight. School period consciously or unconsciously introduces the child into a world of fantasies, thoughts and actions. Now that the child has started attending school, he or she begins to de-emphasize parental interests and turn them to the outside world, mixing and making friends with other people. The development is natural and needs to be guided. In this sense, Dr. Nwachukwu Udaku noted:

> *This is where I am most concerned, because any child or group of children that is unrestrictedly exposed to high and underscored television programmes and movies, is being subjected to an unawarding process of half education. And half education as, has always been known crystallizes in madness of whatever kind. A good number of our good children are in this situation already; most of them have gone, so to say, mad (2009:66).*

Parental responsibilities over their children are symbiotic processes that benefit both parties. For instance, children who abandon their parents at any stage of their lives may not have the skills to run healthy relationships. This is where spiritual psychology and Moral Instructions play classic roles in school systems by constantly reminding the students of the need to be disciplined, respect themselves, their parents and society at large.

e. Genital phase puberty + - maturation of sexual orientation (Adolescent period)

This is a period of great need for SP and Moral Instructions because; this stage of character formation and judgment of conscience must be guided. Sigmund Freud calls it adolescent period. The child naturally develops feelings for the opposite sex at this time and can now differentiate the male from the female and may begin to have boy and girl friends. I call this critical period of a child's personality development "the risky period of I don't care syndrome - RPIS". A child at this stage feels he or she has all the powers to decide for him or herself. But this has never been true. For instance, according to Dr. Nwachukwu Udaku:

> *In some homes, children, not their parents have absolute control over the TV set, the Channel and programmes, and even the type of movie to be watched. In homes where the above is the case, you will hear the parents instruct, when you are tired, switch off and go to bed. Do well to go to bed early. Is this a loving admonition, from a caring parent? ...too much televison viewing can have adverse effect (on children) such as more violent and aggressive behavior, poor school performance, obesity, early sexual activity, and drug or alcohol use prevents them from engaging in activities they need to help them develop their bodies and brains (2009:67-68).*

In case a child fails to fully develop in the first three stages of his or her life especially at the phallic stage and does not resolve them properly, definitely he or she will have difficulty in shifting his love for his parents and relatives to other people. This happens in marital lives where partners scarcely figure out why the two cannot agree on most issues. They may have everything, wealth, education and children. Unfortunately, relationships are beyond the bounds of sexual relations and material possessions.

On the other hand, if the child fails to shift his or her focus of development from himself, family and relatives to the outside world, he will be immature and may develop temper tantrum. People of this nature easily show a form of sensitive personality characteristic by getting flared up in anger when things are not done the ways they want them. Healthy relationships cannot prosper with such people. The child achieves psychosocial maturity once he or she is able to shift the focus from him or herself and family to other people (Cf. Op.cit. 1994:7-9; 1998:114). The shifting, in this sense, has to be half and half or balanced to have a holistic personality in relationship.

However, Erik Erikson has eight stages of self or ego-centered personality development, as summarized here in Sonderegger, namely:

> *Birth to 1year (Trust vs. Mistrust) - Oral-sensory*
> *2 to 3 years (Autonomy vs. shame and Doubt – Muscular - anal*
> *3 to 5 years [Initiative vs. Guilt] - Loco-motor - genital*
> *6 to 11 years [Industry vs. Inferiority] - Latency*
> *Adolescence [Identity vs. Role Confusion] - Puberty*
> *Young adulthood [Intimacy vs. Isolation] - Young adulthood*
> *Middle age [Generativity vs. Stagnation] - Adulthood*
> *Old age [Integrity vs. Despair] - Maturity (1998:115).*

The main reason for adding Erik's personality development is to note the antithesis of life and emphasize how important these stages are in the development of each person and how they affect his or her relationship later in life. For instance, in the light of Erik's eight stages of personality development, in stage one, the child learns to trust and rely on him or herself as the source of his or her comfort and gratification with some obstacles or mistrust. Each stage of a child's development needs to be guided. In stage two, he learns to exercise some freedom of choice and independence and self-control. While the child initiates doing something or actions in stage three, he feels more comfortable carrying out activities in stage four. In stage five, he sees him or herself as useful to him and herself and to other people. In stage six, he or she develops the sense of commitment with society and the moral implication of his or her actions. In stage seven, as an adult, he tries to make a contribution to society that may serve as a model for future generations. In the final stage, the person begins to integrate his experiences in life as ways of self-fulfillment and life lived in conformity with the moral standards of society and feels free from blames or despair. These very stages challenge us as regards how far we have assisted in making society a home. Thus, in these 8 universal life stages, there are always societal oppositions [specific psychological dilemma occurring at each stage] fighting the development, or critical turning points (crises) resulting from the ego's will to live amidst parental and societal influences. These uncertain critical issues of the environment (parents and society) shape the dialectic nature of each person's development. Hence, a person may become good or evil; react positively or negatively in a relationship due to these influences.

From the analysis of the eight stages of a child's personality development in Erik's perspective, being self-centered in relationships does not always augur well. Just as human relationships, the parents, environments and society at large have vital roles in a child's personality development. That is why each of the stages of human developments has its role to play in peoples' relationships with others.

Due mainly to failures to resolve each personality development properly, individuals will always try to appear innocent with regard to Truth, Justice and Peace - TJP. For instance, most criminals want good names. Some tend to be generous to society just to avoid bad names or being associated with ills. Even, a terrible boss, worker, husband or wife, tends to see him or herself as a wonderful person. This is the problem with some relationships today. When everybody claims to be trustworthy, responsible and reliable, it becomes very difficult to account for the ills that plague society on daily bases. Cases continue to mount in their thousands in human behaviors where a thief always tries to protect him or herself from blames and punishments, either by denying the fact, putting up good reasons or defense mechanisms like, 'it is actually lack of employments that I joined this gang or out of hunger that I ate the food'.

Generally, defense mechanisms are natural and seem to have a theological foundation. For instance, when the Lord God asked the man and his wife: "Have you been eating of the tree I forbade you to eat", the man replied "It was the woman you put with me: she gave me the fruit and I ate it" When the blame seemed to have been shifted to the woman "What is this you have done", she answered: "The serpent tempted me and I ate" (Genesis, 3: 1-13). At the final analysis, both the man and his wife freed themselves by denying the fact and eventually shifted the whole blames to the serpent. This non-confrontational approach to relationships does not help all the time. An individual or partner who is always in denial of his or her bad behaviors will never think of fixing them. Openness and clarity dispel the darkness of ambiguous life styles in human relationships. As long as some people do not call a spade a spade, the devil will always find ways and openings to scatter their relationships. Briefly, we studied these defense mechanisms, understandably operative in human relationships and their effects thereupon.

J. The role of ego defense mechanisms in human relationships

These are unconscious and prompt manners we defend ourselves in the face of blamable alternatives and behaviors. As Bangley would have it:

> *Human psychology provides us with an arsenal of weapons with which to defend ourselves against anxiety. Often they come into service automatically (1992:7).*

Invariably, once a person is free from blames, he or she asserts him or her integrity and honor. Yet, it is worth noting that whichever way we live our lives has some imprints on our inner strengths, relationships with ourselves and other people. Therefore, according to Hawkins D: "Falsification of reason is indicative of non-integrity and also a primary characteristic of psychopathic personality traits" (2006:228). Martin Heidegger in Macquarie referring to the role of conscience in this regard, noted: "Conscience is precisely the disclosure to someone of what he ought to be, of his authentic self… the existence has a relation to himself, he has an idea of himself and can either be atone with himself or estranged from himself" (1968:32). Evidently speaking, an inauthentic person or a psychotic, - a person with mental disorder marked by some loss of contact with reality and out of alignment with social functions hardly makes valid judgments concerning his or her relationships. By implication, when people opt for authentic existence, it means they are being realistic to their identity as rational beings. Any relationship that is short of being realistic and fails to carry the imprints of self-commitment and image is more of a failure already.

Surveys and experiences show that we get involved in self-deceptions and inauthentic living because we unnecessarily simulate our identities, even against our own goals in life. For instance, a sex maniac who could not lure a particular girl for his selfish ambitions may jump into a marriage contract with empty promissory advances. Yet, inasmuch as his primary aim is to have sex with her, no matter how beautiful, rich, well behaved the girl might be, once he satisfies his urge, definitely the relationship crashes thereby destroying a trustworthy young girl for life. Spiritual psychology, therefore, calls for authentic existence as a way to make the best out of the various stuffy stages and experiences most girls and honest people go through in their lives. As it were, SP precisely serves as guidance and counseling just as Nwachukwu noted it in these words: "Guidance, therefore, is a service that makes the recipient to take a look at himself and examine his abilities, aptitudes, personality characteristics... It is a part of total continuing educational process that helps an individual to develop self-esteem and find a meaning in life" (1996:2).

Therefore, to understand and appreciate some of these personality characteristics and stages in development, as already noted, we must also study these defense mechanisms in details. According to Sonderegger:

> *During a child's development, the ego strategically uses defense mechanisms to deal with the anxiety produced by conflicting impulses from the id (operating on the pleasure principle) and the superego (using internalized representations of the parents' value system), (1998:123).*

Put differently, defense mechanisms are the instinctive measures we adopt to cover and protect some defects and our self-esteem, ignorance, respect, and defend ourselves against excessive anxiety when faced with failures, frustrations and conflicting situations. For instance, an aggressive driver will always blame other road users for bad driving. We employ these mechanisms more in our relationships. Practically, there are moments in our lives, when we tend to deny whatever memories, impulses and actions, which sound self-belittling. This is where most of us fall victims in our relationships. In situations like this, we begin to look for good reasons to defend our weaknesses or a way out instead of confronting and facing our problems and responsibilities squarely.

On the contrary, we tend to take credit and smile for whatever appears fine and noble in our behaviors. When a rapist tells a girl "you are most beautiful" she smiles and says "thank you" not knowing that she has been flattered. Of course, no girl is ugly in appearance but can, in manners. Defense mechanisms are not bad in themselves. They are natural ways of existence and living. However, they could lead to an inauthentic existence if not properly handled. Hilgard and Atkinson expressed the same view in these words: "All of the mechanisms are to be found in the everyday behaviors of normal people…. They increase satisfaction in living and are therefore helpful modes of adjustment… but when they become the dominant modes of problem solving they indicate personality maladjustment" (1967:646).

Consequently, we are constrained to study the various classifications of defense mechanisms and how they affect human relationships in general. Thanks to Romero & Kemp in particular and few other sources, that guided our survey in this order:

a. Aggressivity - aggressiveness or displacement

This is a defense mechanism in which one purposely hides his or her feelings as a way of self-esteem. In a 'layman's' understanding, such a person is said to be bragging. Aggressiveness could be displayed externally and internally. For instance, imagine yourself being irritated by your boss or school principal at workplace or school. At times, instead of reacting directly to him or her, you may displace your anger, annoyance, and hostility and transfer it to your partner at home or school children. Such behaviors are not intentional. But they happen. In professional and marital relationships therefore, individuals and school children should pause whenever their partners or teachers yell at them for no reason or cause. In the case of the boss just described, the ego, being aware of the need for the teacher or worker to keep his or her job, handles or controls the id impulse to fight back. In this way, the id is satisfied with the ego's intervention without conflicting with the superego's knowledge that fighting the boss can get him or her fired, (2007:91). This is purely on the external level.

Sometimes, an individual can impose punishment on him or herself in order to win back or regain his or her self-esteem, either by refusing to smile or accept gifts from the boss. That attitude is regarded as internal aggressiveness. In Igbo land of Nigeria, most husbands show their external and internal aggressiveness by refusing to accept food from their wives. In Igbo culture,"not to accept food" from one's wife grievously includes *"alukwaighi M"* which suggests that, "the marriage is ended". This type of defense mechanism should generally and diligently be guided because a wife with quick temperament or anxious personality can equally overreact, boil over her husband's unfriendly attitude and unconsciously create conflicts in their relationship. Some parents have victimized their kids as ways of showing revenge on their partners. This is evil. Benson remarked: "Episodes of anger and hostility can translate into stomach ulcers and heart attacks because our thoughts are intimately related to our bodies", (1996:39). That is, whatever happens to the body affects the mind as well. Eventually, this may develop into a definite loss of the feeling of self-esteem with an accompanying impulse of committing suicide. Faced with this type of situation, some partners may feel that their personalities are lost and being trampled upon. In order to make up and regain their personality, they can get involved in all sorts of inauthentic living, laughing aloud, just to attract the attention of others, annoy those they have no regard for, promiscuity and other social ills. However, spiritual psychology recommends that in extreme cases of disappointments, the individual should not take the matter to heart, but rather, he or she must affirm him or herself first as the only person who matters in the entire universe. Of what significance is life or the universe to any one who is not appreciative of it, his or her life?

b. Evasion

Often we get into some difficult situations in which a way out becomes a problem. We encountered this in our treatment of perplexed conscience in which the mind withdraws from making valid judgment of any course of action. In evasion, we react by withdrawing or letting go the situation. That is the way most partners dodge their responsibilities by giving one excuse or the other. Excusing oneself from a reasonable course of action is a sign of inadequacy to affirm self. Evasion takes either of these two forms:

i. Repression

In repression, we unknowingly hide our faces against any disgraceful thing we might have done in the past. As such, we rarely think and speak about them in any form of conversation. This is an unconscious process and therefore difficult to recognize. Some refer to it as active forgetting. Most often, we have memories of certain critical and tragic events and their accompanying unpleasant feelings. People tend to repress the natural inclination of unfavorable feelings, by "preventing the dangerous or painful thoughts from entering consciousness" (1998:123). Eventually, this tendency could lead to unanticipated and even traumatic outcomes. Openness demands that partners tell each other how they feel. Similarly, Dalrymple presented the danger of repression in these words:

> *Repression is an involuntary running away from a situation, a preconscious failure to face up to the frequently ugly truth about one's instincts...It is resisting evil by denying one's involvement in it, brushing it under the carpet, and this causes psychological trouble, because we cannot pretend that we have no involvement in evil, (1970:66).*

The feeling of guilt and unresolved issues about the ugly things we have done may be repressed with at least, a temporary escape from them. This is where discipline and self-evaluation play vital roles.

ii. Projection

This is another form of evasion as defense mechanism, which is very common in many relationships today. Each person knows his undesirable traits or qualities, which he or she does not even acknowledge to him or herself. This is bad. For instance, a man cannot blame his wife for allowing mice to enter their house and destroy things, when he is the very one who returns late at nights and keeps the doors open. In projection we protect ourselves from recognizing these undesirable qualities by assigning them in an exaggerated degree to other people. In this instance, we feel we are not to blame for any wrong we do. These are the major causes of conflicts in most relationships. There are various ways we project those unhealthy traits that are not known to us, to other people. For instance, a lazy husband feels more comfortable to compare himself with those who have no jobs than emulating the hard working people. At times, he projects himself in such statements like "I know I am lazy, but Mr. Tony and his wife are the laziest people I have ever seen" without thinking of the ways to fight his own laziness first. By shifting blames to others he or she affirms him or herself.

c. Rationalization or avoidance

Everybody wants to appear dignified in his or her relationship and act reasonably on the basis of acceptable motives. When things do not work the ways we want them, rationalization surfaces. In such situations, we often tend to assign logical reasons and plausible excuses for what we do impulsively. Rationalization does not mean acting rationally or irrationally. Rather, as Hilgard and Atkinson expressed it: "In search for the 'good' reason rather than the 'true' reason for what we do, we can bring forward a number of excuses" (1967: 516). In order to make a lie appear truthful, we tell more lies and at the end it remains a lie. It is risky rationalizing ones behavior in relationships. This type of behavior leads to an inauthentic living and self-deception. The reasons are that, while the excuses are seemingly plausible and the circumstances they justify quite true ones, they simply do not tell the whole story. For instance, a married man who has been out there, late with a girl friend may come back complaining of being sick and tired of tedious schedules at work place. Attitudes such as these do not encourage any healthy relationship. No wonder, Hilgard and Atkinson jointly added that:

> *In rationalization, one fools oneself instead of others, such excuses are within ones volition to have made use of them to put oneself in a favorable light with others"* (1967:416).

Again, a person who is not allowed to have his or her way in his or her company and to hold an important office there, may boast that members of his staff are envious of his ingenuity or afraid of his intelligence and competence. He, alone, knows in his heart that he is not reliable. The issue has nothing to do with positions but accountability and trustworthiness. This mechanism features prominently in all walks of life, including marital states too. In order to avoid blames, we rationalize our positions and appear innocent and capable. A fool who appears dignified in his or her attire has simply succeeded in exposing him or herself the more. This is also true of unreliable people or leaders who think money is everything.

d. Regression

In regression, we unconsciously and regrettably avoid remembering our unfavorable moments in life. In this mechanism, we tend to revert to the memories of those earlier and happier periods in our lives and adopt behavioral patterns that match our present feelings, especially when faced with difficult situations. This attitude is quite common among children and the aged. Little children show regression when they get new baby brother or sister because all the petting, calling of heroic names like "Dady's own child, king child" [In Igbo of Nigeria, "Nwa Dady, Eze Nwa"] et cetera are now to be shared, if not denied them. Equally, whenever the aged remember their youthful periods they regress because; they now feel like resetting the clock back to their earlier years when they had less worries and problems. This experience happens to people who seem to have become failures in their lives and relationships. For instance, a man who failed to sufficiently plan and organize his life, when faced with financial pressures from the members of his family normally regresses, complaining and narrating to them how all those he assisted in life have paid him with ingratitude. By eliciting the feelings of sympathy, he feels invigorated as a responsible, caring father and husband. Regression is a sign of fear and uncertainty as regards what the future holds in stock for one.

e. Substitution

Psychologically, this creates problems in relationships. Some people seem to proffer easy solutions to tough problems they have no idea of solving, instead of facing them squarely. They do this by reducing the apparent tensions without exposing the motives and tendencies that are compatible with societal approved guidelines. For instance, a person who is not talented enough to study and engage in scientific studies brags to his partner that he or she loved science subjects especially mathematics but his or her parents could not afford to train him or her. When a man begins to substitute his responsibilities in the house with convincing excuses, obviously, his relationship faces extinction. Relationships are action-oriented. Hilgard and Atkinson adequately expressed it, thus:

> *Substitution is a mechanism whereby approved goals are substituted for unapproved ones... activities for possible success are substituted for activities that are doomed to failure"* *(1967:519).*

In this way, substitution encourages complacency and lack of concern. It frustrates relationships. There are two forms of substitution:

i. Sublimation

This occurs when the societal unacceptable motives, impulses and sentiments, especially sexual ones are redirected and re-channeled to those acceptable in society. For instance, some individuals who indulge in cheating their partners in marital relationship, at times and as a cover up, sound so soft-spoken, caring and helpful in the minutest needs of the house. This is a sign of living in falsehood.

ii. Compensation or overcompensation

At times our best efforts to overcome certain handicaps end up in failures. Therefore, we look for other satisfying goals by accepting what is available without bothering for our targeted goals and the desirable. Any situation where a person is unable to reach certain goals in life, but lives on the denial of his or her weaknesses and difficulties by trying to excel where he or she is weakest is called compensation. As already noted, compensation is not helpful in relationships. For instance, an alcoholic or drug addict who is not ready to quit his bad habits is not fit enough to represent his group in religious and moral matters. According to Romero and Kemp, such a person will "either cover up a perceived weakness by overemphasizing some other characteristic, or making up for a frustration in one area by over-gratifying oneself in another area" (2007:92). For instance, an uncaring husband will always remind his wife, as the luckiest woman on earth, of how beautiful women admired him and the number of fiancées he dated before he finally wooed her to marriage. In compensation, to love one's partner becomes a favor or privilege and not a right. This is sad too.

f. Identification and introjections

In identification, individuals seem to live inauthentic existence. This is a situation where a person derives his joys or sorrows through the experiences of others. For instance, a lazy man tends to appear important and spend more of his time with people of worth. In times of grief, he expresses sympathy as if he has lost a person himself. But, in introjections, one may decide to go extra miles in one's relationships just to avoid being reminded of anything or ordered around. As we already pointed out, this is where the need for spiritual psychology - SP or counseling in relationships becomes urgent. According to Nwachukwu: counseling "is an open – ended, face-to-face problem-solving situation within which a student, with professional assistance, can solve personal problems" (1966:3).

g. Fantasy

In a situation like this, a person meets up with unfulfilled desires by imagination or gratifying frustrated desires in imaginary achievements and scenarios. For example, "a child who was abandoned by a parent may fantasize that the parent is really a spy who had to leave for the child's security" (2007:91). In this way, the child's ego, his or her being secured, handles the id's impulse that he or she is being hated and abandoned by his or her parents with the superego's knowledge that he or she is precious and needs every amount of care and love. On the other hand, a wicked man whose wife divorced, feels glad to tell people that he is now liberated from trouble when actually; he greatly feels the loss and support of a hardworking woman, the main source of his livelihood, and wishes she could return.

h. Denial of reality

Denial is a threat to relationship. It could happen among people with life threatening sicknesses. For instance, when a lazy partner refuses to perceive the reality and problems of his family and acts as if nothing is happening and does not work hard to support her, we say he is in denial. Thus, he protects himself from the unpleasant situation of his household by refusing to perceive it as such. Again, an addict hardly believes there is anything wrong. Therefore, by his or her denying this fact of addiction, his or her reality principle or ego calms the id's impulse for addiction and its deadly consequences not to conflict with the awareness of the superego, that generally, addiction can destroy his or her life and relationship.

i. Intellectualization or isolation

This is where one seems to separate emotions from threatening situations by thinking and acting impersonally or indifferently. For instance, the wife of your boss who works in the same department with you is so beautiful to you that you get attracted to her sexually but because of fear of being fired in case her husbands discovers your illicit intentions and advances, you tend to isolate your feelings and religiously present yourself to her as a born again Christian. This kind of mechanism blinds relationships. Instead of living an inauthentic existence or in make beliefs, it is better one positively expresses one's feelings in a more polite manner, "my boss, your wife is so beautiful, and I do admire her a lot".

j. Undoing

The mechanism of undoing does not promote relationships in any level. It is bad for a person to atone for his or her unacceptable desires and actions by trying to do "good deed" as a way to cover up his or her suspicious life pattern. From our survey, we discovered that men easily get involved in this mechanism more than women. For instance, when a man lavishes his resources on promiscuous living, he would always complain to his wife and children how the economy has reduced the value of money to nothingness as a way of covering his expenses rate. In this way, his ego - money is meant to be enjoyed, resolves the id's impulse of squandering it and blocking the future of the family or wasteful living so that it does not conflict with the superego's awareness that he should take care of his family and spend wisely.

k. "Doubt"

As a state of the mind, it also features in defense mechanism in which a person tries to shun certain relationships by way of keeping aloof or silent. For instance, a man knowing that his wife would be going for shopping in the afternoon, and being a stingy person, delays to return home in the disguise that there was so much to do in the office. Thus, by keeping his wife in suspense as whether he is about to return and bring money or not, helps him to relax as a caring husband and also to protect himself from possible blames.

l. Reaction formation

In this situation, one tries to prevent dangerous desires from being expressed by endorsing the opposing attitudes and behaviors and using them as barriers and as one's defense. For instance, a drunkard will always tell his or her partner the efforts he or she is making to quit drinking completely. In this way, the ego – the joy he derives from drinking resolves the id's inabilities to quit drinking with the superego's knowledge and awareness that drinking can kill. Again, most of those ministers who seem to be sex maniac in their ministries always preach against sexual practices in their sermons. By so doing, the ego – sex is good, resolves the constant id's impulses to naturally get attracted to sexual activity with the superego's knowledge of the need for authentic ministry and practices of the Gospel message. This equally happens when some unintelligent and lazy students carry voluminous Encyclopedias and books around as proofs for working hard. Consult Sonderegger & Romero and Kemp for details.

Therefore, excessive adherence to defense mechanisms result to phobias - abnormal fear and active anxiety that often attracts restlessness in relationship. Hilgard and Atkinson beautifully articulated these sentiments in these words:

> *The chief characteristic of the antisocial personality is a lack of moral development or conscience, and an inability to abide by the laws and customs of his society" (1967:541).*

The inability to morally abide by, and integrate the ethical values and principles of TJP – Truth, Justice and Peace into one's life and behaviors is mainly responsible for antisocial personality disorders experienced in most relationships today. Every person or partner should be conscious of others' values and feelings, bearing in mind that, fundamentally, "I am, my own self, and you are, your own self" in every relationship. In this capacity, relationships become holistic, especially when each partner imbibes parts of the other's values and feelings.

Having extensively studied the various factors that influence the ways we behave, act and relate to one another, we are bound to trace, and "scientificize" our survey by examining and stating the methodology we employed in getting to this level.

Chapter three

* * * *

Methodology

This chapter generally presents the methodology that is employed in every research work. In our survey of human relationships, it examines and validates the statement of problem, the hypothesis or thesis statement. Thus, "It is possible for human beings to amicably relate with one another". As an academic work, it includes the design of the study, the population, the sample and sampling technique, instrumentation, the method of data collection and the techniques for data analysis. Similarly, every human relationship demands a procedure, planning, a methodology and a particular language or instrument that measures its progress rate. Methodology, therefore, guides every research work and relationships to healthy conclusions.

A. The design of the study

The book sought to identify the psychological and ethical implications of human relationships and to determine the extent to which individuals are prepared for the challenges involved thereupon. The book equally took into account the impact which religious conflicts; immoral behaviors, personal mannerisms and idiosyncrasies have in human relationship. The focus of this design, which was a survey approach, was to elicit the opinions and responses from some professionals regarding the immoral practices in society today using appropriate research instruments. The data analyzed were gathered mainly from the teachers, lawyers, doctors, judges, and engineers or summarily put, the

"Middle Class", particularly from the Western and African cultures. Apparently, those data generally revealed the causes of conflict in human relationships and the positive measures and techniques individuals could employ to eradicate them. In the design of this book, besides the academic research concerns and perspectives, we took few vital points into consideration as they personally concern the individuals involved in any given relationship as food for thought, such as:

1. Can I actually relate and share with others, based on my own values?
2. What are my standards and preferences in comparison to others?
3. Do I see my life patterns and myself better than every one else?
4. In case I am hurt in the course of my relationship with others, am I naturally and likely to forgive?
5. Do I have any spiritual or physical loopholes that I need to address first?
6. What happens to my relationship when I run out of emotional credit?
7. In times of need, sickness and death, am I able to put my heart, thoughts, energy and feelings together for another person?
8. Am I ready to create some sacred space for and respect others' views?
9. To what extent have I already related with other people and what were the results and how did they feel about me?
10. Have I always based my successes and achievements on my strengths alone or have I benefited, somehow, from the cooperation of others?
11. Assuming my partner is not religious as such, how do I cope with him or her?
12. I love to have children and pets. What shall be my reactions if the person I love or relate to hates all these?
13. Can I engage in "trial" relationships to determine what works for me?

There are thousands and so many questions each person can individually ask him or herself in building healthy relationships. These pre-liminal steps and personal background checks are the energies and taproots that hold the liminal and post-liminality of all relationships together.

B. Area of study

Generally, every relationship operates within its own environment and state. For instance, marital relationships or friendships principally involve two supposedly conscious and free human beings; a man and woman who intend to share their lives together. Likewise in every other level of relationship, organization, political, social, economic, religious et cetera, sharing is involved. Therefore, due to the fact that this book is essentially based on fieldwork, life experiences that are scientifically measured, our area of study includes foreign (Western) and African based data such as the following:

1. Medical Centers, Hospitals and Clinics et cetera, especially New York University Medical Center.
2. Seventeen Secondary or High schools [within fifteen autonomous communities in Igbo of Nigeria, precisely in Ezinihitte Local Government Area] and few from the US.
3. Civil and Ecclesiastical [Courts] Tribunals.
4. Few Shell BP Engineering Companies.
5. The academic staff and alumni of the International Institution, Cloverdale and Graduate Theological Foundation, GTF, Indiana, USA.

In order to achieve our desired goal in the discussion, we utilized the various data gathered from our Questionnaires in investigating the levels, nature and pattern of misconduct and misgivings that seem to have generally affected human relationships.

Moreover, every relationship involves some areas of concentration and emphasis such as: spiritual stability, religious affiliations, financial status, pathological histories, individual idiosyncrasies, family histories, images, objectives, the means towards achievements, personal preferences and needs, ambitions versus resources, desirability versus availability et cetera. Spiritual psychology, as life GPS system and centered practice, touches all aspects of human industry particularly on interpersonal relationships. Human relationships are basically the true tests for healthy living, the realization of the meaning for life.

C. The population

In John Powell's book, entitled "Why am I afraid to tell you who I am?", he elaborately stated:

> *Person is resonant to person.... If I am willing to step out of the darkness of my prison, to expose the deepest part of me to another person, the result is almost always automatic and immediate: The other person feels empowered to reveal himself to me. Having heard of my secret and deep feelings, he is given the courage to communicate his own. This, in the last analysis, is what we mean by 'encounter' (1969:85) or relationship.*

The personhood of the individuals we relate to matters so much. A person's partner is intrinsically the population of his relationship. Only the individuals and persons involved in a particular relationship understand the weight of it all, where it pinches or not. The allusion that man is a bundle of possibilities remains scientifically proved because an individual is capable of mystification in any particular relationship. Yet, in healthy relationships, especially the marital, a partner alone can constitute a quorum.

Similarly, on a more scientific and experiential level, the population of our study in this book comprised of 323 teachers, academic and medical doctors, lawyers, judges and engineers drawn from different Institutions, including the 17 secondary and high schools as mentioned. The choice of this population is determined by the appropriateness of these Professionals, the Middle Class to furnish us with authentic and reliable information regarding the enormity, nature, cause, measurement, management, and effects of conflicts and role of moral values in human relationships in general. More importantly, these groups of people are significant individuals in the social, political and religious lives of society who have acquired sufficient and global knowledge as regards the issue at hand.

D. Sample and sampling technique

A sample of 164 individuals was drawn from the total population of those 323 professionals or Middle Class, including the teachers in the 17 secondary and high schools from the Igbo of Nigeria and America. Moreover, a simple random sampling technique was used to select the research sample as such. The study also adopted a stratified sampling procedure to ensure adequate representation of the Middle Class or professionals, males and females. Also, relationships need stratified procedures in which members of any party are given equal opportunities to prove themselves and make their voices heard.

E. Instrument for data collection

The instrument used in the data collection for this study is a questionnaire titled, "Middle Class Perception of the Possibilities for keeping Human Relationships Healthy Questionnaire" (MCPPKHRHQ). MCPPKHRHQ is a 26 item self-report questionnaire designed to elicit specific information on the respondents' opinions on varied issues concerning the factors that promote or destroy human relationships. It is divided into two major sections – A and B.

Section 'A' taps information on the demographic and ideographic variables.

Section B contains the 26 items of the questionnaire. The 26 items are distributed into 7 sub-sections. Each sub-section is presented in a form of checklist, that is, statements to which each of the respondents or the Middle Class tick the one(s) that most represent his or her opinion.

The scoring of the instrument is done by calculating the percentage of responses for each item in the sub-unit.

F. Development and validation of the instrument

The development of the "Middle Class Perception of the Possibilities for Keeping Human Relationships Healthy Questionnaire" (MCPPKHRHQ) is a product of several months of intensive study of materials related to keeping human relationships together. The development of the questionnaire took the following steps:

1. To isolate from the large pull of literature a number of items that focus on causes, characteristics, consequences and factors that influence and hamper human relationships.
2. To ask a good number of those Middle Class to write in short sentences, specific factors and practices that create harmony or conflicts in human relationships in general.
3. From the data collected from these two sources, a total of 59 items were constructed and these constituted the preliminary form of the questionnaire. This initial form of the questionnaire was then given to a few of the Middle Class who re-examined the instrument for ambiguity, content and relevance.
4. After effecting the corrections, the questionnaire came from 59 to its present form of 26 items.
5. The final stage that we adopted was the process of validation. The face validity is obtained by the approval of the Middle Class who are satisfied that the questionnaire is capable of measuring the various dimensions and factors that influence human relationships.

G. Reliability of instrument

A test-retest reliability index of 164 was finally established for the study. This was done by administering the instrument to another 22 Middle Class drawn from the same research population of 323, but who were not originally among the 164 used as samples for the study. After an interval of two months, the questionnaire was re-administered to the original group. The data and standard scores collected from the first test and second test were correlated using "Pearson Karl's Product-Moment Correlation Coefficient" (IR 1857). The high reliability indexes obtained indicate that the questionnaire can consistently measure the Middle Class views on keeping human relationships together. Similarly, in an organization, legal issues and ministries, when enough evidences for any particular item and case have been established and confirmed, common sense demands that the matter be concluded as authentic. For instance, partners cannot insistently adopt positions and values as right when the general public has condemned their actions as immoral. Compromising one's love with indecency and illicit relationships is evil in itself.

H. Method of data collection

The author, researcher or I, personally visited the various establishments that were selected for the study and administered the questionnaire directly to the Middle Class (MC) sampled for the survey and interviewed a lot of people. The author equally collected the Questionnaires administered to respondents on the spot. This process served as a check for unnecessary loss of the instrument. To accomplish this task was extremely difficult, time and energy consuming.

I. Techniques of data analysis

The data collected from the respondents were analyzed using descriptive statistic - percentages. That is, "by multiplying each response figure by 100 and dividing the total by the reliability index gives the percentage of our over all responses" [that is, each MC's response x 100/164].

Chapter four

*   *   *   *

Data presentation, analysis and interpretation of results

This chapter has two sections or phases: The first phase presents the results of the study and the second involves the Interpretation and Comparative Study and Discussions of Results.

A. The presentation and analysis of data

The results are arranged research - question by research - question. Effort was made to present the results in the form of tables to which references are made. Finally, the results are summarized and some conclusions drawn from them and therefore presented as summary of findings.

Research Question I: What is the enormity (level) of conflicts in human relationships?

Table 4.1 Responses on the enormity (level) of conflicts found among people.

Question	Mode of Response	
Among which category of human relationships have you observed serious misgivings?	Frequency (No)	%
a. Among Married people b. Among ministers c. Among establishments d. Among friends/peers	64 16 34 50	39.02 9.76 20.73 30.49
Total	164	100

Table 4.1 above indicates that 64 (39.02%) respondents confirm that they have observed serious misgivings among married people alone. 16(9.8%) point their accusing fingers to the ministers of the Gospel. While 34(20.73%) of the Middle Class maintain that mishaps exist more among establishments, organizations, political, social and economic circles, 50(30.49%) of them apportion the blames on friends and peers.

Research Question II: Which of the following misconducts have you noticed?

Table 4.2: Responses to elicit the nature of conflicts easily observed among individuals in their relationships.

Question	Made of Response	
Which of these ills/misconducts have you noticed in peoples' relationships more frequently?	Frequency of Responses (No)	Percentage of Responses

a. Dishonesty/Cheating/No Trust	52	31.71
b. Lack of commitment/ Deception	26	15.85
c. Lack of respect for & attentive listening to each other	60	36.59
e. Gossips, Yelling & Quarrelling	26	15.85
Total	164	100

From the above responses on table 4.2, 52 of the Middle Class, representing (31.71%) say that they have observed incidents of dishonesty, cheating and lack of trust among so many parties. 26(15.85%) of the professionals confirm the incident of deception and lack of commitments as being instrumental to the misconducts in relationships. 60(36.59%) present lack of respect and attentive listening to each other's concerns as being responsible for misconducts in relationships. 26(15.85%), attribute gossips, yelling and quarreling to the ills that affect relationships.

Research Question III: From where do you think the bad airs and manners in relationships originated?

Table 4.3: Responses to find out the sources and causes of indiscipline in human relationships.

Question	Made of Response	
From where do you think all these acts of indiscipline originated? Choose from the list below:	Frequency (No)	%

a. Poor upbringing and education [family/other factors-associations, environs.]	52	31.71
b. Lack of moral & religious values	48	29.27
c. Wrong priorities/Choices	22	13.41
d. Lack of self-knowledge/ supervision.	42	25.61
Total	164	100

Table 4.3 reveals that 52(31.71%) of the Middle Class (MC) trace the acts of indiscipline and conflicts to poor up-bringing and education. 48(29.27%) of them agree that lack of moral and religious consciousness is responsible for the problems encountered in relationships. Only 22(13.41%) professionals hold that wrong priorities and choices create conflicts in relationships, while the remaining 42(25.61%) of them attribute the problem to lack of self-knowledge and supervision.

Research Question IV: [As noted in the question box]

Table 4.4: Responses to ascertain whether religious conflicts and disunity can totally be stamped and crushed out of human relationship.

Question	**Made of Response**	
Do you think that conflicts and misunderstanding can totally be crushed out of human relationships?	Frequency of responses (NO)	Percentage
Yes	78	47.56
No	86	52.44
Total	164	100

From table 4.4, it is clear that 78(47.56%) agree that conflicts and disharmonies can totally be wiped out from relationships. Whereas the respondents who vote "No " to the question are 86 in number, representing (52.44%) of the over all population.

Research Question V: (As indicated in the question box).

Table 4.5: Responses to the various measures through which disunity in the community can be arrested

Question	Made of Response	
Through which of these measures can harmony be achieved in relationships?	Frequency (No)	Percentage
a. Living by examples	54	32.92
b. Trust in oneself, others/God	44	26.83
c. Being responsible & there for the other	20	12.20
d. Obeying one's conscience	14	8.54
e. Being flexible/Ready to help	32	19.51
Total	164	100

From the author's table 4.5 of response, 54(32.92%) of the MC acknowledge that living by example is the best education that can easily bring back order and peace in relationships. 44(26.83%) of them maintain that parties need to trust in themselves first, trust other people and their God as ways to build healthy relationships. 20(12.20%) suggest being responsible for one's goals and just being there for the other in case of the uncertainties of life. 14(8. 54%) of the Middle Class hold that obeying one's conscience is helpful in keeping relationships on track, while 32(19.51%) of them opt for and suggest that parties or people be flexible in their judgments before jumping into any decision and action and be ready to extend helping hands whenever the need arises.

Anthony O. Nwachukwu

Research Question VI: (As indicated in the question box).

Table 4.6: Response to know whether these conflicts and disharmony in relationships hamper the progress of society generally.

Question	Made of Response	
Do you think that conflicts in any relationship do affect the progress of the individual parties and the general public?	Frequency (No)	%
a. Yes b. No	164 -	100 -
Total	164	100

From the above table of response, 164 (100%) of the respondents unanimously concur that social, racial, economic, political and religious conflicts and disharmony will always remain a stumbling block to the progress of interpersonal relationships and the development of the whole human race at large.

Research Question VII: (As indicated in the question box).

Table 4.7: Responses to ascertain the factors that can assist individuals restore their relationships.

Question	Mode of Response											
	A Personal Efforts & Sacrifices		B **Religion & Faith in God**		C Material Comforts/ Things		D Churches & Ministers		ABCD The 4 put together		Total	
	No	%	No	%	No	%	No	%	No	%	No	%
Which of the factors do you think can help parties curb conflicts and bring unity in relationships?	62	37.80	18	10.98	8	4.88	36	21.95	40	24.39	164	100

This is the last research question the author asked the professionals or the respondents (Middle Class). It is a context analysis. From the responses shown on table 4.7, five distinct categories were suggested. Among the variables, while 62(37.80%) of the MC are of the opinion that personal efforts and sacrifices will do it alone, 18(10.98%) suggest religion, 8(4.88%), material comforts and things, 36(21.95%), the churches and her ministers and 40(24.39%) think that unity in relationships can only and easily be restored when the four bodies work together.

B. The interpretation

The second phase of this chapter deals with the author's interpretation and discussion of the findings on human relationships obtained from the data analysis. In all, there were 7 research questions and 26 variables that were presented and analyzed. Consequently, the results of the presentation and analysis were interpreted as the final summary of the observations of our respondents.

Eventually, the results obtained from table 4.1 showed that misgivings in relationships occur more among married couples than in other categories of relationships. The analysis is true because marital relationships are primarily and fundamentally the basis for all other human relationships. It is a primordial relationship. The fact that 39% of the overall population of respondents agreed on this fact is indicative that the frequency of misconducts in relationships in society is highest among them. The implication is that, there are a lot of issues going on among married people that need to be resolved in order to balance their relationships. No wonder, the saying goes that parents are their children's' first teachers. The influences of parents on their families greatly shape and determine the relationships of society at large. The interpretation equally suggests that more consideration should be given to married people in this book because they are largely responsible for sound education of their children. From the analysis, some parents have failed in this regard. Therefore, couples are hereby called upon to examine themselves, work hard, and live by good examples in order to maintain healthy relationships. From the analysis, friends and peers scored 30% of the misconducts that plague relationships thereby taking the second place in the analysis. The simple implication is that there are notable elements of competitions, rivalries, and ambitions among them that need to be addressed. That such high percentage of conflicts was recorded among friends and peers challenges the concept of friendship in general.

Contextually, the analysis has revealed a striking piece of information regarding the relationship that exists between society and the ministers of the Gospel.

While 21% of the misconducts in relationships falls within various establishments, political, social, organizational, economic et cetera, only 10% is traceable to the ministers of the Gospel. From the level of misconducts encountered in society, it is clear that, according to Raab, the Gospel message and her ministers do not actually affect the ways people tend to lead their lives. Again, that the ministers of the Gospel scored only 10% reveals that the misconducts in their relationship are minimal and insignificant. A lot of things are implicated here. In the first place, it reveals that some people in leadership positions, politicians, and heads of certain establishments sound egocentric, self-centered, and self-opinionated and seem to be fighting for their own gains and not for the general public. That is to say, for this class of people to maintain their status quo, friends and families, they get involve in embezzlements of public funds as we have witnessed lately in some establishments. This analysis brings the crime rate and insatiability in society within the confines of married people and peer groups. Consequently, the analysis reveals that despite the scandals some ministers get involved today, the general public or society still counts on them for spiritual edification and role models. In other words, the immorality that plagues some relationships today is traceable to various individuals in society and not necessarily to the ministers.

On another level, the results obtained from table 4.2 showed that 32% of the ills we find in relationships and society today stem from dishonesty, cheating and lack of trust in others. Thereby, partners and individuals are called upon to examine how sincere they are in their relationships with other people. The interpretation is that most people are not as faithful as they should be in their marriages and establishments. The issue of trust is very important in every level of relationship. It is number one disease in human relationship. No wonder it took the 2nd place in the rating and analysis. In the analysis, 16% of the ills in human relationship springs from lack of commitment and deception. Non-commitment attitude to relationship is deceptive, evil and deadly. It is another form of cheating and dishonesty. The highest percentage of 37 comes from lack of respect for each other and attentive listening ear.

The inability to listen to others in relationships is physically sickness. Once a relationship, be it marital, social, economic, political, religious ceases to be attractive, appealing and inviting to the other, it dies. The interpretation is that, the best gift a partner or any person could give to the other is to listen and hear the feelings enshrined in his or her spoken words. Whenever a person or partner is always in a hurry to sit down and listen to his or her partner, to the happenings of the house, in their organizations, establishments, et cetera, it simply means that healthy relationship is lacking there. To listen is principally, to respect and be proactively involved. Getting involved in a relationship with someone, a company or an association one does not respect is baseless. In this sense, Lauder Robert made the following remarks:

> *To listen profoundly to someone requires that the listener be in control of himself to some extent, that the listener is able to be still and not preoccupied with himself or with what he is going to say when the speaker is finished (1978:56).*

As a consequence of the lack of attentive listening, the respondents hold that 16% of the ugly experiences in relationship comes from gossips, yelling and quarreling, tallying with the number that condemned lack of commitment and deception in relationships. The interpretation is that, once a person indulges in deceptive acts, he or she feels that others are fools, not knowing that he or she is the very fool in question. The resultant effects of lack of commitments and deceptions are gossips, picking of quarrels and yelling at others because of one's sense of insecurity, unresolved instincts and urges in ones personality traits. Generally, once individuals are open and sincere in their relationships, all forms of hypocrisy, misconducts, disunity, conflicts and misgivings will be given mortal blows in society.

Based on the results obtained from table 4.3, 52 of the respondents, representing 32% of the total survey confirm that acts of indiscipline observed in human relationships today come from poor upbringing and education, including the family phase, biological, associations, and the environmental factors et cetera. In this context, the interpretation reveals the importance of spiritual psychology – SP and parental or family up bringing in the education of their children towards healthy relationship. Education in this understanding equally includes the orientation of the young ones to the culture of their land and its implication for religious, moral practices and interpersonal relationships. That was precisely why the missionaries who brought the Christian message to the Igbo people of Nigeria failed. They never cared about the peoples' value systems and bounced on "cut and nail" evangelism. Knowledge of the family history and culture of any people are important in any relationship. In the light of this, Kinzer Mark noted:

> *Most modern families have significantly less discipline, commitment, and stability than did families in scriptural times. This affects individual self-worth because the family is the most powerful formative influence on human personality development. Stable, committed families usually produce more secure and confident children, whereas weaker families produce children with less confidence (1980:24).*

These revelations are vital in relationships. Here again, the words of Socrates become urgent: "an unexamined life is not worth living". The association an individual keeps and the environment in which he or she is raised, as noted earlier on, tremendously affect and influence his or her relationships. 48, representing 29% of the respondents hold that the conflicts encountered in relationships today come from lack of moral and religious values, while 22 maintain that wrong priorities and choices are the major problems. The interpretation is that, lack of moral and religious values in one's decisions and actions are fatal in any human relationship. This is where the freedom of the will comes into play in human relationships because it is inconceivable and unthinkable to have a human relationship that is devoid of morality and freedom.

Basically, it is the lack of adequate application of the moral, eternal, natural moral principles in individual decisions and actions that leads, mainly our children to wrong priorities and choices. That is why only 13% of the overall respondents apportion the misconducts in relationships to wrong priorities and choices. The simple implication of this low percentage is that people no longer obey their consciences. For instance, a person who is not conscious of what pleases or offends his or her partner can hardly understand what it means and takes to make him or her happy. On a unique level, 42, representing 26% of the respondents agree that lack of self-knowledge and supervision are responsible for the misconducts in relationships. Out of the four categories analyzed and presented here, 26% taking the 3rd place points out that lack of self-knowledge leads to affected ignorance and ineffectiveness in relationships. It is only when people properly understand who they are, their personality types and temperaments that they can dispose themselves to relate with others. That is why self-reflection and supervision are necessary in relationships.

As can be observed from table 4.4, it is remarkable that while 48% of our respondents say that misconducts and conflicts can totally be crushed or wiped out from human relationships, 52% oppose the possibility of such proposals. The interpretation of the 78 respondents positively anchors on the fact that, once individuals set aside their economic, social, political and religious differences and accept one another in the unity of one heart, human relationships can always be healthy. In other words, the above assertions imply that if people could be more responsive, listen and obey the voice of their inner selves – conscience, they would appreciate the reasons for good behaviors and lasting relationship. The position of these 78 respondents who hold that misconducts can totally be crushed in relationship seems to make much sense. Their message is clear. Humanity needs to put aside all differences and embrace each other in peace and love. However, on a second analysis, the 86 Middle Class who hold that misconducts in human relationships have come to stay and nothing can be done about it have their reasons too. The first value interpretation as regards this second group is dimensional. The rate of evil in society today is so evident that many people seem to have lost the sense of moral values. While their responses could also be viewed as being pessimistic and negative, there is a possibility that some of them are indirectly involved in establishing the present day network of indiscipline and apathy in society.

The conclusion anyone may draw from the interpretation, might be that, these 86 respondents belong to the political, high-class who might be single or wealthy citizens and do not care whether human relationship progresses or collapses. Their position raises such questions as: "Is it true that conflicts in our relationships cannot be settled? What is it in our nature that prevents us to accept one another as such? Does it mean that there is no ideal relationship in any level? If conflicts will always abound in human relationships, then, of what significance and importance are religious values, ethical principles, the golden rules, the Gospel, God and the purpose of creation and this life?" In this light, only the individuals that are involved in a particular relationship understand this analysis better. Human nature may sound incorrigible and inadaptable, yet it can correct itself especially in the face of uncertainties. For those who try to abide by the ethical principles in respecting other peoples' values, our 78 respondents are in order. But, as for the 86, representing the highest percentage of 52, are solidly in support of spiritual psychology in creating awareness that even when things seem to be moving fine in our relationships, we can always expect the unexpected therein. In support of this vital observation, the need for flexibility in human relationships, McDonald and McDonald stated:

> *When life goes well (in our relationships-mine), when purpose and meaning govern the daily agenda, positive energy flows freely. Activities are meaningful and fulfilling...Insert unwelcome change into the agenda, however, and energy flags. New questions bubble to the surface of awareness, giving distinct form to the panic within (1997:15).*

The result obtained from table 4.5 shows that 54 Middle Class, the highest in number, out of the 164 of them suggest that the only way and measure that can guarantee order, peace and unity in human relationships is living by examples. As already noted, if we want our partners and friends to be good to us, we must first approach them in that spirit. It does not matter whether they reciprocate or not. We set the pace for peaceful interpersonal co-existence. By unanimous agreement, in keeping with the principles for our measurement in this table, our thesis statement, that is: "It is possible for human beings to amicably relate with each other" is hereby validated. In line with this interpretation, 44, representing 27% of our respondents suggest that individuals must first and foremost trust in their nature. This is, to trust in one's capacity to be good, to relate with other people and trust them with some benefits of doubt as important human documents.

More importantly, individuals must trust in their destinies and identities, as beautiful and unique creation on a specific purpose and mission on earth with the firm belief that even if others disappoint, they still belong to a source that is immutable. In a sense, putting up one's best in relationships has its own rewards that cannot be quantified in physical terms or words. In this light, 20 opted that being responsible and just available in relationships will go a long way to bring peace, harmony and understanding. 14, representing 9% of our respondents hold that obeying one's consciences will, as the last resort, bring harmony in one's relationship. The second value interpretation here has revealed a sticking and serious matter for individual considerations. That human conscience is given only 9% in the over all analysis has proved Raab right, that most people are not influenced by their belief systems and religious practices. The conclusion, as noted earlier, is that many people, young and old do not obey their consciences any more. We can now understand why there is much chaos in society today. A conscienceless society is a violent one. On a special manner, 32, holding the 3rd place out of the total number that assisted in this measurement, maintain that flexibility and hard work can bring harmony in human relationships.

The value of flexibility cannot be overemphasized in human relationships. There is flexibility when partners openly welcome suggestions, criticisms, corrections, and are ready to adapt to changes. Any relationship, in which decisions and behaviors tend to be rigid and static, collapses. Thus, individuals are called upon to be industrious and hard working as to enjoy a variety of choices that may surface and advance their relationships. Moreover, the overall interpretation reveals that some of the Middle Class themselves are not satisfied and happy with what is going on in many relationships today. Thereby, they invite individuals and partners to live by examples, trust themselves by being hard working, responsible people, open to new ideas and listen to each other as belonging to the same rational family of human beings.

However, on a different note, the results presented in table 4.6 revealed that none of the Middle Class agrees that conflicts, misgivings and indiscipline can ever encourage mutual cooperation, warm relationships, community progress and developments. Unanimously, 100% of the entire respondents agree that conflicts in human relationships and society will always affect economic growth and progress. This unanimous confirmation supports the hypothesis of this book that human relationships are possible once the partners comply with the moral and created order. The simple interpretation is that society generally, irrespective of religious and political affiliations must come together and say "no" to disunity and indiscipline in their relationships.

Finally, table 4.7 presents the result of context analysis, whereby the author makes a clarion call to various bodies that can help society and individuals in question to imbibe the culture of good behaviors in their relationships. For instance, the results obtained from the last table, like in table 4.5, rank personal efforts and sacrifice highest with 38% of the overall responses regarding what can help curb conflicts and bring unity in relationships. This interpretation confirms our earlier assertion that individuals decide the nature of their relationships. The efforts people make in studying, understanding, accepting and putting up with one another, to a great extent, are the keys to healthy relationships. The number that presents religion as the only solution is 18 or 11%. Such interpretation, here, reveals that relationship is fundamentally psychological than religious. The way an individual feels about others, their life patterns, situations, condition and environments, whether they have a religion or not, determines how he or she relates to them. That is to say, healthy relationship is not necessarily dependent on any religion but in one's ability, here and now, to apply general moral principles and religious values, to ones decisions and actions. Fundamentally, for this 11% of the overall responses, religion and God are necessary in any healthy relationship. The interpretation as regards this low percentage on religion and faith in God indicates that humanity has lost contact with her primary source and urgently calls for radical change of hearts and attitudes.

Again, 8 representing 5% of the respondents agree that material comforts and possessions have insignificant role in curbing conflicts and bringing unity in human relationships. The interpretation is that, while riches, affluence, wealth and money are essential in every relationship, love among parties is indispensably more powerful than money, thereby confirming table 4.5 of this survey. It is surprising to note that 36, representing 22% of our respondents hold that the Church and her ministers can do it alone, when only 11% of them approve of religion. The first value interpretation that comes to mind is that the Church is the human face of God that radiates such images as peace, unity, forgiveness, love et cetera. The Churches in this context are clearly understood in terms of actions-oriented bodies that address and guide human prospects, conditions, progress and properly shape the Christian religion to its end. In other words, religion without adherents is of no significant value. As noted in table 4.1 of this survey, little or no serious misconducts were recorded among the ministers of the Gospel or the churches, which means they are trying.

The reason is that no matter how sinful the Church and her ministers may be, their primary function is to bring peace and harmony in peoples' relationships. In all fairness, most denominations have justified this mission. Similarly, 40 of our respondents, representing 24% of them, occupying the 2nd place in this survey, prefer the four bodies and categories combined as the only way to curb conflicts and bring unity in relationships. For this 24%, the interpretation is that personal efforts, religion, material comforts, the Church and her ministers alone cannot achieve unity in relationships. The four have to come together. Consequently, the interpretation has revealed a type of dichotomy between the four categories presented. That, there are some divisions among these bodies and categories equally point to the fact that neither of them or the individual is totally free from blames of the conflicts in society today. The interpretation, therefore, suggests that individuals, religious bodies, organizations, ministers should supervise themselves and lead honest lives in order to keep society more peaceful, trustworthy and safer. Basically, the interpretation has revealed that this book has created the awareness and the various ways to achieve healthy relationships. It is left to individuals to apply the strategies and principles outlined here for their own success. Thus, conflicts in human relationships are still within each individual life styles and habits.

Having presented and analyzed our data, the Interpretation, Comparative Study and Discussions of Results, we are inevitably compelled to launch "The Summary of work and Findings". This is going to constitute the chapter five of the book like in any other research work.

Chapter five

*   *   *   *

Summary of work and findings

This chapter is divided into A & B. While A discusses the summary of work, B presents our findings.

A. Summary

The book begins by establishing that life is precious and needs to be preserved despite the fact that man is a bundle of possibilities, who is constantly and continually in search for meaning and in a process of decision-making. This is the decision to act rightly or wrongly in his relationship. We also studied the various characteristics and dynamics of an individual as to ascertain the cause of conflicts and misconducts in his or her relationships. To accomplish this set goal, through research methodology, and relying principally on our area of study – Spiritual Psychology, we approached the issue of human relationship from psychological and ethical perspectives. In this process, we underlined the highlights that assisted us proffer some therapeutic solutions to the problem.

The book is not limited to any level or type of human relationship. Due mainly to the fact that Spiritual psychology belongs to the area of psychological practice; it fundamentally studied the various aspects of human values, socio-religious, political, educational, economic and cultural, et cetera. This is an attempt to integrate these values through psychological and ethical perspectives into a system of self-trust that yields positive results for the individual agent in particular and society in general. Spiritual psychology is particularly very critical of religious hypocrisy and maximizes the Heraclitian and Tillichian ideas of the paradoxical co-existence of the good and bad in preparing a generation of individuals that may objectively reflect integrity and honesty in their behaviors and relationships. This work is better described as a revolutionary handbook of moral instructions, discipline, order, justice, truthfulness, and an educational opportunity for college and research students, irrespective of religion or religious affiliations. The book is therapeutically designed to revive and resuscitate broken relationships and maintain the healthy ones.

However, the book is the product of several years of hard work, fieldwork and research based on analysis and findings and substantially incorporates and maximizes experience and research from various fields of study for individual applications. Daily experiences show that there is no perfect human relationship anywhere. To be aware of this 'expected' and the 'unexpected' quality, paradoxically inherent in all human behaviors is the yardstick for measuring the success rate of healthy relationships.

It attempts to underscore the factors that assist individuals achieve meaningful results and avoid conflicts in their relationships. Holistically, it seeks to study the influences the individual characteristics and dynamics exert on his or her relationships and how these influences can assist him or her in relating with others. It raises such concerns as how far does one's behaviors affect oneself and relationships with other people. There is no gainsaying that society needs a change in behavior, especially today that most of the young ones have gone very wild in crimes. For instance, there are so many broken homes and marriages, cases of divorce, single parenthood, separated children, disappointments, conflicts, embezzlements of public funds, political and cultural disparagements, maladjustments of policies, sex scandals, religious injustices, crimes, insecurity, debilitation of the very bases of human life, quarrels and bickering in our time. Yet, everybody claims right. This is disgusting and needs a scientific attention.

Therefore, the book empirically aims at offering management and maintenance strategies, which every reasonable person, irrespective of age, gender, position, religion and status, may employ in his or her particular level of relationship to bring positive changes in his or her relationships and deal with other life threatening events. Consequently, spiritual psychology urgently challenges each person to tap in his or her inner strengths, energies and put on his or her thinking cap for self-supervision and evaluation. Spiritual psychology is all about revival and transformation of stony individual hearts to soft ones.

Moreover, these days, some ministers of the Gospel seem to commercialize their work as if God is a commodity. Nothing seems to be perceived as sacred anymore. Our young generation appears to be heading to the wrong direction due mainly to the negative influence of the global village syndromes. Morality, which is core and central to all rational beings, has become an appendage to most human behaviors. In some high quarters, reasons are sacrificed at the altar of selfishness. The net result is that the innocent are falsely accused, prosecuted and punished, while the offenders go Scott free. How can there be healthy relationship when the old wounds of hurt are still fresh, and justice without truth, fairness and equity?

The effects of cultural diversities and moral implications of individual actions on other people substantially led us to study human conscience as a springboard for human relationships and interpersonal co-existence. Because of these differences in human actions, we discovered that each person behaves true to type. The complexities of the human nature seem to make human relationship difficult to understand. Paradoxically, in applying the Heraclitian and Tillichian principles of co-existence of the good and bad for interpersonal co-existence, each person is at liberty to make rooms for the "despite of" the conflicting an un-conflicting occurrences in human life. In order to delve into this aspect of human management strategies, we adopted some ethical standards, the Traditional, Christian and moral principles and values as our measurement in the book.

However, we studied the individual person vis-à-vis his nature, with particular reference to the Western and African cultures as our case study. Considering mainly the the implication of studying human relationships from psychological and ethical perspectives for interpersonal co-existence, we delved into chapter one of the book. This was essentially the statement of problem, which the book set out to address. This guided us to ascertain to what extent human relationships have been possible among individuals in society. To achieve the said objective, we mapped out our parameters, which included the background of the study in which the culture of the Igbo of Nigeria featured prominently, purpose of study, the scope and significance of the work. In a nutshell, the statement of the problem or thesis statement or hypothesis, namely: "It is possible for human beings to relate amicably with one another" was thoroughly examined. Conclusively, that hypothesis was measured through data analysis, presentation and validated in chapter three of the book - the methodology.

The statement of the problems or the background of the study examined the spiritual typology of three groups of people in society as to ascertain the level of their rational orientations. However, there could be more typologies, traits, type classifications in society but the author considered the three groups in view of the three major problems he believed that have stagnated human relationships, peace, unity and progress. The problems include those that arise from the nature of man himself, from the magnitude of the present immoral practices and conflicts in society and those resulting from the wrong application of missionary strategies in the Nigerian case. It was precisely within this aspect of the background of our study that we elaborately treated the disorientations and disorders which Christianity and civilization created in the religious consciousness of the Igbo of Nigeria as such. In the light of this development, the African culture with particular reference to the Igbo of Nigeria was extensively examined and given attention as a guide to the effects of science and technology in the ethical and religious consciousness of any peaceful group of people.

The fundamental and traditional values of the people seem to have been violated and neglected by the missionaries who introduced the Christian religion to them. The situation resulted to conflicts, disunity, and lack of faith, syncretistic practices and immoral behavior in their relationships. Such matters demand urgent attention for a global understanding, interpersonal co-existence and relationships. Besides, the purpose of this book was explicit. It was an urgent call to integrate the various factors, skills, religious, ethical and personal values to make human relationships healthier. Due to the nature of spiritual psychology and the diversity of the topic at hand, our scope was limited to the study of human relationships, holistically touching everybody, gender, age, color, language, ethnic groups, race or national origin, family status, the economic, political, social, religious and other establishments and organizations.

The significance of our survey anchored on the relevance and impressions the book would make on each partner, particularly, on the reader. It elicited such questions as: "Has the reading of this book broadened my perception of human relationship, in the family circles, establishments, and school systems? Is it possible that lack of moral guidance in our relationship could be responsible for most of the ills experienced in the school systems and society today? Can we, at this point, tell ourselves the truth that this book is actually a self guide to human relationships, a life GPS system?" On a more practical note, the significance of the book lies on the individual's ability to read it, reflect on it, and share the knowledge gathered thereupon with other people, especially to deepen and bring about the change we need today to make our relationship holistic and lively.

Consequently, in chapter two, the author consulted different sources that are significantly relevant to human relationships. That took us to in-depth study of the various factors that influence individual relationships and behaviors. Such factors include: conscience, its religious, cultural, philosophical, [ethics and psychology], perspectives, the state of the mind in knowledge and application of ethical principles, et cetera. Different experts in psychology, ethics, religion and philosophy were consulted and scientifically examined. In the midst of all these disciplines, "Spiritual Psychology", the area of our specialty was considered most appropriate and adequate to address and approach the conflicts and immoral behaviors that plague human relationships and society.

Although, authors varied in their expressions on the nature of human relationship, they all agreed that it typically and fundamentally belongs to rational beings to set the pace. Therefore, we were constrained to study the nature of peoples' consciences and relationships from various epochs in history, the state of the human mind in knowledge, as already noted, in order to appreciate the "whys" and the diversities in human relationships and the necessity for each person to anticipate eventualities in relationship. For an action to be rational or human, we were necessarily challenged to study the ethical principles that guide it. Eventually, many opinions were sought regarding what could assist this scientific investigation to resolve conflicts and misconducts in relationships and in society at large. In order to alert and prepare individuals for the unexpected challenges that may suddenly and surprisingly spring up in their relationships, we examined other human dynamics and mechanisms. Such studies included personality structures, types, temperaments, characteristics, developments, stages, and the various defense mechanisms or the unconscious behaviors some partners apply in their relationships to dodge blame and some of their responsibilities. It is important to note that the book did not claim to resolve the issue of conflicts in human relationships as our analysis and interpretation indicated. However, it has created the awareness for individuals to be ready and prepared to appreciate challenges in their relationships, even when they think nothing is amiss. In a sense, our study of human personality in general has become an asset to understand why people tend to behave true to type and the need to address conflicts from there.

Chapter three presented the methodology that was employed in this book. The methodology involved, not only, the Internet and library research, but also fieldwork through distribution of constructed and validated Questionnaires. Eventually, the instrument for data collection was developed and presented.

Chapter four analyzed, interpreted and discussed the results presented. The responses we gathered from our Questionnaires through the Middle Class served as our reference points that went beyond library research to the practical approaches that could guide every human relationship. By this approach, the hypothesis, data analysis and interpretation of results were measured and validated. Thus, "it is possible for individuals to relate amicably" as long as they respect each other's bounds, values and belief systems. Percentages were used for the analysis. Moreover, while chapter six examined the "work yet to be done" by other researchers, chapter seven acknowledged the sources or bibliography. Chapter eight recorded the Appendixes [Instrument or Questionnaire] and glossary of terms that featured in place of the book index.

B. Findings

Our findings have revealed the various factors that affect interpersonal relationships especially among individuals. Therefore, part of the results and findings of our data analysis are summarized and presented as follows:

1. Married people have major role to play in human relationships. Thus, serious misgivings in relationships predominantly occur more among them (39%) than among friends (30%).

2. Misconducts in relationships range from lack of attentive listening (37%) to dishonesty, cheating and lack of trust (32%).

3. Misconducts and conflicts in relationships are isolated as originating from poor upbringing - education, family, biological, associations, environments, et cetera (32%), lack of moral and religious values in one's decisions and actions (29%) and lack of self-knowledge and supervision (26%). Education is very essential for the success of all relationships. In all, students are responsible for their own learning because they decide what they want to be or gain from education.

4. Surprisingly, no matter how diligent and careful partners may be, misunderstanding cannot completely be ruled out from relationships (52%). However, with the guidelines SP has already provided in this book, people can avoid conflicts in their relationships (47%).

5. All the same, lasting peace can be achieved in relationships once people live by examples (32%), trust themselves, others and their source of being - God (27%), being responsible human beings, assisting each other at every condition that springs up (12%), obeying their consciences (9%) and avoiding being dogmatic, but flexible and hard working (20%).

6. Disharmony, conflicts and irresponsibility are major obstacles to all relationships, peace, safety, progress and advancement of society at large (100%).

7. Relationships are fundamentally and intrinsically personal. The personal efforts and sacrifices people make are the energy and engine of their relationships (38%). Healthy relationships are never dependent on affluence or wealth (5%). Rather, religion (11%), the Church and her ministers (22%) are more important, especially when the entire bodies are put together (24%).

8. The Middle Class expressed varied opinions on measures that can restore interpersonal relationship and peace in society. However, a dominant opinion is centered on moral upbringing and education of our young ones as effective solutions to and remedies for social and domestic violence encountered in human relationships.

9. The findings we gathered from our data analysis stress that everybody needs good moral life in order to build and maintain healthy relationship. It is also revealed that the cause of conflicts and immoral behaviors at schools and in relationships today is partly from societal influences and partly from the individual choice levels.

We could not from our studies in spiritual psychology claim to have exhausted such a classic topic that hinges on a complicated and religious animal (*homo religiousus*) as man. Therefore, we were forced to state our limitations and recommended other areas and avenues for more scientific studies in the issue of relationship.

Chapter six

*   *   *   *

Work yet to be done

As we have rightly and already noted, the author did not claim to have exhausted the study of relationships from the psychological and ethical perspectives for interpersonal co-existence. In this light, therefore, the following facts were considered:

A. Limitation of the study

This book does not claim to have covered all the areas of study in this scientific enquiry on: "Keeping Human Relationships Together: Self Guide to Healthy Living" [*Studies in Spiritual Psychology vis-à-vis Human Values*]. The topic from the onset essentially suggested universal values that are typical of human beings in every cage and cave, irrespective of status, color or gender. The audience of the study includes people from various tribes on the planet. Besides, the fact that the population of this research involved only the Middle Class of society is a limitation. For instance, why did the survey omit the ministers of the Christian religion, world religious leaders, nurses, titled men and women, traders, students of different institutions et cetera in the questionnaire? The author failed to explain why he concentrated more on the Christian religion instead of focusing on the rich values of other world Traditions. Again, only a sample of 164 Middle Class was drawn from a total of 323 individuals on whom our 26 instruments were administered, to measure the entire society. That is equally a limitation.

Besides, the author employed percentages only as the statistical technique instead of involving Chi-square or Correlation techniques.

More importantly, the issue of human relationship is such a vast one. The author failed to address in details the relationships that exist between parents and their children, the Church and the Government, International Communities, et cetera. Besides, the book seemed to suggest that the treatment of human relationship as a general issue needed more elaboration. The author actually studied the Western and the African cultural values especially those of the Igbo of Nigeria vis-à-vis the Christian religion among one of the three alternatives in the background of this book. Why did he fail to extensively study the multicultural systems, media, and technology of the Western world as important vehicles for interpersonal relationships? The language of the book sounds more British than American and other civilized countries of the world. That is also a limitation. The author eventually mapped out the educational implications of the study.

B. Educational implications of the study

The book is fundamentally designed to guide individuals, college students, seminarians and society in various capacities towards total realization of goals and meanings in their relationships. There are conflicts, ill feelings, anger, misconducts and misunderstanding today in relationships because, either:

1. What we naturally expect in others does not follow that way; And,
2. Due clearly to our own unexamined lives, we tend to misjudge the actions of others, hence the conflicts OR
3. Human nature being what it is, we can assist people live honest lives and not to change them totally.

As a consequence, the findings we made so far in this study have tremendous implications for solid relationships, the advancement of the human society and educational objectives, especially in the area of moral education and instruction. For instance, teachers, parents, the first teachers of their children, the Church and her ministers are expected to transmit sound education and knowledge of morality to the young generation. Regrettably, from our survey, most of them have failed in this regard because of personal interests, selfishness and wrong priorities. It has become necessary that both the teachers and the taught, including ministers of all religions be conscious of their combined responsibility over the enhancement and advancement of society. Failure to prepare society as regards the need for sound interpersonal co-existence and the relevance of education, the future of our young generation will be jeopardized.

Evidently, the survey revealed that most people no longer respect that vital aspect of human life, their conscience, which identifies them as rational beings. For instance, any education, be it formal or informal, that does not take the development and application of the human conscience into consideration is bound to fail. Human relationship has to do with sound moral living. The first education every rational being needs is fundamentally to cultivate the culture of good moral consciousness. This quality of self-reflection and awareness is expedient in every human endeavor because the greatest challenges society faces today emanate from complacency, nonchalance and self-righteousness.

In this light, spiritual psychology calls humanity to wake up from the sleep of ethical ignorance, ethnic differences and embrace order, moral consciousness, and become less judgmental and argumentative in relationship because no two people are the same. Relationships need some sacred spaces to function. We need to pray for blessings on the spaces we share. Enough rooms have to be given to others also for some benefits of doubt because mistakes do occur. In the married state, couples can amicably marry when they keep only one eye open to avoid suspicions and other contingencies of life. Hence, there can never be a perfect relationship. Relationship progresses more when it internally guides and heals itself, step by step.

The dichotomy and lack of rapport that recently exist between the Church and the Government in certain moral matters need to be bridged. Any Government and organization that tend to neglect the roles of the Church, the moral consciousness and arms of society normally end up leading a society of jungle ideologies. Moreover, it is one thing to study relationship from ethical points of view, and another, for individuals to cultivate positive attitude towards good moral living. From our analysis, the Church, religion, her ministers, and the Government jointly have irreplaceable roles in safeguarding the public safety, infrastructures, spiritual and material comforts, especially the young ones.

C. Recommendations and the epilogue

For greater awareness of the need to bring unity and peace to human relationships, it is necessary to make the following recommendations:

1. Moral instructions should be made compulsory in the school curriculum in order to curb the surge of immorality, cultism, promiscuity, spread of venereal diseases, avoidable abortion and divorce rates, misunderstanding, disunity and conflicts in human relationships and restore peace in the world at large. In this light, our young ones, the future of tomorrow will be challenged to apply moral diversities and principles in their decisions and actions. They will, as well, consciously and unconsciously appreciate and imbibe the value of respecting other people, peace and harmony in their relationships.

2. Spiritual psychology – which holistically integrates the various psychological and ethical values and resources in the guidance of the individual person, irrespective of age, color, race and gender, should form part of the school curriculum.

3. The Government should, as a matter of obligation, promptly provide enough employment for her citizens, effective security, infrastructures, and promptly pay workers' salaries, especially in developing countries like Nigeria. The Government should encourage individual initiatives and creativity as powerful means of enhancing order and harmony in relationships and society.

4. There should exist in all the various seminaries, communities and States, inter-friendly dialogues between the NGOs, and representatives of the Christian and Non-Christian religions to discuss common matters that encourage interpersonal and global relationships.

5. Sex education should be introduced in the school systems to clear some of the wrong impressions, opinions, doubts and fears most of the young generation generally have about God's greatest gift of sex by which his creation endures forever. In other words, to mess up with sex, as noted before, the forbidden apple reserved for the highest sacred function of life and powerful means of procreation is to play jokes with the most costly aspect of one's life.

Therefore, as a matter of urgency and emphasis, we suggest the following important areas for further readings, studies and research. Such areas include:

a. The capacity for one to relate with others after posttraumatic experiences, coping with life after a cherished relationship abruptly comes to an end, bereavements, grief after the loss of jobs, beloved ones, single parenthood, effects of intensive and acute sickness, infertility in marriage, accidents, alcoholism and drug addictions, et cetera.

b. Studies on the population of this book as already noted can be increased, from the Middle Class to probably marital and school peer relations, traders, and celebrities – social and spiritual, who face the heat and challenges of relationships on daily bases.

c. Researches and enquiries on topics like "Keeping human relationship together: Self guide to healthy living" are open-ended that can never be totally exhausted by an author. Thus, I invite other scholars also to specifically research on related topics like "keeping relationships together' on international level, communities, among nations, the clergy, between the churches and their ministers, families, men and women, parents and their children, separated and single parents and children, youths, peers, polygamous (more than one wife) polygynous (more than a mate or spouse) and polyandrous (more than one husband at a time) families, Christians and Traditionalists and various religions, cultures, et cetera.

d. Relationships of the heavenly bodies, astrology, among the poor, musicians, various sports, middle class citizens, the wealthy, the elites, professions – ministries, water spirits and natural forces, educational, medical and legal levels, politics, partisan and bi-partisan, alcoholics, drug addicts, gays, lesbians, pedophilic cases, transgender, pets, animals in general et cetera, are possible areas of study too.

e. Relationship of the victims of sex abuses and offenders.

f. Relationships of Vampires (blood drinkers) and Pimp Girls and Prostitution rings are possible areas for research too. Eating habits and disorders – humans who eat objects and things normal people can't.

g. Sexually healing relationships, objectum sexuality (sexual attractions to objects), ethics in international health research and bioethics equally make interesting topics, reading and research in this area of study.

h. Works of this magnitude, as noted above, that involve human behaviors, dynamics, belief systems, socio-religious and cultural diversities could not have been presented without some seemingly conflicting opinions on the subject matter, designs and contents, omissions, repetitions, contradictions, flaws, exaggerations, inadequate acknowledgment of resources, doctrinal fracas et cetera. Therefore, prospective researchers, individuals and organizations who are interested in this important campaign to keep human relationships together as self guide to the healthiest and authentic manner of life are hereby challenged to improve on missed target objectives of the book.

i. Finally, the positive changes we expect from research can only come about when we decide not to take the status quo that has failed society.

At this point, we are challenged to acknowledge our resources and Bibliography in the following chapter seven.

Chapter seven

*   *   *

Resources and bibliography

Abubaka, M. 2001, September. "School girl in ritual murder saga" in *The Leader*. Vol. XLII, No. 16.

Achebe, Chinua. 1994. *Things fall apart*. New York: Anchor Books.

Agwulonu, Fidelis I. 2001. *The Creative Intelligence*. Onitsha: Mid-Field Publishers.

Aguh, N. Reginald, Unpublished works on *The Ethico-Religious Approach to Science in the Light of The Igbo of Nigeria*, FH/Oxford, November 2008.

Akubueze, T. 1998. *Bible Concordance and Topical Guide*. Port Harcourt: Obchikel Publishers.

Alexander, J. (ed). 1966. *The Jerusalem Bible*. Darton: Longman & Todd Ltd.

Allison, E. Peers. (ed.). 1960. *The Life of Teresa of Jesus [Autobiography of St. Teresa of Avila]*. New York: Image Books. A division of Doubleday & Company, Inc.

Anscombe, G.C.M. 1958. *Intention*. Oxford: Blackwell.

Anyagwa, J. 2001. "Odenigbo". Lecturer "identifies cause of immorality among Youths" in *The Leader,* vol. XLIV, No. 6, April, 2002.

Aquinas, T. 1949. *The Soul.* (A translation of Aquinas *De Anima* by Rowan, J. P) London: B. Herder Book Company.

Arinze, Francis A. 1970. *Sacrifice in Ibo Religion.* Ibadan: University Press.

Don, Asselin. 1989. (ed). *Aristotle – Biography,* The Philosopher's Lighthouse, Aristotle's Life. *Human Nature and Eudaimonia in Aristotle,* NY: Peter Lang.

Au, Wilkie. 1989. *By Way of the Heart: Toward a Holistic Christian Spirituality.* New York, New York: Paulist Press.

Aumann, Jordan. 1985. Christian Spirituality. Wipf and Stock Publishers

Austin, F. (ed). 1975. *Vatican Council II, the Conciliar and Post Councilliar Documents.* Dublin: Fowler Wright Book Ltd.

Awoniyi, T. 1979. *Principles and Practice of Education.* London: Hodder & Stoughton.

Ayandele, Emmanuel A. 1988. *The Missionary Impact on Modern Nigeria 1842-1914.* London: Longman.

Azorji, Eugene E. 1986. *The Concept of the Sacred in Igbo Traditional Religion.* Rome: Urban University.

Bahm, Archie J. 1965: *Theories of Conscience. Ethics, Vol. 75, No.2.*

Bangley, Bernard. 1992. *If I'm Forgiven, Why Do I Still Feel Guilty?* Illinois: Harold Shaw Publishers.

Baunoch, Joseph (ed). 2006. *Foundation Theology 2006.* South Bend, Indiana: Cloverdale Book Publishers.

Benson, H. 1997. Timeless Healing: The Power and Biology of Belief. New York, NY: A Fireside Book Publishers-Simon & Schuster.

Beecher, Ward. Henry. 1886, February 25. *New York Times.*

Bellow, J. 1981. *Basic Principles of Teaching Education in Africa.* Ibadan: Spectrum Books Ltd.

Benedict XVI. Pope. 2009. *THE PRIESTHOOD Spiritual Thoughts Series.* Vatican: Libreria Editrice Vaticana.

Berkeley, G. 1975. *The Principles of Human Knowledge.* Warnock, C. J. (ed). London: William Collins & Sons Ltd.

Bluestein, Jane & Katz, Eric. 2005. *High School's Not Forever.* Florida: HCI Teens, An Imprint of Health Communications, Inc.

Bly, Robert. 1992. *IRON JOHN: A Book about Men.* New York: Vintage Books.

Bochenski, I.M. 1966. *Contemporary European Philosophy.* London: Berkeley & Los Angeles.

Bouquet, A.C. 1933. *Man and Deity,* Heffer: Cambridge.

Bourke, V. J. 1951 *Ethics* New York: the Macmillan Company.

Bowker, John. 1988. *IS ANYBODY OUT THERE? Religions and Belief in God in the Contemporary World.* Maryland: Christian Classics, Inc.

Bridgegewater College. 2007. *Philosophy and Religion.* Virginia.

Broccolo, T. Gerard & Thompson, B. Susan. 1990. *Vital Spiritualities: Naming the Holy in Your Life.* Indiana: Ave Maria Press.

Buckingham, Jamie. 2000. *Power For Living.* USA: Arthur S. DeMoss Foundation.

Carl, Anderson. 2008. *A Civilization of Love: What Every Catholic Can Do to Transform the World.* New York: HarperCollins Publishers.

Cary, Philip. 1999. *Philosophy and Religion in the West, Parts 1-111, Lectures 1-32.* Chantilly, VA: The Teaching Company.

Cary, Philip. 1999. *Philosophy and Religion in the West, Video Series, Parts 1-111,* VA: The Teaching Company.

Castrovilla, Mari. (Ed.). 2000. *A Guide to Religious Ministries For Catholic Men and Women 21st Edition.* New York: Catholic News Publishing Company.

Chilagorom, Desmond. N. 2006: *Family Life in the Light of the Gospel.* Gainesville, Fl: InstaBook Corporation.

Cho, Yonggi. Paul. 1978. *Successful Home Cell Groups.* New York: Bridge Publishing, Inc.

Coffey, F. James. 1993. *Seeing With The Heart.* New York: Healy's Graphic Ark Publishers.

Colman, Andrew M. 2003. Oxford Dictionary of Psychology. New York: Oxford University Press.

Dalrymple, J. 1970. *Theology and Spirituality.* Wisconsni: Clergy Book service.

D'arcy, E. 1961. *Conscience and its Rights and Freedom.* London: Sheed & & Ward Ltd.

Dedewo, M. March – June, 1993. "Children in Today's Nigeria" in *The Catholic Ambassador, vol. 14,* No. 1.

Don, Asselin.1989. *Human Nature and Eudaimonia in Aristotle.* NY: Peter Lang.

Donceel, J.F. 1961. *Philosophical Psychology.* London: Sheed & Ward, Inc.

Doniger, Simon (ed). 1967. *Pastoral Psychology.* NY: Meredith Publishers.

Donze, T. Mary. 1998. *In my Heart Room: 21 Love Prayers for Children.* MO: Liguori Publishers.

Dossey, Larry. 1993. *Healing Words.* NY, NY: Harper Collins Publishers.

Douglas, J. D. & Hillyer, N. (eds). 1992. *New Bible Dictionary Second Edition.* Wheaton: Intervarsity Press.

Dourley, John P. 2008. *Paul Tillich, Carl Jung & the Recovery of Religion.* Routledge: Routledge Publishers

Dumm, L. Thomas. 2008. *Loneliness as a Way of Life.* Cambridge: Harvard University Press.

Eamon, Tobin. 1993. *How to Forgive Yourself and Others: Steps to Reconciliation. Revised and Expanded.* MO: Liguori Publications.

Edeh, M. P. Emmanuel. 2006. *Peace to the Modern World.* England: Our Savior Press Ltd.

Edewor, C. E. June – December, 1997. "Sex Education must form the conscience of children" in *Wisdom Satellite.* vol. 5, No. 1.

Edward, Paul. (ed). 1967. *Encyclopedia of Philosophy Vols. 3-8.* New York: The Free Press.

Ehusani, G. May, 2002. "Responding to the challenges of University Cults" in *The Guide* vol. 4, No. 4.

Ejizu, Christopher I. 1984. "Continuity and Discontinuity in African Traditional Religion" in *Cahiers des Religions Africaines.* Vol.18. No. 1.

Ekennia, Justin N. 2003. *Bio-Medical Ethics, Issues, Trends & Problems.* Owerri, Nigeria: Barloz Publishers Inc.

Ekezie, R.E.C. 1984. *Philosophy of Education for Nigerian Students.* Owerri: Onyenze Press.

Ekweh, Christian I. 2002. Righteousness: *An Insightful Commentary on Proverbs Ch. 3.* Jos: Deka Publishers.

Ekpunobi, E. 1982. *A handbook for the Teaching of Religious and Moral in Schools and Colleges.* Kaduna: Baraka Publishers.

Ellis, Albert & Harper, Robert. 1975. *A New Guide to Rational Living.* CA: Wilshire Book Company.

Engels, F. 1965. *Russian Philosophy first Edition.* Quadrangle: Quadrangle books.

Erik, H. Erikson. 1980. *Identity and the Life Cycle.* New York: W.W. Norton & Company.

Ezeonyia, Vincent V. 1998. *Tears of Misfortune, Pastoral Letter.* Ehi: Sibros Printing Press.

Fagothey, A. 1963. *Right and Reason.* London: The C.V. Mosby Company.

Farrant, J. S. 1980. *Principles and Practice of Education.* Essex: Longman Group UK Ltd.

Flannery, B. Raymond. 1995. *Post-Traumatic Stress Disorder: The Victim's Guide to Healing and Recovery.* New York: The Crossroad Publishing Company.

Genicot, E. 1931. *Institutiones theologiae Moralis, Vol. 1.* Paris: Brussels, Desclee Publishers.

George, Harris. 1999. *Agent-Centered Morality, An Aristotelian Alternative to Kantian Internalism.* Berkeley, California: Univ. of California press.

Giffin, Emily. 2008. *Love the One You're With.* New York: St. Martin's Press.

Gill, J. James & Co. Eds. 1990. *Human Development: The Jesuit Educational Center for Human Development. Vol. Eleven. No. 3.* NJ: The Jesuit Educational Center.

Goldberg, M. & Jay, P. 1983. The Story of Our Values and the Value of Our Stories. MN: Collegeville.

Gruber, F. C. 1834. *Foundations for A Philosophy of Education.* New York: Thomas Y. Crowell Company.

Hall, Todd W. & McMinn, Mark R. (eds). 2000. *The Journal of Psychology and Theology.* California: Rosemead School of Psychology.

Hall, Todd W. & McMinn, Mark R. (eds). 2002. *The Journal of Psychology and Theology.* California: Rosemead School of Psychology.

Hamlyn, D. N. 1970. *The Theory of knowledge.* London: The Macmillan Press Ltd.

Hannah, Arendt. 1958. *The Human Condition.* Chicago: Univ. of Chicago Press.

Haring, B. 1964. *Christian Renewal in a changing world.* New York: Desclee Company, Inc.

Haring, B. 1964. *The Law of Christ Vol. 111.* New York: Newman Press.

Haughey, C. John. Ed. 1977. *The Faith That Does Justice: Examining the Christian Sources for Social Change.* New York: Paulist Press.

Hawkins, R. David. 2006. *Transcending The Levels of Consciousness: The Stairway to Enlightenment.* AZ: Veritas Publishers

Hayes, M. John. 1994. *The Fundamentals of Family Mediation.* New York: State University of New York Press.

Hellwig, K. Monika. 1981. *Understanding Catholicism.* New York: Paulist Press.

Henry, Veatch B. 1974. *Aristotle: A Contemporary Appreciation.* Bloomington: Indiana Univ. Press.

Heraclitus, (Stanford Encyclopedia of Philosophy*). 2007. *Studies in Heraclitus* by Graham Daniel W.

Heraclitus, (C 536 BC - 475 BC), Talk: *Heraclitus – Wiki quote*, July 2, 2009.

Heraclitus, *Internet Encyclopedia of Philosophy &* in Stumpt, S. E. (1977).

Herbert, J. 1963. *A philosophy of Education.* New York: MicGraw Book Company.

Higgins, T. S. 1948. *Man As Man.* Milwaukee: The Bruce Publishers.

Hirst, P.H. & Peters R.S. 1980. *The Logic of Education.* London: Routlege Kegan Paul.

Hobbs, Dayton. IGS. *The Christian Conscience and the Chain of Command.*

Hubbard, Lron. 2001. Assists For Illness and Injuries. CA: Bridge Publications Inc.

Hybels, Bill. 1966. *EVANGELISM: Becoming Stronger Salt and Brighter Light.* Michigan: Zondervan Publishing House.

Idowu, Bolaji E. 1976. *African Traditional Religion, A Definition.* London: SCM press.

Ilega, Daniel I. (ed). 2000. *West African Religious Traditions,* Ado-Ekiti: Hamaz Global Ventures.

Ilo, C. Stan. 2006. *The Face of Africa: Looking Beyond* The *Shadows,* Bloomington, IN, USA: AuthorHouse Publishers.

Ilo, S.C. "Sexual Morality today" in *Wisdom Satellite,* Vol. 5, No. 1,

Isichei, Elizabeth. 1977. *A History of the Igbo People.* London: Macmillan Press.

Iwuchukwu, Boniface C. 1993. *Philosophy of Education, A First Course, Volume One.* Owerri: Orji Luton Press Ltd.

Jackson, Charles J. 2005. *Jesuit Spirituality.* USA: Quintin Publications.

Jamison, Kaleel. 1989. *The Nibble Theory and the Kernel Power: A Book about Leadership, Self-Empowerment, and Personal Growth.* New York: Paulist Publishers.

Johann, O. Robert. 1966. *The meaning of Love.* New Jersey: Deus Books Paulist Press.

John Paul 11. 1995. *Evangelium Vitae.* Vatican: Vatican Press.

Josef, Pieper. 1965. *The Four Cardinal Virtues; Prudence, Justice, Fortitude, Temperance,* (tr. Richard & Clara Winston), NY: Harcourt, Brace, and World.

Kahn, Charles H. 1979. (ed.) *The Art and Thought of Heraclitus.* Cambridge: Cambridge University Press.

Kant I. 1992. *Foundations of the Metaphysics of Morals.* J. Ellingen edition, Indianapolis: Hacket.

Karol, Wojtyla, Pope John Paul 11. 1981. *Love and Responsibility.* Willetts H. T. (Tr). NY: Farrar, Straus, Giroux.

Kennedy, E. C. 1974. *The Pain of being Human.* New York, a Division of Doubleday & Company, Inc.

Kilgard, E. R. & Atkinson, R.C. 1967. *Introduction to Psychology 4th Edition.* New York:: Harcourt, Brace & Word, Inc.

Kinzer, Mark. 1980. *The Self-Image of a Christian: Humility and Self-Esteem.* Michigan: Servant Books.

Knight, Kevin. 2007. *The Advent. The Catholic Encyclopedia*

Koterski, Joseph W. S.J. 2001. *Philosophy & Intellectual History: The Ethics of Aristotle.* Chantilly, VA: The Teaching Company.

Koterski, Joseph W. 2001. *The Ethics of Aristotle, Video Series, Tapes 1-111,* VA: The Teaching Company.

Kraut Richard. 2005. "Aristotle's Ethics" in *Stanford Encyclopedia of Philosophy.* (Internet Guide Selection-I.G.S.).

Kuhse, H. 1997. *Caring: Nurses, Women and Ethics.* Great Britain: Blackwell.

Kwasi, Wiredu. 2007. *African Studies Quarterly, The Online Journal for African Studies,* "Toward Decolonizing African Philosophy and Religion".

LaHaye, Tim F. 1988. *Why You Act the Way You Do.* Tyndale House Publishers.

Lauder, E. Robert. 1978. *Loneliness is for loving.* Indiana: Ave Maria Press.

Lawrence, J.P. 1972. *Individual Instruction.* London: Mcgraw Hill Book Company.

Lennox, James G. 2001. *Aristotle's Philosophy of Biology: Studies in the Origin of the Life Sciences.* Cambridge: Cambridge Univ. press.

Levis-Strauss, Claude. 1978. *Myth and Meaning.* New York: Schocken Books.

Lindesmith, A. R. & Strauss, A. L. 1956. *Social Psychology.* New York: Holt, Rinehart & Winston, Inc.

Lucas, C. J. 1976. *What is Philosophy of Education?* London: The Macmillan Co.

MacNutt, Francis. 1992. *The Power to Heal.* Indiana: Ave Maria Press.

Macqurrie, J. 1968. *Martin Heidegger.* London: Lutterwork Press.

Macquarrie, John. 2001. *Twentieth-Century Religious Thought.* London: SCM Press.

Maikklem., Lara & Co. Eds. 1998. *Sister Wendy's Book of Meditations.* New York: A DK Publishing Book.

Marlin, J. George. & Co. Eds. 1989. *The Quotable Fulton Sheen.* New York: Doubleday Publishing Groups, Inc.

Mbefo, Luke. 1985. "Theology and Inculturation: Problems and Prospects-the Nigerian Experience" in the *Nigerian Journal of Theology West Africa,* Vol. 1.

McDonald, J. Patrick & McDonald, M. Claudette. 1997: *Out of the Ashes: A Handbook for Starting Over.* New York: Paulist Press.

McGrath, Alister E. 1999. *Christian Spirituality: An Introduction.* Blackwell Publishers.

Mckenny, Gerald P. (Issue ed). 1999. *Christian Bioethics. Non-Ecumenical Studies in Medical Morality Vol. 5, No. 2.* Netherlands: Swets & Zeitlinger Publishers.

McKenzie, J. L. 1966. *Dictionary of the Bible*. London: Cassoll & Co. Ltd.

Mead, S. Frank. 1965. (ed). *The Encyclopedia of Religious Quotations*. New York: Books, Incorporated Publishers.

Meliaender, Gilbert. 19981. *Friendship*. Notre Dame: Univ. of Notre Dame Press.

Michael, De La Bedoyere, 1966. *The Future of Catholic Christianity*. London: Garden City Press.

Mkpa, M. A. 1991. *Contemporary Issues in Nigerian Education*. Awka: Mekslink Publishers.

Morgan, John H. 2003. *Unfinished Business. The Terminal All-But-Dissertation Phenomenon in American Higher Education*. Bristol Indiana: Cloverdale Corporation.

Morgan, John H. 2006. "Being Human and Being Good: The Psychodynamics of Personhood" (Co-ed). *Religion and Society. Summer Programme in Theology 2006*. Indiana: Cloverdale Corporation.

Morgan, John H. & Neitzke, Russell. 2007. *From Beginning to End. Internet Research and the Writing Process: An author's guide with CD-Rom*. South Bend, IN: Clover Books.

Morgan, John H. (Ed.) 2009. *Foundation Theology 2009 Student Essays for Ministry Professionals*. Mishawaka, Indiana: The Victoria Press.

Murray, M. V. 1960. *Problems in Ethics*. New York: Holt & Company, Inc.

Nietzche, Fruedrich. 1910. *Joyful Wisdom*. London: Herder Books.

Norman, Doidge. 2007. *The Brain That Changes Itself: Stories of Personal Triumphs from the Frontiers of Brain Science*. New York, New York: Penguin Books.

Nwachukwu, F.J. & Ugwuegbulam, C. N. 1966. *Guidance and Counselling: An Introductory Survey.* Benin: Barloz Publishers, Inc.

Nwachukwu, John U. 1991. *Oji Ezinihitte Cultural Festival.* Owerri: Alvan Ikoku College of Education.

Nwachukwu, Anthony O. 1994. *FIRE! The Active Life Of the Spirit.* Owerri: Assumpta Press.

Nwachukwu, Anthony O. 1995. What a Model is MARY: The Mother of Jesus. Owerri: Assumpta Press.

Nwachukwu, Anthony O. 1999. *The Devil Has Come To Church Part 1.* Owerri: Good Samaritan Press.

Nwachukwu, Anthony O. 2001. The 50 Steps to Happy Marriage (2nd Edition). Owerri: Assumpta Press.

Nwachukwu, Anthony O. 2002. *Salvation in African Context.* Owerri, Nigeria: Barloz Publishers.

Nwachukwu Udaku, Ugoeze, Josephine (edited by Victoria U. Nwigwe). 2009. *The Presidency of Mama JO, Reflections and Adminotions.* Nigeria: NCCWO Publishers.

Nwankwo, U. 2001, September. "Bravo! Prof. Anwukah" in *The Leader, vol.XLIII, No. 17.*

Nwigwe, B. E. 2001. *Elements of Philosophy.* Port Harcourt: PAM Unique Publishing Company Ltd.

Obiora, Fidelis K. 1998. *The Devine Deceit Business in Religion.* Enugu: Rex Charles & Patrick.

Ocho, L.O. 1988. *The Philosophy of Education for Nigeria.* Enugu: Harris Publishers.

Ogunu, M. 2002. June. "Moral Crisis in Our Institutions of Higher Learning" in *The Leader, Vol. XLIV, No. 10.*

Okechukwu, S. T. 2001, October. "Riot in Nigerian Campuses" in *The Leader, Vol. XLIII, No. 19.*

Okeke, C.C. 1989. *Philosophy of Education, Concepts, Analysis and applications.* Owerri: Totan Publishers.

Okonkwu, T. 2002, April. "Uwa Ohuu n'usoro Ndu ndi ntorobi" in *The Leader. Vol. XLIV, No. 6.*

Omoregbe, Joseph I. 1996. *A Philosophical Look at Religion.* London: Joja Press.

---------------------------- 1999. *Comparative Religion Christianity and Other World Religions in Dialogue.* Lagos: Joja Press.

Onwubiko, Oliver A. 1999. *African Thought, Religion and Culture. Vol.1.* Enugu: Snaap Press.

Owen, A. N. 1928. *Ethics: General and Special.* New York: Macmillan Company.

Panikkar, Raimon. 2007. *Religion, Philosophy and Culture.* Polylog.

Paulin, C. H. 1992. *Salvific Invitation and Loving Response: The Fundamental Christian Dialogue.* Lagos, Academy Press PLC.

Philips, Simpson, Peter L. 1997. *The Politics of Aristotle, tr. with introduction, analysis, and notes.* Chapel Hill, NC: Univ. of North Carolina Press.

Rahner, Karl. 1964. *Nature and Grace-Dilemmas in the Modern Church.* New York: Sheed and Ward, Inc.

Rahner, Karl. 1982. *Encyclopedia of Theology, The Concise Sacramentum Mundi.* (ed). New York: Crossroad Publishing Company.

Renard, H. 1948. *The Philosophy of Man*. Milwankee: The Bruce Publishers.

Restak, Richard. 1991. *The Brain Has a Mind of Its Own. Insights from a Practicing Neurologist*. New York: Harmony Books.

Romero, Anna A. & Kemp, Steven M. 2007. *Psychology Demystified, A Self- Teaching Guide*. New York, NY: McGraw-Hill.

Ross W. D. *(tr)*. *Nicomachean Ethics by Aristotle 350 BC, Books 1-10*.

Russell, B. 1977. *Roads to Freedom*. London: Unwin & George, Allens Publishers, Ltd.

Sandford, John & Paula. 1977. *The Elijah Task: A Call to Today's Prophets and Intercessors*. Ok: Victory House, Inc.

Sanford, A. John. 1982. *Ministry Burnout*. New York: Paulist Press

Sarpong, Peter K. 1985. "Christianity Meets Traditional African Cultures", in *Mission Trends. No. 5*.

Schollimeier, Paul.1994. *Other Selves: Aristotle on Personal and political Friendships*. Albany: SUNY Press.

Sharon, L. Johnson. 2004. *Therapist's Guide to Clinical Intervention: The 1-2-3"s of Treatment Planning. Second Edition*. London: Academic Press.

Shaw J. & Morgan John H. 2006. *Religion and Society, Summer Programme in Theology 2006*. Indiana: Cloverdale Corporation.

Sheffield, Anne. 2003. *Depression Fallout: The Impact of Depression on Couples and what You can Do to Preserve the Bond*. New York, NY: HarperCollins Publishers.

Sherman, Nancy. 1997. *Making a Necessity of Virtues: Aristotle and Kant on Virtue*, Cambridge: Cambridge Univ. Press.

Shlemon, Leahy Barbara. 1982. *Healing The Hidden Self.* Notre Dame, IN: Ave Maria Press.

Singer, P. 1979. *Practical Ethics.* Cambridge: Cambridge University Press.

Sonderegger, Theo. 1998. *Cliffs Quick Review PSYCHOLOGY.* NY, NY: Wiley Publishing Inc.

Spring, Abrahms, Janis. 1996. *After the Affair-Healing the Pain and Rebuilding Trust When a Partner Has Been Unfaithful.* New York: HaroerPerennial/ HarperCollins Publishers.

Stravinskas, M. J. Peter. 1998. *The Catholic Answer Book 3.* Indiana: Our Sunday Visitor Publishing Division.

Stumpt, S. E. 1977. *Philosophy: History and Problems.* New York: Mcgraw-Hill Company.

Sue, W. Derald & Sue David. 1990. *Counseling the Culturally Different: Theory & Practice (Second Edition).* New York: A Wiley-Interscience Publication.

Svoboda, Meannie. 1996. *Traits of a Healthy Spirituality.* CT: Twenty-Third Publications.

Tavris, Carol & Elliot, Aronson. 2007. *Mistakes Were Made (but not by me) Why We Justify Foolish Beliefs, Bad Decisions, and Hurtful Acts.* Orlando: A Harvest Book – Harcourt,Inc.

Tillich, Paul J. 1957. *Dynamics of Faith.* New York: HarperCollins.

Tillich, Paul J. 1948. *Shaking of the Foundations.* New York: Charles Scribner's sons.

Tillich, Paul J. 1955. *The New Being.* New York: Charles Scribner's sons.

Anthony O. Nwachukwu

Tillich, Paul J. 1952. *"The Courage To Be"* An outline edited, Abridged & Expanded by Richard Schwartz.

Tillich, Paul, (1886 – 1965). From Contributed Quotations and Lecture by Author.

Ware, Corinne. 1995. *Discover your Spiritual Type.* NY: An Alban Institute Publication.

Webster, M. 1979. *Webster's New Collegiate Dictionary.* Massachusetts: G. & C. Merriam Company.

Whitehead, D. Barbara. 1997: *The Divorce Culture; Rethinking our commitments to Marriage and Family.* New York: Alfred A. Knopf, Inc.

Whitson, Robley E. 1995. *The Center Scriptures.* Bristol IN: Wyndham Hall Press.

Wiener, Norbert. 1950. *The Human Use of Human Beings.* New York: Doubleday & Company, INC.

William, G. Rutler. 1995. *A Crisis of Saints.* San Francisco: Ignatius Press

William, T. 1929. *History of Philosophy.* New York: Ginn & Co. Inc.

William, J. Grace. 1965. *Response to Literature.* New York: McGRAW-HILL Book Company.

William, J. Whalen. 1979. *Separated Brethren: A Survey of Protestant, Anglican, Eastern Orthodox and other Denominations in the United States.* Indiana: Bruce Publishing Company.

William, Frankena K. 1980. *Thinking of Morality.* Ann Arbor: Univ. of Michigan.

William, A. Barry. 1990. *Now Choose Life: Conversion as a Way to Life.* New York: Paulist Press.

William, A. Barry. 1992. *Spiritual Direction & the Encounter with God.* New York: Paulist Press.

William, J. Knaus. 1994. Cited: in *The World's Greatest Treasury of Health Secrets,* 1998. CT: Boardroom* Inc.

Winslow, L. 2007. *Religion and Philosophy for $200 Bob* under EzineArticles.com.

Wolman, B. B. (ed).1973. *Dictionary of Behavioral Science.* New York: Litlon Educational Publishers.

W. F. R. Hardie. 1980. *Aristotle's Ethical Theory.* Oxford: Oxford University Press.

Yancey, Philip. 1997. *What's Amazing about Grace?* Michigan: Zondervan Publishing House.

Yves, Simon. 1992. *The Tradition of Natural Law.* Bronx, NY: Fordham Univ. Press.

Zelinski, Ernie J. 1997. *The Joy of Not Working.* CA: Ten Speed Press.

The Internet *Encyclopedia of Philosophy, Aristotle (384-322 BCE.): Ethics.*

The Catholic Bishop's Conference of Nigeria. 2004. *I Chose You-The Nigerian in the Third Millennium.* A publication of the Catholic Secretariat of Nigeria.

The Catholic Encyclopedia, Vol. IV. 1908. NY: Robert Appleton Company.

The Catechism of the Catholic Church. 1994. Vatican: Paulist Press.

Britannica, Internet Guide Selection, 1997-2002. *Aristotle: Ethics and the Virtues.* Garth Kemerling.

Anthony O. Nwachukwu

Federal Republic of Nigeria. 1981. *National Policy on Education (Revised)*, Lagos: Federal Government Press.

The Society of Gentlemen. 1968. *Encyclopaedia Britannica. Vol. 6.* London: William Benton Publishers.

Chapter eight

*   *   *   *

Appendices and glossary of terms

A. Appendices

Appendix 1: The 'MCPPKHRH' Questionnaire

The MCPPKHRHQ is designed to elicit information on the 'Middle Class Perception of the Possibilities for Keeping Human Relationships Healthy'. It is not a pass or fail assessment instrument but a research tool that would help to determine if psychological and ethical values could help to curb immoral behaviors and conflicts from society for healthier relationships. You are therefore requested to respond to the questions as honestly as possible. Your responses would be treated with utmost confidentiality.

Section A: Personal data

Name (optional)..

Age.................................. Sex....................................

Nationality...

Type of Profession and Marital status (1) Retired------- (2) Current------- (3) Single------- (4) Married---------

Length of time in your Profession.......................................

Highest Qualification/Position in your area of specialty..................

Indicate your State/Country/Autonomous Community/Village......
....

Section B: Main body of MCPPKHRHQ

B1: Level and enormity of conflicts or indiscipline in relationships

Kindly indicate your opinion(s) from the items below, among which category and level of relationships have you observed serious misgivings and misconducts?

1. Seriouus cases of misconduct and disunity are very high among married people alone.
2. Serious cases of misconducts and indiscipline are observed among ministers
3. Serious cases of misconduct and disunity cut across various establishments alone.
4. Serious cases of misconduct and disunity are very high among friends and peers alone.

B2: The nature of misconducts that are frequently observed in relationships

Which of the ills have you noticed among the people more frequently?

5. Dishonesty/Cheating/No Trust
6. Lack of commitment and deception
7. Lack of respect and attentive listening
8. Gossips, Yelling and Quarreling

B3: Sources (causes) of misconduct and disunity found in relationships

Choose from the items, numbered 9 – 12, what could be the source(s) or cause(s) of misconduct and disunity in peoples' relationships.

9. Poor upbringing, education [family, biological, association, environment etc]
10. Lack of moral and religious values
11. Wrong priorities and choices
12. Lack of self-knowledge and supervision

B.4: Possibility of total eradication of misconducts in relationships

From the two options indicate your opinion. Is it possible to completely eradicate misconduct from relationships?

13. Misconduct and disunity can totally be crushed out from human relationships
14. Eradication of disunity and misgivings in relationships would be impossible

B5: Management of misconduct or immoral behaviors in relationships

Please indicate, which of these is the most plausible option(s) in the control of misconduct and immoral behaviors in relationships?

15. Living by examples
16. Trust in oneself, others and in one's source of being - God
17. By being a responsible person and available for each other in all conditions
18. By obeying one's conscience
19. By being flexible and hardworking

B6: Effects of disharmony on human relationships and the progress of society

Do you agree that disharmony and misconduct have any effect on individual's relationship and the progress of society at large?

20. Indiscipline and immorality have hampered human relationships and the progress of society
21. Conflict, disunity and immorality have no effect at all on relationships and societal developments

B7: The role of personal efforts/sacrifices, religion, material things, the Church and her ministers, the four bodies combined

Identify by ticking the factors that can play crucial role in the control of misbehavior and disunity in relationships

22. Personal efforts and sacrifices
23. Religion and God alone
24. Material comforts and possessions
25. The Church and her ministers
26. Combination of all the four factors

B. Glossary of terms

Epilogue

IR	Internet Resources
GPS	Global Positioning System
IEP	Internet Encyclopedia of Philosophy
Taba	Greek word referring to God's "covenant of friendship"
Hesed	Greek word referring to God's "covenant of love or solidarity"
Yada	Greek word indicating man's response to the "covenant to serve God"
Nemo dat quod non habet	No one gives what he has not
Qua tale	Latin expression meaning "as such"
CP	meaning Capital Person or Partner
Ab initio	from the beginning or start (Latin)
Initiarum pervum sunt	things are small when the begin (Latin)
DOCMI	deliberate opportunity cost for moral irreversibility
Pari passu	side by side or at an equal pace
Homo Religiousus	religious man/animal
W-A-A	whole and whole
Dict. Def.	Dictionary Definition

Chapter one

Ezeji	a title in Igbo land for a prosperous yam farmer
Nze	Igbo name for a titled person with certain moral and social etiquette
Amadioha	Traditional substitute for the true God of Thunder, Lightening and Vengeance
IGS	Internet Guide Selection, that is, (information accessed from the Internet website)
Age quod ages	do that which you do well (Latin)
Omniscience	all knowing (knowledge), referring to God
Omnipontence	all-powerful, referring to God
A priori synthesis	anything or action likely to happen in future
Conatus essendi	a natural inclination (Greek)
Id	the selfish part of man in his personality Development (Sigmund, Freud)
Et tu Brute	and you Brutus (conf. Julius Caesar)
OBT	obtaining by trick
Westners	refer to all white people – Europeans, Americans and other Caucasians who live outside Africa
IM	Ima Madu, (expression in Nigerian context for the mentality of covering up or favoring a person due to familiarity

Theophoric names	Igbo names that are God related or oriented
Telepathy	Ability to communicate between individual minds without employing mental processes, sensory perceptions or other mental means
L.G.A.	Local Government Area

Chapter two

N.C.C.W.O.N.	National Council of Catholic Women Organization of Nigeria
Poiema	art (Greek – confer the creation account)
Kpom	an Igbo expression to indicate "exactness or just that"
Web.def.	Website definition
NACC	National Association of Catholic Chaplains
JPT	Journal of Psychology and Theology
Anawim	The poor of society that seek God's favor
Op.cit	Opus citatum (from the work cited).
Ibid.	Ibidem - the same place as cited
Homo homini lupus est	man is a wolf to every other man (Thomas Hobbes)
Pericardum	outer layer or lining of the human heart

Myocardum	the muscles or flesh layer of the heart
Endocardum	the inner lining or layer of the heart
Nic.	Abbreviation for Aristotle's 'Nicomachean' Ethics
Ethos	habits (or a habitat - Greek)
Ithos	character (Greek)
Conscientia	Latin word for conscience
Synderesis	The Greek word for conscience, meaning "innate awareness or knowledge of the general Moral Principles"
Scire	The Latin verb root for "to know"
Vulgate	The Greek version of the Bible
GS	Gaudium et Spes [Pastoral Constitution on the Church in the Modern world, promulgated by Pope Paul VI on December 7, 1965]
LG	Lumen Gentium [Dogmatic Constitution on the Church]
Actus humanus	human acts (rational)
Actus humanis	acts of man (brutes)
W, IFE	Wikipedia, Internet Free Encyclopedia
CBCN	Catholic Bishops Conference of Nigeria
EIA	Ecclesia in Africa that is, Church in Africa
Modi operandi	modes of operation

Fictio mentis	The Latin expression meaning "object of the mind" i.e. not being concrete
Ako na Uche	The Igbo name for conscience, meaning "Wisdom and intellect put together
Ethike	the singular of ethea – etymology of "ethics"
Nihil est in intellectu quod non prius fuerit in sensu	"nothing in the intellect that does not first pass through the senses" (Aquinas, Thomas)
Mores	from where morals or manners derive their meaning
Gnoseology	science of knowledge
SP	Spiritual Psychology
Cafeteria (religion)	pick and choose
Primum Movens	First Mover or the unmoved mover
Causa in causata	Uncaused cause
Choice of focal options	A choice of course of action or item among many other important variables that are equally relevant to the agent
Per se	for instance or so to say
Egos	reality principle in one's personality development that needs to be guided
Tufiakwa	An Igbo tribal way of expressing a shameful behavior
Ex opere operato	works by itself or without one's efforts (Latin)

Ex opere operantis	works out of one's knowledge or efforts
EIDN	Eternal Identification Number
Summum bonum	the highest (supreme) good of Aquinas
LCM	Lowest Common Multiple
Katholikos	universal, Catholic (Greek)
USC	Unity school of Christianity
Ad rem	A Latin expression for "properly suited" or "to be applied here"
Philosophia ancilla Theologiae est	Philosophy is the handmaid of theology (Latin)
Esse est percipi	to be is to be perceived (Greek)
Mouvaise foi	bad faith (French)
Anomoi	lawless (French)
Tabula rasa	plain or clean slate
Dialogos	the etymology of the Greek word dialogue
Omne agens agit propter finem	every agent acts for an end
Ali alia facunt	different people do different things
Sine qua non	that which must be done or an irreplaceable point
Apophatic	The same Greek, a way of seeing God as a mystery
Kataphatic	The Greek expression for a way of approaching God in concrete terms

Tember tantrum	an unanticipated expression of anger (very common among toddlers [aged 1 - 3] and animals
Alukwaighi M	Igbo expression to indicate discontinuance of marriage or end

Chapter three

Pre-liminal	the preliminary stage, the beginning
Liminal	the action in its full process and completion
Post-liminal	the after effect of the action or process
MCPPKHRHQ	Middle Class Perception of the Possibilities for Keeping Human Relationships Healthy Questionnaire
Middle Class	refers to the Professionals / Respondents: teachers, lawyers, medical doctors, judges, and engineers

Chapter four

NGO	Non Government Organization
PTA	Parent's Teachers Associations
Aladimma	The Customary moral Principles

Chapter five

Traditional Religionists	Adherents of the religion of the ancestors or morality

About the Author

Anthony O. Nwachukwu, Ph.D., Psy.D.

Anthony O. Nwachukwu is Professor of Counseling Psychology and West African Studies and Chairman/Head of the New York City Ph.D. Thesis Defense Panel. His areas of research, writing and teaching include ethics, religion, spirituality and psychology. He has taught Latin in Bigard Memorial Major Seminary (Nigeria) an Affiliate of Urban University, Rome, as well as a wide range of courses in religion at St. Peter Claver and Mater Ecclesia Seminaries, both in Nigeria. Ordained a priest in 1987, Dr. Nwachukwu is Nigerian and has served as pastor for thirteen years in Nigeria, during which time he published several works of scholarship. In 2008, he was awarded the Dorothy Day Prize in Pastoral Care and Counseling from the Foundation. He holds the B.A. Honors in Divinity and Philosophy from the Bigard Memorial Seminary (an affiliated Institution of the Urbanian University in Rome), the Post Graduate Diploma in Educational Technology and the Master of Education in Educational Philosophy from Imo State University, the Master of Divinity from the Catholic Institute of West Africa, the Ph.D. in Religious Studies from the Federal University of Port Harcourt, Nigeria, and the Doctor of Psychology from the Graduate Theological Foundation. Dr. Nwachukwu is a certified Chaplain member of the National Association of Catholic Chaplains, First Recipient of a Nursing Department Safety Award, "the first award ever given to a Chaplain at this hospital" – Director, and has served for over seven years in the New York University Medical Center. He is also a Retreat Moderator, First Assistant Administrator of Mater Ecclesia Diocese, a Theological Vicariate Examiner, and Judge in the Diocesan Marriage Tribunal (Ahiara, Nigeria).

nwagod1@hotmail.com
www.gtfeducation.org

Books

- Questions and Answers in Philosophy (1982)
- CABIA: The Church and the Bible which First? (1992)
- LOVE Biko Bia: Is Love a Risk? (1993)
- Call no one on Earth your Father' Matt. 23:9. Why Rev. Fathers? [1993]
- Igba Nkwu Nwanyi And the Church: Where Do we Stand? A talk first delivered to KSM, Aba Diocese Nigeria (1994)
- FIRE: The Active Life of the Spirit (1994)
- ENVY: A Deadly Sickness, has only one Medicine (Part 1) - 1994
- What a Model is Mary, the Mother of Jesus (1995)? A talk first delivered to the COMITIUM. The Legion of Mary, Kano State, Nigeria
- Whose Cross and whose Glory? (1996)
- Christ at 2000 Years in Nigeria, Has His Coming Become a Failure: Why Mary's Apparitions Now?? (1997)
- The Devil Has Come To Church (Part 1)-1998
- The 50 Steps To Happy Marriage (1999) & Reprinted 2001; A talk first given to The Catholic Women Organization of Nigeria
- Salvation in African Context (2002) – Ph.D. Dissertation of 378 pages

CPSIA information can be obtained at www.ICGtesting.com
Printed in the USA
267111BV00001B/4/P